This book is due for return on or before the last date shown below.

HOPE
DIES
LAST

HOPE
DIES
LAST

The Autobiography of
ALEXANDER
DUBCEK

*Edited and
translated by*
JIRI HOCHMAN

KODANSHA INTERNATIONAL
New York • Tokyo • London

Kodansha America, Inc.
114 Fifth Avenue, New York, New York 10011, U.S.A.

Kodansha International Ltd.
17-14 Otowa 1-chome, Bunkyo-ku, Tokyo 112, Japan

Published in 1993 by Kodansha America, Inc.
in collaboration with Farrar, Straus & Giroux,
19 Union Square West, New York, New York 10003

Printed in the United States of America

93   94   95   96   97   6   5   4   3   2   1

Grateful acknowledgment is made to the Estate of Alexander
Dubcek, Archive Photos, Associated Press (AP), Vladimir Benko,
Pavel Breier, The Czech News Agency (CTK), Oldrich Jaros, Vlado
Krajci, *Narodna Obroda*, Network/Mike Abrams, and
United Press International (UPI) for permission to reproduce
photographs used in this volume;
and to MAN-ART for the 1968 invasion map at
the end of Chapter 20.

Library of Congress Cataloging-in-Publication Data
Dubcek, Alexander, 1921–
Hope dies last : the autobiography of Alexander Dubcek / edited
and translated by Jiri Hochman.
p.   cm.
Includes index.
ISBN 1-56836-000-2
1. Dubček, Alexander, 1921–1992.   2. Heads of state—
Czechoslovakia—Biography.   3. Czechoslovakia—History—1945–
I. Hochman, Jiří.   II. Title.
DB2221.D93A3   1993
943.704'2'092—dc20
[B]   93-2646   CIP   AC

Book design by Janet Tingey

The text of this book was set in Electra.
Composed by Pagesetters, Incorporated
Brattleboro, Vermont

Printed and bound by Arcata Graphics
Fairfield, Pennsylvania

CONTENTS

Contents

Photographic inserts may be found between pages 146 and 147 and pages 242 and 243.

EDITOR'S ACKNOWLEDGMENTS

IT NEVER once occurred to me during the period between April 1990 and August 1992, while Alexander Dubcek and I worked on this book, that the task of writing these acknowledgments would one day devolve upon me. I am sure that if the author were still alive, modest as he was, he would strive to share credit with every appropriate person. If there are any omissions, I can only apologize in advance.

Special acknowledgments belong first to Mrs. Helen Rees, the literary agent in Boston who had the idea at the very beginning that Dubcek's memoirs must be put into writing.

I feel gratitude toward those people in Mr. Dubcek's office in the Czechoslovak Federal Assembly in Prague who always did their best to work around the chairman's tight schedule so that he and I could sit down and cover some more ground in the story of his life. Of them, Dr. Oldrich Jaros and Mrs. Maria Horna most deserve my thanks.

The help of many historians was also extremely valuable. Dr. Vera Jarosova in Prague shared with me all the documentation she had gathered for an intended critical biography of Dubcek. I am also grateful to researchers at the Czechoslovak Government Commission for the Investigation of the Events of 1967–1970 who permitted me to study their archives, especially Professor Vojtech Mencl and Dr. Josef Belda. Mr. Vladimir Krajci in Trencin, Slovakia, an old friend of Alexander Dubcek, helped in nailing down early episodes. Dr. Jan Uher in Bratislava aided significantly by reviewing the manuscript for possible factual errors or omissions. Also of help in Bratislava were Dr. Ivan Laluha and Dr. Pavol Pollak.

In helping orient the book to an international audience, and for stylistic

ALEXANDER DUBCEK'S CZECHOSLOVAKIA

POLAND

EAST GERMANY

Elbe R.

Dresden

Legnice

Terezin

Karlovy Vary

Cheb

Milovice

Prague

Labe R.

B o h e m i a

Pilsen

Vltava R.

M o r a v i a

Brno

Morava R.

WEST GERMANY

Danube R.

Mauthausen

Vienna

Bratislava

AUSTRIA

0

100 miles

0

100 kilometers

polish, Alan Williams deserves large credit. For accelerating the manuscript review process and gathering valuable family photographs as well as stepping in at a time of crisis, thanks must be paid to Pavol, Peter, and Milan Dubcek, especially to Milan's linguistic abilities.

I would never have found enough time to devote myself to this work without the understanding of Dr. Walter Bunge, the then director of the School of Journalism of The Ohio State University. I remain grateful to him.

I also feel obliged to acknowledge the publishers' great patience and understanding throughout the uneasy labors on this book. Any time there was an unexpected technical problem the heads of Kodansha America, Inc. and Farrar, Straus & Giroux—Minato Asakawa, Roger Straus, Jr., and Roger Straus III—and the editorial director of Kodansha America, Paul De Angelis, were ready to help. Of further assistance to the publishers were, in alphabetical order, Pavel Breier, Susan Brown, Louise Young Dye, Michael Heim, Jonathan Howell, Joyce Kay, Judy Klein, Jean Macdonald, Marc Romano, Danielle Rozgon, Kendra Schwartz, Jean-Emmanuel Shein, Eva Simeckova, Martin Sindelar, and Gordon Wise.

Finally, my wife, Suzanne, who was with me in Prague during the crucial time the bulk of the book was written helped in innumerable ways.

HOPE
DIES
LAST

1

HOW A MAN'S FATE IS MADE

THE question of how much we make our own fates, and how much is determined for us, will be argued forever. My family's restless journeying certainly had a strong and early effect on me. I was conceived by a pair of Slovak socialist dreamers who happened to have emigrated to Chicago. Before I was born, they returned to their native Slovakia. I can't remember how I put up with the ship's rolling.

I was born in Czechoslovakia (of which Slovakia had become a part in 1918) almost exactly three years after the First World War. Of course I have almost no early memories of Slovakia, since I was only three years old when my parents took me on another long haul. This time we traveled 4,000 miles east by railroad, to Soviet Kirghizia, close to China.

We stayed in Kirghizia until I was twelve, and most of my early memories go back there, to a place then called Pishpek. Later we moved to Gorky, in central Russia on the Volga River, where we lived another five years. When I was seventeen, my father finally brought me back to Slovakia. My idea of Slovakia was based entirely on my mother's and father's reminiscences. It was 1938; Czechoslovakia was being dismembered by Hitler and Slovakia turned into a separate state. The storm of World War II broke just as I came of age. Everything I was to do afterwards was marked by the sum of all my previous experiences. Could it be otherwise?

My memories of my early years are random and sketchy. Like anyone else, I could see my past life more clearly as I grew, though sometimes it seems like a film that unwinds, some parts faster and others slower.

Naturally, there were situations that I did not understand at the time, and in some cases it took me many years to get at their meaning. Also, there were happenings that I am still trying to grasp. I often rethink my past reactions and behavior, and I would be lying if I said that I am satisfied with all I did. While I believe I have never betrayed my conscience, I still relive certain episodes again and again for the heightened perception that can come with the passage of years. Sometimes earlier views are turned upside down. But knowledge and understanding come gradually, and one must, unfortunately, make many decisions without really knowing everything one should.

Both my parents were born in west central Slovakia. From the fall of Great Moravia in the tenth century until 1918, Slovakia had been a part of Hungarian Crown lands. From 1526 on, Hungary itself was part of the Habsburg Empire. * The administrative and political systems of Austria and Hungary were quite different, especially after the *Ausgleich*, or compromise, of 1867. In Hungarian-dominated lands, political as well as nationalist oppression was much worse than in the western part of the Empire, made up of Austria, Bohemia, and Moravia. Modernization also lagged behind in Hungarian Slovakia, adding underdevelopment to misrule.

The birthplace of my father, Stefan, was a village called Uhrovec, about two miles northeast of the then district seat, Banovce, where my mother, Pavlina Kobydova, was born. This picturesque area of wooded hills in the western part of the Strazov Highlands, east and south of the White Carpathians, had limited farming resources and only small manufacturing to provide precarious subsistence for a growing population. Uhrovec derives its name from the word meaning "Hungarian" in Slovak. The local population had applied the designation to a redoubt that a group of Hungarians built there in the eleventh century, shortly after their coming to the Danube valley from Asia.

By the turn of the twentieth century, Uhrovec was a purely Slovak village of about a thousand people. Alongside a Catholic majority there was an unusually large Protestant minority, composed of Augsburg Lutherans. Later statistics even show a Protestant majority in Uhrovec, rare in predominantly Catholic Slovakia but less so in the central region, where Protestants had found refuge from the Counter-Reformation in Bohemia in the seventeenth century. My great-grandfather Andrej Dubcek was listed in the

---

* The name *Hungary* is historically ambivalent. In Slovak as well as in Czech, two different terms are used to address this ambivalence. *Hungary* means Hungary proper, without the territories later conquered. *Uhry* also includes all other parts of the St. Stephen's Crown, including, for instance, Slovakia and Croatia.

Protestant parish register of Uhrovec as well as in the district register of taxpayers in the early nineteenth century.

There was some small manufacturing in Uhrovec at that time—a saw-mill, a spinning mill, a cane-making workshop, and even a little glassworks—but farming was still the main occupation. Overall, jobs were scarce, and many young people had to look for work elsewhere. My grandfather was a glassmaker at the local glassworks. There were three children in the impoverished family, two boys and a girl. They had no house of their own, they owned no land, so they depended entirely on my grandfather's work. When the children were small he died of tuberculosis, and the burden of bringing them up fell on my grandmother. Fortunately, she was permitted to take her husband's place in the glassworks.

The little house in which my father's family lived at the time—inhabiting a ten-by-ten foot room with no indoor plumbing—still stands. In this cramped space, my grandmother raised her three children, and she raised them well, taking care that each learned real skills. My father was trained as a carpenter, his younger brother, Michal, as a tailor, and their sister, Zuzana, as a seamstress. It meant great sacrifice on my grandmother's part, but she never wavered; many people then did not have such strength and perseverance and left their children without any useful skills.

In my father's time there was a two-class Catholic elementary school and a five-class public school in Uhrovec, with Hungarian as the language of instruction. Slovak was taught for only two hours a week in the elementary school. Attendance, however, was generally limited to children from better-off families, and I am not sure how many classes my father could go to.

I am sure that the poverty of my father's childhood spurred him all his life, predetermining both his behavior and his views of the world. Growing up, I saw him as an energetic, enterprising, fiercely independent man, but thoughtful and almost always in a good mood. He was also physically very strong and skillful, and I always watched closely what he did and how he did it. I soon noticed that other adults respected him. In other words, he was the kind of father whose authority came easily. I accepted his judgment unreservedly.

Poor or not, my father was a political animal from his early years. This was not accidental. I knew from him, as from my mother, that in this region, with its long patriotic tradition and relatively high literacy rate, people took a lively interest in the political and social events of the outside world. They were particularly proud that Ludovit Stur, the founding father of modern Slovak national consciousness, was born in Uhrovec in 1815. Stur was the younger son of a Protestant teacher, and his landmark efforts at

national revival—culminating in the fateful years of 1848 and 1849—were
well known throughout the country.

As a nation without statehood, clearly drawn borders, or even autonomy,
the Slovaks were naturally restive. They resisted the policy of forced Hungarization imposed by Budapest and fought for their identity, their culture,
and even the preservation of their language. In that respect, the views of the
educated political elite and the populace converged. The Slovak working
class was especially concerned with social justice. Socialism and industrial
democracy were in the air. When my dad was learning his craft, there were
already various workers' interest groups in Uhrovec as well as a cell of
Slovak Social Democracy, founded in 1905.

In 1910, at the age of nineteen, my father walked south along the Vah
and Danube rivers to Budapest in search of work. He knew Hungarian, and
soon he found a job in a furniture factory. There he quickly joined a group
struggling to organize a Hungarian Labor Party cell in the factory. This was
a young party with a program combining Lassallian and Marxist concepts,
similar to the Gotha Program of German Social Democracy. To the
Hungarian authorities, the HLP was dangerously radical, and my father
lost his job after only a few months.

It was then that, like thousands of young Slovaks before him—and more
in the years to come—my father decided to go to America. America looked
to them, as to so many Europeans, like a promised land. It was a republic,
which in itself was refreshing viewed from a Europe still half-governed by
autocratic monarchies. America was a democracy, too, and that was even
more admirable. And it was big, and opportunity seemed to be waiting
there for all hardworking people.

My uncle Michal went along. They arrived in 1912 and went to Chicago,
where there was a large Slovak community in the northern part of the city.

In his first years in America my father held various carpentry jobs, made
about twenty-five dollars a week, and took an active part in Slovak social
life, mainly in the Slovak section of the American Socialist Party. At that
time this party, with over 100,000 members, was at its peak, and the
Chicago branch included several ethnic sections. In addition to campaigning in city and state elections, the party's Slovak section in Chicago organized many activities. My father attended lectures and courses in English
and public oratory, did gymnastics in a Slovak workers' club called Spevo-
kol, and acted in plays.

In 1915, when he was twenty-four years old, my father found a job
paying forty dollars a week in a musical instruments factory at Webster and
Ashland streets, north of North Avenue. Most workers in this factory were
Hungarians, and it was lucky that my father knew their language well.

By 1916 my father seems to have decided to stay in America, and he became a citizen. Apparently, he then lived relatively well. An old friend of his wrote me years ago, remembering how my father had shared his streetcar tickets with him every workday, passing his transfer from the tram's window at Ashland station. Another friend recalled how my father refused to abandon his landlady, even though his room had no bath, because she was a widow with four children and his rent was her only income.

This quiet but largely satisfying life was upset in 1917 by America's entry into World War I, which was a great shock to socialists in the United States. Themselves firmly opposed to all war, they had been convinced by Woodrow Wilson's and the Democratic Party's campaign promises of 1916 that these views would prevail. In fact, the Americans were the only party in the Socialist International to keep faith with the International's long-standing antiwar policy, even after the United States entered the war.

My father sincerely shared these pacifist sentiments. An old friend of the family remembered how my father had reasoned that, if he were drafted and sent to a European battlefield, he might well have to shoot at other Slovaks serving in the Austro-Hungarian Army. Such a possibility appalled him.

Under such circumstances, my father and a Slovak friend, Jozef Griger, decided to dodge the U.S. draft by waiting out the war in Mexico. In Laredo, Texas, they met many Quakers and other conscientious objectors trying to get across the border. But my dad and Griger did not find the right connection and were caught, put on trial, and given the choice of eighteen months in jail or a fine of $1,000. Unable to pay the fine, they went to jail.

When they appeared before the judge, they were offered the option of promising to join the army. On principle they refused. When the war ended, they were still in jail. After his release, my father returned to his job in the musical instrument factory in Chicago. It was then that my parents met, at the Slovak Workers' House, and they soon got married.

My mother had come to Chicago even earlier than my father. My mother's parents, Samuel and Anna Kobyda, lived in Banovce, not far from Uhrovec. There my mother was born in 1897, the youngest of six children. Hers was a poor Catholic family, landless like my own father's. Of her five siblings, three had come to America between 1902 and 1904—her brother, Michael, and sisters Katharine and Antonia.

My mother followed them on the long journey across the Atlantic in 1909. She arrived, at the age of thirteen, in the company of strangers. But in Chicago she found her sisters and brother, and they helped her to start a new life.

My mother worked as a cook and housemaid in the home of a wealthy Jewish businessman. The fact that both my parents had come from the same part of Slovakia almost surely added to their mutual natural attraction. My mother, self-taught and with a highly developed sense of justice and of the good and truthful, leaned spontaneously toward socialist ideas. After all, in many ways they were very close to her Christian upbringing. She, too, was active in the Slovak section of the Socialist Party.

In some respects, she was even more strong willed than my father. I remember her above all as a woman of unlimited kindness of heart, always ready to sacrifice. A true homemaker, she never failed to make our always modest accommodations warm, clean, and appealing. Flowers were never missing, wherever we lived. I was closer to my mother, in some respects, than I ever was to my father. I did the chores around the house, and I was not always cheerful about it, but she used to tell me, "You are the one I can rely on."

My brother, Julius, was born in December 1919, amid the post-World War I turmoil that struck ethnic life in Chicago. The Socialists broke into several factions, with ethnic groups moving toward a more radical course on the Leninist model. It was not surprising that ethnic groups were mainly responsible for this split; they were simply not yet well rooted in American ways. Anyway, the split carried the movement even further from the mainstream of American life and presaged the coming agony of the whole American Left. Both my parents soon joined one of the two newly established Communist parties, which one, I cannot tell. It was my mother, I was told, who brought my dad to the study of Marxism, which he soon accepted as his own creed.

I can imagine how exciting this time must have been for them: the revolution in Russia seemed to open a new era. Until then, socialism was just a dream. But in Russia, as they were told in one stormy meeting after another in Chicago, the November Revolution was turning dream into reality.

At the same time, their old country, Slovakia, had finally ceased to be a Hungarian colony. It was part of a new, democratic republic: Czechoslovakia. This, too, had to affect my parents' views and plans. Contrary to what many think, the idea of union with the Czechs did not originate in the aftermath of World War I. It had been proposed as far back as the mid-nineteenth century. The closeness of both nations and their languages, and the Czechs' tireless support for Slovak national aspirations in the past, made the union natural.

Moreover, there was no other realistic way to extricate the Slovak nation from the thousand-year-old Hungarian yoke, and even that was only made possible by the defeat of the Central Powers and the collapse of Austria-Hungary. Either way, it was not quite incidental that a secret Slovak conference met in Turciansky sv. Martin and approved the idea of a joint Czecho-Slovak state toward the end of May 1918—only a few days before Tomas Masaryk and representatives of American Slovaks signed the Pittsburgh Agreement, which also endorsed the idea of Czecho-Slovakia.

For the thousands of Czechs and Slovaks in Chicago, this was a welcome development. In early 1921 my parents decided to return to Slovakia. They took their savings and sailed back across the ocean—with Julius, who was then fifteen months old, and myself on the way. The passports they carried were American. I missed being born in America by only a few months.

But large parts of both my parents' families stayed in America, and today I have many relatives there whom I have never seen—cousins, nieces and nephews, the descendants of aunts and uncles. There are undoubtedly some I've never even heard of, because, during the years of the Stalinist regime in Czechoslovakia, one was not supposed to have relatives in the West, and to correspond with them was dangerous. It is only now that I have begun receiving letters from these "lost" relatives. Some of them still live in Chicago; others moved to Michigan and Florida.

Back in Uhrovec, my father found his old home uninhabitable. Fortunately, my parents were able to move into a small apartment in a house owned by the local Protestant parish. Until their arrival, it had been occupied by the church organist, Alexander Trancik, who also administered the parish school. Trancik, a good man, vacated the apartment so my parents could use it. He became my godfather when I was born there on November 27. In fact, my parents had planned to give me the name Milan, but they changed it to Alexander in his honor.

That little village house was quite significant, because it had also been the birthplace of Ludovit Stur. Was it my destiny to be born in the same house as the greatest Slovak of the previous century? This long arm of coincidence became a cause of great irritation for the Husak regime after they declared me an enemy and a nonperson in 1970.

2

IN SEARCH OF A DREAM

W HEN my parents went to America, they were subjects of the Emperor Franz Josef, and Slovakia was not even on the map of Europe. When they came home in 1921, everything seemed upside down: there was no Austria-Hungary anymore, they were citizens of the United States, and their old country was part of one of four European states to emerge from the war. Czechoslovakia was born of the political order created by the Paris Treaties, and its security—its very existence—was made dependent on the maintenance of that system. In the long run, this proved fateful.

I can only guess at my parents' thoughts and feelings about all these changes, but I imagine that they needed time to sort them out. That the times did not allow for such reflection one can deduce from the troubled historical record.

From a Slovak point of view, the main result of all the changes was not only that Slovakia was free from Hungary for the first time in a millennium but also that its borders were clearly drawn and internationally recognized in the Trianon Treaty, which Hungary had to sign in 1920. Within Czechoslovakia, Slovakia was an administrative unit of its own—no longer a vague geographic notion with a pejorative name, Horne Uhry, or Upper Hungary.

And, according to its recently approved constitution, the new Czechoslovakia was a democratic republic with legislative powers vested in a two-chamber parliament. Tomas Masaryk, a democrat with socialist leanings, was the president and a great moral authority in the whole country. In the first parliamentary elections in Czechoslovakia, in 1920, the Social Democratic Party, which still united all socialists, won over 25 percent of the general vote, becoming the strongest political force in the country. One

8

might add, of course, that even before the war the socialists were by far the strongest parties in Bohemia and Moravia, getting as much as 40 percent of the vote in the elections of 1907 and 1911. Their strength in Slovakia before the war cannot be reliably estimated.

At least some policies of the new state were consequently enlightened and positive. The land reform of 1919, for example, was certainly a step toward a more equitable system of landholding. It decreed the maximum area of privately owned land to be 250 hectares (370 acres), of which 150 hectares could be cultivated. It is interesting that the Czechoslovak Land Law of 1991 returned to similar criteria. Another example of the new state's social policies was the August 1921 law on enterprise councils, a step toward industrial democracy. And, for Slovakia, it was of great importance that a law of November 11, 1919, established the first national university in Bratislava, the Slovak capital city.

Not everything, however, was roses. The new constitution was based on a unitary idea of the state. It spoke of only one Czechoslovak nation. The Language Law also spoke of only one, Czechoslovak language. That was a Czech political exigency aimed at minimizing the significance of large non-Slavic minorities both in the Czech lands and in Slovakia, but it was also an awkward fiction, insensitive toward the Slovaks' striving for recognition of their national and cultural identity. In the long run, it did no good, as the events of 1938, 1939, and even 1992 were to show. Various Slovak factions immediately opposed the whole idea, including the unitary constitutional setup, and demanded autonomy instead.

There were other serious problems as well. As my parents were returning home, hundreds of Slovak families were bound west across the Atlantic. The postwar economic recession had afflicted Slovakia as early as 1920, a year before it hit the rest of Czechoslovakia. Production was in decline, and unemployment was rampant. Understandably, this crisis reinforced my parents' socialist views.

While the Social Democratic Party lost some strength in the elections of 1920 compared with the prewar period, important segments of the labor movement were highly radicalized by the hardships of a long war, the postwar recession, and the deluding example of the Russian Revolution. In 1920 and 1921, parties on the Left all over the world were splitting, and Czech and Slovak Social Democrats were no exception. While the moderate minority remained in the old party, the radicals founded a Communist Party on the Bolshevik model and accepted the twenty-one conditions of membership in the Third International laid down by Lenin.

The Communists were particularly strong in Bohemia and Moravia, but even in Slovakia the radical, revolutionary forces represented substantial majorities in much of the Slovak socialist movement. Such was the case in Uhrovec. My parents soon found out that the local political air was not unlike that of the ethnic Chicago they had left behind.

As my father later told me, he had hardly adjusted to the time difference between America and Europe when he found himself in the middle of a stormy political debate about the past and future of the labor movement. Then, on September 25, 1921, he chaired a meeting of the local cell of the Slovak Social Democratic Party at which the main agenda item was the party's future affiliation. It took little time to accept the political platform of the Third International.

The main speaker was a certain Balastok, a Slovak deputy of the newly formed Communist Party of Czechoslovakia. Under the circumstances, he probably needed few persuasive skills. It was decided to found a local cell of the Czechoslovak Communist Party, and my father was elected its chairman. My uncle Michal, who had returned from America with my parents, was one of the elected committee members.

In retrospect one wonders how much the people of Uhrovec knew about the issues before them. These were simple folk, making all judgments from their own personal and historical experience. But wasn't the same true in countries presumably more politically mature—in France, Germany, Italy, and, of course, Bohemia? Everywhere on the Left at this time there sprang up an uncritical enthusiasm about virtually all things Russian. Whole parties with seasoned leaderships embraced Bolshevik doctrine, forswearing political independence.

Undoubtedly there was an alternative, as we can see when rereading the polemics between Lenin and Kautsky on the problems of democracy, socialism, and dictatorship. But I, for one, doubt that alternatives were seriously contemplated; they had almost no chance in an air charged with emotions rooted in justified grievances, old and new. Quick and radical solutions fit this atmosphere much better than calls for reason and moderation. Everything looked simple: a victorious working man's revolution was rising in Russia, the dream of social justice put into practice. Now it was all good souls' task to give that endeavor their support—complete, immediate, and unselfish.

My parents' part in Interhelpo is a good example of this attitude. Interhelpo was a cooperative venture of several hundred workers from Czechoslovakia who went to Soviet Russia, in five groups between 1925 and 1932, with the idea of helping to build a new society.

Politically, this movement strove to discourage further military intervention, like that of the Allies in 1919, to Russian affairs and to overcome the isolation of the new Soviet state. Economically, the movement organized campaigns to help Soviet Russia with money, goods, and a variety of medical and technical services. This overall endeavor was coordinated by the International Workers Relief, which had its headquarters in Germany, and was best known by its German name, Internationale Arbeiterhilfe, or IAH.

The IAH campaign was launched in 1921 as a response to an appeal from Lenin to bring relief to the victims of famine. While the IAH was undoubtedly directed from Moscow, its main offices stayed in Berlin until 1933. It grew into a large international organization by 1926, when it claimed over 15 million members.

While the idea to send a cooperative of qualified workers to Soviet Russia was pursued in other countries as well, Interhelpo was a strictly Czech and Slovak initiative, coordinated in its aims with the IAH but administratively quite separate.

My father first learned about Interhelpo from the Party press in late 1923 or early 1924. By then the organization had started to negotiate with the Soviet government. The cooperative's chairman was Rudolf Marecek, a former prisoner of war in Russia. Marecek had experienced the Bolshevik Revolution and the ensuing civil war in Russian Central Asia. It was he who conceived and pursued the idea of dispatching the cooperative to the easternmost part of Soviet Turkestan, later named Kirghizia (and today called Kyrgyztan).

Marecek traveled among workers' houses in Czechoslovakia, giving lectures on the idyllic conditions in Central Asia. Using a projector, he showed photographs of a sparsely populated, thriving country of fertile farmland, rich in raw materials. His audiences were impressed by the images of thick forests, orchards with trees loaded with apples and peaches, vineyards with ripe, burgeoning grapes, and camel caravans.

My father attended these lectures in the nearby towns of Handlova and Trencin and was, like many other workers, convinced and delighted. He was not just a revolutionary, he was a romantic. He told my mother about the project, and they decided to join Interhelpo. Distances and unknown challenges could not discourage them: they were already seasoned travelers.

In addition to occupational skills, membership was contingent upon a deposit of 3,000 Czechoslovak crowns. Working qualifications included expertise as a carpenter, mechanic, electrician, turner, tanner, baker, butcher, and so on. Craftsmen brought with them their tools. My father took everything he needed for a cabinetmaking and carpentry workshop. Only a few single members of the cooperative did not have any specific professional training.

Three thousand crowns was a lot of money in 1925; individual members of the second group had to contribute even more—5,000 crowns. My parents could have bought a house and set up a cabinetmaker's workshop with their membership fee had they thought in more practical terms. But they decided otherwise. Many members deposited all their life savings; others sold houses, land, and other property. The cooperative was dependent solely on its members' contributions.

With these dues, the cooperative acquired a complex collection of machinery and tools, including a steam locomotive, a forty-horsepower generator, a Ford truck and tractor, as well as complete facilities for woodworking and metalworking shops, with lathes and cuttermachines, equipment for a brick field, textile machines, and tannery fixtures. More than a dozen railroad cars were needed to carry this equipment to the Soviet Union, and transportation costs also had to be paid by the cooperative. My parents, like most other members, sacrificed everything they had.

I have the distinct impression that only a few of the organizers were solely inspired by ideological zeal. Most of the rank-and-file members were seeking a job and a decent existence, opportunities they could expect in a country presumably ruled by workers. Fleeing widespread unemployment and bleak prospects at home, the men and women of the cooperative were honest and self-sacrificing, devoted to the idea of a promised land with no masters, plentiful jobs, and no worries about daily subsistence.

In August 1923, the leaders of Interhelpo offered to send the cooperative to the Turkestan Soviet Republic. They also applied for papers for all its members.

An affirmative answer from the Soviet government arrived in February 1924, and in August 1924, two officials of Interhelpo traveled to Moscow to negotiate the actual agreement. The head of the delegation was a Communist member of the upper chamber of the Czechoslovak parliament, Senator Vaclav Chlumecky; he was accompanied by Rudolf Marecek. Chlumecky's role in the enterprise implies that it was sanctioned by the Communist Party of Czechoslovakia. But membership in the Communist Party was not a condition of membership in Interhelpo, and Party committees do not seem to have screened the members of the cooperative.

After the negotiations in Moscow, Chlumecky fell ill and Marecek went on alone to Tashkent to reconnoiter. Tashkent was the capital of Soviet Turkestan, which included the whole territory between the Caspian Sea and the Chinese border. This was the former Russian Turkestan, which had been conquered by the czarist Russian Army only in 1881 and then reconquered by the Red Army in 1920.

Obviously, Marecek did not initially envisage a large industrial coopera-tive but rather a smaller and more mobile expedition. The place he had originally proposed as the home of the cooperative was a town called Przhevalsk, on the eastern shores of Lake Issyk Kul, in the foothills of the Pamirs. A contemporary story in the Slovak Communist daily newspaper, *Pravda Chudoby*, described the location as a "climatically healthy region," a characterization probably supplied by Marecek himself. If so, his infor-mation could most charitably be termed misleading.

While in Tashkent, Marecek found out that the railroad went no farther than Pishpek, some 500 miles west of Przhevalsk. One has to wonder how he ever imagined that several hundred people, including women and children, even without all their heavy machines and equipment, could have traveled on foot through desert and wilderness for several months to reach the place that he had so colorfully described. Even the railroad as far as Pishpek had only recently been completed.

Marecek now went to Pishpek, where he signed an agreement with the representatives of the Turkestanese Council of People's Commissars. It was confirmed in Moscow in November.

Marecek's negotiations in Tashkent and Pishpek were complicated by the concurrent reorganization of the administrative division of the whole re-gion. The Soviet Union had been constitutionally established only in January of that year. The Turkestan Republic now ceased to exist, and the area around Pishpek became an autonomous region of Soviet Uzbekistan. Just two years later, in 1926, it was raised to the status of the Autonomous Republic of Kirghizia. It did not become a union republic of the USSR until 1936.

It is difficult to say to what extent Marecek understood all these shifts. On his return to Czechoslovakia, he reported the change of the planned location to the cooperative. This apparently caused little concern, since Marecek was the only person to have any conception of the places involved.

Members of the cooperative discussed and approved the agreements concluded with the Soviet side at a plenary meeting in Zilina, in western Slovakia, in November 1924. The meeting also made final allocations of funds and decided to dispatch the first part of the expedition early the next spring.

Thus, on the rainy Sunday morning of March 29, 1925, the Interhelpo train set out on its journey. In a cloud of steam and smoke, a locomotive pulled twenty-four railroad cars out of the Zilina station straight to the east. Ten coaches accommodated the members of the cooperative and their families; fourteen freight cars carried their equipment.

There were 303 people in that expedition, representing all major ethnic groups of Czechoslovakia—163 Czechs, 101 Slovaks, 18 Hungarians, 13 Germans, and 8 Ukrainians. Neither my brother, Julius, nor myself, would have a clear recollection of that morning. And I carried away only scant memories of the place where I spent my first three years and four months: the faces of a few friends and relatives, the image of the house where we lived and of the courtyard behind it, which was my first playground.

Strangely, as a child's memory may work, I also remember one little episode of those early days in Uhrovec. On a Sunday afternoon when we were supposed to visit some relatives, my mother dressed both Julius and me in our holiday best, blue navy jackets with wide, white collars. In those outfits, we were sent out to the backyard to wait for her. Alas, there was a wooden washtub filled with dirty water in the yard, and in no time Julius and I climbed into it, to play sailors afloat. What followed, instead of the planned Sunday agenda, was the first thrashing I can recall.

I also distinctly remember our St. Bernard dog, which I loved and we had to leave behind, and a majestic, tame deer in an enclosure behind the church which I watched with great awe. The deer's name—Apita—has stayed with me forever.

There were nearly 140 children in that expedition, 80 of them under the age of three, and I doubt that any of them had a clear idea where we were going, and why. But at least their parents knew: they were searching for a dream.

3

A NEW HOME IN KIRGHIZIA

D REAMS rarely match reality. They tend rather to the ominous or the optimistic. The Interhelpists' dream was of the second kind. What awaited us was quite the contrary of Maracek's paradise. The fact that the enterprise did not end in complete failure testifies to the Interhelpists' endurance. How much of my memory of the journey to Pishpek is my own recollection and how much is my parents' tale I cannot tell. In any case, the journey is stored in my memory in great detail, as if I remembered it all myself.

The expedition had to change trains at the Polish-Soviet border because of the Russian wide-track railroad system. Everything the cooperative was bringing with it had to be reloaded onto the wider Russian freight cars, and the Interhelpists moved to Russian coaches that would be their home for the next three weeks.

In the interwar period, the Polish-Soviet border was much farther east than it is today because Galicia was part of Poland. It was the Prut River that separated Poland from the Ukraine. To transfer everything from one set of cars to another took a day and a half, but then we started moving again. The train puffed through Ukrainian snow-covered birch forests to Kiev and then to Russia proper: to Kursk and Voronezh. My father later showed me the route on a map, and he told me that he and my mother wondered why all the homes along the tracks were built of lumber; brick or stone houses were rare.

In Penza, my parents told me, a stopover halfway between Voronezh and Samara, the locals remembered the Czechoslovak legionnaires whose trains had passed through in 1918 on their long, dramatic journey back home through Siberia.

My mother and the other cooks were busy feeding everyone—no easy task, of course. But local people were very friendly wherever the train stopped, resupplying the Interhelpists with food and water.

The train crossed the Volga—later to be my swimming pond—at Samara. It was renamed for Kuibyshev, a leading Bolshevik, after his death in 1935. The old history was at odds with the new one at that time. Today the process seems to be in reverse.

Beyond the Volga, spring was in full swing. And, with each day of the journey, we realized how huge and manifold was our adopted country.

Forests thinned when the train approached the southern foothills of the Urals, and a vast steppe with tracks of desert took their place as the railroad turned southeast after passing Orenburg. Already we were in Central Asia or, as it was then called, the Kazakh Soviet Autonomous Republic. Camel caravans could be seen crossing the endless space; otherwise there seemed to be nothing along the railroad but telegraph poles and occasional water tanks. Each stop looked like a marketplace—stalls and shops where people from miles around haggled over what they came to sell or buy. This was the Interhelpists' first encounter with the Oriental bazaar.

Aralsk, a larger town on the northern tip of the Aral Sea, was an important stopover. Rows of yurts, large, circular tents, were evidence that a significant number of the Kazakh population still led a traditional nomadic life-style. In the local bazaar, my mother told me, the Interhelpists tasted *kumys* or mare's milk, for the first time, but there was no cow's milk to buy for the children—a great concern for her as chair of the women's committee of the expedition.

Beyond Aralsk, a track of sand and rock called the Hunger Desert seemed to have no end, causing some to voice their first misgivings about the expedition. But then came Arys, at the southern edge of the desert, and Syr Darya, a powerful river flowing north from the Pamirs and the Hindu Kush to feed the Aral Sea.

Greenery soon returned, along with the view of white tips of giant mountains on the distant horizon. This was Tian Shan, Chinese for "Heavenly Mountain Range." Most of the range lies in Sinkiang. Crystal clear streams suddenly appeared here and there, then woods, meadows, and huts of Russian settlers surrounded by gardens and fields. My parents often remembered how the morale on the Interhelpo train rose as sand turned into meadows and forest.

It was sleeting at dawn on April 24, 1925, as the train arrived at the end of the tracks. It had taken twenty-seven days to get to this point. Now, where was Pishpek? The train had stopped seemingly in the middle of nowhere. There was no station building, only a few low Russian shanties and around them bare steppe. I later frequently heard repeated somebody's dispirited comment: "Here we have arrived at the end of the world."

This was not quite true, of course. Pishpek was only about two and a half miles farther east, on a caravan route leading to the western shores of Lake Issyk Kul. One could speculate that Marco Polo had passed there centuries ago on his way to China. Why the railroad builders stopped so short of the settlement I don't know.

Pishpek, soon to be our new hometown, was then still mainly a "station" for the nomadic people inhabiting the region. Of course, its center was a lively bazaar where almost everything—grain, rice, fruit, vegetables, corn and chicken, even sheep and cattle—was bought and sold amid much haggling.

I can't say how many permanent residents the place had in 1925. A pre-World War I Russian encyclopedia put the number at about 15,000. By the time of our arrival, it had probably grown somewhat, what with the new railroad.

The representatives of this first Interhelpo group, namely its chairman, Filip Svolik, had to go from the end of the railroad to Pishpek to announce our arrival and get an idea of how to start. It must be said that the local soviet was understanding and very helpful so far as its limited resources allowed. Very soon several Interhelpists, including my father, became members of the town's soviet.

A letter of May 25, 1925, sent by Chairman Svolik to Rudolf Tesar, a member of the second group of Interhelpo, which was just about to set off on its own journey, sums up the situation a month after arrival:

We arrived in Pishpek on April 24, 1925, and we were disappointed by [the contrast with] Marecek's reports. Neither the country nor the climate agrees with his reports. We are in a region with very primitive economic conditions. We are quartered in a former military encampment, which consists of about ten little decaying barracks. We have repaired these barracks, and now it is somewhat more cheerful. We have a contract to use these barracks until the end of March next year. To stay there during wintertime is [however] impossible, so we will very soon start building family houses.

The contract signed by Marecek was not enough, and we had to conclude another one . . . to secure land for the construction of family houses as well as for our industrial workshops along the railroad. The land Marecek contracted for is only good for farming, which we have already launched. Local authorities do their best to meet our needs. We hope that in spite of the difficult start we will manage [to accomplish] the things most needed in a short time.

There is no industry here whatsoever. There is only a [Russian] brewery, which we will fix up because their mechanical equipment is in very bad shape. Bring your duvets and kitchen pots and dishes, because everything is in short supply here, and nights are quite cold.

One of the first concerns was to generate income. When the cooperative arrived, their cash amounted to only 332 rubles. Individual members had no cash of their own. Production, however modest, had to be launched immediately. Shoemakers were the first to market their products. Their boots were bought by the town's police or militia. Tailors and cabinetmakers soon followed; my father managed the woodworking workshop. Their work made it possible to buy lumber, building stone, and coal, all of which had to be brought from as far away as Samara. Then the Commercial Bank of Kirghizia provided a loan of 20,000 rubles to finance the construction of the tannery, for which the cooperative had brought all the machinery.

The arrival of the cooperative caused a great sensation among the population of Pishpek. The Kirghiz and the Tajiks, who had never seen an automobile or a tractor, were very excited. When one or the other came along, raising a cloud of dust, the locals ran away in panic, shouting, *Shaitan, Shaitan,* "Satan, Satan." But after a while they got used to machines, and the Interhelpists' relationship with the native population was mostly very friendly.

The harsh conditions on arrival forced the cooperative to function for some time as a commune. No wages could be paid in the first several months; there was only a collective kitchen, and all had to live in barracks built twenty years before by Japanese prisoners of the Russo-Japanese War. Not only were roofs leaky but they had big holes, doors and windows were either entirely missing or broken, and floors were in many places rotten. At least one family decided to return home immediately after seeing these "facilities." Only the most important repairs were made in the temporary accommodations. Construction of family houses was obviously a priority, along with building workshops, and planting and harvesting the first crops.

Safe drinking water was another serious problem. Local people took all their water from a weak and shallow stream and apparently did not know how to drill wells. No one knew at what depth water could be found. Fortunately our people reached water at about sixty feet, but it remained in short supply all the time we were in Pishpek.

Family houses had to be built before winter. Because the brickyard was not yet completed, bricks had to be baked in the sun and tied with wet clay and straw; there was no quicklime or cement. Everybody worked, including children. I remember vividly mixing the wet clay. Houses were planned as square structures, each for four families. There was one room per family, a joint kitchen and a small enclosed hallway. Roofs were made of lumber and covered with metal sheets. The chessboard street plan and numbered streets bore the imprint of my father's American experience.

In these early times, food was not plentiful. One of my earliest memories is of the huge flocks of omnipresent sparrows. When we arrived at the old military camp, we flushed out thousands of them that had been nesting on the broken roofs and even inside the barracks. Many more perched in large poplars behind the nearby cemetery. What they were feeding on was a mystery to us. Their eggs were everywhere, and we, the children, our stomachs never full, ate the eggs raw, sometimes even with the shell. We grilled captured sparrows over campfires and ate their little meat.

To help in feeding the pigs, we muddled through the waste dump for scraps. There, I had to brush teeming maggots off my feet. Of course, we went around barefoot most of the year, and the soles of our feet hardened so much that we could walk over a field of thistles and feel nothing.

Because almost everything was scarce, we had to take good care of all property, tools, and implements. A bucket, for example, was a treasured thing. When we dumped it in the well, we had to angle for it until we got it out.

After a year or so, conditions improved, and there was more to eat. Food from the cooperative's farm was occasionally supplemented by what our men shot on hunting trips in the neighborhood. They had brought their own guns from Czechoslovakia, and hunting licenses were no problem. A Kirghiz brought us an ancient, broken rifle, and our people greatly impressed him by fixing it. He remained a good friend.

There were, though, also serious and painful setbacks. The climate in Pishpek was much harsher than Marecek had predicted, especially in the summer, when it was extremely hot and humid. There was no physician in the first expedition, and when almost everyone contracted malaria in early summer, there was little to fight it with. Before the end of the first year, thirty children died of the disease.

Neither Julius nor I was affected, and I do not recall either of our parents ever being sick in Pishpek, or subsequently in Gorky, or back in Slovakia.

Another setback was a fire, which destroyed many of our workshops in 1926. All had to be built again, and strict precautions were taken to prevent future blazes. In the face of these misfortunes, some families left for other parts of Russia, and some returned home.

Among those who soon gave up was Marecek himself, who moved on to

Przhevalsk, the place he had originally planned to go, where general conditions were much better. There he settled down and took a local woman. I heard no more about him until after the Soviet occupation in 1968, when he suddenly appeared in Prague to be celebrated as the great hero of Interhelpo. The Husak regime even gave him a high decoration for his "merits." Those who remembered his real behavior were very angry, but there was nothing they could do.

In that context, I should say that my parents and I later often pondered the reasons for sending the cooperative to such a distant, inhospitable, and primitive environment. With its modern machinery and highly skilled members, Interhelpo could have been much more useful in a better chosen place, in the Ukraine or Russia proper. To go to Kirghizia in the first place was no doubt Marecek's eccentric idea, but those in Moscow who had the power of final decision could have easily changed that. Why they did not, I cannot tell. But it could well have been that given their xenophobia, they liked the idea of dispatching foreigners far away.

In November 1925, an additional sixty people arrived. My father met this group, on behalf of the cooperative, in Arys and accompanied them to Pishpek. In 1926, another group arrived, consisting of over 600 people, including two Czechoslovak physicians, Drs. Birnbaum and Lovas, as well as two teachers for the cooperative's school. One of them was the well-known Slovak writer Peter Jilemnicky, who was with us for several months.

Altogether five groups eventually came to Pishpek: two in 1925, one in 1926, one in 1928, and finally one in 1932, a total of 1,078 people. Among them was the family of my future wife, the Ondrises, who came with the largest group in August 1928. I came to know Anna Ondrisova well in Pishpek. Then our paths crossed again, for life, at the end of the Second World War in Slovakia.

School in Pishpek started from scratch—fifty children attended the same class in the first year. At the beginning, teaching took place in one of the smaller barracks of the encampment, and there were no textbooks, paper, or pencils. But that soon changed. The school moved to a newly built house, and the second expedition brought books and supplies, even music paper and a world atlas. I started school in Pishpek when I was eight years old, in 1929.

Initially, Slovak and Czech were the sole languages of instruction. All basic subjects were taught, including algebra, physics, history, and geography. In 1928 the school introduced instruction in Russian, not only because of pressure from local Soviet authorities but also for the practical reason that all higher education was in Russian. Before 1930 or so, most members of the cooperative thought in terms of a permanent stay in the Soviet Union.

I had mixed feelings when I saw that my Kirghiz and Tajik classmates could not be taught in their own language, and I felt sympathy for them. One of the Kirghiz boys, named Asherbey, became a good friend of mine. He was among the first to associate with us; when he later learned a craft, he worked in Interhelpo's textile factory.

I also remember how outraged I was when one of our own boys tried to provoke a native classmate by putting a bacon skin on his desk. The Kirghiz and the Tajiks were, of course, Moslems, and they never ate pork. When the class was over, the joke resulted in a fistfight, and I did not hesitate to fight on the locals' side against jokers of my own kind.

Julius and I soon adopted Pishpek as our hometown, and having few memories of the places we came from, we could hardly view anything around as "exotic." All the same, we were entirely fascinated with camels.

Once—I was hardly five years old—my brother and I came upon a camel hitched to a two-wheel Kirghiz cart. The owner was nowhere in sight. The camel stood motionless and it looked as if it was sleeping, which it probably was. What else could it have been doing? Julius, always enterprising, had the bright idea of climbing on the cart to see what the world looked like from that command post. He first helped me up, then climbed onto the cart himself. We had barely seated ourselves when Julius found a whip and cracked it over the camel's rump. At that, the animal woke up and started to run like a racehorse—through a few streets and out into the steppe. Maybe it knew where it was going, but we certainly did not. Soon Pishpek vanished behind the wavy landscape. The camel ran and ran. Behind it the cart jumped up and down and from side to side, with Julius and me terrified and hanging on for dear life.

I cannot recall how long the animal ran, but it did not stop by itself. A Kazakh on horseback suddenly appeared, cracked his long whip in the air, and curled it around the camel's neck, bringing the animal to a halt.

Julius and I climbed down from the cart as quickly as we could, much faster than we had gotten into it, and started running away, along the cart's trail back to Pishpek. I don't remember how long it took us to get home, but it was quite dark when we arrived, and everybody was looking for us. Our adventure, of course, brought the predictable consequences.

Julius was always more hotheaded than I, and he rarely thought twice before acting. Once, testing how thick the ice was, he almost drowned in a half-frozen pond behind the tannery. Winters were never too cold in

Pishpek, and, when Julius got to the middle of the pond, the ice broke. All we could see of him were his hands on the edges of the hole in the ice as he desperately tried to keep himself above water. Again, a Kirghiz ran to his rescue. He brought a long ladder, laid it on the ice, and inched toward Julius, finally pulling him out.

Life steadily improved as the cooperative established itself. Interhelpo worked hard and effectively to build Kirghizia's basic industries: the first power station and foundry, the first textile factory, mechanical tannery, a brickyard, and a furniture factory. Interhelpo's construction team designed and built the government house of the Kirghiz Republic, the state bank, a hospital, a school building, and a large house of culture with a 600-seat auditorium. The cooperative also introduced sugar beets to Kirghizia.

In 1926, Pishpek was renamed Frunze after the Soviet military man, opponent of Trotsky, and people's commissar of war, who had been born there and had died the year before. The population of the city grew to about 50,000 toward the end of the 1920s, according to a contemporary Soviet source. And, as the consolidation of Soviet power continued, there was an increasing emphasis on modernization and urbanization. But, after the defeat of the moderates in Moscow in 1928, Stalin started to impose his radical policies. Collectivization, which was launched in 1929, reached Kirghizia in 1930.

As a cooperative, Interhelpo was not directly affected in either its farming or its industrial sectors. But its governing practices were those its members had known from Czechoslovakia—a democratically elected board and chairman—and that was soon bound to run up against the Soviet practice of appointments. In 1928 Interhelpo had to join the centralized Soviet cooperative organization, and in 1930 it had to accept new statutes that corresponded with the Soviet model. In 1932 Interhelpo was divided into seven cooperatives.

Collectivization announced itself by the arrival of peasants deported from their homes in the Ukraine and in Russia and dispatched in freight cars to Siberia and Central Asia. I remember dreadful scenes at the Frunze railroad station. Some died en route, and those who survived, including children, looked like living corpses. They were so hungry that they ate fodder for pigs and poultry that was teeming with maggots. I can never forget the sight of a dead man with his belly blown out. I asked my mother what the man had died from, and she said, "From hunger." When I asked why he was so bulky, she explained that that had happened only after he died.

I don't remember anyone who understood what was causing this misery.

It was very disturbing for all of us, children as well as adults. At the same time, of course, we continued to live our normal lives. The grown-ups worked hard, from sunrise to sunset most of the time. We children went to school and did our homework, helped around the house, and played our little games. But life was not quite the same as before. A shadow of unknown origin loomed over whatever we did.

As the collectivization measures reached Kirghizia, they provoked widespread resistance. Kirghiz farmers formed armed groups known as *basmachi*. Some hid in towns and villages, some took to the mountains. At night they launched attacks on Russian officials, army units, and the militia. We saw some of their victims hanging from posts. Again, this violence was beyond comprehension, especially for a ten-year-old.

Collectivization and violent repression disrupted the whole life of the region, particularly the economy, which had been so visibly improving. A new tax imposed on fruit growers was followed by mass liquidation of orchards. I remember the fruit grower from whom we used to buy apples and other fruit. We arrived at his orchard one day only to see that he had cut down almost all his trees. Why? my mother asked him. "They are imposing a new, high tax on us, and I cannot afford to pay it," he said. "So I cut down most of my trees. The few I left are just enough for my family."

So fruit disappeared from the market. All agricultural production was severely affected, as forced collectivization and requisitions discouraged peasants from producing more than they needed for themselves.

In 1932 Interhelpo sent my father to Moscow for some professional training. At that time, I guess, he was already thinking about moving us. But the next move came very suddenly. In 1933 we moved west, to the city of Gorky.

I did not leave Frunze and the little house where we lived, the only home I really remembered well, without regret. I recall feeling insecure and fazed when I learned about the move. As we packed our belongings, I was quite sad. But the fact that the whole family was going was somewhat reassuring. After all, I was just twelve years old, and my curiosity about new places and people prevailed. Still, memories of Kirghizia never faded away.

Interhelpo continued to function, in its changed and fragmented structure, until December 1943, when it was dissolved and its factories taken over by the Kirghiz Ministry of Agriculture. That was in the middle of the war, and most members of the former cooperative stayed in Pishpek. Many remained even after the war, and, as far as I know, some of them, with their children and grandchildren, continue to live there today.

4

YEARS IN GORKY

Gorky is a historic Russian city at the confluence of the Volga and Oka rivers, about three hours by train from Moscow to the east. It had been known as Nizhniy Novgorod until the year before our arrival, when it was renamed after the great Russian writer Maxim Gorky. (He died in 1936. In 1991 the old name was readopted.) The city had almost a million inhabitants, and it certainly was the biggest place I had seen. It was an industrial center, especially for shipbuilding and textiles, and its university was one of Russia's oldest.

An automobile factory under construction was known as GAZ, the acronym of its full name, Gorkovskiy Avtozavod, or Automobile Works of Gorky. My father's job there was pattern making, preparation of body fillings and panels for cars and trucks. Fillings were then still made of wood, so skilled carpenters were in great demand; plastics replaced wood only much later, even in the West.

It helped that my father spoke fluent English, given the group of engineers and mechanics from Ford Motor Company who had come to oversee the introduction of a Ford-style assembly line. My father was often called on to interpret. Both my parents got to know several of the Americans, who occasionally came over for dinner or a chat and a glass of vodka. They were friendly and cheerful fellows, and I regret that I have forgotten their names. Maybe some of them are still alive. Julius and I watched these Americans with great curiosity, because America enjoyed enormous respect among the Russians.

We lived in an apartment house in Ruttenberg Village, a city quarter built especially for the employees of the automobile works. My mother did not go to work at that time. She took care of the household, as she had in Pishpek even while working full-time at the canteen.

Julius and I went to a much better school, a high school with smaller classes, stricter discipline, and distinctly better qualified teachers. The school also benefited—at least temporarily—from the new all-Union educational reform curriculum, which stressed traditional teaching methods and values. I took a growing interest in learning, and I think I was a rather good student. I certainly expected to pursue a college education, though I had no clear idea of what I would like to be. Julius was a year ahead of me, and usually we walked to school together.

I remember especially the more sports-minded of my classmates. I exchanged letters with two of them, Misha Zakharov and Valentin Belov, after the war. Because the parents of most students in the school worked in the automobile factory, GAZ supported our teams. I played water polo and soccer on a GAZ team and competed in sailing on the Volga and Oka. In winter we went skating on the frozen rivers, but the only kind of ice hockey we knew how to play was with a tennis ball and a bent stick.

Early in 1935, our family life was disrupted by an affair that may look trivial now but at the time seemed very grave. My brother, then fifteen years old, got involved in a street fight with boys from another neighborhood and injured one of them. My parents were afraid that Julius might be very severely punished—and under Soviet law. It was decided that my mother would take Julius back home to Czechoslovakia. They left almost overnight. In the end, nothing too serious happened and the injured boy recovered, but, for the rest of my stay in the Soviet Union, I was alone with my father.

My mother and brother went to Uncle Michal's house in Trencin. After Uncle Michal had returned from America, he used his savings to found a successful tailoring cooperative. He called the enterprise, of which he was the manager and main shareholder, the American Tailoring Cooperative. With his support, Julius finished school and was trained as a fitter. After 1948 the cooperative was nationalized. Uncle Michal lost everything, and in the end he took his own life.

Things were never the same after my mother's and brother's departure. I missed them in different ways. With Julius the constant companion of all my childhood games was suddenly gone. I also missed my mother deeply. She was the real homemaker, and without her the apartment looked empty and cool. Nevertheless, I had to cope with the new situation, taking on some of Mother's housework. And, naturally, I continued to go to school.

Looking back at my years in Soviet schools, I can see that, even when instruction was good in strictly pedagogical terms, it was too heavily burdened with Marxist-Leninist ideology and hardly conducive to independent thinking. Such indoctrination made it especially difficult to develop objective approaches to social studies and history. Matters were better in the sciences, but even there the political situation threw its long shadow. Still, I learned a lot, and I have admiration for quite a few teachers in Gorky.

I was little more interested in politics than other boys of my age, yet my family's background made me more aware of public affairs and developments abroad. At school teachers strove to drum officially approved views of current Soviet and world affairs into our skulls, and at home a small radio brought us unceasing news, commentaries, and speeches, so the air was thick with politics. Even the least news conscious of us became as concerned about the rise of Nazism as our elders.

I remember distinctly when the Soviet Union joined the League of Nations in 1934, and when it concluded its alliances with France and Czechoslovakia a year later. We were very happy, for we knew that we were on the right side of the struggle. But then the Spanish Civil War broke out, and relations between friends and foes became complicated; tensions within the Soviet Union also increased, and the future looked bleak and uncertain.

In spite of everything, the years in Gorky were for me mostly a time of childhood games, sports, and joy. In addition to organized sports, I went swimming in the Volga and the Oka from early spring to late fall with friends, both boys and girls. In winter we often went to the theater or cinema. But even these good times were overshadowed by the strange and disturbing things happening around us from mid-1936 on. The implications of these events lingered like a heavy cloud—growing and darkening. It was impossible to be wholly carefree.

Revolutionary heroes whom we had been taught to admire were suddenly declared villains, put on trial, and executed. In school we were instructed to cut whole pages from our textbooks as truth changed, often overnight. I vividly remember some of the textbooks we were using at that time, particularly one with a photograph of Marshal Tukhachevsky in full regalia—that page had to be cut out with scissors after his execution in the spring of 1937. The removed pages were meticulously collected and counted by our teachers.

Before Tukhachevsky there had been the trial of Zinoviev and Kamenev in August 1936, then Radek and Pyatakov in January 1937; and after the trials of Tukhachevsky and other senior commanders came those of Bukharin, Yagoda, and Rykov in March 1938. This last trial I remember especially clearly, since it was broadcast on the radio. The spectacle of so many well-known Soviet leaders being turned into traitors made us sad and confused.

And there were other disquieting events, nearer at hand. Parents of some of my schoolmates suddenly disappeared, and when I asked their sons or daughters what had happened, they were never able to explain. As time wore on, more and more were afflicted, and an atmosphere of fear and mistrust descended on the whole community. It did not take long to learn that behind the "disappearances" were the secret police, the GPU and the NKVD—forerunners of the KGB.

The whole picture could not be put together for many years. For many of us it was Khrushchev's historical revelations in 1956 that finally made it all clear. But that was twenty years later. During the years 1936 to 1938, all political news in the Soviet Union, domestic or foreign, came from Soviet media, our teachers, newsreels, and compulsory lectures. Soviet methods of socialization were very thorough, and even gossip seemed to disappear, as people feared informers.

My father was a simple, straightforward man, not an intellectual with the ability to sort things out and arrive at an independent conclusion. Withdrawn and serious, he chose not to talk too much about these affairs with me. Under the circumstances, whatever confusion I felt had little chance of rising to serious doubts. The idea that the executed could all be innocent victims of state-sponsored murder was simply too ghastly to think about. It may seem naive to younger generations today, but in 1938 even that skeptical humanist Lion Feuchtwanger, the German novelist who then lived in exile in France and had attended the trials of Radek and Bukharin, believed the accused were guilty.

Throughout the purge years, the drumbeat of Soviet propaganda was ceaseless, publicizing the achievements of the system—the construction of factories and dams, electrification, new housing. With this came the repetitious litany of (what were described as) external threats from the international capitalist conspiracy bent on destroying the Soviet Union, the only socialist country on earth. And above everything hung the fatherly figure of Stalin, whose cult bore all the traits of hypnotic Orthodox ritual, though I was not sufficiently versed in medieval history to recognize the Byzantine origin of this practice.

Claims and accusations were pounded into the minds of a poorly informed people. Until late 1938, Nazi Germany was presented as the most imminent enemy, which seemed to be close to the truth. Developments after June 1941 added more weight to this argument.

In between, of course, was the Nazi-Soviet Pact of August 1939 and the nearly two years of collusion between the countries that followed. I was back in Slovakia when this was happening, and I had neither time nor means to pay much attention to international developments. Frankly, I was not quite

sure what to think about the pact, but the prevailing explanation I heard
from our friends was that Stalin was playing a game with Hitler, just waiting
for the right time to destroy him. This was a comforting theory, of course.

It was only many years later that I tried to tie it all together into one
rational perspective—the repressions I lived through in the Soviet Union,
Stalin's pact with Hitler, and my then growing doubts about the application
of Soviet practices in postwar Czechoslovakia. But that takes the story too
far ahead.

Soon after Germany's annexation of Austria (which coincided with the
Bukharin trial in March 1938), the Czechoslovak crisis became the talk of
the day. Naturally, my father and I were riveted by this development. I have
to point out that at no time during our stay in the Soviet Union did our
awareness of our national identity weaken. My parents always retained their
Czechoslovak citizenship, which, of course, also applied to Julius and
myself. Julius, having been born in the USA, was also an American
citizen, and my parents occasionally brought that up, at times in jest, at
times seriously.

We always spoke Slovak at home, and our life-style and customs remained Slovak. This was easier, of course, while we were with Interhelpo in Pishpek, surrounded by so many compatriots, but even after
moving to Gorky we were essentially Slovaks living abroad, not aspiring
Soviets. On such nationality questions, my father and mother had entirely
identical views.

It was in the course of the Czechoslovak crisis that the Supreme Soviet
decided to order all foreigners living in the Soviet Union to either accept
Soviet citizenship or leave the country. The official decree to that effect was
promulgated in the summer of 1938.

In Pishpek, my parents, like many other members of the cooperative,
had believed that their move was for life. This outlook had started to change
in the early 1930s under the impact of developments in the Soviet Union,
and I remember hearing allusions from both my parents to a possible return
home. I do not think, however, that they reached a firm decision on the
matter until 1938, even after my mother's and brother's exigent flight home
in 1935. After all, their underlying concerns about jobs and subsistence
were still valid. They had left Slovakia in 1925, and the economic situation
at home did not start to improve until 1936 or 1937, as they knew from the
letters of relatives and friends.

In 1938, faced with the necessity to choose between his Czechoslovak
citizenship and becoming a Soviet citizen, forever blocked from returning

home, my father hardly hesitated, despite his resolute belief in socialism. He was not blind to what was happening around him, and he could not avoid critical thoughts and doubts. Moreover, even if he had accepted Soviet citizenship, he knew he would remain a foreigner in the eyes of Soviet authorities, and 1938 was not a good year for foreigners in Russia. That he was a Communist meant very little; thousands of foreign Communists fell victim to senseless repressions in the Soviet Union in those years, and their fate was no secret even then. The possibility that my father would be snatched away was very real. There was no rationale in the selection of victims of terror, and it did not stop even with the fall of Nikolai Yezhov in December 1938.

Thus, at the time of the Munich crisis our return was already decided, and even Czechoslovakia's uncertain future did not change it. In November 1938 we were to go home.

Of course, the place my parents always called "home" was real to me mostly at second hand, from their remembrances and anecdotes. Nonetheless, the image was intimate, warm, and inviting, and I knew I belonged there. After all, everyone there spoke the language my mother had taught me as a child. I had been born there, as had my parents and their parents before them. Now even my mother and brother were waiting there for my father and me.

At the same time, I was leaving behind the only country I had really known so far, the country to which almost all my memories, good and bad, were tied, the country of so many of my friends. Russia—to me it meant houses, trees, sunsets, my life's experience. Beside it "home" was an uncertain notion of vague contours.

With all these thoughts jumbled in my seventeen-year-old mind, I sat on the train at my father's side. He, too, was obviously buried in thought. At the last station before the border, my father suddenly asked whether I had any rubles with me. I did, and he told me it was prohibited to take them out of the country. I hurried into the railroad station, put the money in an envelope, and mailed it to a classmate in Gorky.

When we arrived at the border crossing, however, I realized that I had still more Russian money in another pocket—the change from what my father had given me to buy myself a pair of pants. I remember how frightened I was at the thought that they would find it on me during the thorough frisking all people entering or leaving the Soviet Union had to endure. Walking to the customs office at the crossing, I threw the money into a wastebasket.

Somehow I repressed the memory of these moments for years, but I never lost it entirely. It would come back many years later.

5

WARTIME IN SLOVAKIA: FROM DESPAIR TO HOPE

W E returned to Slovakia several weeks after the signing of the Munich Pact. Czechoslovakia was forced—in absentia—to cede the Sudetenland, some two fifths of Czech territory, to Nazi Germany. This region included the Republic's main defenses, which had been built at great cost. The Munich Pact not only destroyed Czechoslovakia's defenses but also undermined its will to fight. For all good patriots, Czechs or Slovaks, it was a time of despair.

And soon encroachment came from other quarters as well. Poland took the opportunity to grab a part of northern Moravia, and Hungary hurried to reclaim its "right" to Slovakia. More than fifty years later, I can see how completely we were trapped in a quagmire of history. We were running from a bad situation to one even worse.

After crossing the Czechoslovak border, my father and I went directly to Trencin to join my mother and Julius, who were still staying with Uncle Michal and his family. It was a very happy reunion for all, and I was overjoyed to see my mother and brother after three years. I had little difficulty fitting in to my new-old surroundings. I had not expected that it would be so easy and natural. Unfortunately, the glow of family reunion did not last very long. More calamities soon rolled into our lives.

Hitler aimed to finish swallowing Czechoslovakia at the earliest opportunity. He needed to bring Central Europe under full control as a springboard for further conquests. At the same time, he wanted to do away with the rest of Czechoslovakia in a manner that would not too obviously defy the Munich settlement or hamper his plan to deal with one victim after another. Thus, he proceeded to separate Slovakia by secession, turning it into a vassal state with formal sovereignty. The remaining Czech parts of the state in the west, disfigured and defenseless, would then be easier to swallow as a "protectorate."

In this game plan, it was crucial for the Nazis to secure the cooperation of some of those Slovak political representatives who had never given up their 1918 demands for autonomy. For two decades, some Slovak politicians had entertained the idea of full separation from the Czechs but were constrained by their fear of Hungary. The possibility of German guarantees presented a new option. When the Nazis came to woo such nationalists, they could not fail to find sympathetic ears—and not just among the fascists, who represented an insignificant fraction, after all. More important was the People's Party, the strongest political force in Slovakia, supported by the Catholic Church. The church had never forgiven Masaryk's anticlerical policies in the early years of the new Czechoslovak state.

In this framework, the secessionist platform of the Slovak Right quickly took shape after Munich. Predictably, the separatists traded on some justified national grievances (the root of which was the unitary form of the Republic), but they also openly displayed a loathing of Czechoslovakia's democratic system. This platform fit the demand for "national self-determination" so recently employed in Saarland, Austria, and the Sudetenland, and also put the Slovak Right in line with the spread of fascism throughout Europe.

The Slovak fascists looked particularly to Mussolini and his "corporate state" for ideological inspiration, though in 1938 and 1939 Germany was the one calling the shots in Central Europe. It mattered little, however, since the two totalitarian regimes, while they differed in style and structure, shared so much in practice.

Slovakia's political autonomy after Munich was symbolized by the renaming of the overall state as Czecho-Slovakia. An autonomous Slovak government—now only nominally part of a broader entity and in practice untied from Prague—assumed power in Slovakia with a Catholic priest, Dr. Jozef Tiso, at its head. This new "state" launched its predictable agenda without delay. Political opposition was gradually suppressed or silenced.

The Communist Party and the Social Democratic Party were dissolved and banned. Remaining Slovak political parties were herded into one "unified" party—the Slovak People's Party. Outside the SPP, only the parties of the German and Hungarian minorities were allowed to exist. A representative of the Deutsche Partei, a pro-Nazi party of Slovak Germans, became a member of the Tiso government.

Tiso, who was then fifty-one years old, had become chairman of the Slovak People's Party in 1938. His separatism was initially not as outspoken as that of some more radical leaders. When summoned to Berlin by Hitler on March 14, 1939, he refused to declare Slovak secession before it could be approved by the Slovak parliament; the Czech president, Dr. Emil Hacha, put up no such resistance. But Tiso's actions have to be seen in a longer view. As president of the Slovak State from 1939 to 1945, he bore direct responsibility for the heinous record of his government and was justifiably declared a war criminal by the Allies.

In November 1938, Slovakia was forced to cede its southern region to Hungary after "mediation" by Germany and Italy, known as the Vienna Arbitrage, but that did not remove the threat of Hungarian irredentism to the rest of Slovakia. Hitler used this threat to speed up the liquidation of Czechoslovakia. In mid-March 1939, the secession of Slovakia was formalized under German guarantees—and German dominance. Germany occupied the Czech lands, and Hungary was permitted to annex the Subcarpathian Ukraine, the easternmost province of prewar Czechoslovakia.

Some historians see the Slovak secession and the declaration of the Slovak state as an alternative to recolonization by Hungary. The fact is that Hitler preferred a trimmed Slovak puppet state to a larger Hungary. He also liked to cultivate disagreements between both these states and their nations, and thus keep both in check. Immediately after the separation from Czechoslovakia, the Slovak government allied itself openly with Nazi Germany. Czechs, Jews, Communists and Social Democrats were declared public enemies. Remaining civil and political rights were terminated and anti-Semitic laws promulgated. In September 1939, Tiso's government declared war on Poland and joined the Pact of Three—Germany, Italy, and Japan.

The internal *Gleichschaltung*, or equalization, was carried out under German dominance but also at the initiative of the new Slovak rulers, who accomplished their task in Slovakia more promptly than did the Nazis in the disfigured and occupied Czech lands. The Hlinka Guards, armed detachments of the Slovak People's Party fashioned after the Italian Blackshirts, became the political police. One of the first items on their agenda was the seizure of Jewish property and a witch-hunt of political opponents.

It is essential today to understand exactly what kind of regime it was. This regime made Slovakia an accomplice of Nazi Germany in its war of aggression; it declared war on the Allied powers and sent three divisions of the Slovak Army to help the Germans on the Eastern front. It launched totalitarian terror against its own people, destroyed the political and human rights its citizens had enjoyed in democratic Czechoslovakia, and sent almost 60,000 Slovak citizens of Jewish origin to certain death in Nazi extermination camps. I am proud that my father, my mother, my brother, and I, like many other patriotic Slovaks, opposed this state and did not hesitate to offer our lives in the struggle.

It is also appropriate to say that had the Slovak State not been defeated in 1945, had it not been openly challenged by the Slovak National Uprising in August 1944, and had its deplorable behavior not been generously ignored by the victorious Allies as a favor to the restored Czechoslovak Republic, the Slovak people would have shared the fate of other defeated Nazi client states and been burdened for years with the stigma of war crimes and demands for reparations.

From the first days of his return, my father sought his place in the rapidly changing situation, re-establishing contacts with his old friends in the Communist Party, and rejoining their ranks. There was no other group suited to him. The Slovak Communist Party was the only organized body in clear and unambiguous opposition to fascism, Munich, and all its consequences. It is true that there were other opponents of secession and fascism in Slovakia. For example, a part of the Agrarian Party establishment had distanced itself from the collaborators and their policies. But in 1939 the Communist Party was the only truly organized force of resistance.

It needs to be noted that, until the breakup of Czechoslovakia, there was only one Communist Party in the Republic, the Communist Party of Czechoslovakia. The Slovak Party had the status of a regional organization, and Party business was tightly controlled by the Czech Party apparatus in Prague. This reflected both the unitarian political system of the Czechoslovak Republic and Comintern rule, which permitted only one Communist Party in each country. It was not a satisfactory situation, of course.

During the 1920s, the Comintern zigzagged on this matter, basically encouraging a separatist political line for the Communists in Slovakia but executing this policy through the Czech Party officials who dominated the Slovak Party apparatus. In the 1930s, the Comintern line narrowed, and the Czech-dominated Czechoslovak Party was tightly centralized, causing growing resentment, especially among young leftist-oriented Slovak intellectuals. In practice, the Slovak Communist organization, already illegal and operating underground, gained a degree of independence from Prague only after March 1939, when it was recognized by the Comintern as a section on its own. It then lost its autonomy again after the end of the Nazi-Soviet Pact in June 1941. I am explaining these things because the relationship between the Slovak and Czechoslovak Communists has long been an historically crucial aspect of Czecho-Slovak relations.

From its inception in spring 1939 until March 1940, the Slovak Communist program consisted largely of three clear points: nonrecognition of the Slovak State, overthrow of fascism, and restoration of the Czechoslovak Republic. These aims were clear enough for me, at the age of seventeen, to follow my father's example and advice and join the Party in mid-1939. His two friends who later became members of the first illegal Central Committee of the Slovak Party, Ludovit Benada and Jan Osoha, were my "guarantors," as Party statutes required.

After so many years, the reader should perhaps be reminded that joining the Communist Party at that time was not like joining a pigeon breeders' club. It was a very dangerous step that promised only negative rewards. It was nothing like jumping on the bandwagon of a victorious party the day before it comes to power. In 1939 there was no sign of light at the end of the tunnel. Hard times were ahead, and no one I knew expected the situation to change for the better any time soon.

Since the Party was outlawed, all its activities had to be conducted secretly. Our work at that time consisted mainly of distributing illegal publications, delivering them from one place to another, and one person to another. My mother, I recall, carried leaflets to the marketplace in Trencin hidden deep in her shopping bag. Occasionally, we had to keep a new shipment of papers and leaflets at home for some time, and we were always looking for new hiding places. I do not remember who came up with the idea of using our doghouse. Fortunately, my family was almost never without a dog, and when one died, to the grief of all, another soon took his place. The doghouse proved to be a perfect hiding place. The police searched our flat a number of times and turned everything upside down— they even tore off tiles around the stove—but they never looked into the doghouse.

When I returned from Russia, Julius was already training as a latheman in the Skoda Works in Dubnica, a complex of armament and ammunitions factories built in the 1930s with French assistance. In 1939, of course, these facilities were already controlled by the Nazis. Some of the factories were spread out over miles, and some were equipped with underground production lines and storage spaces. In 1939 I, too, found employment in Dubnica, and, like Julius, I was soon training as a latheman.

There is no need to say that after the breakup of Czechoslovakia the factories in Dubnica had little choice of customers. While the Skoda Works in Pilsen continued to fill Soviet orders for many months, with the Nazis' consent, Slovak factories were left with only German orders. But industry in

Slovakia was still underdeveloped and overdependent on arms production, and in the whole area there was hardly any other place to find a job. Dubnica, by the way, was only about nine and a half miles from Trencin.

That same year political repression continued to intensify, and my father had to go into hiding to avoid arrest. Until the end of the war, I was to see him only twice—once in 1940, when he was still free, and once in 1943, when I received permission to visit him in prison in Nitra. I was the only member of the family to see him in all those years. It was too dangerous to try to maintain family contacts.

But we soon renewed our friendship with the Ondris family, whom we had known well from our days in Pishpek. They lived in Velcice, a village about twelve miles northeast of Nitra and about forty miles—in a straight line—south of Trencin. In 1940 the Ondrises hid my father for a while, and that's where I met him. There I also met Anna, my future wife, again. She, too, worked in the Skoda Works in Dubnica. Her name was actually Anna Borsekova, after her mother's first husband, who had been killed on the Italian front at the end of World War I. Anna had never known her real father.

I found Anna very attractive—I think it was love at first sight—and, fortunately, it was reciprocated. Not only was Anna beautiful but she was also a very kind and friendly person. It was then that we started to date, and our relationship grew even closer after the summer of 1941, when my family moved to Velcice.

That move was not voluntary. Because of my father's political beliefs, we were ordered to relocate to a village with no more than 200 inhabitants, where we would be more isolated. The Ondrises helped us greatly, finding us a place to live with the Protestant pastor in their village. He had a workshop on one side of his house, which we adapted for living. There we stayed—my mother, Julius, and myself—until the Slovak uprising in August 1944, when my brother and I left.

From Velcice it was much farther to Dubnica than from Trencin, of course, and from Monday through Saturday we had to get up at three o'clock in the morning to walk to the nearest railroad station, about five miles away. The train then did not go to Dubnica directly but made a circular detour to the Vah River to the west, then north via Trencin. From the Dubnica railroad station, we had to walk another two and a half miles to the factory. To make the trip twice a day was tiring for all of us, especially Anna.

Anna worked in the ammunitions factory, Julius in the arms factory, and I in the toolmaking workshop. So when we arrived in the morning, we had to part; after the shift we met again for the trip home.

People have often asked me about the practical implications of the August 1939 Molotov-Ribbentrop Pact for our illegal Party work. Naturally, we knew about the pact from newspapers and radio, but we did not take it very seriously. At least rank-and-file Party members generally believed that, for the Soviets, the agreement was just a tactical maneuver to gain time as the Germans bled in their war with France and England.

After the fall of France in June 1940 and the German advance in the rest of Europe, reports about the continuing Nazi-Soviet understanding made us uneasy. Even then, however, we never thought that Russia took this collusion seriously. I can see now that my own thinking was wishful, but in 1940 we knew either nothing or very little about the extent of Stalin's cooperation with Hitler, and everything was overshadowed by the growth of Nazi power; even my mixed memories of the last years in Russia lost relevance in the face of the more immediate menace. In his memoirs, President Benes, who was in London and knew much better, indicates that he reasoned along similar lines at the time.

For Slovak Communist leaders, the time between August 1939 and June 1941 was by no means as simple. The ink was hardly dry on the pact when the Comintern adopted a political line that reflected the new realities in the relationship between Berlin and Moscow. The war in the West was characterized as "imperialist," and in some messages to underground Communist parties in Europe, the Comintern even called for fraternization with the soldiers of the *Wehrmacht*, describing them as "proletarian brothers in German uniforms." This wording was also included in a resolution of the Executive Committee of the Czechoslovak Communist Party in Moscow in December 1940, which was then sent to Prague. Very few people in German-dominated countries, however, including rank-and-file Communists, had any knowledge of this outrageous policy.

I suspect that the underground Communist leaders made deliberately little effort to promulgate these instructions. Instead they made formal shows of obedience, adopting resolutions with no practical consequences. Like others, the Slovak Party leadership found themselves obliged to change their line according to instructions from Moscow. But one can trace hesitance, if not reluctance, in the way they accepted Comintern policy.

Party documents of the period indicate that the illegal Slovak Communist Party must have received new instructions from Moscow some time between November 1939 and March 1940. As late as October 1939, the first underground central Party leadership (composed of Julius Duris, Ludovit Benada, and Jan Osoha) had issued a resolution demanding a "free Slovakia in a free Czechoslovakia in a new Europe." This resolution came three months after the signing of the Nazi-Soviet Pact and two months after the Soviet recognition of the Slovak state, which amounted to a de facto approval of the breakup of Czechoslovakia. This adds to my impression that even Slovak Party leaders perceived Soviet moves at the time as only tactical maneuvers.

The next Party pronouncement, issued in March 1940 and prepared by the same Central Committee, finally adopted the new Soviet line. It characterized the previous demand for the restoration of the Czechoslovak Republic as an "imperialist" and "anti-Soviet" scheme. Why, it did not explain. The document also called for an "independent Slovakia," a 180-degree turn.

This new course, unenthusiastically accepted by the Slovak Communist leadership, was fortunately very short-lived and probably never reached lower Party levels. Foot-dragging at the top aside, circulation of Party literature had become far more difficult in 1940. In any case, I never saw the pro-German Party line in print.

My father was then at the middle level of the illegal Party structure, and, while he knew about the new line, he never took it seriously. As he later told me, he simply stuck to his old beliefs. I think he could not even pretend to be opportunistic.

The document carrying the changed Party line issued in March 1940 was, as much as I know from my father, drafted by Jan Osoha, who simply copied the instructions from Moscow. Trained in the blind discipline required by Leninism, Osoha followed orders without putting any faith in them.

During the Nazi-Soviet honeymoon, the illegal leadership of the Slovak Communists issued only one other known document, a new Party program adopted in May 1941. It was also drafted by Osoha, and it called for a "Soviet Slovakia." This program seems to have reflected false hope that Nazi Germany would permit further Soviet territorial expansion in Europe at its own expense. Today we know that Hitler did propose to Molotov, in Berlin in November 1940, that the Soviets push south, against Iran and India, but that Stalin wanted to go after Romania first. Hitler's reaction to such ambitions was to set in motion the Barbarossa Plan for the invasion of Russia.

Naturally, the situation changed abruptly in June 1941, when the Nazis invaded Russia. I remember hearing about it at work in Dubnica—it was a great piece of news for all of us, of course. Stalin returned hastily to the "united front" line of the last congress of the Comintern in 1935. The Slovak Communist Party status changed again, and the Comintern also began to revise its recognition of the Slovak Party as independent.

That revision, however, was not complete. The Soviets realized that conditions in Slovakia differed significantly from those in the Protectorate. So the Slovak Communists continued to be recognized as a distinct part of the Czechoslovak Communist Party, not just a regional organization. Still, by January 1943 they were once more formally politically subordinate to the Czechoslovak Party leadership, then in exile in Moscow. The termination of the Comintern in December 1943 changed nothing in this respect.

New instructions along these lines were brought to Slovakia's Communists by Viliam Siroky, a Slovak member of the Moscow Party leadership, as early as July 1941. Siroky, by the way, was arrested very shortly after his arrival, and a month later, the Slovak secret police fell upon the first illegal Slovak Party leadership group, arresting two of its three members, Duris and Benada.

A second leadership group was formed in September 1941, composed of Jan Osoha, Otto Krajnak, and Vincent Skrabala. It was broken up by the police in April 1942, when Krajnak and Skrabala were captured. My father then came to the fore as a member of the third illegal Slovak Party leadership group with Jan Osoha and Jozef Lietavec. By that time, Barbarossa seemed to confirm the belief of many that the Nazi-Soviet Pact had all been just tactical maneuvering.

This third illegal leadership group had an even shorter life than the two previous bodies; all its members were arrested in less than three months. Even Osoha, who had successfully avoided arrest since 1939, was captured. All three were taken to Bratislava, then brought to Nitra, where they were held until 1945, even during the Slovak Uprising.

In the years preceding his arrest, my father hid in many places, including barns in Velcice and, later, in a room in his sister Zuzka's house in Topolcany. He could not stay there long, so the Party found him an illegal hiding place in the apartment of a widow, also in Topolcany. At that time, a relationship started between this widow, who had an adult daughter, and my father, and that relationship proved lasting. My father never returned to us.

It was while hiding in Topolcany that my father was instructed to move to Bratislava for the formation of the third illegal Party leadership group. Until his arrest three months later, he lived in a secret apartment with Jan Osoha. He was captured during a clandestine meeting in a city park in Bratislava in July 1942.

As I mentioned, I saw my father in Nitra in 1943, in prison. I had applied for a visit, using the excuse that I wanted to get married and was seeking his consent. A short visit was granted; we sat separated by a grille in a partition. Two policemen listened to everything we said, but I could at least see him, and that was good, since I could not know whether I would see him again.

While we talked, I was appalled to see the police drag by us a prisoner with a red armband, the identification of political prisoners. The man's clothes were stained with blood. Looking at his pale face, I recognized Ludovit Benada.

Spring and summer 1942 was probably the worst period of internal terror in Slovakia. It was also the time of mass deportation of Slovak Jews to the extermination camps in Poland. Between March and October that year, 58,000 were forcibly sent to Auschwitz and other camps; most of them never returned. Slovak prisons, too, were full of political opponents, among them hundreds of Communists.

The Slovak Communist Party was hard hit again in April 1943, when the whole fourth illegal leadership group was arrested, together with eighty leading functionaries. The Moscow leadership of the Czechoslovak Communist Party then sent to Slovakia two instructors, one of whom, Karol Smidke, formed the fifth and last underground Central Committee in the summer of 1943.

After Barbarossa and Pearl Harbor, the war tide slowly turned against the Axis. In August and September 1942, Britain and the French government in exile declared the Munich Pact invalid, and soon afterwards the Czechoslovak government in London was recognized by all three principal Allies—the USSR, the United States, and the United Kingdom. In February 1943, Germany lost the battle of Stalingrad, and the Western Allies soon landed in Italy. In Slovakia, as in other parts of German-dominated Europe, hope was rising again.

During the time between my return to Slovakia and the Uprising, I lived a rather quiet life, going to work in Dubnica and taking part in various activities of the small Party cell at the factory. That was the dangerous part, because the police were very watchful in such a sensitive workplace. We managed to establish and maintain contacts with underground Slovak Party groups in other factories, namely in Banovce, my mother's birthplace, where a stronger Party cell had been formed in the nearby Bata shoe factory.

Workers in Zilina and Ruzomberok staged significant strikes during this period, and several isolated partisan groups started to operate in remote mountainous areas, organized mainly by Soviet prisoners of war who had escaped from internment. Other guerrilla organizers parachuted into Slovakia as the Soviet front came closer. But more significant guerrilla activity did not start until the spring of 1944.

From the first signs of change on the battlefields in 1942, we anxiously watched the slow but inexorable death of fascism. I remember how eagerly we studied the map of Russia, where the Germans were meeting their first defeats. We tried to locate places where the Germans insisted they were "shortening the front"—a euphemism for retreat. On a forbidden shortwave radio set, we tuned to news from London and Moscow. In Italy the front did not seem to move at all during the long standstill at Monte Cassino, but we knew that a big Allied invasion in Western Europe was imminent. In early spring of 1944, we could scent it in the air: the end was not far away.

I turned twenty-two in November 1943, and, on the eve of the Uprising, I was grown up and impatient. The war had been like a long, dark night without dawn. But now the daylight was coming.

6

THE POLITICS OF 1944

T HE Slovak National Uprising of 1944 and the termination of the Hungarian yoke in 1918 are the two most important events in Slovakia's modern history. By rising against the Tiso regime and the Nazis, we joined the struggle of all freedom-loving nations against fascist aggression. The Uprising also ended that most shameful episode in our history, the "Slovak State."

As a historic event, the Uprising is shrouded in both legend and oversimplified interpretations. I was, of course, just a foot soldier, unable to see its larger contours. But ever since that time I have been curious to learn how it all happened, and why it happened the way it did. It was difficult for many years for me to see things clearly, and it was really only during the long years of my internal exile after 1970 that I could give the Uprising serious reflection. Naturally, the bitter experience of August 1968 opened my mind to new interpretations.

I read a great deal during that time, and I could see that of the many officially sanctioned books and studies published in the past about the Uprising, only a few were more than propaganda. I think that serious and honest works about the struggle written and published in Czechoslovakia only started to appear in the mid-1960s. After 1968 falsehood and silence descended again. When Husak came to power, rewriting of history was the common practice, and hundreds of historians, including quite a few of my friends, were persecuted.

Rereading everything at the slow pace my seclusion permitted, I found many interesting facts that I had earlier overlooked. Occasionally friends brought me the kinds of "unofficial" publications to which I had had only

very limited access in earlier times. So I widened my knowledge of the
period and tried to separate less important facts from those of real significance. Piece by piece, I put together a more complete and accurate picture
of the Uprising, shedding many previous assumptions as I went.

Preparations for the revolt began in early 1943, by which time the
restoration of Czechoslovakia had won official support from the principal
members of the anti-Nazi coalition, including the Soviet Union. It is hard
to be sure how widely this was known in Slovakia at the time, but I would
assume that politically active circles were not ignorant of it. At the same
time, the Tiso regime had discredited itself internationally by its collaboration with Nazi Germany and lost much acceptance at home.

The non-Communist opposition groups in Slovakia—namely the Social
Democrats, liberals, and Agrarian dissenters—established regular radio
contact with the Czechoslovak exile government of President Benes in
London in early 1943, agreeing on the restoration of Czechoslovakia and
the overthrow of Tiso. First steps were taken by antifascist officers of the
Slovak Army, all of whom had been raised in democratic Czechoslovakia
and trained in the military academies of the Czechoslovak Army.

President Benes had, since 1939, led an untiring diplomatic campaign
for nullification of the Munich Pact and rerecognition of the Czechoslovak
Republic. Manifestations of resistance both in the occupied Czech lands
and in Slovakia were of crucial importance. The need for a spectacular act
of anti-Nazi defiance in the so-called Protectorate helped inspire the assassination of Reinhard Heydrich in May 1942. Heydrich was the head of the
Sicherheitsdienst, or SD, the Nazi secret service, and was sent by Hitler to
Prague in early 1942 as the ranking German officer in the occupied Czech
lands.

Benes and his chief of army intelligence in London, General Moravec,
chose two noncommissioned officers of the Czechoslovak Army in England to parachute into the Protectorate and execute Heydrich. It was no
coincidence that one of them—Jozef Gabcik—was Slovak, and the other,
Jan Kubis, Czech. This pairing was meant to symbolize the continuing
mutuality of Czech and Slovak national interests.

Understandably, the existence of the Tiso regime in Slovakia and its
support for the Nazis were an even more acute embarrassment to Benes's
efforts. He was anxious to encourage the pro-Czechoslovak underground in
Slovakia toward open activity against the Tiso government.

At the time of these early contacts between Benes and the Slovak non-
Communist opposition, the Communist underground was decimated by
the mass arrests of April 1943. Also, the policy of the underground Slovak
Communists toward the restoration of Czechoslovakia was not as clearly

formulated as that of the non-Communists. This confusion originated with the Comintern, which did not explicitly abandon Soviet recognition of the Slovak State until January 1943. Six more months passed—mainly because of difficulties in communication—before the change was implemented by Slovak Communist underground leaders.

In fact, the Soviet government, in various diplomatic acts, such as full rerecognition of Czechoslovakia and President Benes's status, had terminated this policy earlier, shortly after the German invasion of the USSR. The Comintern's slowness may have been accidental—caused, for example, by the German advance on Moscow and general disruption of the Comintern's bureaucratic machinery. But it also may have served a political purpose. Both lines, of course, were basically decided by the same person: Stalin.

The resumption of a "Czechoslovak" course for Slovak Communists was set forth in the January 1943 resolution of the Executive Committee of the Comintern, putting the exiled leadership of the Czechoslovak Communist Party in Moscow in charge of Party affairs both in the Protectorate and in Slovakia. This resolution also called for cooperation with non-Communist, democratic forces, reflecting the post-Barbarossa Soviet alliance with the West. In practical terms, this also tacitly revoked the policy of a "Soviet Slovakia."

In July 1943, the Moscow Czechoslovak Communist Party dispatched emissaries to both the Protectorate and Slovakia. In Slovakia, the new policy was entrusted to Karol Smidke and Karol Bacilek, senior representatives of the Slovak Communists in Moscow. Smidke's role was more political; Bacilek was mainly responsible for the coordination of the partisan movement. Shortly after his arrival, Smidke formed a new Central Committee of the Slovak Communists. With most other experienced Party activists in jail, he chose two new men to serve with him on the new leading Party body: Ladislav Novomesky and Gustav Husak.

Novomesky, then forty years old, was a well-known Slovak poet and cofounder of DAV, a prewar leftist literary and artistic group centered on a cultural journal of the same name (*dav* means "crowd" in both Slovak and Czech). Husak, ten years younger and a lawyer by profession, had also belonged to that group.

Neither had been in hiding since the creation of the Slovak State in 1939. Husak even became a public figure of sorts in the Slovak State and worked in the Bar Association in Bratislava. This bizarre situation can be explained by the complex relationship between some segments of the Slovak extreme right and extreme left in the late 1930s, when ideological and political interests occasionally intertwined because of dissatisfaction with the way Slovak national interests were treated in pre-Munich Czechoslovakia.

In the fall of 1943, this fifth, imported Slovak Communist leadership, encouraged by both London and Moscow, established contact with the non-Communist underground. A substantive understanding was reached in December 1943 and embodied in the Christmas Agreement. The document contained a clause outlining the principle of equality of Czechs and Slovaks within the renewed republic, which was the basis for the formation of the Slovak National Council (SNC) as the central leading body of the underground opposition.

At the beginning, the council had six members, three Communists (Smidke, Novomesky, and Husak) and three who represented the non-Communist opposition: Matej Josko, Jozef Lettrich, and Jan Ursiny. This composition reflected the proportional strength of the groups in the antifascist opposition, but I think it also anticipated the influence the Communist Party would have after the country's liberation by the Soviet Army.

During the Uprising, the council was enlarged to fifty members, but the Communists continued to hold about half the seats. The same applied to the Board of Commissioners, the council's executive organ. Also during the Uprising, the council vested all legislative and executive power in Slovakia in the Commissioners—a gesture toward Slovak nationalism of some significance to both the Tiso regime and the Benes government.

The Christmas Agreement coincided with President Benes's visit to Moscow, where he and Stalin concluded the Czechoslovak-Soviet Alliance Treaty and he and the Moscow leadership of the Czechoslovak Communist Party set forth a simplified postwar political structure. It was these agreements (rather than those reached at Yalta fourteen months later) that effectively delivered Czechoslovakia into the Soviet sphere of influence, subordinated the state's external policy to Moscow, and decisively affected Czechoslovakia's internal political processes for almost the next half century. One of the most far-reaching decisions created new organs of local power called national committees. These resembled the early soviets in the USSR, when they still had a facade of political plurality. It seems clear now that the Moscow leaders of the Czechoslovak Party saw these as their instrument of control. President Benes, however, fully accepted the national committees and endorsed them in his radio messages from London.

In tandem with the political planning, military preparations for the Uprising were under way. Beginning in summer 1943, the London government's Ministry of Defense and President Benes were in personal radio contact with certain high officers of the Slovak Army, especially Colonels

Urban and Golian in the Land Army Headquarters in Banska Bystrica. Benes entrusted Golian with the overall planning of military action. Toward the end of 1943, the conspiratorial officers' network in the Slovak Army was firmly in place.

At the same time, the partisan movement in Slovakia took shape and grew. The partisans, however, were never controlled by either London or the SNC but were under the Soviet partisan command in Kiev, headed by Nikita Khrushchev. This divided chain of command later posed very serious problems.

In May 1944 President Benes and the SNC appointed Colonel Golian the chief of insurgent military forces in Slovakia. In June the SNC prepared two variants of the Uprising. The first and much preferred one proposed to coordinate the timing with the advance of the Soviet Army; the second conceived of the Uprising as a response to the German occupation of Slovakia, when and if it should occur. Coordination with the Soviets was crucial for both variants (but especially the first), and on August 4 the SNC sent Karol Smidke and Colonel Ferjencik, a Slovak antifascist officer, to Moscow to reach agreement on the next steps.

In retrospect, it is not surprising that the Smidke-Ferjencik mission failed to achieve its aims. The organizers of the Uprising expected that the Fourth Ukrainian Front of the Soviet Army would soon resume its offensive in the sector northeast and east of Slovakia. Such an offensive was originally planned for August 28. But on August 23, Romania went over to the Allies, changing the strategic picture. Stalin postponed the next full-strength push of the Fourth Ukrainian Front for seven weeks.

Then Bulgaria, another German ally in the Balkans, collapsed, and the Soviet High Command redirected the next main thrust from Slovakia to Hungary, where the conditions were much more propitious for a large-scale tank operation.

These events were not the only or even the major factors affecting Soviet attitudes toward the Uprising. For instance, I no longer discount paranoia, the Soviets' propensity to be suspicious of any actions over which they did not have complete control. The Warsaw uprising, which broke out on August 1 that year, is a clear example, the Soviets refused to help the Polish insurgents. I admit that for many years I refused to believe that the Soviets were capable of such behavior. But gradually, as I acquainted myself with more of the facts, my eyes were opened. When I read the memoirs of the then Soviet chief of staff, Marshal S. M. Stemenko, published in Prague in 1974, I was shocked that he characterized the organizers of the Slovak Uprising as "bourgeois putschists," a view that undoubtedly agreed with Stalin's.

Only this attitude can explain the Soviets' failure to supply the insurgent forces with war materiel; certainly references to "poor weather conditions," as they appear in biased accounts, are duplicitous. Soviet airplanes flew freely in and out of the liberated territory to take representatives of the Czechoslovak Party leadership, such as Jan Sverma and Rudolf Slansky, to Moscow and to drop supplies to Soviet-controlled partisans. Also, the Soviets refused to give the British Royal Air Force permission to drop supplies for the Uprising.

Some have claimed that the Soviet aloofness might have originated with the so-called Catlos affair, but this strikes me as entirely improbable. I should explain: when Smidke took the SNC's proposals to Moscow, he also carried a "memorandum" prepared by the minister of defense of the Tiso government, General Catlos. I do not know why Smidke agreed to do this. Catlos was a traitor who had sent over 50,000 Slovak troops to aid the Nazis on the eastern front, and he was high on the Allied list of war criminals. Now he proposed to switch sides, offering to carry out an anti-German coup, to "cancel" the war against the USSR, to declare war on Hungary, and to establish a military dictatorship in Slovakia, which would "coordinate" Slovak internal politics with Soviet interests. The Slovak National Council distanced itself unequivocally from Catlos's proposal, as did President Benes. It was unthinkable to them to mix the democratic opposition forces in Slovakia with Catlos. I do not imagine that Stalin, however treacherous himself, would have harbored any illusions about such a man.

There was, however, another factor, a memorandum prepared by Gustav Husak that Smidke took to Moscow. It discussed alternatives to the renewal of prewar Czechoslovakia, one of which was the incorporation of Slovakia into the Soviet Union. Husak claimed that this was the desire of "at least 70 percent of the Slovaks."

To Stalin, who had recently signed the alliance treaty with Benes committing him to the restoration of Czechoslovakia, this proposal must have sounded suspicious and adventurous. To be sure, a few months later, the Soviets annexed Ruthenia, also a part of prewar Czechoslovakia, under quite deplorable circumstances. But Slovakia was a different case. In his zeal, Husak completely overlooked the changes in the Soviet and Comintern policies in place since the middle of 1941, and his proposals contradicted the political platform of the Moscow leadership of the Party. That it merely muddied the political waters, and did nothing to increase Soviet sympathy for the Uprising, is all but certain.

At any rate, no framework for coordination of the Uprising with the Soviets was created, even though the SNC mission—originally scheduled for a week—spent a whole month in Moscow. I now believe that the Soviets were simply not interested in such coordination.

Completing the picture is the fate of two Slovak divisions in eastern Slovakia, which were prepared, from mid-July, to go into action in the German rear and facilitate a Soviet breach through the Carpathians. The distance between the Russian front and the Slovak border in that sector was then about thirty miles. The Soviet High Command was informed about this plan by General Pika, President Benes's representative in Moscow, as early as July 17. Pika received no answer. A limited Soviet thrust in that direction was not launched until September 8, a week after the Germans had surrounded and disarmed the two Slovak divisions.

The supposed commander of these Slovak divisions, Colonel Talsky, was afterwards accused of substantial responsibility for the failure of the Uprising. But in fact the commander of these divisions was General Malar. Colonel Golian had assigned Talsky to assume the command of these two divisions, but the action failed before Talsky could arrive. And I am now inclined to ask what he could have done without any clear idea about Soviet plans.

In utter contrast to their restraint toward the SNC's more formal insurgent forces, the Soviets were positively aggressive in provisioning the predominantly Communist guerrillas. In the weeks before the Uprising, they dropped more and more groups and supplies at night to the growing partisan forces.

It was the unauthorized attack of a partisan group on a small German garrison in Vrutky in northwestern Slovakia on Thursday, August 24, that triggered the Uprising. This was exactly what the SNC had feared. As late as August 20, they had asked the Soviet-controlled partisan staff in Slovakia to postpone similar actions, to avoid giving the Germans a pretext to occupy Slovakia. The Soviets knew about the preparations for the Uprising; they were urged to wait until the revolt could be thoroughly prepared and coordinated with Soviet operations. Why did they ignore the plea? This question bothers me, even after so many years.

The SNC had desperately tried to coordinate their actions with Soviet moves. After the attack in Vrutky, there was no time left: The German Army started moving into Slovakia, and Colonel Golian, the newly appointed chief of staff of the Czechoslovak Army in Slovakia, had no option but to issue an order to resist. The Slovak National Uprising began.

For two months, the Slovak partisans and Czechoslovak Army tied down the German forces, but whatever the assistance to guerrillas from Khrushchev's base in Kiev, the hoped-for advance of Soviet troops failed to materialize. The liberation of Slovakia would come only in March 1945, after Yalta, after American troops had pulled back from a "premature" liberation of the Czech lands, when Soviet troops under Marshals Malinovsky and Konev routed the last remnants of the Nazi and Tiso forces.

And so the Uprising, painted as a glorious but unsuccessful revolt, was not allowed to share credit for the liberation of the country. In objective terms, its failure weakened not only the non-Communist forces in Slovakia but the domestic Slovak Communist resistance and Slovak national interests as a whole. I am not, of course, trying to exaggerate the part the revolt could have played in the defeat of Germany. A well-timed Uprising could, however, have greatly aided the cohesiveness of the central sector of the anti-German front and saved many lives.

But that, it appears, was not part of the great game: I remember reading a document about Gottwald and Molotov in Moscow in September 1944 in which Gottwald was comparing the political positions of the Slovak National Council with Tito's policy in Yugoslavia. Independent attitudes enjoyed little sympathy in Stalin's entourage.

One might add that the outcome of the Uprising also weakened the Slovak claim to a more equal partnership with the Czechs in the new republic. But that, unfortunately, seemed to be against the interests of all the main players at that time: not just the Soviets but the Benes government and the Gottwald leadership of the Party as well. For different reasons, they all preferred a centralized political system in Czechoslovakia. Slovak aspirations for autonomy in a federated state were delayed by another twenty-four years, not to be achieved until the dismal conditions of Soviet occupation of the whole Republic in 1968.

Forty-five years later, I think that one fact needs to be repeated: ordinary people like me then had no awareness of the larger picture. We simply accepted the defeat of the Uprising as a misfortune brought on us by the vagaries of war. Knowing nothing about the politics behind the scenes, we were left with the basic fact that, by and large, it was the Russians who had beaten the Germans. Until the Allied invasion of Normandy in June 1944, we saw Germany being defeated only on the Russian battlefield, one far larger than the fronts in Italy or North Africa.

In 1945 this spectacle of overwhelming Soviet power was my generation's primary impression of the war. The Soviets' ability to recover from their initial military disasters and to strike back with force was obvious and undeniable. This perception easily translated into illusions about the whole Soviet system, political as well as economic. I still remember what an older man told us about the Russians during one of our many hushed discussions on the train that took us to work every day: "People do not fight with such resolve for a regime they dislike." It was not, however, that simple, as we later learned.

Naturally, I had not forgotten my early Soviet experience, but the memory of its dark side tended to recede in the face of the war. Moreover, I was not immune to the propaganda to which I had been exposed in high school in Gorky, at the time of the purges, when their victims—from Zinovev and Tukhachevsky to Bukharin—were presented as Nazi or even Japanese agents. From a 1945 perspective, the "antifascist" message from those times seemed to make bizarre sense.

As for the memories of the Nazi-Soviet Pact, they had faded soon after June 1941, and even after the liberation no one, certainly not the Czech or Slovak press, drew attention to that period. Avoiding public criticism of the Soviet Union was a generally accepted policy of all political forces in postwar Czechoslovakia well before February 1948, and exceptions were very rare.

Thus, the war strengthened in me the socialist convictions of freedom and social justice instilled by my parents. Like them, I never sought power or material rewards, only the modest goal of a decent life—a safe job and a small house where my wife and I could raise our children. But that, I think, was almost everybody's little dream, and for most people it still is.

The importance of a secure job is universally understood; unless one is born very rich, a job is a matter of subsistence. Freedom loses its meaning if a person does not have the basic means to exercise it. I have never wavered in this belief; at the time it reconfirmed my socialist ideals, and reinforced my belief that the old system could not provide that essential of life.

Of course, I first came to Slovakia as an adult in the fall of 1938, and I had no direct knowledge of the situation there in normal times. I did hear many complaints about unemployment and the misery it had caused. There had been some improvement in Slovakia in 1936 or 1937, when the newly built arms factories started up, and in 1939, after the breakup of Czechoslovakia and the beginning of the war, the arms industry continued to supply jobs and revitalize other sectors of the Slovak economy. Also the Tiso regime needed a sizable state apparatus to maintain itself, including large and well-paid police forces.

To some segments of the Slovak population, this relative, precarious, and short-lived prosperity appeared as a positive legacy of the Slovak State. But that is a very misleading concept, because it overlooks the more important, long-term, and entirely negative consequences of that era, including its human and moral price. Even at the time, I neither saw a general rise in well-being nor heard people delight in their living conditions. Indeed, more thoughtful folk wondered where the jobs would go once the war was over. They could not escape their long memory of misery.

Myself, I had very few standards of comparison in making my political choices. My only previous experience was in Soviet Russia, and there—as I remembered—unemployment, at least, had not been a problem.

7

IN THE UPRISING

On QUIET nights in the late spring and early summer of 1944, when the Russians came close to the Slovak border and Allied airplanes flew freely overhead, people in eastern Slovakia could hear the sounds of war. It was obvious to everyone that the next Russian offensive could push the front across the Carpathians and into Slovakia. The Western Allies had landed in France in early June. It looked as if the war could be over in a few weeks.

Naturally, we lived in a state of expectation, as overoptimistic rumors made the rounds every day. We knew little about large-scale political happenings or underground preparations for the Uprising. The struggle looked simple from the window of the railroad car that took us back and forth to work every morning and afternoon.

In the weeks before the Uprising, the many guerrilla organizers and supplies that the Soviets dropped in different parts of Slovakia fueled the impression that partisans were almost everywhere. Contacts between underground groups intensified, and I learned that, once fighting broke out my small group from Dubnica and a Party cell in Banovce were to join forces with the partisans. I had the comforting impression that everything was well prepared and coordinated. We would have to fight, and some of us would be killed or wounded. But it was a war, wasn't it?

The signal came on August 29, when Colonel Golian, soon to be promoted to general by Benes, issued an order to resist the Germans who were moving in to occupy Slovakia. I did not hesitate—after all, I had made up my mind long before.

August 29 was a Tuesday, and I came home from work early. My mother already knew what was happening. She was standing by the kitchen stove when I told her that I was joining the fight. She turned to face me, looked me in the eye, and after a few seconds of silence she said, "Of course you have to go." I understood what was happening inside her: in a certain way, I was almost all she had at that time. But she was always a woman of substance. I put a few necessities into a haversack, she added some more, we embraced, and I left. Her eyes at that moment, when I sensed rather than saw her tears, will stick in my mind forever.

The situation, of course, was not as clear as I had expected; it never is. As we mustered and marched north to Banska Bystrica, at the center of the insurgent territory, the Germans were already rapidly on the move. Within hours they secured the whole south, where the Tiso regime had kept its most loyal forces, and in a few days they took important towns in all strategic directions: Zilina, Vrutky, Liptovsky sv. Mikulas, Presov, Kezmarok, and Topolcany. Topolcany was close to where my group had helped form defense lines at the southern edge of the liberated territory.

By moving so fast, the Germans secured their supply routes for further operations. They soon brought in more troops from the Protectorate in the west, from Austria and Hungary in the south, and from Poland in the north, but their main thrust continued from the south.

I thought constantly of my father; Nitra, where he was in jail, was only some twenty miles south of Topolcany. Would he be able to escape? The fact is that the Uprising had barely started when the Germans moved in. But, as I learned after the war, my father and the other political detainees in Nitra had had an opportunity to escape shortly after the Uprising was launched. The guards had become so demoralized that all the prisoners could simply walk out; the gate was wide open. Local antifascist groups even prepared trucks to carry the prisoners to freedom. My father's old friend Ludovit Benada had already left his cell and was sitting in a truck, waiting for the other prisoners. At that moment a messenger arrived with instructions from Gustav Husak, in his role as member of the fifth underground Slovak Party Central Committee, asking them to await the simultaneous release of all political prisoners from jails in Slovakia, which would be arranged.

So they waited; even Benada returned to the prison. Party discipline was absolutely firm. With Smidke in Moscow, Husak represented the highest Party authority. Before long the Germans arrived, the Slovak prison guards returned to duty, and the opportunity to escape was lost. After a few weeks, these political prisoners were transferred to Bratislava, and from there most of them, including my father, were shipped, some months later, to the Mauthausen death camp, where over 120,000 prisoners were murdered. My father barely survived.

Some old-timers have always thought the main motive for Husak's unfortunate order was ambition: that he did not want to have other senior Party leaders return when he was moving to the center of power. In all fairness, such a claim cannot be substantiated, and Husak was never publicly accused of this, even at the time of his worst trials in 1950. Many years later I myself asked Husak about it. Why did he issue such a foolish order? He replied that he had not then believed that the Germans would invade Slovakia, and he did not want to provoke them by releasing political prisoners. I shrugged at his answer: he had to have known better. I should add here that Smidke cannot be held responsible for this decision. Once I got to know him, I became convinced he would not have endorsed such an instruction.

In the early days of the Uprising I met up with my brother, Julius, by mere chance and for the last time. It was somewhere between Novaky and Prievidza, in the valley of the Nitra River. I was assigned to an artillery unit, and we were ordered to support our infantry in holding the German advance. Our emplacement was on a small plateau above the highway, facing south. The Germans were expected to come from the southwest; in fact, they soon came from the southeast as well, and we saw our infantry retreating on all sides. At that moment Julius appeared suddenly in front of me, looking very soldierly and solemn. This expression quickly changed, though, into a broad smile—we were both delighted to see each other.

Julius had joined the Uprising a day or two after I left. Now he wondered what my unit was doing there behind our field guns. "Don't you see that the infantry is already running away?" he asked. I told him that we still did not have orders to retreat. But his group was on the move, and there was little time to talk. He had to join his unit.

Julius had two handguns; before he walked away, he pulled one out of his belt and gave it to me. "You may need it in this weather," he said, in his usual joking way. I kept the piece with me throughout the Uprising. We embraced and parted. I, of course, had no idea that it was our last farewell.

My unit did not stand around the guns much longer. As Julius went north, my group marched northeast and then east in the direction of Handlova. The heart of the insurgent territory, Banska Bystrica, was some twenty miles farther east in a straight line. The whole front was formed up as a protective circle around it.

As we retreated toward Handlova, German tanks cut a road that we had to cross, very close to a village called Sebedrazie. I kept company with Jano Bulko, who came from a town not far from Uhrovec. The two of us crawled through a culvert to the other side. The rest of our company soon followed. Beside the road was a row of berry bushes, but then there was an open space, at least half a mile wide, before the edge of the next row of forested hills. On our left, some three hundred yards away, where two roads converged, stood a German tank with its conning tower slowly turning.

We saw that we would have to run for our lives across the open space before the German infantry arrived. After catching our breath, we jumped up and started running. Almost instantly we heard the rattle of German machine guns as bullets pocked the dust left and right. I felt a light sting in my back, but it did not slow me. However, I soon found out that what I thought was just sweat had blood mixed in it. Finally, there was the foot of the hill, the edge of the forest, and safety. As we moved deeper into the forest, my companions looked at my wound. Fortunately, the bullet had gone through my belt, which must have slowed it down somewhat, and entered back muscle without hitting the spine. They treated the wound as well as they could under the circumstances, and we marched on.

As sporadic fighting continued, we slowly retreated to Handlova, then southeast along the Handlovka River to Sv. Kriz (whose name was later changed to Ziar nad Hronom). From there, on October 18, the Germans launched a general offensive against our insurgent territory. They pushed us back through the Hron River valley east to Zvolen, which they took on October 26, then north to Banska Bystrica, which we had to leave a day later. Part of the remaining Slovak forces then withdrew farther north to the mountains, establishing another temporary headquarters in Donovaly, about ten miles in a straight line from Banska Bystrica.

The Germans had crushing supremacy in all materiel, especially tanks. We lacked heavier weapons, most of all antitank weapons. The Soviets sent some supplies, but not enough to make a difference. The paratroopers of the Second Czechoslovak Airborne Brigade in the USSR, about 1,700 men, arrived quite late—September 25—and did not enter action until October 8. At that time the insurgent territory had shrunk radically and was encircled on all sides. The fate of the Uprising was already largely decided. We did not even know that the Soviets had finally launched a limited offensive in the mountain passes of the main Carpathian chain, but it was bogged down and did not make any significant advance before the end of November.

With the fall of Banska Bystrica, the organized phase of the Uprising was over. All remaining Slovak forces, which at this peak consisted of as many as 60,000 lightly armed men, went over to guerrilla warfare. Some units went east and west, to the mountains and forest massifs of central Slovakia. My own unit went west, where we had come from.

This time, of course, all paved roads were controlled by the Germans. We had to avoid all larger settlements. To reach the Strazov Highlands, we bypassed Kremnica, Handlova, and Prievidza, moving from the woods of one set of hills to another.

It was a slow march and a game of hide-and-seek with German patrols, which were by now mopping up the lower levels of the mountains in search of us. Occasionally we exchanged fire, but we avoided large encounters. We were not more than a squad when we reached the Strazov Highlands sometime in early December. We were hungry and tired, and nights were getting dangerously long and cold for sleeping in the open without campfires.

Crossing the German-controlled roads in the valleys was especially dangerous, but we eluded the enemy successfully until we reached a narrow lowland by a village called Motesice, halfway between Banovce and Dubnica. We were headed for Mnichova Lehota, about ten miles beyond Motesice, where Jano Bulko had a cousin, a solitary cottager with whom he thought we could hide for a few nights and pull ourselves together after the long retreat through the wilderness.

Motesice is a crossing of two mountain roads. Watching from the forest, we realized that the Germans had built a machine-gun emplacement at the intersection, commanding the narrow lowland north of the village, which we had to cross. A shallow creek ran from north to south, parallel to one of the roads.

We chose a track by which the distance to the next forest was the shortest, and we managed to ford the creek without being noticed. Between us and the road was a field with deep furrows. We decided to crawl through those furrows to the road, then run over it and across the remaining open space toward the forest. We always crossed like that; only the details differed.

This time the distance between the road and the forest was quite short, hardly more than 500 feet. As we crawled on our bellies through the furrows, the Germans must have spotted somebody's knapsack, because we were hardly halfway to the road when they started firing. Protected by the furrows, we reached the road miraculously unharmed, and the shooting ceased for a while. But now we were trapped between the road and the Germans in the emplacement, who had assuredly alerted their command. We could not wait until dark for our next move.

The forest seemed very close, so we decided to jump up all at the same time and run. Bulko was in front of me, and two others were behind me. Once the machine gun resumed firing, the rest of the squad stayed where they were. We ran as fast as we could to the edge of the forest, Bulko always ahead, myself a few steps behind him. We were almost there when a bullet hit me again—this time in my right foot. Instantly, my shoe filled with blood.

Once inside the forest, we waited only a short while before moving again, up the hill to get away from the road and the searching Germans. We did not get too far before we heard something. Boars, I thought at first, but soon we heard dogs barking. A German patrol was approaching. They must have arrived very quickly after we crossed the road. We jumped into a nearby pit, quickly covered ourselves with fallen leaves, and waited. Then the noises diminished and ceased. They had not spotted us.

I remembered that moment many times in later years when I was hunting and watched a forester lick his forefinger to test the direction of the wind. That day in the forest on Ostry Mountain, we were saved by the fact that the wind was blowing toward us and away from the dogs.

After a while, we started to move again, cautiously, and after another five miles or so—it was quite dark already—we reached the cottage where Bulko's cousin lived. Bulko went to see him while we waited in the forest. After a few minutes he returned and told us that we could stay overnight, but no longer. There were Germans all around, they were searching houses, and people hiding refugees were savagely punished. The Germans were killing whole families and burning their houses down. We spent the night in the hayloft and I did not even dare to pry the shoe from my wounded foot. When Bulko's cousin came to wake us before dawn, we almost shot him by mistake.

From there we had to walk another five miles through thickly forested hills to Selec, where Bulko's family lived. My wound made walking quite painful, so I found myself a long stick for support. At the end of this track, there was another open space and another paved road, where we saw German trucks and motorcycles passing up and down. We took advantage of an interval in the traffic and ran across a field, the road, and another field. This time, I do not remember how I hobbled and ran across 1,500 feet of field and a creek with a bullet in my foot. As I got behind it, I fell to the ground. My companions told me afterwards that as long as I was running, with the stick in my hand, I obviously had felt no pain. From there, fortunately, it was not too far to the Bulko house where they finally cut the shoe from my swollen foot and treated the wound with some leaves—a village folk remedy.

In Selec they put me in the house of a family with children, which made me very uneasy, because I was obviously a danger to them. I begged them to take me back to Velcice, since I did not know of any other place to go.

Soon they arranged for a complicated transport; I remember best being hidden in the side panel of a threshing machine pulled by a white horse. Finally they got me to Velcice and hid me in the house of a friendly family named Peter, who had no children. Naturally, I had other friends in

Velcice, and, best of all, Anna was there, caring for me when I could not walk.

But my foot looked awful when I arrived—blue, red, and swollen—and I needed a physician. My mother, who had moved back to Trencin, tried to get me a surgeon, but he wasn't willing to risk treating me. At least he did not report my mother to the police.

In the end they found a district doctor named Bojko from a nearby village called Melcice. His parents, White Russian exiles, had come to Czechoslovakia after the revolution in 1917. Dr. Bojko, a brave and decent man, came regularly to see me until my foot was healed.

As soon as the war was over, I decided to look up Dr. Bojko and to thank him for what he had done for me. But in Topolcany I learned that the Russians had arrested him and deported him to the Soviet Union. "Why would they do that?" I asked. "They were picking up all Russian exiles," I was told. "They had them all on a list."

I was appalled, but there was nothing I could do at the time. However, I could not put Dr. Bojko out of my mind. As soon as possible, I started looking for him, using all possible contacts I had, writing to the Soviet Embassy in Prague, to friends and acquaintances in Moscow and Kiev, and campaigning for his freedom. But it took a long, long time before they let him out of the Gulag.

Dr. Bojko returned in 1957, his health undermined. I was in Banska Bystrica at the time, and I arranged for his treatment in Piestany. Unfortunately, he did not live long after his return. The fate of this brave and good man has never ceased to fill me with sorrow.

I was limping around the house at the time of the first thaw, in February 1945, when I learned that Julius had been killed. After our parting in the thick of battle he, like me, had made the transition to guerrilla warfare. He had stayed with his partisan group, which in late fall of 1944 retreated to the wooded area between the Nitra and Hron rivers; we had not been far from each other. There he was killed by a German patrol on January 28, 1945.

Julius had not been a political person—just a decent, regular fellow. He fully shared my parents' and my beliefs but never joined the Communist Party. I think he did not want to lose any of his independence, being basically a free spirit. From childhood on, he had been irresistibly spontaneous, at times even rash. He did not try water twice before jumping in. And I'm sure that was how he died. Since the news arrived that February, I have never stopped remembering my brother's last smile as we parted on that hill above the Nitra River, less than six months before liberation.

While for me the war was over, my father's worst time had just started. In February 1945 the Tiso government handed him, with other political prisoners, over to the Nazis, who took him to Mauthausen. Later I learned that the train carrying almost 200 prisoners was bombed on its way through Austria. Some prisoners were killed, notably Jan Osoha, one of the senior Slovak Communists and a longtime friend of my father. Others, including my father, managed to escape, but not for long. Before reaching the Slovak border, they were caught again and brought to Mauthausen. My father weighed less than a hundred pounds when he returned in May 1945.

It was a warm spring, there was peace, everybody, including me, was looking to the future. There was also a lesson at hand, overlooked at the time, which I've never ceased pondering since: one should always strive to understand the past before presuming to look into the future.

But I was still young, and I was disposed, by my upbringing, to great expectations: in the new, socialist order, economic growth would be planned, production would be evenly distributed, and everybody would get a fair deal. That looked not only good but also credible.

Obviously, I had only vague ideas how such a new world would be built and function. But the Party, which I had joined at the age of seventeen, claimed to know all that; it claimed to have a scientific system for accomplishing its historic mission. All it asked for was patience, discipline, and hard work. My belief in socialism was complete, and I was prepared to give it my heart and soul to bring about a better world.

8

THE POSTWAR YEARS

T HERE is a creek between Velcice and the neighboring village of Choc-
holna, and the front moved several times in both directions in that sector
before the Russians pushed the Germans out for good. That was in the early
weeks of 1945, when I was still in hiding, limping along at night from one
shelter to another across the village backyards.

I spent almost the entire time with two families, striving not to be seen by
anyone else. But, soon after the fighting was over and I could go out, I
learned that the whole village—which was predominantly Protestant—had
known I was there. There was no traitor in Velcice.

Anna continued to go to work in Dubnica until the front came very close
and the factories had to stop operating. We saw each other almost every
night; she brought me food and news about the outside world. There was no
radio nearby, and I was anxious to know what was happening. My ears at
least told me that the front was closing in.

Soon after the liberation, Anna and I decided to get married, setting a
date a few months later, after the dust of the great war had settled. Our
wedding took place September 15, 1945, in Velcice. The ceremony was
conducted by the local Protestant pastor, Mr. Kolesar, and my best man was
none other than Alexander Trancik, my godfather from Uhrovec, after
whom I had been named nearly twenty-four years before. He was still at his
post, working for the church as teacher and organist.

Fond and sorrowful memories of that wedding have often welled up in
me since the time, in the summer and autumn of 1990, that I sat by Anna's
hospital bed watching her life coming to its end. She was a faithful
companion, patient and brave, a good mother to our three sons, and a good

wife to me. I miss her very much, but I am grateful that at least she lived long enough to see the end of the Soviet occupation of our country and the restoration of our dignity.

Though separated, both my parents attended our wedding—my father still weak, pale, and half his normal weight. He was then recuperating in Piestany, a spa resort in central Slovakia. I went there to see him as soon as the authorities informed us about his return. I cannot describe how happy I was to see him alive.

He told me that he had learned about his sons' fates during the Uprising, while he was in Mauthausen. One day another Slovak prisoner had come to him and asked, "Is your name Dubcek?" "Yes," he replied. "Well," the man said, "I am Jano Bulko, and I met both your sons in the Uprising." It was my comrade-in-arms from the flight through the hills and forests after our defeat. Soon after he'd helped me to my refuge in Velcice, the Germans had arrested him and sent him to Mauthausen. He never told them about me, and I remain grateful to him. He himself never returned from the camp.

Anna and I moved to Trencin a few weeks after we were married, and I found a job in the local drozchiarna or yeast factory. The factory had about 500 employees at the time, and I worked as a maintenance man and operator of the distilling system. The enterprise had just been nationalized according to the Nationalization Act of October 28, 1945, promulgated by President Benes on the twenty-seventh anniversary of the declaration of Czechoslovakia's independence.

Anna also worked there until before the children were born. We did not have much luck with parenthood at the beginning. Our firstborn son died of pneumonia when he was only a few weeks old, in the winter of 1947. Then Pavol was born in 1948, followed by Peter in 1950, and Milan in 1953. Jokingly, I told Anna once that I would like to have enough sons to make a volleyball team. No sports fan, she asked, "How many is that?" I replied, "Just six," and she seemed to accept that.

Working in the yeast factory until the summer of 1949, I was hardly more than a spectator of the dramatic developments of the early postwar years. Like most of my co-workers, I supported wholeheartedly the policies carried out by the governments since the liberation: on the whole, they promised a better life, and nothing was more important. What we saw was old injustices redressed by steps such as land reform, nationalization, and general health insurance. With most other people, I also believed that the plague of unemployment would not come back in a system of economic planning that had started with the Two-Year Plan of 1946.

Perhaps I tended to simplify things and to hold some naive expectations, but ours was still essentially a belief in fairness and decency—nothing more and nothing less. Freedom was certainly not absent from that concept, only we thought that to enjoy it we needed a full stomach and a roof over our heads. Actually, I don't believe that ordinary people think differently today.

During those postwar years, I was politically active only at the grass-roots level, in the factory cell of the Communist Party. I had never thought of becoming a professional political worker until a day in June 1949 when I was called to the district secretariat of the Party in Trencin and offered a full-time Party job. Like other political parties, the Slovak Communist Party also had an administrative staff, mainly to manage its internal affairs. That was what I was supposed to do.

This offer came at a bad time, since I was about to become the deputy director of the yeast factory. Because I was proving a quick learner of the rules of good management, I stood a good chance of replacing the director in two or three years, when he was to retire. And there was another disadvantage: Party pay would be less than half what I was earning at the factory. This was not without importance, because Anna was expecting our second child, and we were hoping for more children later.

I agonized over the offer with Anna, and, to tell the truth, we considered the move first from a practical angle—how reasonable it was, under the circumstances, to give up my well-paid, secure job at the yeast factory. But the Party, of course, was more than a possible employer to me; it was the embodiment of what I believed in. For that reason it was extremely difficult to decline the offer. Anna knew that. So in the end, with her encouragement, I accepted. There was no calculation in the decision. We both thought of it as a necessary sacrifice, and we expected it to be temporary, like any other duty in the Party cell. I did not have a very clear idea about professional political work at that point.

Thus, I soon left the yeast factory to start my new job. At the Trencin Party secretariat, my duties consisted of the scheduling of meetings, membership registration in local and factory cells, recruitment of new members, collection of Party dues, and so on, and so on. I was appointed organizational secretary, a secondary position, in the district office; there were three other secretaries—specializing in problems of industry, agriculture, and ideology—who worked under the district secretary. Office work was new for me, and it took me several weeks to adjust.

After about three months, once I began to feel confident in my ability to handle the job, they sent me for a six-month course to Harmonia, a recreational resort about fifteen miles from Bratislava. The course was administered by the Central Committee of the Slovak Communist Party, and consisted of lectures on various aspects of the Party program and ideology, the history of the labor movement, and the structure and the organizational system of the Party.

When it was over, in March 1950, I had only a few days at home before I was summoned for reserve duty in the army. For three weeks, I took part in an exercise that consisted mainly of running over the hills in a military zone in Bohemia.

It was at this time that a sad event overtook our family—Uncle Michal took his own life. He was only in his late fifties and still a leading official of the tailoring cooperative in Trencin. The cooperative had been founded in the early 1920s by American Slovaks returning home and was self-managed, as were most organizations in the cooperative movement in Western and Central Europe. In 1949 there was some infighting among officials of the enterprise, and my uncle was falsely accused of discrepancies in his bookkeeping. A proud and honest man all his life, he could not take the accusations and threw himself before a speeding train. Shortly after his death, an audit of the records found the cooperative's finances in perfect order. I was deeply saddened by the tragedy.

Soon after my return from my military duty, I learned that I had been appointed first secretary of the district Party organization in Trencin. I spent over a year in that position, until October 1951. That was a sad and troubled time, reminding me of the purges of my youth in Gorky. The ideological pretext for the repressions was an alleged "intensification of the class struggle," which, as we now know, became Stalin's notorious obsession in his final years. Between 1950 and 1952, a number of well-known politicians, including Communists, were removed from their positions, accused of improbable deeds, put on trial, and sentenced to heavy punishment, including life imprisonment and death. Slovakia was not spared.

My father always believed that the initiator of the Slovak side of this persecution was Viliam Siroky, a Slovak member of the Moscow leadership of the Czechoslovak Communist Party between 1938 and 1941. He took over the Ministry of Foreign Affairs after the arrest of Vladimir Clementis in 1950 on a trumped-up charge. Eventually Siroky became Prime Minister. Even in the late 1960s my father was searching for documents that supposedly would have exposed Siroky's intrigues, but he never found them.

My father, by the way, never held any Party office after the war; he did not even work in the Party apparatus. He stayed in Topolcany and, until his retirement in 1952, worked in a large local furniture store utilizing his old cabinetmaking skills.

I must say that, in my role as district secretary in Trencin between April 1950 and October 1951, I encountered no episodes of official political or economic persecution. I do not even remember knowing anyone in my district who was arrested. There may have been such cases, but no one brought them to my attention.

In my position, of course, I had no jurisdiction over either the public security or the secret police, the so-called State Security or StB. They had their own line of command and never asked me anything or reported to me. As I learned twelve years later, during my work on the commission investigating the repressions of the early 1950s, State Security were to a large extent a state within the state, even at the middle level. They often received instructions directly from their Soviet advisers, and the Czechoslovak show trials of the early 1950s were orchestrated by the Soviets. This is how so many district and even regional Party secretaries could disappear, and even the Party's first secretary, Rudolf Slansky, be murdered.

In October 1951, I was transferred to Bratislava as an official in the organizational department of the Central Committee of the Slovak Communist Party. So we moved to the Slovak capital—one of the many moves my family would have to undertake.

In addition to my work on the Central Committee secretariat, I was assigned in early 1952 to stand in for the ailing chairman of the Slovak National Front, Frantisek Kubac. I was probably picked because for two or three months I had been a deputy in the Czechoslovak National Assembly for the Trencin district. That had come about because, during the elections of 1948, I had been voted runner-up by my co-workers at the yeast factory on the National Front candidate list. In 1951 the deputy who had been elected died, and it was my obligation to take his place. Kubac himself had been in his position, which had previously been held by Karol Smidke, for only about a year.

Then, in January 1953, I was promoted to be regional secretary in Banska Bystrica, in central Slovakia. I can't say that I was not surprised, or that I was not pleased. Not that I didn't like Bratislava, but Banska Bystrica was closer to Anna's and my old home and to our hearts. The Slovak Party leadership had been in flux since the demotion and arrest of important Party officials such as Ladislav Novomesky and Gustav Husak in 1950 and the abolition of the office of first secretary in 1951. My father's old friend Ludovit Benada had been back in the secretariat since mid-1952, and he may have been instrumental in my appointment.

I became regional secretary in Banska Bystrica only about two weeks before Stalin's death. A week or so later, Klement Gottwald also died, having contracted pneumonia at Stalin's funeral. Back in Prague, his physicians could not save him, and he ended up embalmed, just like Stalin. The Czechoslovak Communist Party leadership knew no limit in their imitation of Soviet ways.

Many accounts, including the memoirs of Khrushchev, indicate that things in the Soviet Union started to change for the better almost immediately after Stalin's death. However, Czechoslovak Party repression did not lift until much later. Still, some signs of a general turn for the better could be discerned. The war in Korea and the struggle against the French in Vietnam were settled, East and West had renewed efforts to solve the division in Germany by negotiation, and it seemed that the Soviet leadership was about to "review" the case of Yugoslavia. I began to reflect more systematically about the "thaw."

The worst repressions had taken place over several years, but, for those who were not dragged into the mills of violence, everything seemed to happen very fast and forcefully. In retrospect, it was like a film moving backward at great speed. Most of my friends at that time were, like myself, confused and frightened. What had happened to our great dream, and why?

We learned one significant lesson from this development: that socialism is no safer than any other system from abuse by bad, unscrupulous, dishonest people. In my eyes at least, the idea itself did not thereby lose any of its purity and greatness. What was needed, I felt, was to bring the political system of socialism into harmony with its philosophical values. The problem was how to do this.

Life went on in the midst of the purges as if nothing unusual were happening. People went to work and to the movie houses; theaters, ballrooms, and pubs were packed as usual. As regional secretary, I had enough to keep me busy sixteen hours every day. Harvests had to be organized, factories built, production begun. New employees needed housing and services. New highways and railroads had to be laid. I traveled extensively: to cattle and crop farms, forests, and all kinds of local or regional industrial plants then under construction. In meetings, we would decide how to reach the agricultural and industrial production targets set by the state.

To tell the truth, the most vivid memories I have of the time in Banska Bystrica are of my family life. The children were a great joy, and, when weather permitted, Anna and I loved to take them on expeditions to the beautiful countryside. We went to the High Tatra Mountains often, to ski, hike, or pick mushrooms or berries.

By the end of 1954, I was told that I would be sent to Moscow to study at the Higher Political School of the Soviet Communist Party Central Committee. No explanation for this honor was given, but I could guess the reasons. For one thing, I was a prewar Party member, and with significant seniority. I was also exceptionally fluent in Russian. And in my work I was causing no problems. I had no enemies—at least none that I knew about.

For me in 1955, going to Moscow was a mixed blessing. On the one hand, I looked forward to visiting the land of my youth for the first time in almost twenty years, especially when it was changing in exciting ways. On the other hand, I would have to leave Anna and the boys behind. The course was to last three years, and I did not expect to be home more than twice a year. Furthermore, I was already in the sixth semester of external law studies at Comenius University in Bratislava, I was doing rather well, and switching from one field of study to another at my age—I was thirty-three years old at the end of 1954—did not look very practical.

But Anna gave me the encouragement I needed. In the summer of 1955, we moved back to Trencin, where Anna would stay with the children during my absence. Pavol, our eldest, was seven years old then and going into second grade; Peter was five and would start school a year later; Milan, the youngest, was two.

My mother stayed with us during this period, and she was a great help in caring for the children. Anna also had a sister and two or three cousins in Trencin, so she had solid family support. At least I knew I did not have to worry about my wife's and children's well-being as I set out for the Soviet Union of Nikita Khrushchev in August of 1955.

9

STUDIES IN MOSCOW

A DOZEN or so students from Czechoslovakia were sent to the Higher Political School in Moscow in 1955—two or three Slovaks, the rest from the Czech lands. I remember only a few of them today. One was Milos Jakes, a longtime high Party official in Prague who in August 1968 took part in the pro-Soviet conspiracy. In 1988 he became the last Czechoslovak Communist Party first secretary, there to lead the Party's funeral rites, so to speak. More Czech and Slovak students were already studying at the school, like Jozef Lenart, who became prime minister under Antonin Novotny in 1963, and who in August 1968 dishonored himself the same way Jakes did. We may all have read the same books in Moscow, but we did not come back with the same ideas.

It was quite a sentimental journey for me in August 1955. It was easy to relive my past on the train, tracing in reverse the trip I had made in October 1938, when I was by my father's side. Looking at the passing scenery, I thought more about the changing times than about the trees and houses. Seventeen years earlier, the USSR had been torn by an internal conflict my father and I were unable to comprehend, and ahead of us had loomed the heavy cloud of war.

Since then, an eternity seemed to have passed: the long war, with its destruction and death, and the postwar period, with all its contradictory developments. Now it was two years after Stalin's death, and everything seemed to be getting better, as if fresh air was coming through a wide-open window. Whereas that earlier trip had been marked by despair, this one inspired hope.

I had the feeling that I was returning to an old, familiar place but, at the

66

same time, a place with new and unknown features to be explored. Because of my youth in the Soviet Union I was soon able to develop a much sharper view of what was going on there than the other Czechoslovak students, and in the meantime I found answers to some questions that had burdened me for many years.

I had never been to Moscow before, though, and when, after an almost two-day journey, the train pulled into the Byelorussian Railroad Station it was as much a first for me as it was for the others. We looked at our drab surroundings with great curiosity, some certainly hiding their disappointment. I did not have to: all was roughly as I'd thought it would be.

A battered old bus took us and our belongings across town to Leningradskoye Chaussee, close to the Leningrad Station. The school was a compound of about twenty houses built in the typically austere Soviet bricks-and-blocks style of the early 1930s. Everything was in one place—classrooms, library, administration, dormitories.

The Higher Political School of the Central Committee of the Communist Party of the Soviet Union—HPS for short—was organized as a regular university, only its departments were called chairs, not faculties or schools. At the head was a rector, assisted by deputies and heads of chairs. The HPS was supervised by the Department of Education and Arts of the Central Committee. There were about a thousand students at that time. About 10 percent were from Eastern Europe; I do not remember any students from other parts of the world.

There were foreign students at other institutions of higher education in Moscow and in the USSR, and quite a few Czech and Slovak students studied at Moscow State University, Frunze Military Academy, the Higher School of Agricultural Sciences, and other schools. We all met occasionally for functions at the Czechoslovak Embassy.

At the HPS foreign students received a good deal of special treatment. We lived together in separate areas of the dormitories and were assigned to *spetzgroups,* or special learning sections, in which we were given personal assistance. At the beginning, most of us had to study Russian, which took roughly a semester. Foreign students also had smaller course and reading loads and were tested and graded more leniently, to the jealous dismay of the native students.

Such segregation resulted in a certain isolation for foreign students. Soviet students also had their own Party cells, which held regular meetings, while we had no political organization. Luckily, because of my fluent and unaccented Russian, I was not treated as a foreign student. I received no special assistance and had to work with the same rigor as my Russian peers from the very beginning. I remember taking a first, difficult test a few weeks after my arrival and being pleased to get a C. Grading of Soviet students was very strict.

For similar reasons, I was assigned a room with a Russian named Boris, formerly a district Party secretary from a region south of Moscow. The average age of HPS students was between thirty and forty, but Boris was around fifty and had had to fight for his admission. He had applied several times without success and in the end wrote to Khrushchev, who ordered the school to admit him. Boris was a hardworking student and became a good friend.

The school was divided into eight or ten chairs, of which I remember history, political economy, philosophy (mainly Marxism-Leninism, of course), international relations, agricultural science, journalism, and history of the Soviet Communist Party. Students had to take all the subjects in the curriculum. As well as regular courses, consisting of lectures and discussions, there were seminars and individual tutorials.

In addition to the school's faculty, there were lecturers from other universities in Moscow. Various high Soviet officials also came to lecture or to talk informally to students; I remember, for example, B. I. Ponomaryov and L. P. Iliychov. Ponomaryov was in the International Department of the Soviet Central Committee, and Iliychov was deputy foreign minister under Molotov.

From lectures and reading, one was able to amass a lot of facts, but no topic was taught or presented objectively; everything was tightly wrapped in a Marxist-Leninist interpretation. We were told about differing or critical views, but these were always characterized as either "revisionist" or "hostile," and we could never independently evaluate such deviationist critics as Leon Trotsky, Karl Kautsky, or Rosa Luxemburg. All we got were selected quotations, along with the reasons for their inadequacy.

Historic events and personalities were also subject to changing judgment, dependent on current Party gospel. I remembered this practice from my years in Gorky; now, in 1956 or 1957, some of the verdicts from my Gorky days, like that on Marshal Tukhachevsky, were reversed. I often thought about the human tragedy behind such turnabouts, but in many cases I was only speculating. We knew that Tukhachevsky had been executed but even then we were not told what had happened to other such "victims of the cult of personality."

There were a few rare exceptions to the school's biased packaging of unorthodox views. For example, I remember reading with great curiosity the full texts of documents of the old German Social Democratic Party, the Gotha and Erfurt programs. In fact, I came upon these originals almost as if directed by my subconscious. The HPS library did not officially carry any works of unapproved authors, certainly nothing critical of Lenin and his views. I should also say that our assigned reading load was so heavy that we hardly had time to read anything else.

Certain lectures and texts surprised me by their selective and simplistic contents. In agricultural science and political economy, for example, there were no references to the rich and important history of the cooperative movement in Western and Central Europe. It was as if the Soviet kolkhozes were a purely Soviet Communist invention. Moreover, even then, in the mid-1950s, kolkhozes were not really conceived as self-managing cooperatives. Why the Soviets had decided to ignore the nineteenth-century European cooperative movement I cannot tell, but its democratic nature must have looked suspiciously bourgeois in light of Lenin's theories and Stalinist practice. Anyway, the Russians were then obsessed with the idea that they had invented everything from the wheelbarrow to electricity, and their historical isolation made this self-illusion possible.

Examinations at the HPS took place in the middle and at the end of a semester. Each student pulled a card with his question from a cardboard box and was given a while to think about it in the classroom. Then we were called to the professor's office for the exam. There were only oral examinations—no essay tests, no papers, no theses, and no dissertations at the end. The grading scale was A to E, Excellent to Insufficient. The HPS awarded no academic titles, only diplomas certifying attendance and passing of all tests. Diplomas were color coded according to achievement. I was pleased to receive a red diploma, meaning A. In the end, I could not help comparing the rigidities of the HPS unfavorably with the more lenient atmosphere of the Comenius University in Bratislava, but, whatever its drawbacks, I did learn a lot, and was able to read extensively, an activity for which I would otherwise have hardly found the time.

I read mainly in the two subjects that attracted me most—history and political economy, and in both I found the works of Karl Marx greatly enriching. Of all the authors, Marx was the most logical and persuasive. I am not surprised to see that he continues to be recognized as one of the greatest Western minds of the nineteenth century. I read, of course, *Das Kapital*, but I also enjoyed his lesser works, such as *The Eighteenth Brumaire of Louis Bonaparte* and *The Class Struggles in France*. The question of the applicability of some of his ideas to the second half of the twentieth century did cross my mind, but I wasn't sure I had any firm answers.

As I read, I did not consciously compare Marx and Lenin—certainly not at the beginning. The idea that there could be some disagreement between the two did not even occur to me for quite some time. It was probably in my last year that I started to notice subtle variances. Marx's discussion of economic preconditions for a socialist transformation, for example, seemed to throw doubt on Lenin's reasoning concerning Russia, although Lenin's argument was presented as final revelation. Also, Marx—in contrast to Lenin—was emphatically democratic: his idea of the dictatorship of the proletariat was in no way divorced from the concept of majority rule. I realized, of course, that such a concept would make little sense in Russia. But how relevant then were the other references to Marx in Lenin's work?

I was disturbed by these questions, but I never dared come out with them. Outside school times were changing, but inside I did not notice any thawing in the professors' attitudes. Their doctrinaire world outlook had priestly qualities, and Lenin was their god. Any doubt about the authenticity of his Marxism would have amounted to the worst form of heresy.

I think my problem was I believed in socialism no matter what. It was, after all, my heritage. In my reading I was looking not for justification but for ways to understand socialism better, to make it work better. I liked to weigh each idea on its own merits and not treat any work as if it were the Bible or Koran. But fundamentalism was what our professors expected and required. This practice reduced Marxism to a set of infantry regulations.

While still a student at the HPS, I also noticed some contradictions within works of Lenin such as *State and Revolution* and *Leftism: The Infantile Disease of Communism*. There I ran across an idea that struck me instantly as relevant to the mid-1950s. Lenin suggested that once the socialist revolution was victorious in an advanced country—not a backward one, such as Russia—this country would assume leadership in the international socialist movement, and Russia would follow it. I underlined the passage, making a note in the margin: Czechoslovakia? East Germany?

Twelve years or so later, I recalled this passage when Brezhnev and his Politburo were trying to teach us how to conduct our affairs in Czechoslovakia. I mentioned it to my staff during the talks in Cierna in 1968, and I said I intended to bring it up during a formal meeting. But my staffers were horrified, certain that Brezhnev and Co. would be insulted, so I dropped my notion.

Today I ask myself whether the failure of socialism, more than a hundred years after Marx's death, was truly inherent in his ideas. He proposed no fixed model of socialism; in his last years, he even accepted the possibility of a nonviolent transformation of capitalism. His followers then further revised his ideas in accord with social and economic developments in Western Europe that Marx could not have predicted. Cannot the failure of socialism in the twentieth century be better explained by the fact that its realization was monopolized by Russian radicals, burdened with dogmatism and orthodoxy? My reading in Marx indicates that a country like Russia was unfit for the socialist experiment. I also think there can be little doubt of the contribution of Marx and other classic social thinkers to the phenomenal reforms of social injustices that have shaped modern Western life.

Reading was not all that was shaping my ideas and future behavior during those three years. Events in the Soviet Union and beyond had an equal or greater impact. Far-reaching changes were already occurring when I arrived in Moscow. At the end of May 1955, Khrushchev had made a trip to Belgrade during which he addressed Tito as a "dear comrade," which did much more than reverse Tito's standing in the Soviet bloc pantheon. It cracked the foundations of the oppressive system of unequal relations between the Soviet Union and its client states in Eastern Europe as enforced by Stalin in the immediate postwar era. This approach really launched a long process of liberation of these states, which led through the milestones of 1956 and 1968 to the final collapse of Soviet dominance in 1989.

I sensed rather than recognized the historic meaning of Khrushchev's gesture. Deep in my heart, I had never quite reconciled myself to the idea that Tito was the traitor described in Soviet propaganda in the years after his break with Stalin. With Khrushchev's public apology, I felt a great inner satisfaction, even if Tito, his party, and his country did not formally return to the group of Soviet-led states and continued to pursue their own goals, internally and externally. Khrushchev's act legitimized a socialist country's independence from the Soviet Union for the first time.

Next came the Russian people's response to Tito himself, during his visit to Moscow in June 1956. I found this overwhelming: I had never before seen such a spontaneous outburst as the welcome given the Yugoslav leader by hundreds of thousands of Russians as he rode from the airport to the Kremlin. Until recently this man had been caricatured as a vulture-faced figure in Nazi uniform with a blood-soaked ax in his hand and called an executioner and imperialist lackey in all the Soviet media. This explosion of enthusiasm unveiled the shallow impact such propaganda had on the average Russian. And I liked that; it showed that the people's judgment was sound after all.

There were other important events signaling a better era, but the most phenomenal, of course, was the Twentieth Congress of the Soviet Communist Party in February 1956 and Khrushchev's secret speech on its closing day, revealing the criminal nature of Stalin's rule.

Not long after my arrival in Moscow, I realized that the general atmosphere among the students at the HPS was quite different from what I'd left behind. Since I was living with and had been accepted by Soviet students, they spoke openly with me, sharing information and gossip from their discussions in Party meetings.

To tell the truth, I was not quite ready to hear much of what they were saying, and I was shocked when they stated bluntly that Stalin had been a murderer. There were many more shocks waiting to be sure, but this one was too sudden and too momentous—the man had for so many years portrayed himself as the embodiment of everything I wanted to believe in. Now I could no longer separate Stalin from the bad side of things, could no longer assume he did not know. Now it seemed he was the very cause of all the woe.

A major source of these revelations were the prisoners who were then starting to return from the camps of the Gulag. Their stories quickly spread. It was more and more obvious that all of them were innocent, which meant that the other millions, those who could not return, those whose graves were scattered across the country, had also been innocent. This included the best-known victims of the great purges of the 1930s, a time I remembered so vividly. It was a terrifying thing to learn.

Apparently most other foreign students, including those from Czechoslovakia, were insulated from this ferment until well after the Twentieth Congress. I have to admit that I hesitated to tell them what I was hearing from my Russian friends. Since my very young years, I have been inclined to think things through before making a move or a judgment, and this was no exception. It took me time to digest this flood of depressing news and to separate men from ideas and the good from the bad.

My Russian friends learned about Khrushchev's secret speech about two weeks after it happened. A representative of the Central Committee came to the school and read excerpts at their Party meeting. No text circulated. It was a strictly confidential intra-Party announcement, and we foreign students were told nothing, then or later. I, however, learned very quickly about the speech and about many additional details which confirmed rumors that had been circulating for months. Still, it was the official truth that had the greatest impact.

Among my Russian friends, Khrushchev was the hero of the day. The story circulated that he had dared to make the speech before the delegates against the will of the majority of the leadership, who had been involved in the mass repressions. In 1957 they conspired against Khrushchev and tried to overthrow him, but he was smarter and won the struggle against Molotov, Kaganovich, and the rest.

All these developments resulted in such a thorough change in the political climate of the Soviet Union that it is almost impossible to describe. I remember from that time the Russian movie *The Thaw*. The winds of spring were indeed blowing; the thaw was everywhere in Moscow, and everybody was feeling it.

I was overwhelmed by these events, and, as my stay in Moscow approached its end, I thought more and more about the situation back home. I remember complaining about the restrictions on home visits to an official of the personnel department of the Czechoslovak Communist Party Central Committee in Prague at the end of a leave. Her response was: "Nor could we come home to visit from the German concentration camps!" I could not help but tell her, "But we are not in a concentration camp, Comrade. We are at school!" This episode may show how slowly the thaw was making its way into Czechoslovakia.

After graduation I was invited to join a group of foreign students going to the Urals to study Soviet methods of industrial management. We mainly surveyed the heavy industry complex in the Sverdlovsk region, one of the principal Soviet centers of metallurgy and mining. What we saw was much bigger than anything I had seen in Czechoslovakia, but I had little to compare it with.

After this trip, I finally headed home. As the train carried me there, I traveled, figuratively speaking, from spring back to winter.

10

THE ADVENT OF
A STORMY SEASON

In SEPTEMBER 1958, I rejoined my family in Trencin. The boys had grown up since my last visit, and I spent a few quiet and happy days with Anna, my mother, and the children. But soon I was instructed to come back to Bratislava, where I was informed that I had been appointed the regional Party secretary for western Slovakia.

There were some small stirrings in Czechoslovakia's political situation. After the Party became acquainted with an abbreviated version of Khrushchev's denunciation of Stalin, there was heated discussion in many cells, and quite a few voted resolutions demanding an extraordinary Party congress.

Unfortunately, this initiative was limited mainly to the intellectual segments of the Party, and the leadership easily suppressed it. The anti-Stalinist opposition within the Party, which had always been there, was silenced again. But this period of critical reflection on the record of the Czechoslovak Party in the post-1948 period was the beginning of our uphill struggle for reform. To understand the complex passions this review stirred within the Party, it is necessary to look back into those unsettling years, as we at the time were doing.

After 1945, the country was governed by a coalition of eight political parties—four in the Czech lands and four in Slovakia—which were united in the National Front. These were all parties with a leftist or left-of-center political orientation. Understandably, at that time, given Munich and the war, rightist parties were not permitted to operate in the political system.

Thus, Czechoslovakia had moved decisively in the direction of socialism well before the Communist Party assumed full power in February 1948. The nationalization in October 1945 affected all banks, insurance institutions, steel and iron works, companies with more than 500 employees, and, in some cases, factories with only 150 workers or more. The public sector had already been significantly enlarged by the "retribution decrees" proclaimed in May and June 1945, which transferred extensive German- and Hungarian-held property in Czechoslovakia to government control and distributed it gratis to landless peasants—at least in the Czech lands. Another presidential decree of 1945 gave trade union councils, largely dominated by Communists, a significant role in managing industry, both public and private.

In the general elections in May 1946, the Czechoslovak Communist Party, aided by the role it had played in land redistribution, won over 40 percent in the Czech lands, becoming the strongest party there. The National Socialists took 24 percent, the Popular (Catholic) Party 20 percent, and the Social Democrats 16 percent. In Slovakia the Communists won slightly over 30 percent, second to the Liberal Democrats' 62 percent. The voting, however, did not reflect the Communists' organizational power. By the end of 1947, the Czechoslovak Communist Party had as many members as all other political parties combined. In the National Assembly, the Communists needed only the support of the left wing of the Social Democratic Party to control all legislation.

The political crisis in February 1948 and its outcome superseded the partnership model of the National Front with a system entirely dominated by the Communist Party. The National Front was formally preserved, but merely as a shell. In response to the democrats' refusal to go along with some of their demands, the Communists organized a vast display of raw power on February 21, parading their 200,000-strong workers' militia through Wenceslas Square. Klement Gottwald, then premier, demanded that President Benes install a new cabinet, giving the Communists control of vital ministries. On the evening of the twenty-fifth, Benes gave way to Gottwald's demands.

Despite these strong-arm tactics, the events in February 1948 were not followed by any obvious departure from the social and economic directions in place since 1945. Indeed, the most immediate results were the enactment of the national health insurance system, a revision of the land reform of 1920 (still carried out on the basis of individual farming), and the nationalization of wholesale trade, foreign trade, and enterprises with more than fifty employees.

What really mattered for the long term, though we were then not fully aware of it, was the qualitative change in the political system at that time. The Communist Party emerged with a virtual monopoly on power. No matter what its leadership's immediate intentions were, the Party's historical and ideological association with the Soviet Union opened the door for implementation of the Stalinist system. With the Cold War developing, that could probably not have been avoided.

Men like Jan Masaryk and Edvard Benes must have understood this much better than most other people. Masaryk, the first postwar foreign minister of Czechoslovakia, committed suicide shortly after the February crisis. (Many people believed that he was murdered. The case was investigated in spring 1968, but the investigation did not yield any facts to support the theory of a political murder.) President Benes, who was in poor health anyway, resigned his office in June 1948 and died three months later. We did not grasp the ominous meaning of these tragedies at the time.

Doubts remain about the immediate plans of the Czechoslovak Party leadership following the changes in February 1948. Historians of that period say that Gottwald and the other Communist leaders were not very anxious to initiate a Soviet-modeled political course. In fact, Gottwald restated several times his previous program, which was "a specifically Czechoslovak and democratic road to socialism." That may sound today like a slogan devoid of contents, but emphasizing that specificity could not then have meant anything other than an intention to avoid the Soviet "road to socialism."

The departure from that postulate was very gradual and almost inconspicuous; at the grass-roots level, where I functioned at that time, it was hardly noticeable. The Party leadership was in no hurry to provide more explicit explanations of what was happening. In June 1948, however, when the dispute between Stalin and Tito came into the open, Gottwald joined the Soviets in their criticism of Yugoslavia and her claims to "specificity."

Of course, that was also the end of Gottwald's specifically Czechoslovak road to socialism. Soon Party propaganda put more emphasis on the "Soviet experience." Although such shifts indicated that the Soviet system would be the only permissible model, the actual process was one of detours rather than reversals and was difficult to follow for people without substantial political experience. Like most of my friends, I was quite confused by the Yugoslav affair and did not grasp its historic dimension at the time.

The onset of the Cold War in 1948 and 1949, meanwhile, revived the paranoia of Stalin, his henchmen, and some other highly placed Communists. When Matyos Rakosi, first secretary of the Hungarian Communist Party, had his minister of foreign affairs, Laszlo Rajk, executed in a fit of jealousy, he told Stalin that Rajk's conspiracy extended into

Czechoslovakia and Poland. Stalin, of course, was all ears. Unbeknownst even to the Czech minister of the interior, Lavrenty Beria's deputy arrived in Prague in 1949 to search for this nonexistent conspiracy. Where the Polish Communists resisted similar pressure from Moscow, Gottwald and his first secretary, Rudolf Slansky, cast around for victims to fit the script. Eventually this witch-hunt rebounded onto Slansky himself. He was accused of a scheme to withdraw Czechoslovakia from the Soviet alliance—a so-called Titoist conspiracy—put on trial, and hanged with ten others in November 1952. Eleven out of thirteen chief defendants in this trial were of Jewish origin (as Rajk had been).

This madness was a distant if foreboding menace to us in Trencin, where I was serving as district secretary during the height of the arrests. As I said earlier, I knew of no persecutions during my tenure. Later revelations turned up two StB arrests of former Nazi collaborators (or sympathizers), who were unjustifiably forced to serve four-year prison sentences. Slovakia as a whole suffered terribly, however. The pretext used against my elder Slovak fellow Party members was not Titoism but "bourgeois nationalism"—a charge cooked up in Prague and used cynically to settle old scores and, in the process, warn us off support for Slovak aspirations.

The principal victim was Dr. Vladimir Clementis, a highly respected prewar Slovak intellectual and the Czechoslovak foreign minister since 1948, who was accused of espionage, sentenced to death, and executed in December 1952. In fact, as we learned much later, he was simply being punished for his criticism of the Nazi-Soviet Pact of August 1939—Clementis had been in exile in Paris at the time. Gustav Husak and the poet Laco Novomesky, both involved in the Slovak National Uprising, were jailed for years, as were Daniel Okali, Ladislaw Holdos, and Ivan Horvath. Karol Smidke was not put in prison, but he was slandered and destroyed politically.

This so-called bourgeois nationalism was a doctrinal Marxist cliché drawn from the false assumption that all expressions of nationalism have bourgeois roots. Its application to Slovakia and to these three men was particularly specious, since none of them could be called bourgeois. Smidke, for instance, was a Czech worker. Nonetheless, he was expelled from the Party and thrown out of all public functions. He died a year later, in December 1952. Although I had not known him personally, my father had, and we had many mutual friends. His death just a week or so after the Slansky (and Clementis) trial in Prague posed a serious problem for many of his friends.

The State Security terror was peaking at this time, and fear of new accusations and arrests was widespread. But Smidke had to have a funeral, and the question was whether or not to attend. One of the hardest pressed was Ludovit Benada. He was then a secretary of the Slovak Party Central Committee, but he was also related to Smidke; his daughter was married to Smidke's eldest son. Benada undertook the task of persuading someone to make a speech at Smidke's funeral, but he could not find anyone willing to do so. One morning he called me. I don't remember hesitating much in agreeing to the request. Nevertheless, he thought of some precautions. "Draft your speech, then take it to Gosiorovsky for approval," he advised me. Gosiorovsky was then the Slovak Party secretary for ideology.

I wrote a draft in which I eulogized Smidke as everything he really was— a good man, a dedicated revolutionary, and a great leader, whose organizational work in the Slovak National Uprising could not be overstated.

Gosiorovsky made extensive cuts and changes in the draft for me to read at the funeral. I didn't like his changes, and I decided to read my original text. It was a very cold and windy day, but in the end quite a crowd came to bid their last farewells to Smidke. I had no doubt that StB people were also there.

Juraj Spizter, a journalist and a friend of mine, had read the draft before I took it to Gosiorovsky, read the "corrected" text, then heard me at the funeral. After the speech, he told me, "This is going to cause an earthquake." But nothing happened. Probably no one had been assigned to compare my speech with the doctored text. As the old Czech saying goes: Don't go in your pants until you really have to.

Back to September 1958. While I had been in Moscow, personnel had changed at the top of the Czechoslovak Communist Party. Antonin Novotny, first secretary of the Czechoslovak Central Committee since 1953, had been elected president of the Republic in November 1957, after the death of Antonin Zapotocky, an old-guard member of the Czechoslovak Party. This ominous step combined the powerful offices of first secretary and president, thus confounding Party and state.

Novotny was a prewar Party member who had spent four years in Mauthausen. In September 1953, when Gottwald's successors decided to renew the office of first secretary, last held by Slansky, they sought someone unchallenging to their authority. So they chose Novotny, a colorless regional secretary in Prague. Stalin had once been chosen for similar reasons.

When I became regional secretary in Bratislava in September 1958, I needed time to analyze the internal situation, as well as who stood where on various issues. In May 1958 at the Slovak Party congress, I had been reelected, in my absence, both to the Slovak Party Central Committee and as a candidate member of its Presidium. I don't know the exact circumstances of my promotion, but I assume my stint at the HPS in Moscow played a role. In June I had also been elected, in absentia and for the first time, a member of the Czechoslovak Central Committee, which meant I would soon be taking regular trips to Prague as well. Although I was making significant headway within the Party, Novotny was at the apex of his power, and he was an obstinate foe of changes in the political system. To oppose him directly would have been suicide.

The reader will, I think, need to know a bit more here about how the Communist Party system was organized. Each Party's top body was a congress, usually held every four years. A congress decided basic policies for the next period and elected the Central Committee. This was the most powerful body until the next congress. The Central Committee met every other month to discuss specific problems and steps to solve them. The Central Committee elected its Presidium, the first secretary, and the Secretariat to carry out the day-to-day tasks. In the late 1950s, the Presidium had ten to twelve full members with voting rights and several candidate members, who were being groomed for full membership. They took part in the deliberations but did not vote. The Presidium met once a week. The Secretariat had up to ten secretaries and "members" and served as the executive arm of the Central Committee and its Presidium, implementing its agenda. The head of the Secretariat was the first secretary. The Secretariat met twice or even three times a week, and was assisted by a large bureaucratic body usually called the apparatus, several hundred officials working in over twenty departments supervising all government agencies and Party activities.

The decisive power lay in the hands of the first secretary. That was the key characteristic of the Stalinist system. The most important power was that of appointments, promotions, and demotions. A first secretary could gradually affect even the composition of the Central Committee, and thus the composition of the Presidium and the Secretariat. The department heads of the apparatus held more power than ministers of the government, and they were accustomed to interfering with government business on a daily basis and in great detail.

As for the relationship between the Czechoslovak and Slovak Communist parties, I have already mentioned that the Slovak Party was substantially subordinated to the Czechoslovak one, of which all its members were collectively a part.

Soon after returning to Bratislava, I was assigned a one-story family house at 31 Misikova Street, where I brought Anna and the children from Trencin. My mother also moved with us again. I was especially happy that the house had a little yard around it. The boys could play there in the fresh air, and I soon started a bit of gardening, which is one of my hobbies. I have lived in that house ever since.

In technical terms, my work in Bratislava did not differ much from that in Banska Bystrica, but this large and fast-growing city had problems of its own, and I paid little attention to what is commonly considered politics. There was very little one could have achieved there, anyway, because the Slovak Communist Party was firmly controlled by Novotny's chief watchdog in Slovakia, First Secretary Karol Bacilek.

Bacilek had been an organizer of the partisan movement in Slovakia in 1943 and 1944. He was trained in clandestine operations by the Soviets and it was generally believed that he retained close ties to the NKVD. That, at least, was how his appointment to the post of Czechoslovak minister of security was explained. The following story, which may well be true, captures the man and nature of the time: soon after his appointment as minister of security in 1952, Bacilek had made an inspection of the dreadful Ruzyne Prison in Prague, which held hundreds of political prisoners. Going from cell to cell, he happened to enter one holding the Slovak poet Laco Novomesky, whom he had known earlier. Novomesky had no knowledge of events since his arrest, and when he saw Bacilek entering his cell, he exclaimed, "My God, Karolko, you're here, too?" Bacilek, without losing his composure, reached into his pocket, gave Novomesky a cigarette, and walked out.

Besides Bacilek, the Slovak Party leadership included Michal Chudik, a Novotny ally, and Jozef Lenart, the future prime minister who had studied in Moscow with me and was then a secretary of the Central Committee. Occasionally we worked together, and we got along rather well. At that time Lenart was a modern-minded man with good intentions, but his lack of both personal courage and stamina emerged later. None of these Presidium members, with the possible exception of Benada, had any reformist leanings, and Benada was on his way out to take over a non-Party office.

The first major political issue I had to face in Bratislava was Novotny's constitutional reform, announced in 1959 and put through a year later. The new constitution, designed to replace that of 1948, contained several clauses about which I had serious doubts, and some which I considered entirely wrong.

For example, it added the adjective *Socialist* to the name of the state, a description I did not think justified by our stage of development. The document also codified the ruling position of the Communist Party in the state, which I did not think was really appropriate as a legal measure in any democracy, even a socialist one. I could not voice these opinions directly in

1959 or 1960, but during the years to come I pointed out several times in my public appearances that the Party's leading place in the society had not been won forever: it had to be constantly earned by the Party's activities, and reconfirmed by public confidence and support.

The most regrettable clauses of the new constitution concerned the autonomous Slovak political structures created in 1944 and 1945. The Slovak body known as the Board of Commissioners, which was supposed to administer state policies in Slovakia, was abolished completely, together with Slovak branch offices of other central institutions, including the Social Security Administration. The Slovak National Council was reduced to a regional assembly with no actual authority. These measures, significantly increasing centralization in Prague and showing arrogant disregard for Slovak national interests and feelings, ignored the bitter lessons of the first Czechoslovak Republic during the late 1930s. Deep in my heart, I had no doubt that these disquieting arrangements could only seed a crisis in Czecho-Slovak relations.

I also realized that, in the long run, this policy would undermine Novotny and his allies, but, again, it was impossible to challenge their dictatorial power immediately or directly. That such a step would have been suicidal was demonstrated by the Rudolf Barak affair. A junior member of the Czechoslovak Party leadership and minister of the interior, Barak attempted to remove Novotny in 1962 and was sent to jail on spurious charges. I was to free him six years later.

I understood that to oppose Novotny I needed first to make careful preparations and then to choose exactly the right moment to attack. I quietly searched out like-minded people around me, finding many in lower- and medium-level positions of both the Party and government structures. I also made friends with journalists, writers, and scientists whose understanding of the necessity for change went almost without saying.

In 1960, after two years as Bratislava regional secretary, I was transferred to Prague as Czechoslovak Central Committee secretary for industry. So the whole family moved to Prague.

My areas of responsibility included metallurgy and the machine tool, chemical engineering, and construction industries. My office was designed to provide Party supervision of all these branches of the economy, part of the overcentralized concept of management that had recently been buttressed by a "restructuring." Initially, I admit, I did not see why the concept should not work, because I then had almost unlimited confidence in centralized economic planning, thinking the flaws of the system were mainly caused by poor management. All that was needed, I thought, was to make it more ingenious and flexible. Only over time did I come to understand that the problem was the system itself, which had reached the absolute limits of its possibilities. It needed to be dismantled.

Still, those two years in Prague were very useful for me, because I broadened my outlook on many problems, both economic and political, and I became acquainted with a number of knowledgeable people whose basic interests paralleled mine. Some of them, like the economists Ota Sik and Karel Kouba, became my friends, and we worked together again in later years, under much better circumstances, particularly in the spring of 1968.

In Prague I had my first open disagreements with Novotny, during meetings of both the Secretariat and of the Presidium, which I attended as a secretary. These confrontations arose when I dared to offer differing opinions first on investment priorities in Slovakia and later on the rehabilitation of victims of the 1950s repressions. I took care to make my observations in a low voice and keep them strictly to the point, avoiding a polemical tone or offensive criticism; that has been my customary style in any case, but at the time I had to be especially cautious and to avoid larger battles, which I then had no chance of winning.

I had not known Novotny well before. I had only met him officially a number of times as Party secretary in Banska Bystrica. Initially I formed no very specific opinion of him. He seemed an average Party official of working-class origin, not unlike myself before my studies in Bratislava and Moscow. From afar Novotny appeared quite businesslike and straightforward. It was in Prague that I discovered him to be dull and often arrogant, lacking consideration for other opinions and incapable of understanding key political and economic problems of the country.

He was particularly ignorant about almost everything that concerned Slovakia and Czecho-Slovak relations, which was, of course, depressing for me. What was even worse was the fact that no senior members of the Czechoslovak leadership dared correct his obviously wrongheaded views on many crucial problems. Novotny reacted to my own views with irritation and impatience, and I realized that he would be the main obstacle to any changes.

Fortunately, internal developments in the Soviet Union continued to follow a reformist course, and Czechoslovakia was bound to follow. While general pressure for reform was growing, the more immediate issue—which lay like a boulder on the road to further progress—was rehabilitations. Novotny and his allies were dragging their feet as long as they could, fearful that a wave of criticism would sweep them away.

It is fair to point out that in Slovakia we had no equivalent of the secluded recreational compound that Novotny had built for himself and his people by the Orlik Water Dam south of Prague. I visited there two or three times when I worked in Prague in the early 1960s. The place itself was very nice, located in a charming part of the Vltava River basin. But I detested the whole idea of it—the isolated luxury enjoyed by the leadership under police protection.

Most of the weekending party leaders spent their time playing a card game called marriage, at which Novotny himself excelled. To be invited to play at the table with the first secretary, inside a huge beer barrel built in front of his house for that purpose, was the goal of his entire retinue. I do not play cards, so I was in no danger of being invited to the table. I spent my time there playing with children and walking in the surrounding forest.

In October 1961 came the Twenty-second Congress of the Soviet Communist Party, at which Khrushchev resumed and augmented his denunciation of Stalinism, this time publicly. The congress was followed by the removal of Stalin's mummy from the mausoleum on Red Square. This even the Stalinists who dominated the top Party organs in Czechoslovakia could not ignore.

By then all that had been done in Czechoslovakia to correct the injustices of the early 1950s was a quiet release from prison of tens of thousands of innocent people. The Czechoslovak Central Committee had established a commission, headed by the ill-fated Rudolf Barak, to review the circumstances of the earlier repressions, but the commission's report in 1958 was more a cover-up than a serious investigation. Moreover, it was kept secret from most Party members, not to mention the general public. In 1961 Gottwald's embalmed remains were still on display in a Prague memorial, and Stalin's oversized monument was still towering over the Vltava River.

Novotny, who had attended the Twenty-second Congress, was now forced to make a few concessions: Gottwald's embalmed remains were cremated, and a decision was adopted to tear down Stalin's monument. It was another year before further steps could be taken. During that time I had more disagreements with Novotny, especially during discussions in the Presidium or the Secretariat about various aspects of the rehabilitations. I insisted, for example, on the rehabilitation of Slovak resistance fighters and guerrilla commanders from the war; hardly one prominent commander had escaped persecution in the early 1950s.

I also disagreed with Novotny on the lack of financial support for some regions in Slovakia, where underdevelopment continued to be a serious human problem. And, finally, I brought into the open the deterioration of Slovak national political structures caused by the new constitution. Novotny was predictably irritated, and he determined to remove me. However, he could not do so all at once, since I had not given him an overt pretext, as had Barak. So he chose to cut me down gradually.

First I was transferred back to Slovakia by the Czechoslovak Presidium, a move formalized at the Slovak Party Congress in November 1962. There I was elected a full member of the Slovak Party Presidium and appointed a Slovak Party secretary, which looked almost like a promotion. All insiders understood, however, that it was a demotion—from secretary at the central level to secretary at the provincial level.

My situation looked bleak. In Bratislava, I was surrounded by Novotny's loyal cronies Karol Bacilek, Michal Chudik, and Michal Sabolcik. My old schoolmate and associate Jozef Lenart was also there, but he could not be counted on. I did not have much time to build my defenses, so I worked desperately to solidify my position, renewing contacts with old friends and looking for new allies. I knew they were there, though not in the higher positions. I traveled around Slovakia and talked with local officials as well as ordinary people. I proceeded systematically, trying to block Novotny's moves against me.

My tactics proved successful, for at the Twelfth Congress of the Czechoslovak Party, despite Novotny's eminence as first secretary, I was thrust back to the national level, being elected to the Central Committee and named a candidate member of the Presidium. In addition, I was elected a member of the crucial commission investigating the repressions and political crimes of the early 1950s.

Working on the commission was a watershed for me. It was chaired by Drahomir Kolder, the regional secretary of the North Moravian region in Ostrava and a newly elected full member of the Czechoslovak Central Committee Presidium. I was the second ranking member of this group, which became known as the Kolder Commission.

Kolder was a man of limited education and rough manners, but he held reformist positions and supported me. Later he was an important ally in the final struggle against Novotny. Unhappily, he became afraid of the democratic course of Prague Spring and ended as an accomplice of the Soviet-inspired conspiracy in August 1968. I have remained puzzled by his political zigzags.

The Kolder Commission worked intensively for over two months investigating the repression whose victims were Communist Party members (other rehabilitations were handled by bodies established by the government). Many revelations about the methods of the repression were truly shocking.

I learned, for example, that victims were subject to both physical and psychological torture, were deprived of sleep through continuous interrogation, of water, of decent food, of civilized medical treatment. They were kept in cold cells, forced to sleep on concrete floors (even in the winter), threatened with cruel measures against their wives and children if they refused to sign fabricated confessions. I learned also that the personal involvement of the top Czechoslovak leaders had reached almost savage proportions: top Party officials, including Novotny, had divided among themselves the property—down to pots and pans and bedsheets—of their former friends and colleagues whom they had sent to the gallows. The memory is sickening.

I saw documents that established with certainty the lamentable roles of Alexej Cepicka, Gottwald's son-in-law and former Presidium member, and Vaclav Kopecky, a veteran member of the Czechoslovak leadership from the late 1920s. Even Gottwald himself, as well as his successor as president, Antonin Zapotocky, was shamefully involved one way or another, mainly by offering no resistance to such obvious and wholesale miscarriages of justice. Others, like Novotny, not only enriched themselves on murdered men's property but also covered up all cases of unjustified persecution.

Worst of all, actions in this spirit had continued, if more selectively, at the very time that Stalin's successors were changing course, when, for example, the "physicians conspiracy" in Moscow was pronounced a fraud shortly after Stalin's death. Undeterred, the Czechoslovak Party leadership proceeded with the persecution of the so-called Slovak bourgeois nationalists, a show trial in April 1954.

I was dumbfounded by the revelations of what had been going on in Czechoslovak Party circles in Prague in the early 1950s. The Slovak Communist Party always exercised more mutual respect and tolerance than did the national Party. There have been exceptions, Viliam Siroky and Karol Bacilek probably being the worst. But Siroky was directly linked to the Party bureaucracy in Prague, and whether or not he did what my father thought, one of the purposes of the bourgeois nationalism charges was to solidify the power of the national Party leadership over any regional initiatives.

During the worst repressions, State Security was detached from the Ministry of the Interior and assigned to a separate Ministry of State Security, just as in Moscow. Only two men were ever minister of state security. The first was a Czech, Ladislav Kopriva, who was succeeded in 1952 by Karol Bacilek.

My work on the Kolder Commission strengthened my reformist views and my determination to change things. I directed a working group reviewing the case of Marie Svermova, a former deputy of First Secretary Slansky. Svermova, the widow of a prewar high Party official who had lost his life in the Uprising, was falsely accused in 1951 of conspiring with others against the then Party leader Gottwald and held in jail for over six years. Until the commission's findings, nothing had been done to correct this injustice.

I also focused on the Slovak side of the repressions. I do not think I was the same person at the end of the commission's work.

We presented our report to the Czechoslovak Presidium by the end of February 1963, and long discussions followed there and in the Secretariat (of which I was no longer a member). In my remarks I focused on the Marie Svermova case and the Slovak question. I particularly insisted on the full rehabilitation of Clementis, Husak, and other Slovak victims, in clear refutation of the bourgeois nationalism charge. Novotny and his allies opposed me, agreeing only to a civil rehabilitation before the law, in contrast to rehabilitation that would have included the restoration of Party membership. "Ideological deviation" was still being used by Novotny and his allies to keep survivors of the purge out of the Party. I felt that this halfhearted rehabilitation was insufficient, unfair, and malicious. They, however, prevailed and thus further delayed the healing process.

The Kolder Commission Report was put before a plenary session of the Czechoslovak Communist Party Central Committee in April 1963. Novotny presented a summary of the document and proposed, on behalf of the Presidium, to expel from the Party the two men presumably most responsible for the repressions, Alexej Cepicka and Ladislav Kopriva. The other former minister of state security, Slovak Party First Secretary Karol Bacilek, was to be recalled from his post of first secretary of the Slovak Communist Party and stripped of his membership in the Czechoslovak Presidium. A former Czechoslovak Central Committee secretary responsible for the security agenda, Brunno Koehler (the only German still in a leadership position after 1945), was only to be fired as a Central Committee secretary.

I asked for the floor on April 4, the second day of the Central Committee session. Novotny did not permit me to speak, so all I could do was submit my speech in written form, become part of the protocol of the meeting. In this undelivered speech, I pointed out that Koehler, who had been directly involved in the repressions, deserved a much more severe punishment. I directly criticized Klement Gottwald, the Party leader at the time of the witch-hunt: should he not, as head of state, at least have prevented the execution of so many innocent people he'd known personally for twenty or more years?

I also said what I thought about the charge of Slovak bourgeois nationalism. Accusing Husak and Novomesky of trying to restore capitalism at the behest of President Benes was as ridiculous as making any of the accusations against Marie Svermova. And, on behalf of my younger generation of Party officials, I stated that each senior Party official of the period between 1949 and 1954 should shoulder his own, however uneven, share of responsibility for the terror.

This was a clear message to Novotny. My criticism of Koehler touched an especially sensitive nerve: Koehler had worked hand in hand with Novotny, and they had remained close.

The commission report was still restricted; even Party cells were only gradually given access to it, and then only to about 80 pages out of almost 800. Nonetheless, it made a strong impact on the Party and better-informed segments of the population. In Slovakia the report paved the way for important personnel changes in the wake of Bacilek's departure and caused the fall of Prime Minister Siroky, another close ally of Novotny. Finding a successor to Bacilek was a problem for Novotny, who had accepted his removal grudgingly. No compliant replacement would get by the Slovak Party Central Committee. Novotny was in retreat.

In April 1963 the Slovak Party Central Committee Presidium consisted of nine members, of whom three—First Secretary Bacilek, Ludovit Benada, and Pavol David—were leaving for different reasons. Of the remaining six, I was the only one responsive to Slovak national interests, and, with the current mood in Slovakia, this made me the obvious choice for first secretary. I made a speech sharply critical of Bacilek's role in the repressions, with emphasis on the Slovak aspects of the Kolder Commission Report. Here in Bratislava I could not be deprived of the floor.

Novotny hated the prospect of my accession and had vainly lobbied backstage for his preferred candidate, Michal Chudik. But Chudik had no chance of being elected, and Jozef Lenart's chances were not much better. In the end, Novotny had to give in. All he could achieve was to make his man Michal Sabolcik my deputy. I think this was Novotny's first distinct political defeat.

Under these circumstances, I assumed the office of Slovak Communist Party Central Committee first secretary, which was soon followed by my full membership in the Czechoslovak Communist Party Presidium. There I also took Bacilek's place. I had survived the first of Novotny's attempts to bring me down and reached a place from which I could, step by step, pursue my reform plans. But it was only the beginning, and I was still vulnerable. I had to fortify my position before moving ahead.

11

"THE GRACIOUS SUMMER"

THE Twenty-second Congress of the Soviet Communist Party reverberated in Czechoslovakia like the aftershocks of a distant but powerful earthquake. One tremor brought down Stalin's monument in Prague, and another caused the fall of Bacilek. More tremors were to come. At the time I assumed my new post, the Slovak political scene was in motion. Naturally, the most agitated Slovaks were the intellectuals, alert and sensitive to every change, but in fact all society was affected.

Adding fuel to the fire was the clumsy timing of public disclosures. Novotny was afraid that too much bad news at one time might rock his boat beyond control, and he tried to postpone each disclosure as long as possible, a strategy that caused its own problems. Information about the main conclusions of the Kolder Commission Report was withheld until late August 1963, but personnel changes resulting from it had to be announced as they took effect, as early as April. At a time when secrets were impossible to keep, it was ridiculous and embarrassing.

The Slovak press reacted to these developments with growing openness, stretching the barriers of the permissible step by step. In 1963 formal censorship was not yet institutionalized. After 1948 the Czechoslovak Party leadership had been content to control the media by appointments: acquiescent chief editors and their deputies acted as censors, guided by the Central Committee's propaganda department. But that system was cracking. Many editors became vulnerable to public pressure. In 1964 the alarmed central government felt compelled to create a censorship office, the Board of Press Oversight.

In the spring of 1963, the weekly of the Union of Slovak Writers,

Kulturny Zivot, or *Cultural Life,* took the lead in featuring previously taboo subjects. As in the Czech lands, this publication, like the union that was publishing it, enjoyed special status and privileges. Most Slovak and Czech writers had long and sincerely supported the Communist Party. The union's weekly was subject to no heavy-handed prepublication censorship. *Kulturny Zivot* then had a circulation of almost 100,000, and it was the only Slovak publication that was widely read in the Czech lands, mainly by intellectuals.

Negative pieces on official Czechoslovak Communist Party policy soon appeared in a number of other publications, including *Pravda,* the organ of the Slovak Party Central Committee. Because *Pravda's* chief editor was Onrej Klokoc, and everybody knew that he was my good friend, it was not difficult to deduce that I was playing a role—either by encouraging such criticism or by simply giving it free vent. Anyway, I was soon caught in the cross fire between the rebellious Slovak journalists and writers and the Stalinists.

The writers, many of whom were Communists of liberal orientation, were determined to speed up de-Stalinization. The journalists were not far behind them. They knew well that behind them was a large part of the academic and intellectual community, not to mention other segments of the population.

While their goals paralleled mine, occasionally they put me in a difficult position. The resistance to change in the Czechoslovak leadership was still very strong, and I knew we would not break any walls with bare foreheads. Daring was fine, but we also needed patience and political finesse.

Both the writers' and the journalists' unions held stormy congresses, in April and May respectively. Together with their published criticism, these congresses put Slovak intellectuals in the forefront of the reform movement in Czechoslovakia. In the Czech lands, Novotny was still keeping a tight lid on public criticism of his policies.

At the Slovak writers' congress in April, the once purged poet Laco Novomesky made a moving speech in defense of the martyred Vlado Clementis. It was a bitter accusation of those responsible for the terror of the early 1950s, and of those still refusing to reverse criminal judgments.

Long excerpts of Novomesky's speech were published in *Kulturny Zivot,* adding weight to sharp criticism in *Pravda* of lagging rehabilitation. Another and even stronger salvo was fired during the journalists' congress in May, in a speech by the well-known Slovak publicist Miroslav Hysko. He looked back at the trumped-up charges of bourgeois nationalism, and accused Viliam Siroky, then still prime minister and a full member of the Czechoslovak Communist Party leadership, of being their main instigator.

It was the first public denunciation of Siroky. He had been a full member of the Party Presidium since May 1949. Even Novotny—who had played his role in the purges as the regional party secretary in Prague—did not become a member of the Presidium until the end of 1951. Siroky had been there through the whole dark period, and his continued tenure in high Party and state offices as late as 1963 was a disgrace.

Nevertheless, his case was a highly political issue, and I realized that Hysko's criticism spelled trouble with the remaining Czechoslovak Party old guard. They—especially Novotny and Jiri Hendrych—had worked with Siroky for many years. I had to consider the practical side of the problem: was the time ripe for such a frontal attack? And was Siroky the best case to start with? After some pondering I concluded that the answer to both questions was yes.

About a week after the journalists' congress, the text of Hysko's speech appeared in *Pravda*. Its publication there was, in its way, even more significant than the speech itself, since it indicated the Slovak Party's—or at least my own—approval of the criticism. The fact is that Klokoc had not felt it necessary to inform me in advance. That was fine with me.

It was rather quiet for a few days. Even at our next weekly Presidium meeting in Prague, the matter was not raised. Siroky said nothing and made no attempt to talk to me during a coffee break. Novotny also said nothing. But it was clear to me that the case had to be a hot topic out of my hearing in the Secretariat.

Finally, during a break, Novotny came over to me and asked: "So what is happening there?" meaning in Slovakia, of course.

I pretended not to know what he had on his mind and asked back, "What do you mean?"

We stood alone, a few yards from the others, and I noticed that Novotny spoke almost in a whisper. He said, "Well, the writers' congress, the journalists' congress, those articles in the press. Why aren't you keeping it under control?"

I asked him whether he couldn't be more specific, and after a while he hit the main point: Hysko's criticism of Siroky.

I was prepared. I told him, "This is not a simple matter. We both know that in the 1950s Siroky had his fingers in that pie. The Kolder Commission Report makes it clear. Hysko cannot know what we know, but obviously he and others know enough, and his criticism has substance. In such a situation, there's nothing I can do."

He said nothing, so I added, "I think part of the problem is that the public is not informed about the Party's effort to rectify its injustices. They see developments in the Soviet Union and think rehabilitation in Czechoslovakia is going too slowly." This, I knew, was an argument Novotny could not openly reject.

After this conversation, I did nothing to discourage further critical articles in the Slovak press. All I asked was that the writers maintain a calm and matter-of-fact tone.

Novotny, however, was not willing to give up Siroky without a fight. In mid-June he arranged an appearance in the eastern Slovak city of Kosice. Because he was my superior and also the president of the Republic, protocol required that I go with him, and be seated at his side. I sat on the platform, trying to avoid any expression in my face. I must have looked like a complete outsider, but there was little else I could do to make my opinion felt.

Novotny demonstrated again his complete ignorance of Slovak affairs. He said that there was no substance to calls for a revision of the new constitution because the abolished Slovak Board of Commissioners had not worked well. Then he tried to defend the repressions by repeating absurd arguments about bourgeois nationalism, naming Husak and Novomesky again as culprits. This was a political blunder of remarkable proportions, given that the main findings of the Kolder Commission were soon to be published. I wondered what drove him to such silliness.

Novotny also lambasted the Slovak press, *Pravda*, Hysko, and Klokoc. This was an implicit attack on me: wasn't the Siroky case an intra-Party affair? And wasn't I supposed to keep the press under strict control?

I decided to respond to Novotny's speech along two lines. First, I had a resolution prepared and approved by the Presidium of the Slovak Party demanding the creation of a special commission to investigate abuses arising from charges of bourgeois nationalism. It was a carefully prepared demand, and even the Czechoslovak Party Presidium could not refute it. My aim was to ask for a proper review of the entire episode, which could not be done overnight. This would reduce the heat of the polemics and lend weight to the rehabilitation process, since the new commission would prove that the old accusations had no substance whatsoever. Novotny could not have expected any other outcome, but my proposal at least bought him time, and that made it more acceptable to him. Thus, a Czechoslovak Party commission devoted solely to the Slovak "bourgeois nationalism" trials was established.

Next I had to respond to Novotny's accusations about press control and do so without forcing a premature face-to-face confrontation. I decided to focus on the least harmful aspect of Novotny's criticism, his reproof that the rehabilitations were an "intra-Party" matter. I decided to accept the rebuke in general terms in a public speech a few days later, in which I indicated that Hysko should have submitted his criticism to the Slovak Party Central Committee before going public. It was a toothless reprimand, and no one was harmed, least of all Hysko or Klokoc. Moreover, I avoided any statement that would have sounded like a defense of Siroky, and I pointed out that bourgeois nationalism was in itself an unclear notion.

Several weeks later, by the end of August 1963, the report based on the Kolder Commission findings was published. As I had expected, it took more ground from under Novotny.

The commission I had requested started work in July; its very existence signaled the urgency of solving the Siroky problem. It was then that Novotny finally realized that Siroky had to be sacrificed before the new commission issued its report. His recall was presented at the Czechoslovak Communist Party Central Committee meeting on September 20, 1963, ending his ten years as prime minister. Siroky also lost his membership in the Czechoslovak Presidium, so it was clearly a complete demotion. Novotny unconvincingly tried to make the operation less conspicuous by wrapping Siroky's downfall in a number of other, less important personnel changes.

The office of prime minister was taken over by the wavering Jozef Lenart, and Michal Chudik, Novotny's choice for my position, was appointed chairman of the Slovak National Council in Lenart's place. A Czechoslovak Party Central Committee secretary for cultural affairs, Cestmir Cisar, was fired after only five months in office; I mention him because he was made responsible, without real justification, for the relaxed political climate in the spring and summer of 1963. Some called that season "the gracious summer," and it was indeed gracious compared with previous times.

My attention then turned to the work we Slovaks had called for on the question of bourgeois nationalism. Initially the commission was composed of only Slovak members and chaired by Lenart. After the changes in September, Lenart's place was taken by Vladimir Koucky, a Czech official who was a longtime Czechoslovak Communist Party secretary for ideology. The seven other members of the commission were Slovaks. The commission worked in an old Barnabite Monastery in Prague, which housed parts of the state and Party archives. Though not a member of this body—now called the Barnabite Commission—I was regularly informed about its work, and I visited the place once or twice.

Their findings were quite unambiguous: the whole affair of bourgeois nationalism had been trumped up, and all those persecuted on the basis of that accusation were innocent. At the beginning of December 1963, the Barnabite Commission submitted its report to the presidia of the Slovak and

Czechoslovak Communist parties. It recommended complete exoneration of the 1950 Slovak Communist Party leadership and full rehabilitation of all persons falsely accused and unjustly persecuted in the case, especially Vlado Clementis, Gustav Husak, Ladislav Novomesky, and Karol Smidke. The Slovak Party Central Committee endorsed the report on December 18, and a day later the Czechoslovak Central Committee did the same. An ugly chapter in the history of the Communist Party was thus formally closed. The stain of the crime could never be removed, of course, especially given the execution of Clementis. Still, it was a great victory for us and, I could not help feeling, for me personally.

Naturally, rehabilitation raised the question of restitution. Clementis and Smidke were dead, and Novomesky had no political ambitions, but Husak was a different case. He had been released from prison in 1960, when Bacilek was still first secretary of the Slovak Party Central Committee. Bacilek, who should have had Husak heavily on his conscience, did nothing to help him. Husak was assigned a job as storeman in a warehouse for construction materials, where he worked until 1963.

Soon after succeeding Bacilek, I arranged to move Husak to the Institute of History of the Slovak Academy of Sciences in Bratislava. He was assigned several assistants and a secretarial staff and proceeded to work on the history of the Slovak National Uprising, an incomplete version of which, written with the help of Vilem Precan, was published in 1966.

In July 1963 I invited Husak to my office to discuss his rehabilitation. I told him about the Kolder Commission findings, and the ongoing Barnabite investigation. He listened attentively, and responded with queries and comments. I had not known him personally before this meeting, but he had known my father, and he certainly knew who I was and where I stood, so we were not strangers to each other. I was sure that he knew I intended to help him, but, as I had heard from others, he was extremely cool and emotionless. I must say I did not feel I had managed to establish the sort of open relationship with him that has usually been easy for me.

Husak was a key witness for the Barnabite Commission. The whole case of Slovak bourgeois nationalism could not be effectively thrown out without his complete exoneration. While his civil rehabilitation had been achieved on the basis of the Kolder Commission Report, Novotny and his chief ideologue, Jiri Hendrych, were still opposed to Husak's political rehabilitation, which involved his readmission to the Party. They claimed that he had committed serious "political errors," such as nationalism. Under the circumstances, it was crucial to clear Husak of these accusations.

Quite a few well-motivated people were apprehensive about the prospect of Husak's readmission to the Party. They claimed that he had been, and remained, a power-thirsty, calculating, unscrupulous, and dangerous man. I had heard these opinions from many people who had known Husak during wartime and those who remembered him when he was in power after the war. I also knew my father's opinion. Despite all that, I did not believe in judging Husak guilty by association and by supposition of defects in character. In retrospect, that may well be seen as an error. But in 1963 Husak's rehabilitation was an essential step on the road to wider reforms and a more equitable federation between Czechs and Slovaks.

The task of interviewing Husak was assigned to Jozef Lenart. It was September 1963, just before Lenart was appointed prime minister. For reasons of his own, Lenart was truly frightened by the idea that, except for a stenographer, he would be talking with Husak alone. Agitated, he called and asked me to be there with him. I had no reason to refuse, and I asked Husak to come to my office at the Slovak Party Central Committee in Bratislava once again.

The conversation took several hours. At the beginning, we explained to Husak the purpose of the meeting and asked him to give us his version of the cases in which he had been accused of wrongdoing. I had seen his file in the Barnabite monastery, and I knew that the case against him, especially the accusation that he was a secret follower of Tito, was based mainly on fabrications and slander, collected by criminal elements in the ranks of State Security. Still, it was important that Husak give us his own opinion of these accusations. This time Husak seemed very nervous, as if he felt uncertain about the outcome of the meeting. But he regained his calm, and we covered all the points needed.

Soon after this meeting, Lenart and I submitted our report to the commission, recommending Husak's full political rehabilitation. It was included in the final report of the Barnabite Commission to the Czechoslovak Communist Party Central Committee on December 19, 1963.

Early in 1964 Husak was readmitted to the party, and I received him again on February 5 to discuss his situation and his plans. This time he looked very self-assured, but he remained as haughty and cold-nosed as ever. He offered no comments on his plans, but I inferred that he expected to be offered a very high Party or state position. About a month later, the Czechoslovak Party Presidium agreed to offer him the post of deputy minister of justice. I thought it was a good proposal. Husak was a lawyer, and with his recent ordeal I hoped that he could help with lower-level rehabilitations still on the agenda, especially in Slovakia.

On March 13 I received Husak again, in the presence of Frantisek Dvorsky, a Slovak Party secretary. I asked Husak to accept the ministerial job, and I explained how useful he could be in such a position. He refused it flatly. Clearly, it was not enough for him. Instead he continued to work in the Academy of Sciences, and began to establish liberal credentials on the side.

By the end of 1963, I had reason to be satisfied with what had been achieved. I had been in office for nine months; I had survived Novotny's attempt to demote me, and I had made him accept both the exoneration of the Slovak Communist Party from charges of bourgeois nationalism, and a full rehabilitation of all persons implicated in the case. Novotny had also failed to force me to rein in the press and cultural life of Slovakia, as he had done in the Czech lands. Slovakia continued to be a favorable environment for social and political criticism, one at which Czechs looked with envy.

I was determined to stay this course, impelled by my deepest beliefs. I felt that a relaxed personal style was helpful, and I moved around without police protection. I talked freely with people everywhere. I could feel a bond of growing confidence and was encouraged for the struggles ahead. Novotny could not push me around the way he had my predecessors. I knew I was not safe from his further attempts to remove me. But, as 1963 ended, I had managed to make it more difficult for him.

12

THE END OF AN ERA

SHORTLY after my meeting with Husak in March 1964, Novotny launched another attempt to bring me down. He seemed to understand this time that he could not remove a Slovak Communist Party first secretary by administrative fiat from Prague. So he decided to undermine my position first from inside the Slovak Communist Party structure.

Novotny's instruments were his appointees, Michal Chudik, Michal Sabolcik, and the regional secretary in Banska Bystrica, Rudolf Cvik. Novotny showed his support of Cvik by attending his regional Party organization conference, an ostentatious gesture since it came shortly after Cvik had launched an attack on me.

During his previous visit to Bratislava, in March 1963, Novotny had spent over two hours promenading along the Danube riverbank alone with Bacilek. By then it was obvious that Bacilek would have to be sacked, but Novotny still wanted to show his disapproval. From then until his own fall in 1968, Novotny never came to Bratislava—except for an August 1964 ceremonial appearance during a visit by Khrushchev.

At the Slovak Party Central Committee meeting in March, Cvik suddenly took the floor and sharply criticized my "softness" toward writers and journalists. He also blamed me for the activities of Slovak publication of books banned in the Czech lands.

Thus began the guerrilla war Novotny waged against me through Slovak proxies. Although I had a majority of the Slovak Central Committee behind me, I still had to follow certain rules that limited my maneuvering space. I became particularly cautious after April 1964, when I learned from the Trencin district Party secretary, a supporter of mine named Turcek, that my wife and I were under surveillance by the StB. They were gathering "materials" to use against me. This was hardly surprising since Rudolf Barak, who, it will be remembered, had been arrested for his opposition to Novotny in 1962, had just been put on trial in Prague and sentenced to fifteen years in prison.

With varying intensity, Novotny's proxies continued to attack my policies until 1967, but I managed to ward off the onslaught. By mid-1965 my support in the Slovak Central Committee was fairly solid. I felt even more secure following the Slovak Party Congress in May 1966, after which Novotny no longer had the power to bring me down by officially accepted political means. He remained powerful in his own right, however, and he still stood in the way of more thorough reforms. More than another year had to pass before the moment arrived for me to go on the offensive.

The big political event of 1964 in Czechoslovakia was Nikita Khrushchev's August visit. At that time, Khrushchev seemed to us to be firmly in control in the Soviet Union. He was also very popular in our country because of the role he had played in the termination and condemnation of the Stalinist terror. His earthy style and straightforward personal manner elicited favor, especially among the common people. For me, Khrushchev was synonymous with hope. In contrast to the late 1930s in Russia and the early 1950s in Czechoslovakia, I saw what Khrushchev did at the Soviet Party Congress in 1956, and in later years, and I was confident that his endeavors had finally put the socialist system on the right track. I also viewed him as warm and sincere, worthy of a trust that politicians rarely deserve.

At the same time, I took only cursory interest in foreign policy and did not feel qualified to scrutinize Khrushchev's external political ventures. In general, I believed that he pursued a course leading to international peace, and his support of decolonization also appeared to me as a logical extension of socialist thought. After all, weren't most socialists everywhere, including those in Western Europe, opposed to colonialism?

No retrospective view of Khrushchev is complete, of course, without taking into account the Hungarian affair in the fall of 1956. I was in Moscow at that time, admittedly not the best place for an objective view. The whole dimension of the revolt was not entirely clear to me then. As a Slovak, I was still inclined to see Hungarian events through the lens of my nation's experience, right up through World War II, when Hungary fought on Hitler's side to the end. In view of all that, and my positive perception of Khrushchev, I was not disposed to disbelieve Moscow's interpretation of the rebellion as a revival of rightist, even fascist tendencies.

I had met Khrushchev for the first time in October 1961, when I was a

member of the Czechoslovak Party delegation at a congress of the Romanian Communist Party. Later Novotny almost never took me with him—in
spite of the fact that after my accession to the office of Slovak Party first
secretary, I should not have been passed over. All dealings between the
Czechoslovak and Soviet Party leaderships, for example, took place in my
absence—the only exception being a 1964 ceremonial trip to Moscow for
Khrushchev's seventieth birthday.

Normally, trips like the one to Bucharest were simple formalities. One
had to attend congress meetings, listen to boring speeches, go to official
lunches and dinners, and drink innumerable toasts. In Bucharest in October 1961, however, the situation was different. The Sino-Soviet ideological
dispute was intensifying, and a delegation of the Communist Party of China
was there. That they and the Soviet Party would disagree in their messages
to the congress was a safe bet. The importance of the event was signaled by
Khrushchev's presence at the head of the delegation of the Soviet Central
Committee.

As expected, the Chinese delegation severely criticized Khrushchev's
policy of de-Stalinization, even though his final moves to expunge Stalin's
legacy—especially the removal of his remains from Red Square—were still
to come.

At one point, Khrushchev suddenly asked the Romanians to assemble a
closed meeting of all foreign delegations. There was no time to prepare
speeches and have them translated. Novotny's practice of having everything
drafted and approved in advance was a terrible handicap for him and was
compounded by the whole debate's being conducted in Russian. We had to
take a stand in this very direct debate and, as it turned out, I was the only
member of our delegation who spoke Russian. Thus, I had to express the
Czechoslovak Party viewpoint—without prior consultation with Novotny. I
spoke confidently in entire support of de-Stalinization, and there was no
backlash.

This meeting was dominated by the exchange between Khrushchev and
the Chinese, who rejected all criticism of Stalin. In a fit of high temper
directed at the Chinese delegation, Khrushchev invoked Stalin's mummy,
then still at Lenin's side in the mausoleum in Moscow: "Well, if you want
him, you can have him!" The Chinese did not take him up on his offer.

In April 1964 I went to Moscow with a Party delegation for Khrushchev's
birthday celebration. I was pleased that he remembered me and personally
expressed a great deal of friendly sympathy. I looked forward to his trip to
Czechoslovakia in August of that year, especially to the opportunity to
welcome him in Slovakia on the twentieth anniversary of the Slovak
National Uprising. Since Khrushchev had commanded partisan headquar-

ters in Kiev in 1944, I assumed—correctly—that he had clear memories of the event.

Four months later, Khrushchev spent the first two or three days of his visit in Prague. Then he came to Bratislava, accompanied by Novotny, and from there we flew to Banska Bystrica for the commemoration of the Uprising.

In Bratislava, Khrushchev was very cordial to me and constantly sought to have me at his side. That was hardly pleasing to Novotny, who was by then openly hostile and always trying to keep me in the background. Novotny, however, was handicapped by his poor knowledge of Russian. I also surmised that his dull behavior did not appeal to the spontaneous and cheerful Khrushchev. I tried to be as self-effacing as possible to avoid unnecessary problems with Novotny, but Khrushchev kept looking around and demanding my presence.

I was pleased that he was so well informed, not only about general Czechoslovak affairs but also about the situation in Slovakia, including the circumstances under which I had replaced Bacilek. More than once Khrushchev praised my efforts to rectify the injustices committed by the postwar Czechoslovak Party leadership, and he emphasized the importance of complete rehabilitation of all victims.

As we know, he was himself not entirely consistent in this respect, but I believe that this was not his fault. In his campaign against Stalinism, he met a great deal of resistance from his colleagues, who in the end kept him from completing his reforms. Indeed, at the time of his visit to Czechoslovakia, the conspiracy against him was nearing its climax, but of this I was, of course, unaware.

At the airport in Banska Bystrica, the party entered limousines and headed for the amphitheater on the far side of the city. Khrushchev rode with Novotny in one of the lead cars, while I was assigned to a car at the end of the convoy, a position carefully arranged by Novotny's protocol people. The limousines moved slowly through cheering crowds. Everybody was in a festive mood.

Then, suddenly, the whole convoy stopped about half a mile outside the city limits. I lowered the car window, concerned that something had gone wrong. At that moment I saw Soviet Ambassador Zimyanin running back along the row of cars, peering into each limousine. When, almost out of breath, he reached mine, he shouted at me, "Alexander Stepanovich, come quickly with me, Nikita Sergeyevich wants you to be at his side when we enter the city!"

Somewhat reluctantly, I got out of my car. I knew that Novotny would not be happy about this disruption of protocol, but, naturally, I could not refuse, so I followed the ambassador all the way back along the convoy, noticing the curious expressions of the people on the sidewalk. We passed some twelve limousines before reaching the one with Khrushchev and Novotny in the backseat. Zimyanin pushed me inside, to be met by a scowling Novotny and a broadly smiling Khrushchev.

After the ceremony, the whole company went to Sliac, a nearby spa, for lunch. After the meal I saw Khrushchev slip out a side door and walk to the edge of the woods, where he stopped and apparently became absorbed in his thoughts. I understood his need to be alone on such a busy day, but I was concerned as well, and after several minutes I decided to join him, to ask whether everything was all right. As I neared, I could see that he wore a serious, almost sad expression. He brightened and said that he felt well but had been thinking about the many problems awaiting him at home. He added nothing more specific, and the rest of our brief exchange consisted of pleasantries. After a few minutes we returned to the house.

When the news arrived a few weeks later that Khrushchev had been forced out, I vividly recalled our conversation at Sliac. Had he known that a conspiracy was under way against him, or did he just have a sense of foreboding?

At the first Czechoslovak Party Presidium meeting after Khrushchev's fall, I saw that everybody, including Novotny, was disturbed and unhappy. He had long resisted the kinds of changes that Khrushchev had initiated, but over time even Novotny seemed to have been impressed by the Soviet leader's obvious good faith and enthusiasm. None of us had any clear idea of what Khrushchev's fall would mean. A full reversal of de-Stalinization was hard to imagine, and those who had pushed Khrushchev out of office went out of their way to deny any such intention. Their basic complaint had to do with his methods of management. They accused him, in the typical jargon, of "subjectivism," meaning that he acted without the consent of the Politburo.

Like me, most members of the Presidium were fond of Khrushchev not just as a politician but as a person, and we were not convinced by the explanations given for his ouster. We felt embarrassed that he had been overthrown so soon after his visit to our country. We were also very uneasy about the way Khrushchev's own Politburo removed him; for reasons of his own, Novotny had to share this concern.

Under the circumstances, we decided to draft a statement and not just send it to Moscow but make it public. It was not a formal protest, which would have been inappropriate, considering that this was an internal Soviet affair. But we said that we were "surprised" by the "sudden" changes in Moscow. The clear implication of the message was that we did not like the change.

There were rumors at this time that Novotny phoned Leonid Brezhnev and expressed his personal disagreement with the coup, but about that I have no knowledge. The statement we approved was a unanimous action of the Presidium. It is quite possible that Brezhnev blamed Novotny for it, but I do not believe that it played a role in Brezhnev's later failure to support Novotny.

According to some sources, Khrushchev was the first Soviet leader who pressed Novotny to accept a Soviet military presence in Czechoslovakia. In these accounts, Novotny allegedly refused, and he is described as having remained opposed to such plans even after Brezhnev became general secretary. If such discussions took place, I was not privy to them nor, so far as I know, was any other member of the Party Presidium.

The deeper and long-term significance of the changes in Moscow in October 1964 was not clear to me for quite some time. For one thing, I had only met Brezhnev once before he succeeded Khrushchev. That was in mid-December 1963. Brezhnev was chairman of the Supreme Soviet and visited Bratislava for two days after his stay in Prague to renew the alliance treaty initially signed by Stalin and President Benes in Moscow during the war. I had not subjected him to any special scrutiny; no one, after all, could have predicted that in ten months he would take on Khrushchev's mantle. I remembered Brezhnev as outwardly jovial, but subconsciously I couldn't help comparing him unfavorably with Khrushchev, for he utterly lacked Khrushchev's pure spontaneity.

It is Brezhnev who always brings to mind the not entirely welcome Russian custom of male kissing. Although even in Russia the custom tends to be reserved for meetings between relatives or close friends after a long separation, Brezhnev used it constantly, as an act of public relations. When I welcomed him at the airport in Bratislava, there was no reason for him to embrace and kiss me. We had never seen each other before. Five years later he tried to do the same, in public again, under worse circumstances. Someone called this playacting "organized cordiality."

The effects of Khrushchev's removal remained hard to judge. Independent Soviet studies did not exist in Czechoslovakia, and even our diplomatic reports from Moscow, as I later found out, were entirely superficial. Brezhnev and his circle did dismantle certain of Khrushchev's measures, but one could not then see that they were reversing the reform course completely. That became apparent only years later.

That course, I believe, was masterminded mainly by Michail Suslov, the Soviet chief ideologue who held forth in the Kremlin from Stalin's era until the rise of Gorbachev. Suslov, I think, was the éminence grise behind the Politburo's overthrow of Khrushchev and, later, the strangling of Czechoslovakia. As a member of the Politburo, he survived four general secretaries—Khrushchev, Brezhnev, Andropov, and Chernenko—and, had he not died, he might have blocked even Gorbachev's moves toward glasnost and perestroika.

All the same, at the end of 1964 I was not seriously concerned about external threats. To be sure, I was saddened by Khrushchev's departure, but I did not translate it into a bad omen for the future of Czechoslovakia. The fight to reform our system was occupying almost all my energy and attention.

13

WITH THE HELP OF
A MOUNTAIN BEAR

THE years between Khrushchev's fall and the final showdown with Novotny in the autumn of 1967 were marked by struggles on three battle-fields. First was the economy, which continued to deteriorate. Second was freedom of expression, with the dogmatists pressing ceaselessly for strict censorship of the Slovak press, Slovak publishing, and other creative activities. Third were Czech and Slovak relations, repeatedly damaged by Novotny's insensitive policy toward Slovakia. Naturally, all three battle-fields frequently overlapped.

Ever since my 1961–62 stint in Prague as Czechoslovak Central Committee secretary for industry, I had been allied with the proponents of economic reform. While initially I had great confidence in economic planning and central management, the arguments of leading economists such as Ota Sik and Karel Kouba persuaded me that decentralization was essential. I had always paid serious attention to the opinions of experts, and in my work in Slovakia I relied increasingly on their advice.

Although Professor Sik's plan of economic reform was spelled out between 1964 and 1966, I was already convinced of the importance of the independence of enterprises as a stimulant to the initiative and imagination of managers, technicians, and workers. I was also converted to the replacement of "gross production," the traditional Soviet bloc measure of economic results, with profit.

Despite the risks for an economy less developed in Slovakia than in the Czech lands, I was supportive of the reform, known as the New Economic Mechanism or NEM, because I realized that overcentralized management was simply causing stagnation. It was unable to provide conditions for sound economic growth.

Sweeping as the NEM proposals were, the question of ownership did not arise. Even a modest suggestion of privatization would have been ideologically unthinkable and politically unacceptable, and would have drawn accusations of a "restoration of capitalism." The reform thus adhered closely to a system of state ownership, but it was still an important move toward more rational management of the national economy, especially industry. And, quietly, we contemplated strengthening other forms of *public* ownership, cooperative and communal, because both bore the potential for a more flexible economic operation.

Carrying out the reform program was an uphill struggle. Changes in management concepts threatened the power of both the Party apparatus and the ministerial bureaucracy. These entrenched and reluctant forces dragged reform out by all possible means, and in the end they narrowed the scope of the New Economic Mechanism to a minuscule "experimental" variant, which was launched in January 1967. It was termed "the perfected economic system," but, in its amputated form, it was soon obvious that it had no chance to succeed.

The necessity for political reform before economic became increasingly obvious to me at that time. I was convinced that the daily meddling of the central Party apparatus in economic management had to end, that there had to be a clear separation of the functions of Party and state organs. I pronounced these ideas openly, in the fall of 1967, when the political situation finally became ripe for it.

In the course of my striving for economic reform, I forged a political alliance with several members of the Czechoslovak Party leadership who later played a key role in further struggles with Novotny and other opponents of change. Much support came from Dr. Jaromir Dolansky, a prewar veteran of the Czechoslovak Party (since 1954) and a senior member of the Presidium. Among his peers Dolansky was, unfortunately, quite exceptional. But two junior members of the Presidium, Drahomir Kolder and Oldrich Cernik, joined forces with me. They were both former regional secretaries in Ostrava, a metallurgical center in North Moravia. Cernik's position was initially ambiguous, but by the end of 1966 he was firmly on my side. Ultimately, he was a more staunch supporter than Kolder.

A leading proponent of reform was Frantisek Vlasak. An engineer by profession, he was not a member of the Party Presidium but held the important post of chairman of the State Committee for Technology. There were many others in government working for reform, of course, but under Novotny they had virtually no chance to carry out their ideas.

I frequently clashed with the conservatives over investment policy. The central planners and their allies in various economic ministries continued to favor overconcentration of industry. I kept pushing for more investment in Slovakia because it was in the interest of the country as a whole to have more balanced economic development. Given its lag behind the Czech lands, there were even sound reasons to favor development in Slovakia and to urge the creation of more Slovak enterprises producing finished goods, instead of semifinished ones to be completed in Bohemia or Moravia.

An episode that still gives me pleasure is the matter of the paper mill in Sturovo, in Slovakia. It was initially to be built in Steti, in Bohemia, an area already used to capacity for paper production, depleted in both pulp-wood and labor, and with a threatened environment and dwindling water supply. The Slovak alternative I proposed was reasonable and sound, but to carry it through against the bureaucratic opposition in Prague was extremely difficult. As the dispute heated up, I resorted to a trick. In September 1964, I organized a ceremony in Sturovo at which ground was broken for construction of the mill before it had been approved by the central authority. The bluff worked, because Novotny and his allies did not relish the public embarrassment of canceling the project. That episode led to more than a few sour faces.

A similar affair was the construction of a large metallurgical complex in eastern Slovakia that had been planned for the Ostrava region, in North Moravia, already the locus of metallurgy in Czechoslovakia. Iron ore was imported from the Krivoi Rog basin in the Ukraine, which meant that the ore trains passed through the length of Slovakia to North Moravia, a distance of some 200 miles. To build another ironworks complex in the Ostrava region not only made no logistical sense but, given the labor shortage there, would also have made it necessary to import workers to the region. Building an ironworks in eastern Slovakia had been discussed, and dismissed, in the mid-1950s, but, when the need to increase national iron and steel production arose in the early 1960s, I was able to win the plant, with the help of many rationally thinking people, for eastern Slovakia.

In the early 1960s, Czechoslovakia had become a leading producer of machinery of all kinds, as well as weaponry, for the whole Soviet bloc. This production was the basis of our economy, and I had no power to change it— I could only maneuver within its bounds and try to limit its cost to our population. At that time, a new iron and steel works simply had to be built somewhere, and the question boiled down to cost estimates and locations.

No matter how persuasive and objective my rationales for factory locations and other economic issues were, Novotny perceived me as an obsessed Slovak nationalist. His dislike for and ignorance of Slovak affairs and culture left him convinced that someone somewhere in Slovakia was constantly conspiring against him. It still angers me to recall his visit to Bratislava in April 1965, on the twentieth anniversary of the Red Army's liberation of the city. During a lunch at the Hotel Carlton, Novotny made a scene by insisting that the waiter open a bottle of vermouth in his presence before serving it. Then, during a visit to the ancient historic site of Devin, when wine was served, Novotny quickly swapped the glass put before him for that of Michal Chudik's wife, who was sitting across the table. I cannot describe how embarrassed I was to see this. Later I learned that he may have been repeatedly warned by State Security that the Slovaks were preparing an assassination attempt; who was behind that rumor, and why, I never knew.

Novotny's hostility toward me was further strengthened by the relaxed cultural climate in Slovakia, which I tolerated over his frequent objections. This eased atmosphere, characterized by freer public debate on national problems, contrasted sharply with the situation in the Czech lands. Slovak intellectuals became increasingly open in their criticism of Prague's insensitivity toward Slovakia, but the discussion was conducted in a moderate and tactful way, and I decided to keep my hands off.

One may ask why I did not make a formal objection in the Czechoslovak Presidium to the downgrading of Slovak national institutions in the constitution of 1960. Unfortunately, for such a move I needed a united Slovak Party leadership behind me, which I did not have, not even after the Slovak Party Congress of May 1966. Novotny always had the power to impose his men on me in both the Slovak Party Presidium and the Secretariat. Under those circumstances, my main tools were critical public debates and indirect attacks on the injustices.

One such move was my attendance and speech at the October 30, 1965, celebration of the 150th anniversary of the birth of Ludovit Stur in Uhrovec. I have already mentioned that I was born in the same house as Stur, and, under my parents' influence, I had never accepted the official ambiguous view of him. On the one hand, his role in the formation of the modern literary Slovak language, for example, was officially accepted as positive. The same applied to his literary achievements, and even to his activities as a deputy of the Hungarian Diet. But because Stur failed to support the Hungarian revolution in 1848 and instead emphasized strictly Slovak aspirations, he was viewed as a bourgeois nationalist.

This view followed from the simplistic Marxist-Leninist perception of any nationalism as detrimental to the cause of the proletarian revolution. Back in 1849 or 1850, Marx denounced the role of the Slavs in the suppression of the Hungarian revolution, and what he then wrote amounted to a dogma. But the Slovak revolution of 1848-49 could not be compared with the actions of other Slavic nations, namely the Russians and the Croats, which helped the Habsburgs to suppress the revolution in Hungary. Slovakia's very existence was denied by the Hungarians, and the Slovaks had no army, of course. And whom could they have revolted against in 1848, other than their Hungarian oppressors?

The official view of Stur was therefore wrongheaded and unfair, and it was misused by the centralists in Prague to denigrate Slovak emancipation efforts, even after 150 years. Under these circumstances, I thought it was right to claim for Stur the place in history he truly deserved.

In my speech, I placed Stur's actions in their historical context, emphasizing that the Slovak revolt was of Slovak serfs against their Hungarian feudal lords. I also said that there was nothing wrong with national pride in socialism, and that this national pride was "the opposite of bourgeois nationalism." This was as far as I could then go, but nobody could mistake my rejection of the anti-Slovak views of the Prague centralists.

Novotny, who had been attacking me since March 1964, continued to do so through proxies like Chudik, Sabolcik, and Cvik. Several weeks before the Slovak Party Congress in May 1966, I learned that the StB was looking into my part in the construction of the paper works in Sturovo. Even more alarming was their investigation of my activities in the armaments complex where I had worked during the war. I did not know what they were looking for, but I believed it was serious, because it indicated that the StB were creating a case against me.

Their orders had to come from a place as high as the Department for Armed and Security Forces of the Czechoslovak Party Central Committee. That department supervised the army and police in the whole Republic, and it worked directly under First Secretary Novotny. The department's head, Miroslav Mamula, was Novotny's appointee and his right hand.

As soon as I learned of the investigations, I counterattacked on the floor of the Czechoslovak Party Presidium. I asked how it was possible to conduct these probes without approval of the Presidium, and I demanded that the Central Commission for Revision and Control immediately investigate who had ordered them. I warned that such practices clearly spelled a return to the early 1950s, an argument I knew would be effective so shortly after the revelations of the Kolder Commission. Fortunately, I was supported by other members of the Presidium, especially old Dolansky. It was clear to everyone that Novotny was behind the affair, and he had to retreat when he saw that he was running into strong opposition.

Until 1968 the activities of the Slovak Party were closely supervised by the Czechoslovak Party leadership, especially by the Czechoslovak first secretary and the central apparatus he controlled. Among other things, this meant that the Czechoslovak leadership, where I was in a minority, had the power to approve, in advance, documents to be presented before each Slovak Party congress, including my general report and my suggested personnel changes. Novotny's power was, however, not quite unlimited; he needed approval by the majority of the Slovak Central Committee.

Before the Slovak Party Congress in May 1966, I believed I had sufficient support in the Central Committee plenum, but in the Presidium, Lenart joined Chudik and Sabolcik against me, and in the Secretariat, two secretaries, Kriz and Janik, were allied with them. Both in the seven-member Slovak Party Presidium and in the five-member Secretariat, my opponents were a minority, but the power of the Czechoslovak first secretary was such that he could still unseat me. Novotny launched his campaign to remove me well before the Slovak Party congress met. He must have known that many resolutions critical of his policies had been adopted by Slovak Communist Party district and some regional organizations and was afraid that such criticism would be reflected in my report to the congress. This in turn could result in unfriendly personnel changes in the leading bodies of the Slovak Party and complicate his manipulation of the Thirteenth Congress of the Czechoslovak Party a month later.

In reality, I was still pursuing a cautious course because I did not believe that the time had arrived for a direct clash with Novotny. The report we were preparing for the Slovak congress was actually moderate and restrained compared with the resolutions of the lower organizations of our Party. Novotny, however, proceeded from his worst-case assumptions and took aggressive countermeasures.

In early April, a month before the Slovak Party congress, he decided not only that the congressional report would be discussed beforehand at the Czechoslovak Party Presidium but that the whole "political situation in Slovakia" would be reviewed. With sufficient support in the Czechoslovak Presidium, he could have carried out personnel changes in the Slovak leadership even before the congress met, and over its head, especially by removing me in favor of Chudik.

Despite the threat, I nurtured the hope that Novotny was overreaching, and I was right. When the matter came up in the Czechoslovak Presidium, Novotny did not receive the support he needed. Indeed, the discussion signaled his declining hold over the Czechoslovak Party's highest bodies. Of the eight voting members of the Presidium, only Jozef Lenart supported Novotny all the way—despite the fact that he was a Slovak and a member of the Slovak Communist Party Presidium. I noted particularly the ambiguous behavior of Jiri Hendrych, usually Novotny's closest ally. It was clear, at least to me, that these two close allies might eventually part ways.

Novotny received more support from nonvoting Czechoslovak Presidium members, namely Martin Vaculik, Michal Sabolcik, and Antonin Kapek. Vaculik was then the Czechoslovak Party secretary in Prague and was believed to be Novotny's choice to succeed him.

In spite of Novotny's failure to get his plan through the Presidium, my prospects for survival were not entirely certain. My mood was fatalistic, and I needed a rest, so in late April, three weeks before the congress, I headed for a remote High Tatras resort. A few friends came with me, including Frantisek Barbirek, who headed the Department of Industry in the Slovak Party Central Committee. Barbirek was a close and faithful friend, and subsequently I spearheaded his advancement not only to the Slovak Presidium but even to the Czechoslovak one.

We arrived at a small chalet in the Javorina area, very close to the Polish border. The High Tatra Mountains are the highest part of the Carpathians, extending from northern Slovakia into southern Poland. The highest point, the Gerlachovka, is over 8,700 feet above sea level. The whole massif has been designated a natural reserve. It has rich alpine vegetation and beautiful glacial lakes. Deer, lynx, and bears live in remote areas of the mountains.

When we arrived, the snow was still deep and the night was cold. We learned that a hunt was on for a wild brown bear. These bears are normally strictly protected; they are herbivorous and try to avoid humans. But this was a rogue bear that was now attacking herds of sheep on both sides of the border. Polish and Slovak rangers had decided it must be destroyed. That, however, was easier said than done. The bear was obviously cunning and had been avoiding hunters for a couple of years, moving at night from Poland to Slovakia and back. Shortly after we arrived, we learned that the bear had been spotted moving from Poland to our side of the Tatras. I could not resist the temptation: I decided to join the hunt, and others, including Barbirek, followed me.

Hunting such a big and dangerous beast is no small enterprise, and several foresters with trained dogs went out nightly to different locations to lie in wait. We accompanied them, walking in the wet snow up to our knees. After a while the cold started to penetrate our bones, but the expectation that the animal might appear warmed us up.

We waited for two nights in vain, and on the third day the foresters decided to call the hunt off. They knew their job and were convinced the bear must have departed their area.

My friends decided to return to Bratislava, and I almost left with them, but something told me the bear was still around, and I decided to stay and try once more. As Barbirek left, I told him jokingly, "You know what? If I get the bear, it means Novotny won't get me at the congress!"

I went to the forester's house to tell him what I was up to and to obtain his permission and help. Of course, he wanted nothing to do with it. He told me that the dogs and those authorized to take part in the hunt were already gone, along with the bear. It took me a long time to persuade him. I think he had little if any confidence in my clairvoyance.

We left before sunset and took our position under some low trees at the edge of a sharply sloping plain. We waited. It was the night of Good Friday and bitterly cold. We were there for several hours, and I am sure the forester must have thought it was all nonsense and how good it would have been to stay in his warm bed.

Then suddenly, I noticed a dark mass about 200 yards from us. I alerted the forester, putting my hand on his and pointing. Another look through the rifle scope confirmed that it was huge—it was *the* bear, beyond any doubt.

So I aimed at him, waited until he reached an open space among the trees, and fired. We heard the beast roar; he jumped to the side and disappeared in the darkness behind the trees.

The forester now told me in no uncertain terms that I had created a very difficult situation. With no dog to lead us to the wounded animal, we would have to reach a vantage point above the spot where we had first seen the bear.

The forester was in no mood to move ahead, perhaps to encounter an enraged and wounded bear, but I insisted, and led the way. After a thorough search, we found the bear dead. It was a big animal—some six hundred pounds. I have had the bearskin and head on the floor of my living room ever since.

When we got back to the chalet, we celebrated our triumph with toasts according to tradition. I called Barbirek in Bratislava in the morning and told him that I had shot the bear. Given my parting jest, it was for both of us an important political omen.

A few days later, the Slovak Party congress opened, and Novotny failed to get my skin as I had the bear's. Instead, I received full support for my report and even managed to strengthen my position. I was unable, of course, to get rid of Chudik and Sabolcik, but I felt much safer. The Thirteenth Congress of the Czechoslovak Communist Party, a month later, held no surprises. My report there was as restrained as the one to the Slovak congress. I knew that time was on my side.

I now heard that Novotny had initiated an investigation into my shooting of the bear. The police, on orders from Prague, could do nothing but verify that the hunt had been legal and officially approved. It must have been the first bear shooting that had been investigated on direct orders from such a high authority. The news amused me greatly: it was another sign of Novotny's desperation and declining power.

14

OPENING THE ROAD
TO PRAGUE SPRING

B Y 1967 a direct clash between the proponents and opponents of reform was inevitable. And this time the struggle would center on the basic and long-standing malaise of our society—the oppressive political system carried over from the early 1950s.

During the previous year, Novotny and his allies had failed again in their attempts to silence the opposition, especially in Slovakia. Discontent was growing. Early in 1967, we learned from reports of the district Party committees that the public mood in both Slovakia and the Czech lands was increasingly impatient and in favor of change. All three focal points of the crisis—the economy, the cultural environment, and Czecho-Slovak relations—were urgently and openly debated in the Czechoslovak Party Central Committee in the autumn.

The New Economic Mechanism was launched in January, but very soon it became clear that, in its narrow scope, the project would lead nowhere. Moreover, its wider application was not without possible negative consequences for Slovakia because of the continuing imbalance in economic development. Slovak industry's productivity continued to be lower than that of the Czech lands, and even some of my allies, like Frantisek Barbirek, thought the old system provided better protection for the Slovak economy. A debate reflecting this concern broke out in the first months of 1967, and the problem also emerged at the Slovak Central Committee session in May. I was worried by these trends, because they could further delay reform of the political system, which, I believed, was the root problem.

At the end of June, a congress of the Union of Czechoslovak Writers was held in Prague that resulted in a revolt similar to that in Slovakia four years earlier. This was truly significant because some three quarters of the Writers' Union's members—novelists, poets, playwrights, and editors—were Communists who had constituted a prestigious force solidly support-ive of the Party since before the war. The writers, responsive to the degener-ation of the socialist ideal, soon launched an open revolt against the policies of Novotny and Jiri Hendrych, who, as secretary for culture, supervised cultural affairs. Several well-known Communist writers—including Pavel Kohout, Milan Kundera, and Ludvik Vaculik—denounced Stalinist gover-nance and demanded changes in accordance with the country's democratic traditions.

Novotny, Hendrych, and their allies were outraged and called for strict measures against the most outspoken critics, first through the Writers' Union itself. But the leadership of the union was in quiet agreement with the critics and failed to follow the orders of Hendrych and other officials responsible for cultural affairs. The case, including Novotny's and Hendrych's proposal to silence *Literarni Noviny*, the Czechoslovak writers' weekly, was then brought before the Czechoslovak Presidium.

At the Presidium in late September, I opposed this step, but no other member joined me; only Dolansky raised some cautious reservations. No-votny's majority had its way. Shortly afterwards, a group of journalists of dubious reputation, under police protection, took control of the editorial offices of the paper in Prague.

This naturally set the stage for a similar action against *Kulturny Zivot*, the Slovak writers' weekly. Legally, this could have been done over my objections, because the police were then centrally controlled from Prague. Fortunately, time was running out for Novotny, and he had too many other urgent problems. Thus, for several weeks the action against Czech writers in Prague had the indirect result of underlining the difference between free expression in Slovakia and dead silence in the Czech lands. The rebellious Czech writers found the pages of the Slovak press, especially *Kulturny Zivot*, readily opened to them. In itself, this was bound to cause another clash with Prague.

Israel's resounding victory in the Six-Day War also added to the ferment that summer. Following the Soviet lead, the whole Eastern bloc except Romania had sided with the Arabs and broken diplomatic relations with Israel. In Czechoslovakia this was not a popular move, and a well-known Slovak Communist writer and journalist, Ladislav Mnacko, emigrated to Israel in protest. He was promptly expelled from the Czechoslovak Party and stripped of his citizenship. I was opposed, in principle, to these measures for "solving" differences of opinion, but I did not think this was the issue on which to take a stand against Novotny. It involved the state's foreign policy, and that was, under the circumstances, an untouchable area.

Despite the political turmoil, I was able to take two weeks off in July for a holiday with my wife and sons. We went to the forests and mountains of the Low Tatras, north of Banska Bystrica. We hiked and camped along tourist trails. It was our favorite pastime, and we savored the beautiful country and delightfully clear air.

In the middle of his campaign against Czech writers in August, Novotny made an unplanned trip to Slovakia that created a new irritant in Czecho-Slovak relations. This time he displayed an ostentatious disrespect for the foundations of the modern existence of the Slovak nation. The occasion was the hundredth anniversary of the opening of a Slovak lycée in Turciansky sv. Martin. The establishment of this school had been a major event in 1867, when there was only one other Slovak teaching high school in the whole country.

The town (called simply Martin since 1951) lies about twenty miles northeast of Banska Bystrica and is a place of great historical and cultural significance for all Slovaks. It was the traditional center of the Protestant branch of national revival, which later joined with the Catholics to promote and protect Slovak national identity. Martin played a leading role in resisting the brutal Hungarization practiced by Budapest in the second half of the nineteenth century, and it was where Matica Slovenska, an institution almost synonymous with national survival, was founded in 1861. (*Matica* means "mother.") Its purpose was the preservation of the Slovak language and the development of Slovak national literature, and it was formally sanctioned by Emperor Franz Josef in 1862. Both Matica and the lycée were closed down in 1875 by order of the Hungarian authorities and only reopened after 1918, when Hungary was forced to relinquish its hold on Slovakia. Since the 1920s Matica has functioned as the Slovak national library.

Thus, the hundredth anniversary of the foundation of the lycée was an important event in Slovak cultural history. Neither we in the Slovak Party leadership nor the Presidium of the Slovak National Council had taken the initiative to invite Novotny to attend the celebration. I doubted that he had much sympathy for Slovak historical landmarks. It was the idea of leading officials of Matica Slovenska to invite him in his role as head of state. They needed no permission from Bratislava, so they acted on their own. They did not even inform us until after Novotny surprisingly accepted.

Not having been officially informed by either the presidential office in Prague or the Czechoslovak Party, I could avoid going to Martin myself. Still, Novotny was the president of the Republic, so I instructed Vasil Bilak, a Slovak Party Presidium member and the Central Committee secretary responsible for cultural affairs, to attend the event.

By skipping out, I spared myself a great deal of discomfort and even had a moment of incredulous pleasure when I heard that, by accepting the invitation, Novotny had initially intended to improve his image in Slovakia. Instead his visit was an uninterrupted chain of insults to his hosts. He apparently had made no effort to learn what Matica Slovenska was, and when they asked for some financial support, he suggested they move the museum to Prague. His blunders culminated in a refusal to accept well-intended gifts for his wife—a Slovak fur coat and a collection of embroidery. After Novotny demonstrated such total ignorance of the importance of the place and the anniversary, and responded to his hosts' overtures as provocative evidence of Slovak nationalism, relations between Novotny and Slovaks of almost all stripes became irreparable.

A two-day plenary session of the Czechoslovak Party Central Committee started on October 30. The basis for discussion was a report about the Party's place in the political system, presumed to express the collective opinion of the Party Presidium. A draft had been discussed at Presidium meetings on October 19 and 24. Finding crucial parts inadequate, I had asked for changes and corrections.

I had focused on three areas. First, I wanted to see clear self-criticism by the Party leadership; the draft did not go beyond the criticism of district and regional Party committees. Second, I had proposed to complement the report with a delineation between the power of the government and that of the Party. My purpose was to put an end to the Party bureaucracy's daily meddling in government business. And, third, I demanded the early preparation of an action program based on the decisions of the Central Committee.

Today this may look like too little too late, but one has to remember that in 1967 we were still living in a system designed by Stalin to fit his dictatorial needs; we could only dismantle it gradually. Even this "too little" brought an army of 600,000 men and 7,000 tanks in less than a year.

Novotny and others rejected all my criticisms and proposals, especially the idea of an action program, and left the report unchanged. Novotny was certain of majority support, so he simply mumbled, after everybody else had spoken, "Approved." No vote was taken on my suggestions, and I do not recall that anyone supported me.

When the Central Committee session started, Novotny read the report, which was supposed to represent the opinion of the whole Presidium. Then the meeting was, as usual, declared closed, which meant that no journalists or guests were present. When discussion opened, I was one of the first speakers.

Contrary to the many accounts of my speech, especially in the West, I launched no sensational attack on Novotny. I repeated the points I had raised during the preparatory meetings. I demanded substantive changes in how the Party directed the affairs of the society, and I pointed out the need for self-criticism by the leadership.

I touched on the mistreatment of Slovakia, but it was not a major aspect of my speech. It was, however, the issue on which Novotny and his allies chose to counterattack as soon as I finished, leveling at me the tired and discredited charge of bourgeois nationalism. Martin Vaculik also tried to narrow my presentation to Slovak affairs, accusing me of "nationalist deviation."

Fortunately, many members of the Central Committee understood the real problem, and, after I opened the Pandora's box for them, they jumped into the fray. The ensuing discussion soon demonstrated how ripe the time was to start talking about real issues. That day and the next, one speaker after another added weight to my arguments, and it was then that the term *accumulation of offices* was used for the first time. At first, it was an implicit criticism of Novotny's excessive powers, but it soon evolved into an explicit demand that he resign as Czechoslovak Party first secretary.

The debate was the opening skirmish of a struggle that would last for more than two months. I recall with particular gratitude the remarks of Josef Smrkovsky. He was honored in the Czech lands for his part in the resistance during the war. In the early 1950s, he was also a victim of repression, and in 1967 he held the politically insignificant position of minister of water economy. But his taking the side of the reformers at this early stage of the battle was of great significance. Two regional secretaries from Moravia, Oldrich Volenik and Josef Spacek, also came out strongly in support of my stand, as did a number of other members of the Central Committee.

During the second day, around 8:00 P.M., news arrived of a student demonstration in Prague and of police action against it. This was not of great importance in itself—the students were mainly protesting against interruptions of power supply to their dormitories—but it helped to thicken the atmosphere in the Central Committee.

Then came an even more serious blow for Novotny. In the closing hours, a majority rejected the resolution he and his staff had prepared, "theses" based on his opening speech. The proposal was criticized as formulaic and inadequate, and the Central Committee voted to return the document for redrafting and fresh consideration in December. This had never happened before. There could have been no clearer signal of Novotny's declining authority. The body itself seemed surprised by its sudden power. The crisis of leadership was now obvious to everyone.

The session thus ended with no conclusions. The next morning Novotny and other members of the Presidium left for Moscow to participate in the ceremonies marking the fiftieth anniversary of the Bolshevik Revolution, bringing a pause in the unfolding drama. The next plenary session of the Central Committee would not meet until just before Christmas. But the train of events taking us toward Prague Spring was on the move and could be neither stopped nor reversed.

15

NOVOTNY'S RELUCTANT DEPARTURE

Novotny did not return from Moscow until November 10. Contrary to protocol and courtesy, he had not taken me along. Instead he was accompanied by Michal Chudik, his "favorite Slovak."

The length of Novotny's stay in Moscow caused comment at home. He arrived there November 1, attended the ceremonies on the sixth and seventh, and went to a one-day conference of Communist parties of the bloc on the eighth. We assumed that he spent much of the time waiting for an opportunity to talk with Brezhnev about his problems at home, but we learned nothing specific. All we were told after his return was that he had caught flu in Moscow, an explanation or an excuse for his absence from the next two Czechoslovak Party Presidium meetings. Moscow flu had had a special reputation in Czechoslovakia since March 1953, when Klement Gottwald caught his terminal case of it at Stalin's funeral.

In Novotny's absence, discussions about the dramatic October plenary session of the Central Committee dominated Party couloirs. Several Czech members of the Central Committee—Josef Smrkovsky, Vaclav Slavik, Frantisek Kriegel, and others—came to Bratislava to talk with Slovak Party officials. We were in agreement on basic problems, and I could see that a strong pro-reform bloc in the Czechoslovak Party Central Committee was taking shape. Whether it would be strong enough to overcome Novotny's resistance was, however, still uncertain.

Novotny's reaction to the October plenum was predictable. He formed a five-man Czechoslovak Presidium group to investigate my "nationalist deviation." This was a perfect example of his simplistic Stalinist thinking: first I was to be accused of ideological wrongdoing, then found guilty and punished (at least by reprimand); that would be enough to justify my recall from the position of Slovak first secretary. In the end, Novotny could put Chudik in my place.

This commission was composed of Novotny himself, Hendrych, Chudik, Sabolcik, and Lenart. Naturally, Novotny chose those he thought most trustworthy. He must have been wholly confident this move would work. As for myself, I knew that it could not work, and I kept my calm. Novotny's thinking was at least ten years out of date.

After the October plenum, the Presidium started to discuss accumulation of offices. There were ten voting members of the Presidium at that time. Four of us—Cernik, Dolansky, Kolder, and I—were for separating the offices of president and first secretary; Hendrych, Chudik, and Lenart, with Novotny himself, were serving on the "Dubcek Commission" and presumed loyal to Novotny (Sabolcik was not a Presidium member). I needed to get the vote of one of the other two members—Bohuslav Lastovicka and Otokar Simunek—or to change the affiliation of one of Novotny's loyalists. In that event, the balance would be shifted, the opposing sides even, and it would be a whole new game. It looked hopeless to most insiders, and for good reason.

Simunek, though passed over by Novotny for his anti-Dubcek investigation, had been a deputy prime minister for the economy since 1959 and was unswervingly loyal to Novotny, so I ruled him out. Alas, I also had to rule out Lastovicka. A Czech prewar Party veteran and Spanish Civil War Interbrigadist, he had escaped the early 1950s Stalinist persecution of anti-Franco partisans that had snared such figures as Artur London, author of *The Confession*, largely because of Novotny's personal protection, and he remained grateful.

My attention focused instead on Jiri Hendrych, who for some years had been the undisputed number two man in the Czechoslovak Party leadership. He was considered Novotny's staunchest supporter and was thought to have no higher ambitions. In the period after the October plenary session, he had made a point of standing firmly behind Novotny.

But I had had an eye on Hendrych for some time. A short, fat man with thick glasses in heavy, dark frames, he looked like an aging village rector, the very picture of a man without aspirations. He was Novotny's right hand, his main adviser and speech writer. At the same time, he was a strange bedfellow. Unlike Novotny, Hendrych was an intellectual who had completed several semesters of law school at Charles University before the Nazis closed it down in 1939. I sensed that the armor of his outward dogmatism was not without hidden cracks, and I knew he could not be unaware that Novotny's days as first secretary were numbered. I had seen Hendrych vacillate on various occasions, most recently in April, when Novotny had tried to make an issue of my stewardship in Slovakia. Now that, I thought, was significant.

After much pondering, I concluded that Hendrych was the only person on the other side who could be broken. I didn't underestimate the difficulties, for I knew how personally close Novotny and Hendrych had been. They had spent a long time together in the Mauthausen concentration camp, among other things. However, Ota Sik was close to Novotny, too—at Mauthausen he had been even closer to him than Hendrych—yet he stood resolutely against Novotny in this case. That gave me hope.

Some historians have speculated that I had to make a deal with Hendrych to change his mind. The truth is, there was no deal whatsoever, only a seed planted in his mind.

In late November, I told Drahomir Kolder of my surmise about Hendrych. A man of simple outlook, Kolder was completely flabbergasted. He looked at me as if I were out of my head and said, "There is no point in even trying to talk to Hendrych about it. Novotny and he are like twins. You can never change Hendrych's mind. You'll just make a fool of yourself." I trusted my instincts, however, and from Kolder I went directly to Hendrych's suite. A red light was on above the door to his office, and his secretary told me, "He is very busy. He is working on something very urgent and important."

"Well, I also have something very important," I said and went straight to the door, opened it, stepped inside, and closed it behind me. Hendrych was sitting behind his desk reading some papers, but, as he heard me come in, he turned his round face toward me and asked, "What do you need?"

I remained standing even after he asked me to sit down, and I assured him that I would not take much of his time. Then I went straight to the point. I said, "As we both know, the separation of the office of the first secretary from that of the president is just a matter of time. So it occurred to me to ask you, wouldn't you be interested in one of these offices?" He looked like someone who had just been hit over the head. For an interminable moment he remained frozen, and I realized that he had almost certainly never entertained such a possibility.

As he caught his breath, I continued. "One way or another, a solution will have to be carried through. But it would be difficult to replace the president in such short order, so it is the office of first secretary that is at stake, of course. You can't stave it off, and if you go on opposing it, you too may fall."

Still he did not say a word, and I saw only a pencil slowly slipping through his fingers onto the papers before him as I left his office. At least I have put a bee in his bonnet, I thought.

And that I had.

Not long after my incursion into Hendrych's office, Novotny served formal notice that on December 5 I was to appear before the commission investigating my nationalist deviation, and he gave me a list of questions I was expected to answer the next day. They read like an examination at the end of a Party course on nationalism. Considering the rapidly changing political climate, the whole thing was ridiculous. It missed the real point of the dispute and was even in violation of Party statutes.

When I appeared before the commission, I could discern that most of its members were less than enthusiastic about the enterprise. Only Chudik gave full support to Novotny's points. Sabolcik, to my real surprise, took no part in the encounter, and Lenart went no further than a few formal observations. Naturally, I was especially curious to see what Hendrych would do. He cleaned his glasses at least three times and took a lot of notes, but he looked positively aloof and on matters of substance chose to remain entirely neutral. I knew that Novotny must have been annoyed, and I was rather amused.

In spite of a wishy-washy conclusion to my interrogation, I was required to inform other members of the Slovak leadership of it on my return to Bratislava. Everyone present at the Slovak Presidium meeting held the next day decided to reject Novotny's accusations, with one exception—Michal Chudik. That, for all practical reasons, put an end to the affair.

Meanwhile, Novotny had urgently asked Brezhnev to come to Prague to intervene in his favor, and the Soviet leader quietly arrived December 8, the same day the Slovak Presidium threw out the accusation against me. I know that Brezhnev came with the intention of supporting Novotny, because one of his assistants told me so a few weeks later. He also told me how his boss changed his mind.

Before Brezhnev left Moscow, he inquired about "who was actually number two in Prague." Hendrych, they informed him. They also told him that, according to the embassy reports from Prague, this "number two" stood solidly behind Novotny.

Brezhnev came with a list of five people he wanted to talk to—Novotny, Hendrych, Lenart, Dolansky, and me. The list had not been composed with the view of finding a possible successor to Novotny. Instead Brezhnev purposely chose three Czech and two Slovak senior members of the Presidium, and by and large he followed protocol. Nothing more, nothing less.

Hendrych was the first Brezhnev talked to after his meeting with Novotny, and, according to my informant, the meeting was a shock. Brezhnev asked Hendrych to share his thoughts about how to solve the dispute. Hendrych replied, with almost no preliminaries, "Well, I'm willing to take over the office of first secretary." What else they discussed I do not know, but Brezhnev apparently realized that it would be impossible to sustain Novotny in power when even his closest supporter was ready to desert him.

I talked with Brezhnev the next day at the Czechoslovak Communist Party Central Committee building in Prague. (In the West there were erroneous reports that Brezhnev came to Bratislava to see me.) The meeting lasted about an hour. That may have been less than the time he spent with others, but we needed no interpreter. Brezhnev asked me to tell him what I thought about the situation, and I did. I emphasized the magnitude of the problems we had and Novotny's reluctance to solve them. I also mentioned Novotny's intolerance concerning ethnic relations in the country. Brezhnev asked a few supplementary questions but offered no opinions of his own. There was no talk of Novotny's succession.

I think that when Brezhnev came to Prague he had no clear idea about the depth of our problems, and in talking to me he displayed no interest in learning more about them. He listened to what I said but asked no questions that would help him understand the substance of the dispute and its underlying social, economic, and political factors. I think that he looked at the whole mess as a personal squabble among high Party officials. What was even worse, he and his Politburo showed the same ignorance in the months to come. They translated everything into one simple issue, the interests of the ruling Party bureaucracy.

Brezhnev is frequently quoted in Western reports as saying, at the end of his visit, that it was up to us to decide how to solve the problem—*Eto vashe delo*, "It's your business." To whom he said that I do not know. The fact is that he avoided an expected meeting with the whole Presidium. He left December 9, accompanied to the airport by Novotny.

In the end, what Brezhnev said was less important than his avoiding the Presidium, where he could have exerted pressure in Novotny's behalf. Thus, the net result of his visit was a signal failure of support for the expectant Novotny. I have no doubt that it was Hendrych's behavior, more than anything else, that affected Brezhnev.

Even after this setback, Novotny did not give in. For almost four more weeks he held on. On December 11, at the first Czechoslovak Presidium meeting after Brezhnev's visit, the dispute continued with the same intensity and along the same lines as before. I watched Hendrych carefully, but he was passive and showed no signs of changing sides. It became necessary to postpone the Central Committee session scheduled for December 12 until December 19, uncomfortably close to Christmas. Some women members complained that they would have no time to make cookies.

It was at a Presidium meeting on December 17, the last before the December plenary session of the Central Committee, that a breakthrough occurred. I took the floor and said that the positions of only four members of the Presidium—Dolansky, Cernik, Kolder, and myself—were absolutely clear. That was an exaggeration, but I needed it to introduce a clear proposal: let all members of the leadership, including candidate members of the Presidium and secretaries of the Central Committee, say openly where they stood.

There was no vote on this proposal, and it was quietly accepted. Even Novotny raised no objections, apparently hoping that a majority would back him up.

There was no formal order in which members spoke, but the crucial moment came when Vladimir Koucky, a secretary of the Central Committee, took the floor. Koucky, unlike many others, was a well-educated Party official who had taken part in the resistance during the Nazi occupation. He was also very close to Hendrych; he would not do anything without clearing it with him.

Koucky began cautiously explaining how closely he had been following the debate. Then he said that after thinking about it all over and over again, he had come to believe that it was impossible to avoid the separation of the offices of first secretary and president of the Republic.

I could actually see the shock wave of Koucky's final words traveling around the room, and I had no doubt that this was just a foreword to what Hendrych, a voting member, would say. He did not disappoint, saying emphatically that separation of the offices was unavoidable. The cat was definitely out of the bag. The five-against-five division in the Presidium was firmly in place.

The Central Committee session opened on the nineteenth with a speech by Lenart on the economic situation, but everybody was waiting for the second point on the agenda: "reorganization of the leading organs of the Party." On that, Novotny was to report.

He apologized for his attacks on me at the October plenum, and unconvincingly described himself as the ultimate defender of Czecho-Slovak friendship. Then he started to read a text filled with clichés and generalities, such as "external threats to the security of the state." This was a none too subtle one-should-not-change-horses-in-midstream argument against replacing him.

But the Central Committee didn't like it, and Novotny's speech was interrupted by shouts from all sides. A stormy discussion followed, and several speakers called on Novotny to step down. The extraordinary session continued into a second day, and it became entirely clear that Novotny's support was fast dwindling.

The meeting went on for a third day, and it was then, December 21, that all members and candidate members of the Presidium and secretaries of the Central Committee were asked to state their opinions. In this all-male group of fifteen, only four continued to stand behind Novotny: Lastovicka, Simunek, and two lesser known Novotny appointees, Pastyrik, chairman of the Trade Union Council, and Hron, the chairman of the Central Auditing Commission. Among the desertions, the most important was that of Martin Vaculik.

Now, finally, Novotny retreated, to some acceptance of the *principle* of the separation of the two top offices. Specifically, he placed the secretary's office "at the disposal of the Central Committee."

There was no discussion about who might succeed him at that point, but the Central Committee elected an eleven-member Consultative Group to assist the Presidium in the selection of candidates. The group was composed of representatives of all regional committees, and it was chaired by Jan Piller, representing the regional Party organization in Central Bohemia. The Central Committee then adjourned until January 3, 1968, a decision that was accepted with great reluctance by some members, who were afraid that Novotny might resort to illegal methods to save his neck.

Indeed, the fear was justified. Probably with Novotny's knowledge, plans for a coup d'état utilizing the StB and selected units of the army were being laid even as the Central Committee was still sitting.

A center of this activity was the Eighth Department of the Central Committee apparatus, in charge of security and the armed forces. Headed by Miroslav Mamula, Novotny's close associate, this department was said to have compiled a list of several hundred of Novotny's opponents, who would all be arrested by State Security the moment the coup was launched.

A parallel plot was pursued at the ministry of defense by Party Secretary General Jan Sejna. Sejna was a protégé of Novotny and a personal friend of his son. After his defection to the West in February 1968, it came out that he was also a thief who had been secretly selling army supplies of grass seed on the black market. Sejna tried to win over the main Party committee in his ministry to support Novotny. Ironically, he succeeded on January 5, after the struggle was all but over.

Whether Sejna was also involved in an attempt by some officers on the General Staff to dispatch a tank unit to Prague in support of Mamula is not clear. Collusion in all these plans has not been proven, but it should be noted that two influential army generals and candidate members of the Central Committee—Rytir and Hecko—stood behind Novotny until the end, and so did the minister of the interior, Josef Kudrna. Some army generals deserve to be noted for their courageous efforts to foil the conspiracy—Dzur, Pepich, and Prchlik, for example. Later I appointed them all to significant military or security positions.

Happily, the putschist activities failed to save Novotny, and he may himself, in the end, have called them off. It was all too ridiculous: an internal military putsch like this had no precedent in Czechoslovakia, and, above all, it would not have changed the problems the country was facing.

Nevertheless, the time between the December and January sessions of the Central Committee had been very tense, with all kinds of rumors going around. I spent Christmas with my family in Bratislava, and, quite frankly, I never stopped worrying about the proverbial 3:00 A.M. knock at the door.

The Czechoslovak Presidium met again on January 2, in the presence of the Consultative Group, to prepare proposals for the session of the Central Committee scheduled for the next day. Novotny still continued to maneuver; he now demanded that the election of his successor be postponed, at least until the end of February. Novotny's supporters understood the delay as another way to keep him in office. The Presidium remained divided as evenly as before. The meeting lasted over ten hours, until almost 2:00 A.M., and proved unable to resolve the problem.

However, the pressure mounted over the next two days. Novotny started to retreat during a Presidium meeting in the evening hours on January 4, 1968. This meeting was held without the Consultative Group but in the presence of candidate members and secretaries of the Central Committee. Novotny asked all present to write down the names of those they preferred to see elected first secretary.

Until that point, I had not imagined it possible that I could replace Novotny. The principle of fair distribution of top positions between Czechs and Slovaks was not yet established, and, as a Slovak, I had the odds against me. In fact, of the four positions—president, premier, Czechoslovak first secretary, and chairman of the parliament—only one was held by a Slovak, Lenart, who was then prime minister. Thus, I expected that the new first secretary would again be a Czech, and I didn't care, as long as it was someone reform minded, such as Cernik. I preferred him, but he refused even to be considered for the job, preferring to continue as deputy prime minister.

Whether I felt qualified for the job was a different question. I was aware of the heavy responsibilities of first secretary. I had had enough experience in Party work and public administration to know what they traditionally were;

what I would want to change was the direct involvement of the Party in the day-to-day workings of the government. Eliminating that involvement would open the road to reforms.

When the straw vote was counted, it appeared that I was on top: Lastovicka was preferred by four of those present, Cernik by four, Lenart by six, and I myself by seven. This result was handed over to the Consultative Group, which conferred through the night.

The Presidium and the Consultative Group met again at 8:00 A.M. on January 5 and proposed two candidates, Lenart and me. After a rather short discussion, a decisive majority selected me as the sole candidate to be proposed to the Central Committee. Even Novotny reluctantly accepted the decision. The plenary session of the Central Committee then endorsed this recommendation, and I was elected to take over Novotny's job.

It is sometimes quizzically recalled that my closing remarks at the session were polite in both content and tone, and that I thanked Novotny for the work he had done. Now I would like to ask: Isn't it always good to behave in a civilized manner?

The Central Committee also decided to enlarge the Presidium by four, so Jan Piller, Josef Boruvka, Emil Rigo, and Josef Spacek were elected to the newly created positions. This was an important step: none of those elected was a Stalinist hard-liner.

These events have been called the "January" that opened the door to Prague Spring. I had a keen sense of the historic importance of the moment and of the opportunities it offered, but I did not perceive the larger and more threatening obstacle on the distant horizon. Obviously, the idea that I was twenty years too early did not occur to me in January 1968.

There has been incorrect speculation about the way I took over Novotny's office in the Central Committee building. It was no casual matter: I discussed the technical aspects of succession with Novotny shortly after my election, and the whole procedure was clarified and agreed on. I stipulated that all documents and files that were part of the office of the first secretary remain in place and be itemized. I also told Novotny that he could, of course, take with him all his personal belongings. He had until January 8 to move out, and his people and mine took part in the transfer. I treated Novotny politely and with due respect—after all, he remained president of the Republic.

That I gave Novotny an opportunity to remove from his office some secret files is nonsense. There would have been no way other than a strict police search to separate his personal things from official papers, and I wanted to avoid that by all means. Moreover, there was not much to take over in his office, and I believe that most of his archives were already at the presidential office. After January 8, Novotny had no office in the Central Committee building. His only office was at Prague Castle, the president's seat.

When it was all over, I left for Bratislava, quite exhausted. It was early in the afternoon. I have never needed much sleep, but I did need to get away from the tension of the previous days and weeks. I went straight home and spent some time with my wife and children. In the evening, I went to an ice hockey game at Bratislava Winter Stadium. It was a good idea. I enjoyed the game, and I felt good there among the cheerful crowd.

16

BEYOND THE ROADBLOCK

T HE early period of Prague Spring, between January and April 1968, has been the subject of many critical analyses, but from what I have read they all come down to two opposite conclusions. One group of authors says I moved too slowly, and the other says I moved too fast. Naturally, the time gauge they use, in hindsight, is the period between my accession as first secretary and the Soviet invasion.

My problem was not having a crystal ball to foresee the Russian invasion. At no point between January and August 20, in fact, did I believe that it would happen. The hindsight estimates are therefore largely irrelevant. Even looking back after almost twenty-five years, I do not see what I could or should have done otherwise.

On every day of those short eight months, I had to weigh carefully all the conflicting realities in play around me and to prepare my next move accordingly. The balance of forces among the leading Party organs—the Presidium, Secretariat, and Central Committee—was of paramount importance. Then there was reemerging public opinion, which soon became the most important support for my policies. Unfortunately, the Soviets stepped in before I could make full and effective use of this lever to accelerate development. And it could not be denied that Brezhnev's USSR was a constant and interfering factor long before The Five invaded.

Furthermore, even after January 5, 1968, I had no reform-minded majority behind me in the expanded Presidium or in the Central Committee. The makeup of the coalition that had ousted Novotny from the secretaryship was much more complex than that. Many of those who had supported removing Novotny were not prepared for further steps toward reform, as I was well aware.

At the Presidium meetings in January, the air was uneasy and discussions were limited to technicalities. Those who had opposed one another in previous disputes were on guard for signs of further moves by their opponents. Clearly this was a temporary truce.

The four members added to the Presidium on January 5 made only a qualified difference. They all had been solidly against Novotny during the final acts of the struggle, but when it came to support of a principled reform policy, I was sure of only two of them, Josef Spacek and Josef Boruvka. I was particularly impressed by Spacek, the South Moravian regional Party secretary and a well-educated man. As a regional secretary, he had behind him a solid political base. Boruvka was also strongly pro-reform, but as chairman of a farming cooperative he had much less clout than Spacek. Jan Piller, a former deputy prime minister, had vacillated in the past, and I was not sure where his compass might take him. That he behaved with such courage in the crucial moments in August 1968 was a pleasant surprise.

The fourth man, Emil Rigo, was the chairman of the Enterprise Committee of the East Slovakian Ironworks, and he was an even more complicated case. A gypsy laborer by origin, Rigo was a man of undeniable natural intelligence who had graduated from the Higher Political School of the Czechoslovak Party. For better or worse, he was also personally very close to Slovak Party Presidium member Vasil Bilak, with his doctrinaire mindset. Rigo had taken part in the struggle against Novotny, but now he was showing signs of reluctance to support practical reforms. In other words, the addition of these Presidium members did not make much difference when it came to decisions about a new political course. It only shows how thick was the brush through which I was moving.

In the following weeks, the failure of some of my previous allies to support me was disturbing and even mystifying until I deduced that the Soviets were putting pressure on people like Kolder and Bilak. Both these men, and many others, were simple people raised in unquestioned subordination to everything Soviet. They had had no experience or family background comparable to mine. By their lights, socialism did not exist outside the Soviet Leninist model. Any doubts about Soviet ways, past or present, were beyond their imagination, as Bilak's memoirs testify. When men like these were approached by Soviet representatives who objected to this or that aspect of my policy, they clicked their heels and followed the Soviets' "advice."

Judging from various documents now available, such as correspondence of Soviet bloc diplomats from Prague, one can assume that the Soviets launched their lobbying sometime at the beginning of February 1968. In the next weeks and months, their meddling became more obvious and more aggressive. Soon I was able to recognize when Kolder or Bilak was simply repeating Brezhnev's arguments, sometimes word for word.

The unwelcome behavior of many other ranking Party officials, however, had nothing to do with Soviet lobbying. As society opened up, it became increasingly obvious that many bureaucrats would lose their positions—and privileges. Thus, their opposition to changes was simply self-preservation.

Anyway, the initial situation in the Presidium discouraged me from making substantive proposals. I counted on increasing pressure from within the Party and from the general public, which would, sooner or later, first soften the opposition and then permit me to make constructive changes in the composition of the Presidium.

My actions during the early weeks were also slowed down by a bout of flu, which had actually begun in December. I could not get rid of it for weeks, and it returned at the end of February, when I had to attend an especially important public function.

The one thing on which I needed Presidium approval as quickly as possible was the Action Program, for which I had been vainly pushing since mid-1967. This document was meant to set out new guidelines for democratizing our Party and our society. Its essence was to provide a strict definition of the role of the Party and its administrative apparatus, curtailing its power to dictate, and increasing its ability to respond directly to people's needs.

I had not spelled all that out in October 1967, when I first used the words *action program*, and, even after the January 1968 changes, I had to remain vague about my concept of the Party's functions and limits. There was no reason to alarm the conservatives too early. I had to choose my words and moves cautiously. This approach was somewhat facilitated by the fact that the role of the Party had often been interpreted in contradictory ways even in Lenin's works. Nevertheless, I knew this would be the most sensitive part of the program.

Of course, the Action Program also had to promote further economic reform, assure the rehabilitation of victims of political persecution, and address other fundamental issues of our nation, including federalization. But none of this could have been made explicit before I became first secretary, or even immediately after, because of the way the system worked. I needed first to legitimize the very idea of such a program by asking the Party Presidium to approve the establishment of a commission to draft it.

I made this proposal very soon after my election. I argued that documents of the 1966 Thirteenth Party Congress had called for such a commission and program—those documents were, fortunately, so general that they permitted a very stretched interpretation. This proved the right way to "sell" the idea of the commission, which ran into no significant opposition in the Presidium. That body, I must say, was quite apathetic at the time anyway. Thus, in mid-January a special commission was set up to prepare the proposals that would constitute the Action Program.

While the chairman of this "working commission" was Drahomir Kolder, who would soon start turning against me, actual preparation of the Action Program necessitated a staff of experts, and I knew very well that their disposition was friendly and enthusiastic.

The commission created five working groups with specific responsibilities. The most important focused on reform of the political system and the expansion of economic reform. We heard a promising report on the progress of this work at a Czechoslovak Party Secretariat meeting as early as January 24. Only in view of later developments did I realize how much time had been lost in the protracted struggles with Novotny. To prepare the program was a complex and sensitive task; at least several weeks were needed just to write a draft. Other developments may have made the Action Program look trivial, but that is a superficial view; the Action Program was to become one of the most important legacies of Prague Spring.

Meanwhile, political developments accelerated within a fortnight of my appointment, mainly because of the void of concrete information about the Central Committee's last three sessions. Both the official press release and the intra-Party transmission of the news were deficient. A release had been prepared by a commission of the Central Committee used to operating by the old system, under which public information about Party business was viewed as a formality. The original release, drafted when Novotny's defeat looked improbable, was unusable, and a second version had to be prepared at the last moment.

At the final Presidium meeting immediately after my election, there was barely time to discuss the draft, and there was still contention over the explanation for the separation of offices. Thus, the press release said only that Novotny was out and I was in, which was ridiculously sparse considering all the rumors surrounding the event. In any case, the facts did leak out. I asked for further information to be released, but the Presidium was in no condition to reach a consensus. The majority still firmly believed in keeping public information about Party activities to a minimum, and I saw little point in confronting them on this secondary matter.

Strangely enough, the fragmentary nature of both the press release and Party instructions played a positive role in the longer run. It provoked heated critical discussion in thousands of Party cells and thus activated a large segment of the rank and file, which had been very passive in recent years. Soon it also stimulated the rise of healthy public curiosity and concern.

Party cells around the country were informed in person by participants in the October, December, and January sessions of the Central Committee. The informants were from regional and district Party organizations, and cells of central political importance from various government departments, the army High Command, and the Academy of Sciences.

The extent and accuracy of these reports differed depending on the source; even the interpretations varied. Ironically, in mid-January detailed and accurate reports about those last three sessions of the Central Committee, including information about the aborted coup, were published in the West. Naturally, these quickly reached the country by way of foreign broadcasts.

Soon, resolutions adopted by myriad Party meetings expressed strong dissatisfaction with the way information was rationed; they criticized the terse and cryptic press release and demanded a full and open account of what had gone on. I took advantage of this anger and proposed, at the Presidium meeting on January 25, a substantial change in the system of publicity about the activities of top Party organizations. I said we should publish regular reports about all meetings of the Presidium and the Secretariat. Given the national wave of wrath, the Presidium could not kill this proposal, as it certainly would have done a few weeks earlier.

Otherwise, in January I took only modest first steps along my planned path. I fired the conspiratorial Miroslav Mamula, in charge of the StB, and replaced him with the loyal, pro-reformist General Vaclav Prchlik, until then the head of the Main Political Administration of the army. I also asked Jiri Hendrych to reach an agreement with the Union of Czechoslovak Writers on withdrawal of the repressive measures against the union and certain of its individual members, initiated by him and Novotny in 1967. Talks with representatives of the union started in mid-January, but Hendrych dragged his feet, so it was another month before the union's weekly could reappear. Swiftly, there came a growing openness in the media and a relaxation of formal censorship, especially noticeable in the Czech lands, as they caught up with the earlier openness in Slovakia.

I moved to counter any retightening of censorship by administration hard-liners. I knew that I needed a free press to help me open the way to basic reforms, political as well as economic. At the beginning of March, I extracted from the Presidium a revocation of the decision that had legalized the censorship system in 1966. Emerging public opinion also helped me remove Hendrych from control of the ideological sector, including the press.

On January 10, Soviet Ambassador Chervonenko brought me an invitation from Brezhnev for an official visit to Moscow, to take place on the twenty-ninth and thirtieth. It was inevitable if not entirely welcome. After all, we were not living on Mars.

I thought hard about what to tell Brezhnev and the other Soviet leaders. I also wished I could compare notes with the heads of other countries in the bloc, especially Hungary and Poland.

Just at that moment, a call came from Janos Kadar, first secretary of the Hungarian Communist Party proposing that we meet soon. I agreed immediately, and we met January 20 at a place close to Nove Zamky, in southern Slovakia.

It was an informal meeting without other officials or even interpreters, and we kept no notes on what we said. We informed each other about the situations in our respective countries, and Kadar seemed very interested in my plans.

Kadar was then fifty-six, ten years older than I was, and his personal experience with the Stalinist system, I thought, must have made him understanding toward the problems we faced in Czechoslovakia. He had been falsely implicated in an alleged conspiracy intertwined with our Slansky affair and had spent three years in prison before being rehabilitated in 1954. The Russians used him in 1956, after suppressing the Hungarian uprising, as the figurehead of a puppet government, but soon he achieved space in which to pursue a relatively successful course of limited reforms.

I had been closely following the way Kadar had steered his country's economic reforms since the disaster in 1956, and I had no small respect for him. In fact I believed that, of all leaders in the Soviet bloc, he should have been most sympathetic toward my views and plans. His prospective support was very important for me. Nevertheless, at this early stage, I decided to proceed with caution and did not go beyond sharing a rather general outline of my plans. I did not suspect him of treachery but simply thought it wise to listen more than speak. However, I did not hold back in stating my conviction that essential reforms in Czechoslovakia were terribly overdue.

Kadar seemed to understand and to agree with me, and we parted in friendly fashion. Later on he disappointed me profoundly, because he lacked the courage to challenge the Russians by supporting reform in my country. And that disappointment turned into bitterness when I learned, after August 1968, that, immediately after meeting me, Kadar had called Brezhnev and informed him in great detail about our discussion. It now seems probable that the initiative to meet with me came from Brezhnev, and that the Hungarian leader continued tamely on the Kremlin leash until the invasion. To think about that gives me no pleasure.

I went to Moscow on January 29. The invitation was to me alone, but I needed an assistant and took along a staffer of the Central Committee Secretariat. This was a courtesy visit of sorts, but without ceremony or transcription of our talks. I first met Brezhnev alone and then met with most of the Politburo. All the senior members of the Soviet leadership were there: Brezhnev, Podgorny, Kosygin, Suslov, Kirilenko, and Shelest.

Brezhnev asked me to tell them how I viewed the internal situation in Czechoslovakia and what my political plans were. Of course, I had prepared myself thoroughly for this, and, for the most part, I spoke without notes.

First, I tried to explain the historic and current conditions of our nations and what it meant to introduce socialism into a country such as Czechoslovakia, already so industrialized, at least in its western parts. Also, our society had long been accustomed to modern political institutions and a modern political culture. The existing political system did not fit our circumstances, I said, and had led to the growing tensions and conflicts that were the root of the stagnation and current crisis. Changes and corrections were absolutely essential if the socialist system was to function effectively in Czechoslovakia.

I carefully avoided all terms that would trigger hostility from these dogmatic Marxist-Leninists—such as *reform*, *reformist*, or *revision*. Instead, I consistently used words like *renewal* and *revival*, which I knew they could not connect to any "sinful" episode they might recall from the past. Naturally, I also refrained from citing Marx's own observations about the inappropriateness of Russia as a proving ground for socialism.

Nevertheless, as I watched the impassive and somber faces before me, I realized I wasn't getting through to them. These customers were too tough for me. In contrast to early postrevolutionary attitudes, late Stalinism was marked by a self-deceptive arrogance in relation to other countries. Stalin's heirs, like the master himself, believed that what was good for them had to be good for everybody else, and this made any other argument, however rational, quite useless in their company.

Fortunately, I was not unprepared for this obduracy, but I had not thought it would be quite so hopeless. As eloquently as I could, I tried to reassure them, pointing out that nothing my supporters and I planned was in any way directed against the interests of the Soviet Union, the Warsaw Pact, or economic cooperation within the Soviet bloc. What we wanted to do was necessitated by the special internal conditions in Czechoslovakia, nothing else. In conclusion, I asked for their understanding. We needed to be left alone to put our house in order. And that, I said, should be seen as a goal in harmony with the interests of the Soviet Union.

They did not say much, but I could sense that what I had told them was not what they would have liked to hear. Yet, there was no sign of open disagreement. No other problems were discussed, certainly not personnel questions, as Brezhnev was later to imply.

I returned to Prague the next day, and on my desk was another invitation to meet Kadar. As before, he was in a hurry, so we made arrangements to meet twice on February 4, in Komarno, on our side of the border, and in Komarom, across the Danube on the Hungarian side. Various officials joined us for the second meeting, and Kadar asked more questions about our reform plans. Some minor bilateral matters were also on the agenda, but essentially I think this was another probe on Kadar's part.

Almost simultaneously, Wladyslaw Gomulka, the first secretary of the Polish Communist Party, proposed that we get together. We quickly arranged for a meeting in Ostrava, in North Moravia close to the Polish border, on February 7.

I viewed Gomulka as a man who should have almost, if not quite, as much understanding of our problems as Kadar. He had been active in the underground Communist resistance during the Nazi occupation, and after the liberation, until 1948, he was the general secretary of the Polish Communist Party. In 1949 he became a victim of the Stalinist purges. He was not jailed like Kadar but was expelled from the Party and turned into a nonperson until 1956, when a national movement brought him back to power.

In 1968 Gomulka was sixty-three years old, and I knew that he had failed to meet the hopes of his early supporters. At the same time, I did not realize how adamantly he opposed reform; I only discovered this later. For the first and official part of our meeting, I was accompanied by Vladimir Koucky, the Czechoslovak Party secretary responsible for international relations. I described our reform plans in much the same words I had used with Kadar.

After dinner, Gomulka suggested that we two go for a walk. We put on our overcoats and walked around a nearby soccer stadium for over an hour. I do understand Polish, but Gomulka also spoke Russian, so there was no communication problem. I told him that, from shortly after the moment the Communist Party had assumed power in Czechoslovakia, we had been burdened with excessive repression. Horrible injustices had been committed and never redressed. The whole country groans as if under a heavy stone, I said, adding that I believed he would understand this better than people who had not experienced it.

In a quiet voice, he said he understood, so I continued.

"We have adopted no decision on this matter. What I am telling you I have been carrying in my head for a long time. I am determined to redress all the old crimes and injustices, whether they affected Communists or non-Communists, soldiers, civilians, partisans, men or women, Czechs or Slovaks. I believe that this is the indispensable first step in getting reform and democratization under way. There is no other way to renew confidence between the society and the Party."

Gomulka did not reply immediately, so we walked in silence for a while, until he asked me how many people I thought would be affected.

Many thousands, I said. In the first stage, we would engage the prosecution, the courts, parliamentary committees, Party organs, and national committees. Extrajudicial rehabilitation would follow.

"What do you mean by that?" Gomulka inquired.

By that, I said, I mean many people who were never put before a court but were persecuted in many other, often illegal ways.

Again Gomulka remained silent. Finally he said, "I understand in a moral and human sense. But I am afraid that all this would bring about uncontrollable political consequences. It could undermine the position of the Party."

I replied, "I envisage renewing confidence in a socialist society by putting the Party's position on new, democratic foundations."

Again, Gomulka said, "Yes, but . . ."

We parted in a friendly fashion, but I cannot get rid of the suspicion that he, too, hurried to inform Brezhnev about what I had told him. He no doubt felt unable to step over the line that would have allowed him to consider the possibility that the Communist Party could enjoy public support and confidence. In Poland, of course, unlike Czechoslovakia, such a situation was difficult to imagine.

The trip to Moscow and the meetings with Kadar and Gomulka marked a sort of halftime between the fall of Novotny and the breakthroughs that would come in April. It was still February; snow was on the ground, but politically we had just had an early thaw. Sadly, that was soon to change.

17

STOPOVER IN DRESDEN

T WO weeks after my meeting with Gomulka came the twentieth anniversary of the Communist takeover in Czechoslovakia, which, under the circumstances, had to be celebrated appropriately. Representatives of all the Communist Parties of the Soviet bloc were invited. As we worked on arrangements, Brezhnev himself called me, proposing that top leaders of the whole "socialist camp" take part in the celebration.

I didn't really know what the precedents were, but I confess that I welcomed his initiative. For one thing, the presence of all of these heads of state would give us an opportunity to reassure them that our reforms would not threaten their strategic interests, as well as to elicit their tacit approval of our subsequent steps.

Thus, I agreed with Brezhnev's suggestion, and he said that he would inform the other leaders, including Tito and representatives of the Yugoslav Union of Communists. Relations between the bloc and Tito were relatively good at that time. In the end, all the general secretaries came except Tito, who sent his deputy, Vlahovic.

It was customary for the speakers at such ceremonies to exchange the texts of their speeches beforehand, so, the day before the main ceremony, we sent the text of my speech to Brezhnev as well as to all the other leaders. In the speech, I cited the basic tenets of my proposed reform program. I used cautious formulations and employed the habitual jargon, but the ideas were undiluted. It was important to me that they would be articulated in Brezhnev's presence, which would make them automatically more acceptable to my opponents in the Presidium.

Because this was a ceremonial occasion, and the assembled leaders did not have the usual bureaucrats in tow, the sort of staffers who delight in mauling such documents were not on hand. And, time was short, which was also good.

Brezhnev sent my draft back a few hours later with objections to only two paragraphs, which were more explicit than other parts of the text. On rereading, I felt reassured that removal of those paragraphs would not weaken any of my substantive ideas, and I cut them without pain. *

Everything ran its normal, boring course during the ceremonies, the only dissonant note being struck by Walter Ulbricht, the East German boss, who was openly critical of our plans for economic reforms during a dinner at Prague Castle. But this mattered little; no one thought of Ulbricht as an economic expert.

At about this time, our domestic political life was jarred by a scandal of shocking proportions, the Sejna affair. General Jan Sejna, head of the Czechoslovak Party Main Committee in the Ministry of Defense, had been a pro-Novotny plotter during the December and January sessions of the Central Committee. Now the military prosecutor's office had assembled enough evidence about his black market sales of army supplies of grass and clover seeds to start formal proceedings against him.

I did not involve myself with this affair as it took its natural course. I could only imagine how easily Sejna and his best buddy, Novotny Jr., would have suppressed the scandal if Novotny had still been in power. But Sejna and his stolen seeds were not above the law anymore. The wheels of justice turned too slowly, however, and before the anniversary celebration was over, Sejna took his mistress and ran off to the West. Soon news of the defection made headlines across the country. Censors were no longer there to stop it.

The general's connection with the family of President Novotny was, of course, the most sensitive part of the affair. Very soon the media started demanding Novotny's resignation from his remaining office, and pressure for the resignations of his well-known cronies also mounted.

New radio and television programs were now launched, encouraging calls from listeners and viewers. Public meetings attended by thousands of people, especially the young, further broadened the involvement of ordinary citizens in the affairs of state. Thus, the political climate changed dramatically in a few weeks. The most immediate impact, from my perspective, was the weakening of the conservative bloc in the Party Presidium.

I decided to take advantage of all this without delay, and, at a Presidium

---

* In his memoirs, Vasil Bilak makes much of this affair, but he was not aware of the whole context; he only acted as a messenger.

meeting on March 14, I proposed a general rehabilitation of all citizens who had been victimized by past repressions. Again, there was no direct opposition. A formal vote was not taken, but I considered the proposal approved. The task of promulgating the necessary judicial measures was immediately referred to appropriate government agencies. The final version of the Action Program was also approved, as I had expected. It still, however, needed ratification by the Central Committee, which was to meet next at the beginning of April.

At the same time, a number of important personnel changes in the Party apparatus and in public and state organizations became possible. In Slovakia, where Vasil Bilak had in mid-January taken my place as Slovak Party first secretary, there were public calls for the ouster of my old adversary, Novotny's ally Michal Chudik. He was still chairman of the Slovak National Council, but by mid-March, not even allowed to jump, he was pushed from office.

The pressure to replace the best-known opponents of reforms steadily mounted. There were calls to fire Jozef Lenart, the prime minister, and leading officials of the Trade Union Council, the Union of Youth, and the Union of Czechoslovak Journalists were forced to resign. Along with public demands for Novotny's resignation from the presidency came sharp criticism of the attorney general, the ministers of defense and the interior, and other officials in key positions.

The new spirit of openness also revived Slovak demands for a revision of the constitution of 1960 and for renewal of the rightful role of Slovak national institutions. Federalization of the state became the top Slovak priority during Prague Spring. A significant step in that direction was the rerecognition of Bratislava as the capital of Slovakia by a decree of the National Assembly in March.

These developments started to have inevitable international implications and to create unrest among our allies. In East Berlin, Ulbricht and his Politburo had become nervous about our changes as early as January; their reaction was to be expected given their internal situation. For the Soviets, it was somewhat different.

Under Novotny and his predecessors, the Soviets had been permitted to control the Czechoslovak armed forces and secret police in various ways, which included an implicit "right" to approve key appointments. It was apparently not until mid-March that they realized that their proxies might be fired and replaced without their consent and decided to step in. I base this hindsight estimate of their timing on what *didn't* happen at a Warsaw Pact meeting on March 6 and 7 in Sofia, which I attended with Jozef Lenart, Minister of Foreign Affairs Vaclav David, and Minister of National

Defense General Bohumir Lomsky. No one made any reference to the situation in Czechoslovakia, the business of the meeting proceeded as usual, and the only ripple was Romania's criticism of the way the mechanism of the pact was functioning.

The critic was, of course, Nicolae Ceausescu, general secretary of the Romanian Communist Party. I listened to his speech very attentively. I shared his views without reservation, but silently. What bothered Ceausescu was the Soviets' total domination of the pact, with almost no command authority assigned to the allies. Eventually we would have to raise the same question, but in March 1968 we had different priorities from Ceausescu, to whom internal reforms were apparently of little importance. To come out in support of Ceausescu at that moment and on that issue would immediately have been interpreted as a sign of Czechoslovak retreat from treaty obligations, and that, I knew, would be a tactical folly. I do feel obliged to say that no matter what happened in the years to come, Ceausescu's independent stand at that time required great courage, and it was very important for me under the circumstances.

The Soviets obviously decided to apply direct pressure on me between the Sofia conference and March 16, when Brezhnev sent me an invitation to come to Moscow with a full delegation of the Czechoslovak Communist leadership and the state government. Oddly, he proposed no date, but it now seems to me that the Soviet Politburo was not yet quite in agreement on how to proceed with us. Evidence to support this view comes from the fact that, two days after I received Brezhnev's letter, General Lomsky received a similar invitation from his Soviet counterpart, Marshal Grechko, asking him to bring a delegation of the Czechoslovak High Command to Moscow. When Lomsky asked me what to do about Grechko's invitation, I advised him not to accept it for the time being; I wanted to wait for the prospective top-level conference. Before the date could be set, Brezhnev telephoned me and changed the invitation for a bilateral meeting to one for a conference of East European countries to be held in Dresden on March 23. I asked him what the agenda would be, and he said that we would take up economic cooperation within the bloc. There was just enough time for preparation.

I received no further calls or letters from Brezhnev or other leaders of the bloc countries. I composed our delegation with a view to economic affairs. I took with me Prime Minister Jozef Lenart; the chairman of the State Planning Commission, Oldrich Cernik; Drahomir Kolder, the Central Committee secretary responsible for planning the national economy; and Vasil Bilak, first secretary of the Slovak Communist Party.

Dresden used to be renowned for its art treasures, its architecture, and its streetcars, on which, for some reason, a one-hour ride was believed to cure kidney stones. How many of these attractions survived the massive Allied air raid in February 1945 I cannot tell. Ulbricht's hospitality did not extend to sightseeing. It was all strictly business—and unexpected business.

Soon after the conference started, I found out that Brezhnev had lied to me on two counts. First, not all the East European countries were in attendance. The representatives of Romania were not there, and Yugoslavia, which usually sent observers to all bloc conferences on economic affairs, was also absent. As it turned out, economic cooperation was not on the agenda.

Instead of talking about five-year plans and other perennial themes, Walter Ulbricht opened the conference by saying that at issue was the situation in Czechoslovakia. I got so angry at the knavish way Brezhnev had fooled me that I was tempted to walk out, but I forced myself to calm down and wait.

I have read criticism of my going to the Dresden conference because it established the pattern of the "court of The Five." The real question for me is whether it was not a mistake to sit there after it became so clear that I'd been deceived. I am still not quite sure, but the fact is that the Dresden conference established no pattern. There was no court and no verdict. There were accusers and there was a rebuttal, nothing more and nothing less. I believe that the importance of the meeting has been exaggerated.

After Ulbricht's opening sermon, Brezhnev spoke, succeeded by Wladyslaw Gomulka, Janos Kadar, and Todor Zhivkov, the leader of the Bulgarian Communist Party. Each had a thick file of clippings from the Czech and Slovak press, which he occasionally culled for a suitable quotation to illustrate his exasperation. With varying intensity, they attacked us for "losing control" over our situation and permitting a diversity of opinion that, in their view, bordered on "counterrevolution." Mixed in were the usual references to "outside threats to the socialist camp."

I noted with regret that the harshest criticism came from Gomulka, with Ulbricht only a little less arrogant. Brezhnev put on the face of the worried parent, but he was as stinging as Gomulka or Ulbricht in what he actually said.

I noticed that Brezhnev was flanked not only by senior members of his Politburo but also by several marshals and generals of the Soviet Army. This was quite unusual at a conference that was not a formal Warsaw Pact meeting, and I realized they were instruments of none too subtle intimidation.

After they had all had their say, I took the floor. I could not resist observing that the agenda was not exactly what had been announced. I looked at Brezhnev, but he seemed to be busy taking notes. Then I turned to the substance of the matter. I said that it was altogether wrong to confuse the press—and a very selective reading of it, at that—and the policy of a state. Since we had abolished censorship, which was entirely our internal affair, neither the Party leadership nor the government could determine the contents of the newspapers. That was the journalists' business. Our business was to manage the affairs of the state, to protect citizens' rights and well-being, and to run a prosperous economy.

Given freedom of the press, people will always express different opinions. In government, we were having to get used to facing critical views, but we considered this a positive, not a negative phenomenon. A free press was for us a political corrective. Since all that we did was for the people, we felt we should let the people say what they wanted.

I had not heard any criticism of our external policy at this meeting, I continued. We were faithful to our foreign obligations and remained a firm part of the alliance, which was a much more relevant criterion of state policy. Also, we had not changed our fundamental socialist orientation. We were simply adding democratic norms to it.

I paused, then turned to countering the criticism that had been leveled against some of my colleagues, especially Josef Smrkovsky and Jiri Pelikan. I said that these attacks were entirely unsubstantiated. I pointed out that Smrkovsky was an old, prewar member of the Communist Party. He had behaved with great courage during the Nazi occupation and had been one of the leaders of the uprising in Prague in May 1945. He had been unjustly persecuted in the early 1950s, and in the years since had faithfully served his country and the cause of socialism. He was a member of the Central Committee of the Czechoslovak Communist Party and enjoyed the great confidence of the Czechoslovak public. No one had the right to question his integrity and honest intentions.

I similarly defended Jiri Pelikan, who was then director general of Czechoslovak television. I said that for years Pelikan had been general secretary of the International Union of Students, and his loyalty should be well known to all those present.

Finally, I told them that we had accomplished our work on the new political platform of the Czechoslovak Communist Party, the Action Program, and that it would be discussed by the next session of the Central Committee. As soon as the document was published, I said, they could judge for themselves our overall policy plans.

The conference ended in a cool mood. There were no conclusions, no joint declaration, only a very formal final communiqué. We disagreed completely.

Back home I did not allow the Dresden remonstrations to inhibit our reforms. My colleagues and I felt that, as long as we met our external obligations, we could continue to insist on our right to make our own domestic decisions. Thus, reform developments continued to follow their course. The legal framework for a general rehabilitation of victims of past injustices was prepared by the end of March. Free media provided a wide platform for the expression of public opinion for the first time since 1948. Substantive personnel decisions were adopted at the Central Committee sessions that started on March 28 and continued at the beginning of April.

Under public pressure, Novotny now resigned the presidency, and in his place we recommended Army General Ludvik Svoboda, who was elected by the National Assembly on March 30. Svoboda, then seventy-three, was a professional soldier who had commanded the Czechoslovak Army in Russia during World War II. Also a victim of policies from the early 1950s, he had been demoted from minister of defense to accountant in a farming cooperative. Svoboda enjoyed widespread respect, and, despite what happened several months later, I do not think that there was at that moment a better suited candidate for president.

Six of the ten members of the old Presidium—Novotny, Hendrych, Chudik, Lastovicka, Simunek, and Dolansky—were replaced at the April session of the Central Committee meeting. With the exception of Dolansky, this was the hard core of the Novotny team. A new Presidium was elected: Frantisek Barbirek, Vasil Bilak, Oldrich Cernik, Drahomir Kolder, Frantisek Kriegel, Jan Piller, Emil Rigo, Josef Smrkovsky, Josef Spacek, Oldrich Svestka, and myself. All three candidate members selected in April—Lenart, Kapek, and Vaculik—were leftovers from Novotny's times. Vaculik lost his position very soon as a consequence of the election of a new first secretary of the Party's city organization in Prague. The new man was Bohumil Simon, a strong supporter of reforms.

I was confirmed in my post of first secretary, and other new secretaries were also elected—Cestmir Cisar, Drahomir Kolder, and Stefan Sadovsky. Cisar was an intellectual who had gone through several ups and downs in his political career and most recently had been ambassador to Bucharest. Sadovsky, a Slovak, was personally very close to me; we had worked together in Bratislava. Both Cisar and Sadovsky stood on the side of reforms; Sadovsky was more consistent, however; Cisar tended to vacillate, particularly after the invasion.

New members of the Secretariat, who in the end would either execute or obstruct our reforms, also included Evzen Erban, Alois Indra, Zdenek Mlynar, Vaclav Slavik, and Oldrich Volenik. Erban was a former Social Democrat of the pre-1948 era who had held a number of political and administrative positions. He had a reputation as a pure opportunist. Indra, some say, was an obvious Soviet agent from the beginning, and he would play a very nasty role in August. But I remembered him as a man who had occasionally dared to oppose Novotny, and in April 1968 I accepted him mainly because he was recommended by Kolder (at that time still an ally). Mlynar is best known for his memoir of 1968, *The Cold Comes from the Kremlin*. While his account of that year is not very reliable, the fact is that Mlynar's contribution to the preparation of some of the parts of the Action Program was important. Slavik and Volenik supported me completely.

Milos Jakes, a former deputy minister of the interior, was elected chairman of the Party's Central Auditing Commission, a powerful office under certain circumstances. He was to become better known in 1989 as the grave digger of the Husak regime. Oldrich Cernik took over the office of the prime minister, Josef Smrkovsky was elected chairman of the National Assembly, and Frantisek Kriegel became chairman of the National Front, that grouping of Communist and non-Communist political parties important in the years before 1948 but largely ceremonial since then.

Kriegel was a physician who had served as a military surgeon with the Spanish Republican Army. During World War II he served in China under contract to the United States Army as a physician with the Kuomintang forces. Kriegel was born to a Jewish family in Russian Poland before the First World War, but he was raised in Czechoslovakia, got his diploma at Charles University, and was a prewar member of the Communist Party. He was firm and consistent in putting our reforms into practice until the August invasion and even beyond it.

Naturally, not all these departures and promotions were the result of public pressures. I was able to bring into top positions a number of my political allies, and many other appointments were the products of inevitable compromise. After all, we still had the same old Central Committee, which could not be replaced without a Party congress. That was an issue that had to wait. *

Compromise or not, the new Presidium, still the most important institution in the country, differed substantially from the old one. Its core— Barbirek, Cernik, Kriegel, Smrkovsky, and Spacek—now stood firmly behind the reforms. With only one exception, Cernik, all stayed with me until the end.

The situation in the Presidium was admittedly not all roses. Kolder had

---

* The convocation of the congress *before* the regularly scheduled term in 1970 had to be justified by demands from one third of the district and regional Party organizations; this happened in May.

been moving closer to the Soviet position since the beginning of March, and Bilak and Rigo were already there. Piller held mostly centrist positions but tilted to my side. Svestka, the chief editor of *Rude Pravo*, the Party daily, had taken part in the struggle against Novotny but at the time of his election to the Presidium was already moving away from his pro-reform stance. He was very unpopular among intellectuals and even with his own editors and reporters and was frequently criticized in public and in the press. This accelerated his political turnaround between March and August, when he hit the bottom of his career by joining the pro-Soviet conspiracy.

The new government, I should say, was better tailored for the tasks ahead than the Party leadership. In the old system, the government stood below the Party Presidium in terms of actual authority, but it was more in the public eye. The conservative forces were better able to resist reform appointments in the Presidium than in the government. But the government was subject to the approval of the National Assembly, and by April 1968 that was no longer a pure formality. Our new political program gave the government much more direct power and independence.

At least some members of the new government deserve attention here, for they represented the new blood under the still old-line Novotnyite Prime Minister Jozef Lenart, whose days were numbered.

Ota Sik became a deputy prime minister. There were suggestions that he should become a member of the Party Presidium, but I believed that his economic expertise made him much better suited for a place in the government.

Gustav Husak also became a deputy prime minister. As I already mentioned, in 1964 he had refused a ministerial position despite my encouragement. Now he seemed to feel differently. In January 1968, shortly after I replaced Novotny in Prague, he sent me a letter of congratulations in which he said that he was prepared to return to political life. In February I instructed Bilak to ask Husak what he would like to do. Husak's answer was, "Anything, even in Prague." Thus, when the personnel changes were carried out in April, I remembered him.

There was a new minister of culture, Miroslav Galuska; a new minister of education, Professor Vladimir Kadlec; and a new minister of foreign affairs, Professor Jiri Hajek—all three of solid liberal reputation. We also replaced the ministers of national defense and of the interior. The new minister of defense was General Martin Dzur, a Slovak whom I had known rather well and who had actively resisted the coup attempt in December 1967 and January 1968. Dzur's behavior in August 1968 is, however, not entirely clear.

The new minister of the interior was Josef Pavel, an officer in the

International Brigades during the Spanish Civil War and another victim of the repression of the early 1950s. He had spent several years in prison but was never broken by torture, and he was an extremely honest man.

It goes without saying that the Soviets were not overjoyed by these changes. Pavel, for example, soon initiated a number of measures limiting the extralegal activities of State Security. That reduced Soviet control over the secret police, and soon the Soviets put Pavel's name on their hit list. After the invasion, President Svoboda apparently saved Pavel's life by hiding him in the presidential country seat in Lany.

The sessions of the Central Committee at the end of March and the beginning of April represented a watershed of sorts. The first stage of our struggle, begun in October 1967, had been brought to a largely successful conclusion, and the worst internal obstacles to reforms were gone. The Action Program had been adopted, and reformist forces had prevailed in the Presidium. The old Central Committee was still on the fence, but once a new Party congress assembled, with candidates reflecting the massive grass-roots support for our efforts, this blockage too would be gone.

We were seriously engaged in correcting the injustices of the past, and we had a good program to revive our economy. Public confidence in the Party's goodwill and good intentions was rising, as May Day testified. But the clouds of Dresden continued to throw their shadows on these sunny spring days.

(Top): Dubcek's birthplace in the western Slovak village of Uhrovec; also the birthplace of Ludovit Stur, the founder of Slovak nationalism in the early 1800s.
(Above, left): Julius and Alexander Dubcek as toddlers with their parents in Pishpek (now Bishkek), Kirghizia, c. 1924.
(Above, right): Dubcek at age eighteen in Trencin.
Uncredited photos are from the author's collection.

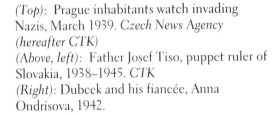

(Top): Prague inhabitants watch invading
Nazis, March 1939. *Czech News Agency
(hereafter CTK)*
(Above, left): Father Josef Tiso, puppet ruler of
Slovakia, 1938–1945. *CTK*
(Right): Dubcek and his fiancée, Anna
Ondrisova, 1942.

(Above): Last known photo of Julius
Dubcek, far left, with fellow Slovak
partisans, 1944.
(Left): Dubcek's emaciated father,
Stefan, on his release from Mauthausen
prison camp, May 1945.

(*Above*): Marchers in the 1950 May Day parade in Prague carry portraits of Gottwald and Stalin. *CTK*

(*Opposite, above*): Trencin, in western Slovakia, where the Dubceks lived from 1945–1951, and again from 1955–1958. *Slovenske Vydavatelsto Literatury*

(*Opposite, below*): Class photo at the Higher Political School in Moscow, July 1958. (Dubcek is seventh from left.)

Группа выпускников – отличников Высшей Партийной Школы при ЦК КПСС. Слева направо М. Пожарскас, П. Петров, А. Карла-бснева, В. Коча, Н. Нлимуова, З. Сояк, А. Дубчек, И. Муртузаев, Ф. Аглов, В. Холявчук, А. Майорова, К. Козуб, И. Микулович, К. Ива-нов, И. Пушкэ, П. Уханов.

г. Москва, июль 1958 года

(*Above*): Family photo from the 1950s showing Dubcek with his three sons, Pavol, Peter, and Milan.
(*Opposite, above*): Bratislava. *Pavel Breier*
(*Opposite, below*): Khrushchev walking between Dubcek and Novotny during the celebration in Banska Bystrica of the twentieth anniversary of the Slovak National Uprising, August 1964, shortly before Khrushchev's ouster.

(Above): The Tatra Mountains, near Javorina. *Slovenske Vydavatelsto Literatury*
(Left): Dubcek and a forester with the famous bear, near Javorina in the Tatra Mountains, 1966.
(Below): Antonin Novotny addressing the Thirteenth Czechoslovak Party Congress, 1966. *CTK*

(Above): Reform economist Ota Sik, 1968. *CTK*

(Right): Antonin Novotny (left) with wavering ally Jiri Hendrych, 1967. *CTK*

(Left): Dubcek with Hungarian leader Janos Kadar, Prague, 1968. *CTK*
(Below): At twentieth anniversary celebration of 1948 Communist takeover: Brezhnev, Dubcek, Dolansky, Novotny, and Ulbricht (obscured) in the front row. *UPI/Bettmann Newsphotos*

Gomulka, Kosygin, Zhivkov, Dubcek, and Brezhnev at the Sofia summit, March 7, 1968.
AP/Wide World Photos

Euphoria: May Day, 1968 (In parade picture from left to right: Husak, Svoboda, Dubcek, Kriegel, Piller). *CTK* (*opposite, below and above*)

Bohemian Forest troop
maneuvers, June 1968. *CTK*
(both)

(Above and right): Czechoslovak leaders and citizens pondering the reply to the hostile July 14 Warsaw Letter from The Five. *CTK (both)*

(Left): Dubcek and Brezhnev at Cierna. CTK
(Below): Smrkovsky and Cernik conferring as Dubcek looks on outside the Cierna train station. *Oldrich Jaros*
(Bottom): Dubcek taking leave of Podgorny at Cierna. CTK

18

FROM SPRING TO SUMMER

SWEEPING as the personnel changes were, the Action Program was the single most important outcome of the Central Committee session in April 1968. Without exaggeration one might say that it was the heartbeat of Prague Spring. The resolution that accompanied the document talked of a new political course "for the nearest future," but even a quick reading today shows that it was much more than that: it marked a historic reversal. It laid the foundations for an entirely new approach to the solution of almost all the basic problems in Czech and Slovak society.

"Nearest future" meant the period between the April session of the Central Committee and the Fourteenth Party Congress, originally scheduled for 1970. The new situation required that the congress be convened much earlier. The question of when now became one of the crucial political issues of Prague Spring.

Naturally, our Dresden critics did not permit the publication of our Action Program in their countries and suppressed all references to it. One could easily understand their apprehensions: the program was a unique document in the history of the so-called international Communist movement. No other Communist Party anywhere had prepared such a comprehensive and principled program of departure from the theory and practice of Leninism-Stalinism. Ours was a plan for gradual return to the concept of democratic socialism, as it had prevailed in the European socialist movement at the turn of the century.

Some Western European Communist Parties—namely in Italy, Spain, and to some degree France—were also shedding the unfortunate legacy of the Communist International at this time, but their situation could not be compared with ours. Their only form of bondage was material support from Moscow (which, in the case of the Italian Communist Party, was already insignificant). In contrast, all Eastern European bloc parties were tied to the Soviet Party by a powerful and pervasive network of loyalists and agents at all levels. As much as these parties were at the center of local power structures, the Soviets not only penetrated each Party's official apparatus but also controlled key positions in the armed forces, security forces, foreign service, and so on, which, of course, made any attempt at independent action extremely difficult.

The Action Program did not even touch on the possibility of an independent initiative in foreign policy; for now this was a secondary issue. It focused entirely on domestic problems, political, economic, or cultural. Even in these areas, however, the Soviets had been accustomed to meddle. It was obvious that they were not happy that the program had been composed without their advice and consent.

Of course, the document could not be a provocation. Czech and Slovak reformers were not out of their minds. Neither domestic nor external conditions would permit outright rejection of Soviet doctrine. The language we used was low key and cautious, and we made a sufficient number of ritual references to customary Marxist-Leninist notions. The program was heretical, but we did everything not to make it look that way.

As stated explicitly in the preamble, the Action Program was rooted in Czechoslovak reality and grew out of our dearly bought experiences over the past years. That may sound obvious today, but to refer to our own conditions as the basis of our actions was in itself a very bold proposition at that time. Until then, Soviet example and practice were the required mandatory models, with ethnic "peculiarities" considered nothing more than decoration.

The program declared an end to dictatorial, sectarian, and bureaucratic ways. It said that such practices had created artificial tension in society, antagonizing different social groups, nations, and nationalities. Our new policy had to be built on democratic cooperation and confidence among social groups. Narrow professional or other interests could no longer take priority. Freedom of assembly and association, guaranteed in the constitution but not respected in the past, had to be put into practice. In this sphere, there were to be no extralegal limitations.

The program proclaimed a return to freedom of the press and proposed the adoption of a press law that would clearly exclude prepublication censorship. Opinions expressed in mass communications were to be free and not be confused with official government pronouncements.

Freedom of movement was to be guaranteed, including not only citizens' right to travel abroad but their right to stay abroad at length, or even permanently, without being labeled emigrants. Special legal norms were to be established for the redress of all past injustices, judicial as well as political.

Looking toward a new relationship between the Czechs and the Slovaks, there was to be a federalization of the Republic, full renewal of Slovak national institutions, and compensatory safeguards for the minority Slovaks in staffing federal bodies.

In the economic sphere, the program demanded thorough decentralization and managerial independence of enterprises, as well as legalization of small-scale private enterprise, especially in the service sector.

This proposal, I should say, was immediately viewed by the Soviets as the beginning of a return to capitalism. Brezhnev made this accusation directly during one of our conversations in the coming months. I responded that we needed a private sector to improve the market situation and make people's lives easier. Brezhnev immediately snapped at me, "Small craftsmen? We know about that! Your Mr. Bata used to be a little shoemaker, too, until he started up a factory!" Here was the old Leninist canon about small private production creating capitalism "every day and every hour." There was nothing one could do to change the Soviets' dogmatic paranoia.

These were, in summary, the main ideas of the Action Program; the document itself ran to over sixty pages.* One restraint has to be kept in mind; we were in no position even to hint at wanting a return to multiparty democracy. In the eyes of the Soviets, that would have been synonymous with the dismantling of socialism. The monopoly of power euphemistically termed "the leading role" of the Party was fundamental to Soviet Communist Party doctrine. In the months to come, their primary objection to our reforms was that we were "losing the leading role." To move out of this fenced area of operation would have required changes in our external situation that were difficult even to imagine; we did not have the conveniently removed geography of Yugoslavia. Even before 1948, our political system had been severely restricted by the exclusive nature of the National Front. But in 1948 the National Front was deprived of its authority as the non-Communist parties lost all influence and independence.

That was the situation we inherited in 1968 and accepted as a point of departure. We proposed to establish a more equal relationship within the National Front. This could have served as a first step toward the revival of a nonexclusive partnership of social and political forces. We could not then go any further, but the principles of full respect for constitutional freedoms,

---

* See The Action Program, p. 287.

rule of law, freedom of the press, and freedom of association indicated clearly our expected direction.

Neither my allies nor I ever contemplated a dismantling of socialism, even as we parted company with various tenets of Leninism. We still believed in a socialism that could not be divorced from democracy, because its essential rationale was social justice. We also believed that socialism could function better in a market-oriented environment, with significant elements of private enterprise. Many legitimate forms of ownership, mainly cooperative and communal, had not been used to any effective extent mainly because of the imposition of Stalinist restrictions.

As for the Party, we believed that by working for the rectification of past injustices, and by honest and truthful political action, it would regain the trust it had once enjoyed. Even in a system of open electoral competition, we believed that we would get the support of a very significant part of the population. It is still my opinion that our self-confidence was justified.

I will never forget the May Day celebration in Prague in 1968. My wife, who watched the parade from a viewing stand, also remembered the day with deep emotion. After years of staged productions, this was a voluntary "happening." No one herded people into columns marching under centrally designed and fabricated catchwords. This time people came on their own, carrying their own banners with their own slogans, some cheerful, some critical, some just humorous. The mood was relaxed and joyful. Colors and flowers, unseen in past years, abounded everywhere you looked. Even Mother Nature blessed the day with sun, warmth, and bright blue skies. I was overwhelmed by the spontaneous expressions of sympathy and support from the crowd as they passed the low platform where the other leaders and I were standing.

I remember the members of two of the new organizations—the Club of Engaged Non-Party People (KAN) and K-231, an association of former political prisoners—who walked around under slogans expressing their full support for my policy. I was truly touched. I think of it occasionally nowadays when I see KAN moving to the extreme Right under the leadership of people who have no idea what the year 1968 was all about.

I couldn't help reflecting on the fact that I was the first Slovak in the office of Czechoslovak first secretary, then the most powerful position in the country. And Prague was a Czech city, and I was reviewing a Czech May Day celebration. For these reasons it was twice as important for me to see such sympathy and friendly support.

✻   ✻   ✻

After assuming Novotny's office, I had taken a single room in downtown Prague in the Hotel Praha, which was then operated by a department of the Central Committee. I spent only a few hours there every night after work. In Prague, as in Bratislava, mine was the last window to go dark in the monumental Central Committee building, on the south bank of the Vltava, where the river bends eastward. Each Saturday when official duties allowed, I traveled to Bratislava to spend the weekend with my family, returning on Monday morning.

After several weeks the protocol officials suggested that I move to more appropriate quarters. My room at the hotel was so modest that I could not even receive visitors there, they said, and wouldn't it also be better if my family could stay with me? I did not pay much attention and said I would think about it. But they came back again in a week or so, more insistent. I agreed on the condition that they find a reasonable place where I could move with my wife and sons.

They showed me several houses that were obviously too big for my family's needs and my taste. After some time they found a modest house in the suburb of Troja, with four bedrooms, a living room, and a kitchen. It belonged to the government and had once been inhabited by Prime Minister Viliam Siroky. In spring 1968 the house was empty. Anna, Peter, Milan, and I moved there in April. Pavol, our eldest son, had just entered Comenius University medical school in Bratislava, so he stayed there, with my mother to care for him.

After the restructuring of the leading Party bodies and of the government in April 1968, we were ready to implement the Action Program. Soviet lobbying and personal considerations were gradually pushing people like Bilak, Kolder, and Rigo to oppose the program's realization. A new configuration in the Presidium took shape very quickly; my most reliable allies in this period were Josef Smrkovsky, Frantisek Barbirek, Frantisek Kriegel, Oldrich Cernik, and Jan Piller. In the Secretariat, the situation was much less favorable, with Drahomir Kolder, Jozef Lenart, and Alois Indra forming an antireform bloc. Only Stefan Sadovsky and Vaclav Slavik were consistently on my side.

The issue always close to my heart was the progress of rehabilitations, which I tried to speed up as much as possible. In mid-May a group of high officers of the Czechoslovak Army who in 1949 had been unjustly purged on the basis of tainted evidence were fully rehabilitated. The best known of these men was General Karel Kutlvasr, a pre-World War II officer who in May 1945 had been the military commander of the Prague uprising.

Before the end of May, a draft law on judicial rehabilitation was endorsed by the government and soon afterwards approved by the parliament. At the end of June, resistance fighters who had been summarily removed from the armed forces in the early 1950s, were fully reinstated. At the same time, several writers and journalists, victims of the same repressions, were also rehabilitated. Among them was the son of the well-known painter Alfons Mucha.

At the end of July, the Supreme Court posthumously annulled two shameful death penalties of the post-1948 era. One of these victims was Dr. Milada Horakova, a National Assembly deputy for the Socialist Party who had been falsely accused of high treason. She was the only woman ever executed for political reasons in Czechoslovakia. The other was Zavis Kalandra, a leftist writer and literary critic. Also, members of the national ice hockey team who were falsely accused of treason in 1950 and jailed for several years were all fully rehabilitated in June 1968. More rehabilitations followed along Party lines in July, and just before the Soviet invasion, on August 19, Josef Pavel, as minister of the interior, created the administrative framework for a general judicial rehabilitation of all innocent victims of Stalinist repression.

We continued to pursue this effort even after the Soviet occupation, and it was not stopped until the Husak regime was installed in April 1969. I was very pleased to see that soon after the collapse of the old regime in December 1989 this effort was renewed and is gradually being brought to completion. Lives cannot be brought back, and suffering cannot be entirely healed or forgotten. But at least we tried to do our best to help those who could still be helped and to set the record straight.

Another internal problem was the demand of a group of younger Social Democrats to be allowed legally to renew their activities as a political party. Alas, this was an internal problem with inescapable external implications. It was the left wing of the Czechoslovak Social Democrats that had split away in 1921 to found the Communist Party. In the interwar period, the two parties remained antagonists, and soon after Munich both were suppressed.

In December 1943, President Benes, while in Moscow signing the new alliance with the USSR, reached an agreement with the exiled leadership of the Czechoslovak Communist Party on a substantial simplification of the prewar party system.

Among the parties permitted to continue operating were the Communists and the Social Democrats. They worked together quite closely until 1947, when a new leadership steered the Social Democrats on a more independent course, although a rather strong left wing still leaned toward the Communists. After the takeover in 1948, the Czech Social Democrats were forced to integrate into the Czechoslovak Communist Party, the same fate that had greeted Social Democratic parties everywhere in Eastern

Europe after the war.

In Slovakia, Social Democrats and Communists had joined in one Communist Party of Slovakia during the Slovak National Uprising of 1944.

The Social Democratic Party demand to be relegalized in 1968 was of course a by-product of the political climate created by our reform policy. The Social Democrats were trying the limits of our policy. In their eyes, it was a test of our good faith. But our good faith was not the only factor; the situation was not so simple.

Since the late 1920s and early 1930s, Stalin and the Communist movement, inspired by Lenin, had been obsessed by a hostility toward Socialists and Social Democrats. Years after Stalin's death, and even after Khrushchev's de-Stalinization, this hostility had yet to be overcome, especially among older Party members. There was no way to ram approval of the renewal of the Socialist Party through the Communist Party Central Committee in the spring or summer 1968. And there is no need to say that, in Brezhnev's Moscow, Socialists remained a full-sized bogey.

I myself had great respect for such Western European Social Democrats of this time as Olof Palme and Willy Brandt. Whether a formal renewal of the Social Democratic Party in our situation was desirable at that time I was not so sure. With our Action Program, we were moving in their direction anyway. I think it's appropriate to mention that twenty years later and under changed conditions it was my natural choice to join the Social Democratic Party in Slovakia.

But in spring 1968 the situation was different. I did not see how we could possibly satisfy the Social Democrats without provoking our opponents both at home and in Moscow to attack us. At the same time, however, I took no administrative measures to discourage the Social Democrats from trying to organize themselves, though I did try to persuade them to wait for a more favorable moment.

Naturally, I could not negotiate with the Social Democrats myself. In the Central Committee there were dozens of questionable characters who watched all my moves. It was less difficult for Frantisek Kriegel, as chairman of the National Front, and Josef Smrkovsky, as chairman of the National Assembly, to discuss the matter with them. I thought it was appropriate to talk to the Social Democrats at the party level as well, so I asked Bohumil Simon, the newly elected first secretary of the Prague city committee of the Party and a candidate member of the Presidium, to do so, discreetly and without unnecessary publicity.

The Social Democrats' spokesmen were Premysl Janyr and Zdenek Bechyne, sons of two older-generation socialist politicians. Simon met them several times. He asked them to understand our situation and to avoid actions that would cause too much public attention. Simon could go further than Smrkovsky and Kriegel, who were bound to the official viewpoint. He assured them that I and other reformers in the Party leadership were well beyond the old Communist hostility toward Social Democrats. We understood the importance of plurality of opinion, but we still had to proceed cautiously. Simon asked the Social Democrats to wait until after the next Communist Party congress, when there should be a friendlier atmosphere.

I think they understood, even when, in June 1968, we had to issue public statements rejecting the idea of the revival of the Socialist Party. No other measures were taken against them—even at a later point, when they created, without authorization, a preparatory Central Committee. At least they did not launch an aggressive public campaign in pursuit of their demands. And soon the intensification of our dispute with the Soviets made our point even more understandable to them.

During this period we also made encouraging progress toward the much needed codification of Czecho-Slovak relations within the Republic. In line with the Action Program, practical steps were taken to federalize the state. At the end of April, the Czechoslovak Communist Party Presidium approved a blueprint of the next steps, including the drafting of a constitutional law no later than June 20. It was also decided to have the law approved on the fiftieth anniversary of the creation of Czechoslovakia, October 28, 1968.

The preparation of Czech national bodies within the new federation was entrusted to a special Czech committee, which was formed at the beginning of May. At the end of June, the National Assembly approved a law on the preparation of the federative framework of the state. In that, the creation of a Czech National Council as a counterpart of the Slovak National Council was approved. A parliamentary commission started to work on a new constitution.

The restructuring of the state was on the agenda of almost every meeting of the Presidium until just before the invasion, the last being on August 13, 1968. Neither the Soviets nor their Czech proxies obstructed this side of our reform policy, but that does not say they liked it. They were simply too busy fretting over other reforms that they found even more alarming, such as the abolition of censorship. But they did oppose the move toward decentralization, and, when they regained full control after 1969, they deprived the new federal setup of any practical meaning. Centralized power was reestablished, and until 1989 federation was to remain largely a formality.

The necessity to convene the Fourteenth Party Congress early, in an extraordinary session, had been clear to me since the moment I assumed the office of first secretary. The congress and its timing were matters of strategic importance both domestically and externally and for both pro- and anti-reformers. If permitted to hold the congress, the reform forces would gain decisive control of leading Party organs; that would, at the same time, substantially reduce the Soviet fifth column in the Party.

Any substantive decision the Party might adopt, including the election of the Presidium and the Secretariat, had to be approved by the Central Committee. The Central Committee that I inherited had been elected in 1966, too many of its members were Novotny's appointees, and its latent majority always remained opposed to reforms. Beginning in March, public opinion helped to force this majority to retreat in a number of ways, but the body remained an uncertain component of further development. The only way to change this situation was to convene an extraordinary Party congress to elect a new Central Committee.

At the same time, I was suspicious of bandwagon reformers and other opportunists. Having freed ourselves from one kind of unanimity, I was not anxious to replace it with another, and I was afraid that, if we went too fast with this process, we might achieve exactly that. What I was looking for was a plurality of opinion, a real discussion of differing views that would lead to a consensus based on actual circumstances. That was why, as early as late January 1968, I resisted the pressure from both Left and Right to convene a "cadre-solving" Central Committee to quickly replace people in high positions. Initially, I must say, the strongest pressure came from the conservatives, the opponents of reforms, and the opposite trend only slowly gained in force.

My top priority remained the Action Program. I saw little sense in changing personnel before we had a binding new political platform. I managed to extract that from the old Presidium, and public pressure made the Central Committee endorse it in April. Then, and only then, I believed, did it make sense to move on.

I put the question of convening the extraordinary Party congress on the agenda of the old Presidium in the early April session of the Central Committee. Then it was discussed again in the new Presidium on April 16. The second half of April was the time of regional Party conferences, and at those a majority of the delegates strongly favored an extraordinary congress. Quite a few regional secretaries were not reelected, but they continued to be members of the Central Committee. That made the need for the congress even more obvious. It would cap our achievements by removing the danger that the reform course could be reversed from inside the Central Committee.

When we decided in early June to convene the congress, the Soviets happened to be urging—not by chance, I think—large-scale war games on our territory, and they went public with their criticism of our internal development. While it was now desirable to convene the congress as soon as possible, I was still reluctant to antagonize the existing Central Committee. That body's power would be intact until the congress, and we could not convene the congress overnight. District conferences had to meet and elect delegates to regional conferences, and regional conferences had to be held to elect delegates to the congress. It was also necessary to prepare congressional documents, resolutions, and personnel proposals, all of which were demanding tasks.

When the delegates to the congress were elected, in the first half of July, the time for setting the date was at hand. This was a very delicate matter. As usual, I thought twice before moving. I did not believe it was essential to convene the congress immediately. I knew how nervous the Soviets were. In Prague, we looked at it as a way of jettisoning reactionary deadweight, but from Moscow it appeared quite different: that deadweight was their spoon in our soup.

I could not know, of course, how the Soviets would react. While I did not seriously imagine that they would invade the country, I was cognizant of their attempts to intimidate us by indirect military and other threats. Thus, I thought it might be wise to announce the date of the congress not too long before its convening, a ploy that now, with the delegates elected, was possible. However, that move was easier to contemplate than to carry through, because I had to have the cooperation of the key Secretariat organizers, who happened to be my opponents Indra, Lenart, and Kolder.

In retrospect, I do not believe that the fate of Prague Spring would have been much different if the congress had been convened at the end of July instead of in early September. What the Soviets did on August 20 they could have done much earlier. The state of their military machine was not the crucial factor in the decision to launch the invasion; they were ready at any time. Soviet documents that have recently become available confirm this conclusion: at all costs they wanted to prevent a congress that would be fully, unreservedly supportive of our reforms.

19

THE WARSAW INTERPLAY

IN mid-April, after the Central Committee session, Soviet Ambassador Chervonenko brought me a three-day-old letter from his boss. Brezhnev wrote that he felt uneasy about developments in our country. The high-priority mail Chervonenko delivered in those months was invariably dated several days before. Whether this was sloppy work or purposeful I did not understand: after all, Moscow was just a two-hour flight from Prague.

Chervonenko was not only a misfit as mailman but also a miserable observer. He seemed to have no clear idea of what was happening in Czechoslovakia, and the reports he sent home—which I was recently able to read—were simply idiotic. I suspected as much from his stupid questions. I also recall the remarks a Ukrainian historian made to our consul in Kiev. This historian, who had just returned from Prague, told our people in Kiev that Chervonenko and his deputy, Udalcov, were completely ignorant about Czechoslovak affairs and that their standard explanation of any change was "counterrevolution."

Responsible, to some extent, for his superiors' views of our situation, Chervonenko was a damaging factor in our Soviet relations. His previous post, by the way, had been in China. One can imagine his contribution to the ruinous state of Sino-Soviet relations!

A dull and smug man, Chervonenko consistently befriended the most notorious die-hards in our ranks, and any list of conspirators against the legal government of Czechoslovakia in August 1968 would be incomplete without his name.

Anyway, I had barely opened the letter that Chervonenko brought me on April 14 when Brezhnev telephoned and invited me to come "to talk." After the Czechoslovak Party Presidium agreed to accept the invitation, the meeting date was set for May 4 and 5. We had some previously planned state business for the second half of April and two rounds of regional Party conferences, so we could not propose anything earlier.

About this time there was an outbreak of political unrest in Poland. The slogan that some Polish students had come up with—"Poland Is Waiting for Her Dubcek"—must have been especially galling to Gomulka. Among documents recently made available by the Russian, Polish, and Hungarian governments is one that quotes Gomulka's complaint, as early as mid-April, that "Czechoslovakia is turning into a bourgeois republic."*

On April 23 a Bulgarian delegation headed by Todor Zhivkov arrived in Prague to sign a renewed alliance treaty. The Bulgarian Party leader, who had been one of my five critics in Dresden, said nothing critical this time. Brezhnev wasn't around, so Zhivkov apparently felt no need to sound off. For us, it was important to cooperate with the Bulgarians to demonstrate that we were not changing our foreign policy. In mid-June our alliance with Hungary also needed renewal, and we traveled to Budapest to sign that.

Zhivkov was still in Czechoslovakia when Soviet Marshal Yakubovsky, commander-in-chief of the Warsaw Pact forces, arrived. During the talks he held with President Svoboda, Prime Minister Cernik, Minister of Defense General Dzur, and myself, Yakubovsky demanded that the large, multination war games originally scheduled to be held on our territory in September be advanced to June.

We did not like the idea, and I argued that, in our current situation, these war games could cause both alarm and political complications. When Yakubovsky insisted, I had to tell him flatly that his demand was unacceptable. He then retreated somewhat, proposing as an alternative a "small training exercise" requiring the presence of only limited staffs. To that I reluctantly agreed, simply to avoid a larger argument. I did not expect them to cheat so egregiously as to bring in 27,000 men and, after the maneuvers, to make clear that they had no intention of moving them out. It then took several weeks of vehement protests before they withdrew. We now know that the purpose of this "staff exercise" was both to intimidate us and to prepare for the invasion.

On May 4, after dealing with Yakubovsky, a group of us went to

---

* From the archives of the Czechoslovak Government Commission for the Investigation of the Events Between 1967 and 1970, Document No. AK L 1353. A report of the Soviet Ambassador A. B. Aristov in Warsaw, April 17, 1968.

Moscow—Cernik, Smrkovsky, Bilak, and I. On the Soviet side, the conference was attended by Politburo members Brezhnev, Podgorny, and Kosygin. Brezhnev repeated the criticisms he had voiced in Dresden and in his recent letter: that the Czechoslovak Party was losing control over mass communications and that our economic reform could lead to a restoration of capitalism. Contrary to some accounts, I am certain that Brezhnev made no direct threats, especially none involving military force.

I replied that we viewed the situation differently. Not only was our Party not losing its leading role but we were gaining more support than ever before—from all segments of society and all nationalities. As for the media, I reminded him that the content of newspapers was no longer the government's responsibility, since we had abolished censorship. Moreover, the press was, in the main, supportive of our policy, and occasional criticism was to us simply an expression of diversity and freedom.

Our economic reforms were designed to assure wide decentralization and enterprise initiative, I said, encouraging increased material rewards for better performance. Such reform, contrary to their suspicions, did not make for an antistate substratum in either industry or personal enterprises; even before the war, the Czechoslovak Communist Party had enjoyed significant support among small craftsmen and shopkeepers.

At this point, Brezhnev again made his reference to Bata and his shoes and expressed concern about our intention to get a hard-currency loan from the West.

Indeed, we had been offered a $400 to $500 million loan from the West, I replied, to facilitate modernization of our industry. "I have already read in your press," I added, "that to accept a Western loan means to sell ourselves out to the capitalist powers. But a loan of $400 or $500 million is very little compared to our overall economy. We need it, and, unlike you, we have no gold reserves to draw on. But if you give us a hard-currency loan, we'll accept it gladly, and then we'll need no loan from the West."

Brezhnev did not react, but Cernik told me that while I'd been speaking, Kosygin had turned to Brezhnev and whispered in his ear, *"Eto by byl podarok kontrarevolucii* (That would be a gift to the counterrevolution)."

It was obvious that we again disagreed on almost everything. It is interesting to note what Brezhnev thought about the meeting. My source is a Polish stenographic record of a briefing Brezhnev gave to Gomulka, Ulbricht, Kadar and Zhivkov in Moscow on May 8. Brezhnev said that in Dresden he had characterized the Czechoslovak reforms "as a counterrevolution." (Well, if he had, it wasn't during the official session.) Then he said that of all members of the Czechoslovak delegation during our talks in

Moscow, only Bilak had "cooperated." "Dubcek," by contrast, "is entirely hopeless, and I do not even want to speak about him."*

When we returned from Moscow, I determined to play down our disagreement, at least in public, and this remained my tactic for months. We needed time, and I thought that moderate, nonconfrontational behavior would serve our purpose better than open polemics. One must realize that we were alone: our ambassadors' reports from around the world showed that we could not rely on any effective support in our dispute with the Soviets from any quarter.

From what we now know and what we could only guess twenty-four years ago, Brezhnev had begun to prepare an invasion of Czechoslovakia well before the Moscow meeting. Marshal Yakubovsky's war games demands were clearly a part of it. The political conspiracy of "The Five" against Czechoslovakia was formalized a few days after our trip to Moscow, during the meeting from which the Polish stenographic record is taken, not in Dresden in March. They had had to wait, because Ceausescu—as he himself later told me—had also been invited to Dresden but had refused to go. In May they no longer had to worry about him. When the Five met in Moscow in May 8, it was for a clear purpose.

Soviet publicity about the meeting of The Five on May 11 was a form of intimidation; so was Kosygin's letter of May 10 to Cernik, criticizing the liberal conditions on border crossings between Czechoslovakia and Austria and West Germany. Kosygin claimed that there were many "agents and saboteurs" among the Western tourists coming to Czechoslovakia.

We reacted with restraint. Cernik assured Kosygin that we were reviewing the system of protecting our Western borders. I called Ambassador Chervonenko to my office and formally expressed my concern that our representatives had not been invited to the conference of The Five in Moscow. My protest was intentionally muted because I had already decided to avoid any more meetings like Dresden. Our pretense that everything was all right was calculated.

In May we received two further high-level Soviet military visits: First, Marshals Konev, Lelyushenko, and Moskalenko, who had commanded Soviet troops on our territory in 1944 and 1945 and who now came to attend the celebrations of the anniversary of our 1945 liberation. During his visit, Konev specifically denied rumors that the Soviet Army planned to invade Czechoslovakia.

A week later, a much less ceremonial team arrived, headed by Minister of Defense Grechko. He brought with him Marshal Koshevoy, General

---

* Archives of New Sources, Warsaw, "Secret," No. 658/4.

Ogarkov, and General Yepishev, head of the Soviet Army Main Political Administration, who had made some very unfriendly comments on our situation before his visit and was getting sarcastic rejoinders from our press. Yepishev and B. I. Ponomaryov, by the way, were the last surviving members of the secret personal secretariat of Stalin. No wonder they did not like what they saw as our disobedience.

Grechko's team claimed that they had arrived to discuss the staff exercise now planned for June. When Svoboda, Cernik, and I received them, the discussion was formal and did not spill over to our internal problems.

Grecko was still in Prague when we learned that Kosygin had suddenly appeared in Karlovy Vary (or Carlsbad), the western Bohemian spa, for a "short rest and cure." We learned about his presence through internal channels; Chervonenko had made arrangements for his stay without our government's knowledge. Why Kosygin used such an Oriental sort of trick to oblige us to pay him a visit we did not understand.

Cernik and I went to see him, but our discussion was just a repetition of previous talks with the Soviets. To say that Kosygin was no charmer would be polite. Sometimes he behaved with moderation and sometimes quite rudely. In Karlovy Vary, we found him rested and more willing to listen, but that did not mean much. He and Brezhnev often changed roles, in a well-rehearsed good cop–bad cop routine. After our visit, Kosygin returned to Moscow, his five-day "rest and cure" over. He had certainly not drunk enough Carlsbader water to make a difference—it is said to take effect only after about a week and if you drink it while walking.

At the end of May, the Soviets started to arrive for the staff exercise, code-named Bohemian Forest. Despite the excess troops, it was more acceptable than the large-scale war games Yakubovsky had initially demanded.

On June 12, I received another letter from Brezhnev, in which he proposed a bilateral, informal meeting somewhere in the border area, on our side or theirs, on June 15 or 16. I replied that I had such a busy domestic agenda that I could not possibly meet him before the middle of July, after the second round of our regional Party conferences.

The reason he had for wanting an early meeting—to increase pressure—was the same one I had for postponing it. Still, any talks with the Soviets, however unproductive, tended to reduce tension. I was therefore pleased that a parliamentary delegation headed by Josef Smrkovsky happened to be going to Moscow, Leningrad, and other cities in mid-June. They held talks with Brezhnev and Podgorny, and, at the end of the visit, Smrkovsky gave a well-attended press conference during which he fielded dozens of questions regarding our reforms. We published a transcript in our media, and everyone could see that Smrkovsky had been very effective in explaining our policy. Unfortunately, the Soviet media paid little attention.

On July 5, Brezhnev called and told me that a conference of the six Dresden countries should meet again as soon as possible. I promised to give him my answer soon, and I chose to do so in a letter. I asked him to clarify the purpose and agenda of the proposed meeting, in writing, because I had to put the proposal to our Presidium. Of course, I was playing for time, but it was a legitimate request.

In his prompt, written response, Brezhnev proposed that the conference meet in Warsaw on July 15. In the next few days, letters with the same proposal dutifully arrived from Gomulka, Ulbricht, Kadar, and Zhivkov. I read all five letters closely, and noticed that they differed significantly in both content and tone. The worst was that of Ulbricht; it was almost insulting, and I thought of ignoring it completely. But I also reasoned that there might be tactical advantages to be garnered from the differences in the letters.

I could hardly refuse the meeting out of hand, but I tried to set certain conditions. First, that we wanted it attended by *all* European socialist countries, which would include Romania and Yugoslavia. Second, that because the letters we received showed differing opinions on the Czechoslovak situation, bilateral meetings should be held with each country to clarify our problems before a general conference.

I put this proposed response to the Party Presidium of July 12. Some members, such as Kolder and Bilak, who must have already decided to cast their lot with the Soviet hard-liners, demanded that we accept the invitation unconditionally, but a majority supported my proposal, and I so informed Brezhnev.

Instead of hearing from him, I got a call from Kadar, who urgently asked for a meeting. Cernik and I met him in Komarom in the late afternoon on July 13.

Kadar, obviously on Brezhnev's instructions, urged us to go to Warsaw. He had not yet received our answer to his own letter, so I informed him that we had a binding decision of the Presidium on the matter and that we thought the conference was premature and too exclusive. Kadar did not seem terribly disturbed by this news, and we parted in a friendly way. After all, he had just been doing his job, right?

Brezhnev and friends met in Warsaw the next day, July 14. A day later they issued a communiqué stating that The Five had met, exchanged views on the situation in Czechoslovakia, and dispatched a joint letter to the Czechoslovak Central Committee.

The letter was a slap in the face to the very idea of "peaceful coexistence" so loudly advertised by the Soviet Union. Predictably, it repeated the criticism of our reform policy we had so many times refuted. It characterized our reforms in threatening terms as the work of "counterrevolutionary forces" and went on specifically to demand that we suppress "antisocialist organizations" as well as freedom of the press.

We discussed the Warsaw Letter—as it would be referred to in the literature about Prague Spring—in the Party Presidium on July 16 and 17. First, we reiterated the reservations set forth in our answer to the original invitation. As before, the Presidium was not totally unified; the Kolders and the Bilaks dragged their feet and said we ought to have gone to Warsaw. Nonetheless, they did not go so far as to criticize the language of the position paper, which was approved.

Next, I decided to make a bold move, unexpected by my colleagues. I proposed that we ask the full Central Committee to vote on the position paper. This led to a strange situation, in which my supporters feared the Central Committee would reject the document, while my opponents feared they might approve it.

As it happened, my opponents' fears were justified. My reliance on the influence of public opinion, by now a decisive political factor, proved well-founded. A poll showed that our reform policy was supported by as many as 78 percent of the people, with only 7 percent against. In the face of their own people, even the diehards dared not show their true faces.

The Central Committee session took place on July 19 and was attended by the president, members of the Central Auditing Commission, and representatives of the elected delegates of the coming Fourteenth Party Congress. Approval of the draft position paper was *unanimous*. In the end, even Kolder, Bilak, Rigo, Svestka, Indra, Jakes, and the rest of the gang voted for it.

This was a significant manifestation of unity. After all, the Warsaw Letter was ostentatiously addressed to the Central Committee, and we could provide an answer at the same level. Could the whole Communist Party be accused of counterrevolutionary tendencies?

I should add that, even before the Central Committee vote but following the Presidium approval, I had called Brezhnev and suggested that they not publish either their letter or our answer, saying that to do so would only increase international tension and serve no one. He listened but did not give a clear answer. The next day the official press in the five countries published the Warsaw Letter.

We decided to publish their letter, too, in full, with our response. They never published our answer. It reminded me of 1948, when the Yugoslav press had published the attack of the Cominform while Soviet papers never carried the Yugoslav Communists' answer.

After Warsaw came the last round of efforts to preserve our right to an independent policy. We had only six more weeks to breathe.

20

TALKING WITH THE DINOSAURS

L IKE everyone else, I often reflect on the causes of the collapse of the Soviet Union. How could this giant power crumble so quickly and so completely? There are many learned theories about it, but I think that underlying all of them is one elementary explanation: the system inhibited change. It fed on dead doctrine and prevented a natural replacement of leaders. When they finally tried to do something about it, it was too late for remedies.

In 1968 we ran into this dinosaur of a system still in working condition. The Politburo held together the external empire that Stalin had grabbed and saw to it that opposition arose nowhere. I had seen it in Dresden in March, and then in Moscow in May. What we were trying to do was beyond their comprehension.

The challenge was to maneuver around them long enough to make them accept us on civilized terms. I thought, optimistically, that we could prevail because their bullying would not exceed certain limits. The 1956 crushing of Hungary was way behind us: this was a different era. I think most of the world agreed with me.

Beyond the Soviets' empty phrases about "counterrevolution," the core of the dispute was not our social system but our *political* reforms. We believed that socialism—in our country at least—could not exist without democracy. But the Soviets wanted us to reinstitute their model of one-party dictatorship. Still, I did not believe that they would launch a war against us just because of this disagreement. After all, we were bound by a valid alliance treaty, and Czechoslovakia was avoiding anything that might throw doubt on her loyalty. Moreover, the Soviets had for years preached the principle of peaceful coexistence and noninterference in the internal affairs of other countries. Was it rational to expect that they would contradict all this by attacking us militarily? I did not think so, and I do not think I was a dreamer. I did not expect that they would commit an act that was bound to carry catastrophic consequences for their own cause (which it did, as no one today would deny). And I simply did not expect the perfidy they were soon to display.

A few hours after the Central Committee's approval of our reply to the Warsaw Letter on July 19, Brezhnev telephoned. He sounded as if nothing had happened, and he proposed a *bilateral* meeting. He did not suggest the time of the meeting but said that it should take place on Soviet territory.

It was significant to me that he seemed less adamantly opposed to the idea of bilateral talks than before, but I did not delude myself that he'd become suddenly disposed to make concessions. It was clear to me that his main aim was to put still more pressure on us, and to deepen the differences in our ranks. Still, I saw it as a possible way to put the Warsaw Letter behind us and reduce tensions.

We discussed the overture in the Presidium and decided to accept, but on condition that the meeting be held on our territory. We could not ignore the broad, growing, and resentful anti-Soviet mood in our country, even within the Communist Party. The Warsaw Letter was especially aggravating to most of our people, who stood wholeheartedly behind our new reform policy.

The Soviets' provocations and intimidation were ongoing. After the staff exercise, we had to ask them again and again to get their troops out. At the time of the Warsaw conference, they were still departing at a snail's pace.

Another example of such intimidation was a Soviet protest, received on June 21, against alleged Czechoslovak demands for the return of the Subcarpathian Ukraine, a part of prewar Czechoslovakia that the Soviets had annexed in 1944. We were unable to find out what it was all about, because no Party organization or government agency of ours had even thought about this matter. But with deadly calculation, the Soviets blew this nonexistent problem out of all proportion.

In mid-July an anonymous caller alerted our police to a cache of five backpacks with about twenty World War II American submachine guns and some ammunition under a highway overpass in western Bohemia. Soviet and East German media, claiming that Americans had sent weapons to "arm our counterrevolution," launched a campaign of alarm even before the police located the hiding place. Our minister of the interior, Josef Pavel, later told me that examination revealed that the guns' packing grease was of Soviet origin; his people figured that the weapons had been stored in Soviet

Army stockpiles in East Germany before being planted by Soviet agents. Now the Soviet government sent us a stern protest, which included a demand that "allied" troops be stationed on our western border.

Another provocation concerned General Vaclav Prchlik, then head of the Central Committee department in charge of national security. During a press conference in mid-July, Prchlik made a mild comment about the uneven representation of member states in the Warsaw Pact High Command. This gave the Soviets one more pretext for pressure. Admittedly this was a sensitive issue, in an area where I was anxious to avoid provocation. The problem should have been swept under the carpet, but we did not agree to demote Prchlik as the Soviets demanded. Instead we abolished the department of which he was head, and Prchlik quietly returned to his duties in the army. After Gustav Husak came to power, Prchlik was purged and spent two years in jail.

All these concocted irritants made for a nervous public atmosphere. Given the abuse we had suffered over the last several weeks, to go to Moscow would look like a humiliating surrender, and we agreed that it would be politically wrong to meet on Soviet territory.

Still, to continue to refuse to meet with the Soviets would be unwise. After due deliberation, I called Brezhnev on July 21 and proposed that we meet in Kosice, a large and accommodating city in eastern Slovakia. Kosice is an important railroad crossing, quite close to the Soviet border, and it has a large airport.

In a few days, Brezhnev came back with a rather unusual counterproposal: let the two full leaderships—the Soviet Politburo and the Czechoslovak Communist Party Presidium—meet in the railroad station at Cierna, a border-crossing point between Slovakia and the Soviet Union with high-capacity facilities for reloading trains on the wider Russian railroad tracks. I told Brezhnev that I wasn't sure we could find appropriate accommodations in such a small place, and he said, Never mind, they'd come in their own train. My God, I said to myself, they'll be camping out!

I was later accused, by Vasil Bilak and others, of having proposed this undignified environment for the conference, but it was in fact Brezhnev's own caprice. The Cierna talks were thus held on our territory, in the railwaymen's clubhouse at the railroad station. Each morning the Soviets would arrive in their train, and in the evening they would pull back across the border.

The conference started on Monday, July 29, and soon came to an impasse. The two sides disagreed as completely as before. Brezhnev and I simply restated our opinions. Other members of both delegations were also asked to speak. A few in our group—such as Bilak, Svestka, and Rigo—

diffidently voiced dissenting, pro-Soviet opinions, but their minority views did little to change the overall picture.

We had agreed that neither side would keep an official record of the negotiations. We kept our word, but the Soviets did not, as we later found out. As they demanded, no journalists were permitted to cover the conference. Brezhnev's Politburo was not fond of publicity when they could not shape it themselves.

Some Soviet potentates, namely Pyotr Shelest, the Ukrainian first secretary, as well as Kosygin and Podgorny, were at moments quite rude. Kosygin, for example, referred to Dr. Frantisek Kriegel, a member of our Presidium, as "a Galician Jew." I rebuffed this insulting remark in the strongest terms.

News about the progress of the conference was scarce, and the Czechoslovak public reacted to Cierna with deep concern. The people strongly opposed any substantive concessions to the Soviets. We received thousands and thousands of letters, telegrams, and resolutions from the whole country, expressing full support for our position. The slogan of the day was "Be with us, we are with you." That solidarity was all-embracing and touching. One night I could not sleep, so I went out and walked through the railroad station. I was immediately surrounded by the railwaymen, who expressed the same sentiments of support as I had read in the mail.

At one point in the debate the next day, I mentioned the extent of this support as proof of the strength of our Party. Brezhnev retorted with his own theory of spontaneity: "If I gave instructions, I too could have a ton of letters here in no time."

On the third day, it was obvious the conference was going nowhere, but it was also clear that it had to have a discernible end. At this point, we were told that Brezhnev was ill and was resting in his car. The conference broke into small groups who walked along the platforms arguing about this and that. I decided that I should try to visit Brezhnev and find out what he was up to.

I found him in bed in dark pajamas, but it was instantly clear to me that his illness was simulated. He complained about fatigue and a headache, but after a while he dropped his pretense and came to the real point: that he still wanted his conference with the other countries of the Warsaw group.

It occurred to me that such a meeting could now conceivably be a way of canceling out the Warsaw Letter, and smoothing the sharpest edges of our dispute, and returning to normality. I figured we needed forty more days of peace, after which the Party congress would bring about an entirely different situation. So I told Brezhnev that in principle we would not refuse such a conference, provided that it would truly offer a new start in our relations. We could not, I said, accept the criticism in the Warsaw Letter, but if we could agree to a conference that would adopt an entirely new document, in which none of the points of that letter would be repeated, we would be willing to drop our demand that Romania and Yugoslavia also attend.

He listened with closed eyes, but after a moment he came back to life and said, "I think we can do that."

In the afternoon, we held a Presidium meeting, and I reported my agreement with Brezhnev, with which the Presidium concurred. The next day, August 1, the delegations met for the last time. I repeated the main points of our understanding, and we agreed to call a full conference of the six countries in Bratislava only two days later.

No other agreement was reached or signed in Cierna; complete disagreement over our internal situation continued. This is very important to note, because of Brezhnev's later lies on this matter.

When the Bratislava conference met, I was curious to see what face Ulbricht and Gomulka would put on the suddenly summoned gathering. This was not a tribunal on the model of medieval Church councils, and we were not the accused, as we had been made out to be in Warsaw. This was just a conference in which we took part as equals.

I have already mentioned Brezhnev's custom of kissing for the camera, and, waiting at the Bratislava airport, I was ready for him. I held a big bunch of flowers in my left hand and was determined to use it as a shield to keep Brezhnev at a safe distance when he stepped off his airplane. It was just as I expected. He went after me, but I fended him off with my bouquet. He settled for grasping my hand holding the flowers and forcefully raising it in the air. That's how we were photographed, but the picture does not reveal the little preceding struggle.

Of course the new joint declaration, which was the whole purpose of the conference to us, quickly became the sticking point. The Soviets presented a draft, which was then reviewed by all the delegations. The language was awful, but I did not expect otherwise. It was couched in the kind of Stalinist semantics that had become one of the main instruments of Soviet political control. Ordinary Russians themselves called it *derevyannyi yazyk*—wooden language.

That day I did not care much about the clichés with which the document was stuffed—the empty references to imperialism, colonialism, and revanchism. I had other concerns. When a second draft prepared by delegation experts appeared on the table, I was satisfied to see that it was in no way tied to the Warsaw Letter. In fact, it read as if that letter had never existed. So far so good. Now I demanded that the document contain a clear declaration that specific ways of internal development in different countries were the business of each signatory.

This was the subject of a heated discussion, with Ulbricht and Gomulka claiming such a clause was unnecessary. I argued that this principle had already been accepted by the international Communist movement, as evidenced in several documents, and that it directly followed from the generally respected policy of noninterference in the internal affairs of other countries.

I made it clear that if the idea was not restated in the document, we would simply not sign it. At that moment, I must say, it was Kosygin who stepped in and offered a compromise. Two telling phrases were incorporated. One said that each Communist Party "would creatively solve the problems of further socialist development"; the other, which was more explicit, restated the principle of "equality, preservation of sovereignty, national independence, [and] territorial inviolability."

Some time later, Soviet propagandists quoted another phrase from the jargon in the preamble of the declaration, which, in their opinion, justified the invasion of Czechoslovakia: that "support, protection, and strengthening" of achievements of nations of the bloc were the "joint international duty" of all. It is easy to see which of the three phrases was to take precedence in Soviet eyes, but an impartial reading of the document in the context of the times bears out my interpretation.

We returned to Prague the day after the conference, and I made a statement on television in which I emphasized that we had accepted no secret agreements either in Cierna or in Bratislava. The declaration was the only document we signed, and it clearly "opened further necessary space for our reforms." At the time I firmly believed what I said. Even now I ask the question any normal, decent person would then have asked: Why would the Soviets have gone to Bratislava to pledge noninterference in our internal affairs if they had quite contradictory intentions? *The Washington Post*, commenting on the Bratislava Declaration a day after its publication, drew a similar conclusion. It described the Bratislava conference as a "Soviet Playa Girón," a reference to the failed U.S.-sponsored Bay of Pigs invasion in April 1961. That is, it understood the conference as a Soviet retreat and a Czechoslovak achievement.

With considerable satisfaction, I read Janos Kadar's speech before the Central Committee of the Hungarian Communist Party on August 7, in which he said that the Bratislava conference represented a turning point in the dispute over Czechoslovak reforms: "In the activities of brotherly Communist Parties, political means have taken priority." Was Kadar also fooled?

The apparent contradiction between the Russian concessions at Bratislava and what was to happen on August 21 can be explained by the habitual and calculated use of confusion. Thus, they could and did employ a retroactive and bold-faced revision of the Bratislava Declaration to justify their actions. It was at a meeting of The Five in Moscow on August 18 that they made their final decision to launch the invasion. We know this from a stenographic record of that meeting that was only recently made available. *

Brezhnev stated that in Cierna "it had been agreed" that the Czechoslovak Communist Party would reinstitute censorship and outlaw KAN and K-231, the organization of former political prisoners. He further said that "it had been agreed" that we would demote Presidium member Frantisek Kriegel; Cestmir Cisar, the Central Committee secretary; and Jiri Pelikan, the director general of Czechoslovak television. Brezhnev added that this "agreement" had been the basis of the Bratislava conference. All that, of course, was the most blatant of lies. The Soviets had presented these demands, but we had rejected them all decisively, and the only agreement we then reached was about going to Bratislava. Nothing else.

At the same meeting, I might add, Brezhnev talked about me, saying that "Dubcek had joined the forces of the Right."

To assume that Ulbricht et al. were tricked by Brezhnev into agreeing with the aggression would be to give them too much benefit of the doubt. They were probably quite happy to hear these lies.

The period between the Bratislava conference and the invasion brought no changes in our internal situation that could be construed as provocation for what happened. There was a general relaxation of tension, a feeling of hope that we had finally been left alone.

On August 9, President Tito arrived in Prague for an official visit and received an enthusiastic welcome from large crowds along the route from the airport to Prague Castle. I could not suppress the memory of his welcome in Moscow twenty years earlier. During our conversations, Tito expressed full support for our policy and our cause. Like many politicians worldwide, he believed that the Bratislava conference was a sign of Soviet retreat. Nevertheless, we agreed that the Soviets would continue to harass us in various ways, trying to slow down and narrow the scope of our reforms. I told him that this had been going on since March and April, that we had had to look over our shoulders before making important decisions about almost anything.

* Stenographic record from a conference of first secretaries of the Communist Parties of Bulgaria, the German Democratic Republic, Hungary, Poland, and the USSR held on August 18, 1968, in Moscow; Archives of New Sources, Warsaw, "Secret," no number.

President Ceausescu arrived for a long-scheduled visit on August 13, and we renewed our alliance treaty with Romania, just as we had with Bulgaria and Hungary. Unlike Yugoslavia, Romania was a member of the Warsaw Pact, so Ceausescu's position was more immediately relevant to us. His subsequent refusal to take part in ganging up against us also had welcome significance for us, of course.

Ceausescu was likewise very warmly received by the crowds in Prague. During our talks, he assured me that Romania would not change her position or take any steps against us. I briefed him about our domestic programs, political as well as economic, and he simply took notice, saying that all that was our own concern. I knew that he was no great reformer himself; for him it was a matter of pragmatic politics, which he had also applied in recognizing China and Israel.

Walter Ulbricht was a different kind of visitor. Along with Brezhnev, Ulbricht was the most unpopular foreign statesman in Czechoslovakia, so he was not the object of a local ovation when he came to Karlovy Vary, and I'm sure he didn't expect to be. He brought with him several Politburo members, such as Erich Honecker and Willi Stoph, so I brought several members of the Czechoslovak Presidium, including Smrkovsky and Cernik.

To agree with the goateed Ulbricht on anything required special tolerance: he was a dogmatist fossilized somewhere in Stalin's period, and I found him personally repugnant. I had heard that he liked to play volleyball, but looking at him I found it difficult to imagine that he could engage in any normal physical activity. All the same, under the circumstances I welcomed the mere fact that we met and talked, even if we disagreed. It was a relatively painless way to reduce tension. I have only a limited recollection of the meeting, but I remember that Ulbricht greatly amused the journalists at his press conference by his statement that there was no censorship in East Germany.

I heard from Brezhnev on August 13. He called to say that he and his friends were not satisfied with the way we were implementing the Bratislava "agreement." Patiently and in detail, I explained that we were conducting our affairs in exact compliance with the declaration. We were especially busy now, preparing for the Party congress, and he certainly knew, I said, how demanding that work was. During our conversation, he made no direct or specific reference to the nonexistent "agreements" from Cierna that he would recite to The Five in Moscow five days later. He knew that was all a fairy tale.

I was not exaggerating when I said that our main concern at the time was the preparations for the Party congress scheduled for September 9. Documents and resolutions were being drafted, and all organizational matters were hashed out during the meetings of the Secretariat and the Presidium. In fact, the last two Presidium meetings before the invasion, on August 13 and 20, were entirely devoted to this agenda.

On Saturday, August 17, Kadar called and proposed that we meet at the border, close to Bratislava, that evening. I saw nothing unusual about this and accepted.

When I met Kadar, he was relaxed and soft-spoken as ever. He cited no special reason for seeing me, and I did not see any reason to press him. The conversation was entirely casual. Kadar repeated the usual suggestion that we do something to rein in press freedom. I told him that we were doing something: that we talked with our journalists both in groups and individually, that we held regular briefings and press conferences, and that that was all we could do in a country such as ours, where freedom of the press was guaranteed by law.

It is important to emphasize that Kadar made no reference whatsoever to the possibility of military aggression against Czechoslovakia. When we parted, I said again that criticism of our reforms had been unjustified from the beginning. He looked at me and replied, "But you know them, don't you?" Now I know, of course, that he had met me on Brezhnev's instructions. In his own way, he was as much a product of "Leninist morality" as any of the others. The next day he went to Moscow to put his seal on the decision to invade Czechoslovakia.

I spent that night in my house in Bratislava and returned to Prague on Sunday. Monday, August 19, I was busy, mainly preparing the agenda for the Presidium meeting scheduled for the next day.

The morning of August 20 was equally uneventful. That Russian tanks might start rolling in on us in a few hours was inconceivable.

For some it was difficult to imagine even when the tanks had arrived. A close friend of mine, the late Anton Tazky, then a secretary of the Slovak Party Central Committee, was returning by car to Bratislava from Banska Bystrica late Tuesday evening. In the streets of the city, Tazky saw strange lights, then tanks, trucks, and soldiers in foreign uniforms: the invaders had come in from Hungary, from the south. He told himself, "They must be shooting a movie here." He made a detour, arrived home, went to bed, and in five minutes somebody called, saying, "The Russians are here."

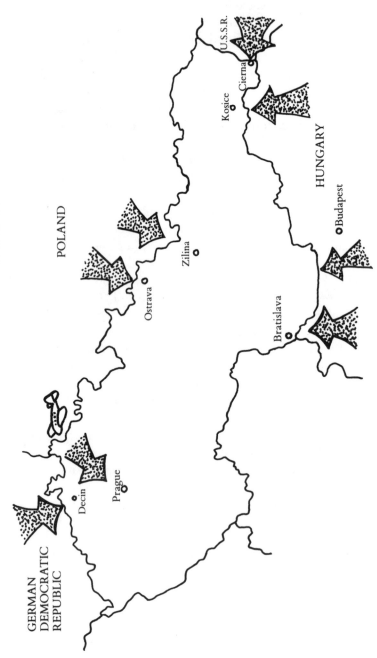

THE INVASION OF 1968

21

THE INVASION
AND KIDNAPPING

T UESDAY the twentieth was a typical late-August day, warm with hazy sun. Prague was full of tourists; whole families were promenading in city parks or sitting on wooden benches. Not only the city but also the country was peaceful. Many were still on vacation, and tens of thousands, taking advantage of the lifting of travel restrictions, were abroad.

The night before, Anna had been in pain—her gallbladder had acted up again—and I had to take her to the hospital on Tuesday morning. When we parted, I reminded her that I had a long meeting in the afternoon but that I would certainly come to visit her the next day. I saw no reason to think otherwise.

The Presidium meeting that afternoon was supposed to be the last before the Fourteenth Party Congress, which was to open three weeks later. The main items on the agenda were drafts of my congressional report and resolution, and the election of new members for the principal Party organs. Had the congress taken place under normal circumstances as planned, it would have put the achievements of Prague Spring on solid foundations, setting the stage for the fulfillment of the Action Program and further reforms.

The meeting started shortly after 2:00 P.M. All full and candidate members were in attendance, except Jozef Lenart, who was reportedly sick. He recovered very quickly, however; after midnight he was extremely busy at the Soviet Embassy. Secretaries of the Central Committee were also there: Cisar, Indra, Mlynar, Sadovsky, Slavik, and Volenik. In the Party system, the Secretariat was an important body but had no right to vote on policy matters. The decision-making power was reserved to the eleven full members of the Presidium: Kolder, Bilak, Svestka, Barbirek, Rigo, Piller, Smrkovsky, Cernik, Kriegel, Spacek, and myself.

In addition to planning for the congress, there was only one other item on the agenda, a follow-up to the "Report on the Political Situation," which had been prepared by a new branch of the Secretariat, the Department of Cumulative Information. I had read the report and found nothing striking in it. Nevertheless, two participants in the previous Presidium meeting, Kolder and Indra, proposed that some conclusions be drawn from the report, and there were no objections. The same men volunteered for the task. Compared with the documents for the coming Party congress, this item was of secondary importance, and I did not pay much attention to it.

In my folder I also had a letter from Brezhnev that had been delivered to me after ten o'clock on Monday night by Ambassador Chervonenko. In spite of the unusual timing of its delivery, there was nothing urgent in the letter. Some leading spokesmen of the "normalization" era imposed on us subsequently, such as Husak and Bilak, later claimed that this letter contained an explicit ultimatum, a clear-cut warning that the invasion was imminent. Such claims are entirely false.

In reality, the letter was a mere replay of the complaints the Soviets had been making since February, and it differed little from previous Soviet messages or calls by Brezhnev. I read the letter thoroughly several times, even after the invasion, and failed to see anything in it that would substantiate Husak's and Bilak's assertions. Anyway, I felt that everything Brezhnev harped on had been settled during the Cierna talks and by the Bratislava Declaration.

Throughout the months of Prague Spring, it had been clear to me that the Soviets' criticism aimed to force me to restrict, if not abandon, our reforms. Yet they never clearly stated, publicly or privately, how *far* they wanted me to retreat. Ambiguity was a trademark of the system. Inter-Party exchanges were often carried on in double-talk, indirect hints, and puzzling allusions to ideological precepts and events in Russian history. This made all communication difficult and agreements unclear. The Soviets' usage of even such basic terms as *democracy* or *sovereignty* either emptied these notions of meaning or turned them into their opposites.

A special favorite of equivocators was the term *the leading role of the Party*. The Soviets brought this up constantly, and a great deal of time was devoted to it in our dealings. While we could not avoid using the same term, we conceived of it, and tried to implement it, in a way diametrically opposed to theirs. They understood the Party as a complete political monopoly maintained by force, making the term itself a confusing understatement. My conception was of a consensus based on free discussion and free choice. In every sense we meant totally different things.

At any rate, each Party's and country's political practice was supposed to be entirely their internal affair, not a subject for international discussions. On that I was adamant; I viewed freedom of our domestic debates as vital to our new political life, and I vowed to defend it. Only principled reforms could extricate socialism from the weight of the "leaden buttocks" the postwar leaders had dumped on our country as they aped the Soviet model. My becoming first secretary of the Czechoslovak Communist Party in January 1968 may have been a surprise, given my history as a reformer, but I was determined to use the opportunity. Even in the first eight months of occupation, I resisted pressures to reinstall the old order.

Almost all communications with the Soviets were fraught with terms as ambiguous as "the leading role of the Party." I think they were explicit on only one major point, the preservation of our alliance and our continued adherence to the Warsaw Pact. Here, I agreed, they were entitled to legitimate concern about their own security. Repeatedly we confirmed the validity of our external obligations. Our reforms had no bearing whatsoever upon the alliance. Even the Prchlik episode did not connote any faltering of the pact. The basic Czechoslovak-Soviet alliance went as far back as 1935 and had been reinforced by President Benes's wartime trip to Moscow in 1943. This did not mean, however, that we had no right to an opinion on how the Warsaw Pact, a later creation, was managed.

The Presidium meeting started with a matter-of-fact discussion of the documents prepared for the Party congress. At one point in the early evening hours, Kolder moved to postpone further consideration of the congressional documents and instead to take up again the "Report on the Political Situation." This motion was opposed by most participating members for practical reasons, even before we knew what was behind the maneuver.

Kolder and his accomplice Indra had no intention of drawing any conclusions relevant to the text of the report. Instead, they presented—to the exasperation of most people in the conference room—a draft of a declaration that was a virtual replay of the criticism in the Warsaw Letter. This was total retrogression from the Cierna conference and the Bratislava Declaration, and was so outrageous that only two other full members of the Presidium—Bilak and Rigo—supported Kolder's motion (Indra, as a secretary, could not vote). Nevertheless, I learned from Bilak's memoirs that they expected their declaration to be supported by a majority! No wonder their conspiracy ended in such a fiasco.

After rejecting the Kolder-Indra proposal, we resumed discussion of the congressional documents. It was already late in the evening; we had a light supper without interrupting the meeting. The atmosphere was electric with fresh rumors about Soviet military moves close to our borders, especially in East Germany. In retrospect, it is odd that we had no inkling of preparations for the capture of Ruzyne, the Prague airport, because these preparations began in the early evening hours, and in fact the invasion started there.

I did not pay much attention to the rumors, considering them an intimidation tactic. But shortly before midnight, Prime Minister Cernik was called to the telephone and told by Defense Minister General Dzur that the Soviets and four of their allies had invaded. Cernik also told us that Dzur had been detained by the Soviets in his office in the Ministry of Defense, which was now occupied, and that he had only been permitted to call the prime minister to inform him about the invasion. Cernik's news was like a bombshell.

I do not have a precise recollection of what I and the others did in the moments that immediately ensued. Naturally, the news caused an excited and chaotic discussion, in which I did not take part. I hurriedly sorted out my thoughts. Our situation was completely changed, and with it my own perspective. My estimate of Soviet intentions had been proven wrong. I struggled to deduce why I had so misread them.

It had been obvious to me in 1964 that the Soviets had not removed Nikita Khrushchev just because he was old and sick, as they claimed. However, Khrushchev, in the pursuit of his phenomenal reforms, had made a number of zigzags and insensitive moves, and I could understand why his own Politburo and Central Committee might have turned against him for reasons other than his policies. Four years later, it was still difficult to determine the extent to which Brezhnev's Politburo would go in reversing Khrushchev's reforms. I was not out of line with most expert opinion, East and West, in thinking that they were not set on a total abandonment of reforms, internally or externally. The invasion changed all that.

In the months preceding, I had been inclined to blame the Soviets' hostility toward our reforms on their different cultural environment and historic experience rather than on a premeditated rejection of reform. Until the last moment, I did not believe the Soviet leaders would launch a military attack on us. To me, that was simply unthinkable. It ran contrary to my deepest idea of the value system I thought governed the relationships between socialist countries. It took the drastic, practical experience of the coming days and months for me to understand that I was in fact dealing with gangsters.

Any parallel with the Hungary of 1956 looked positively absurd to me. In the first place, the times had changed. In the subsequent years, the

Soviets had made great efforts to present themselves as consistent opponents of aggression, and they had vehemently promoted international peaceful coexistence. Would they now decide to destroy that carefully nurtured image by committing such blatant aggression, and against their own ally? Second, Czechoslovakia in 1968 was not Hungary in either 1956 or 1918. Unlike Hungary, Czechoslovakia had not been allied with Hitler but was an early victim of Nazi aggression and a founding member of the United Nations. The international repercussions of unprovoked aggression against Czechoslovakia would be much worse than those resulting from the occupation of Hungary. I did not believe the Soviets would ignore that fact.

I admit that my reasoning was naive, and that it was rooted in goodwill and common decency. Under civilized circumstances, victims usually do not expect a holdup, and until just before midnight August 21, I still believed that relations within the "socialist camp" were essentially civilized. Surely the last thing I expected was that a meeting of the Presidium would end in a hunting down and kidnapping of half its members, myself included.

Some of my failure to anticipate can be explained by how little we knew about the Soviet leadership. We still did not know how much power Brezhnev, as general secretary, had gathered into his own hands and how much of it he had to share with others. After all, Khrushchev had needed some four years to stabilize his power.

Novotny, to be sure, had known more about these things, and apparently he had maneuvered effectively among various factions in the Soviet leadership during the last years of his tenure, especially when it came to their demand to place Soviet troops permanently in Czechoslovakia. In the end, however, even Novotny seems to have miscalculated and underestimated Brezhnev's options. But Novotny certainly did not share his knowledge with me when I succeeded him.

Looking back, I could see that the talks in Cierna had offered some insight, but no person in Czechoslovakia at that time, and certainly no department or institution, specialized in analyzing Soviet developments in a systematic and objective way—that would have amounted to "anti-Sovietism" and was politically unthinkable. So no analyses of Kremlin politics ever reached my desk. I'm not sure how much the West knew about these aspects of Soviet politics between 1964 and 1968, but I believe that even there a clear notion of "neo-Stalinism" appeared only in the aftermath of the Soviet invasion of Czechoslovakia.

The Presidium meeting returned to some order a few minutes after Cernik's announcement. At that point, I remembered Brezhnev's letter, pulled it out of my folder, and read it to the participants. I did this to show that even in this last communication there had been nothing that could be read as a warning of imminent invasion. It was just the old orthodox stuff, complaints about this or that article or cartoon published in the Czechoslovak press. Countries in the mid-twentieth century were not expected to wage war over cartoons, someone observed. No one said the letter had any particular relevance to what was happening.

I felt that we had to adopt a statement expressing our indignation and sense of betrayal. I was keenly aware of my responsibility at that point. The Soviets had taken a giant step beyond polemics and into the realm of war, and a huge army was on the move against us from all sides, obviously determined to crush any resistance. I knew that the Czech and Slovak public were in full support of our reforms and would be passionately opposed to foreign intervention. They would be waiting for a word from us. We had to show a resolute resistance to the aggression but at the same time do everything to avoid fruitless bloodshed. Military resistance was impossible anyway, because our defenses were directed toward the western border to ward off an attack from Bavarian territory. An order to resist would only result in local fighting, and that would justify Soviet accusations about an organized "counterrevolution."

We decided to seek President Svoboda's advice. He arrived within about forty minutes of our call. In the meantime, Ambassador Chervonenko had been to the Castle and formally "informed" him of the invasion. Two secretaries of the Central Committee, Cisar and Mlynar, were instructed to draft a declaration of the Presidium, and it was not long before they brought back a text that firmly expressed the views of the majority. Nevertheless, heated discussion, which led to only insignificant changes, arose. For example, we cut out a sentence that tried to explain why military resistance was impossible. I myself thought it better not to bring up the subject at all.

The declaration was addressed to all people of the Republic, and I quote it in full.

August 21.
Yesterday, August 20, 1968, around 11:00 P.M., the armies of the Soviet Union, of the Polish People's Republic, of the German Democratic Republic, the Hungarian People's Republic, and the Bulgarian People's Republic crossed the borders of the Czechoslovak Socialist Republic. It happened without the knowledge of the President of the Republic, of the Chairman of the National Assembly, of the Prime Minister and of the First Secretary of the Central Committee of CPCz, and of all these organs.

The Presidium of the Central Committee of the CPCz was meeting in these hours and was discussing the preparations for the Fourteenth Party Congress. The Presidium appeals to all citizens of our Republic to keep calm and not to resist the armed forces moving in. Therefore neither our army, security forces or the People's Militias have been ordered to defend the country.

The Presidium believes that this act contradicts not only all principles of relations between socialist countries but also the basic norms of international law.

All leading officials of the state, of the CPCz and of the National Front remain in their functions, to which they were elected as representatives of the people and of the members of their organizations, according to the laws and other statutes valid in the Czechoslovak Socialist Republic.

Constitutional officials convene for immediate session the National Assembly and the government of the Republic, and the Presidium of the CPCz convenes a plenary meeting of the Central Committee of the CPCz to deal with the situation.

When the draft was put to a vote at 1:30 A.M. on August 21, there were seven votes for and four votes against. The positive votes were cast by me, Smrkovsky, Kriegel, Spacek, Cernik, Piller, and Barbirek. Those voting against were Bilak, Kolder, Svestka, and Rigo. Most candidate members and secretaries also supported the resolution, and, as far as I can recall, only Jakes, Kapek, and Indra were against. None openly expressed support for the Soviet intervention; instead they twisted their words in various ways to avoid saying what they meant. They must have known they would be condemned by the whole society. As we later learned, the Soviets had informed these men about the invasion several days earlier, and they had agreed to provide a "legal" justification for it. In that, they failed completely.

They probably already knew that their failure to give the invasion a legal pretext was a blunder of enormous proportions. Unknown to us, but probably not to these quislings, the Soviets had already circulated worldwide an official announcement by the Tass News Agency in which they claimed that the invasion was a response to the request of Czechoslovak "Party and state authorities." This is why our declaration was so important. It exposed the Tass statement as a lie, and the invasion as naked aggression.

With the vote on the declaration, the meeting was over. At about 2:00 A.M., in agreement with the adopted decision, Prime Minister Cernik left for his office, and President Svoboda returned to the Castle.

Next I discussed with Bohumil Simon, first secretary in Prague, the possibility of immediately convening the Fourteenth Party Congress, or at least a conference of the elected delegates. I was afraid that, once gathered, the delegates might be captured and shot, so we agreed that the city committee of the Party should try to convene a conference of the delegates in a secret place.

Two more hours passed. The air was full of the noise of aircraft engines. As we soon learned, the Soviets were landing one airplane a minute at Ruzyne airport, bringing in tanks, armored vehicles, and troops.

It has been asked why we did not leave the building, go into hiding, and assume leadership of a resistance movement. Certainly I considered this possibility, as did Smrkovsky, Simon, and others. But it seemed to us that this would contradict our collective decision to offer only political resistance, part of which was to remain in our positions to frustrate our replacement by traitors. Of course we realized that we could be removed physically, but that was different from deserting our posts. So we stayed in the Central Committee building.

While we were waiting, I walked the spacious corridors of the big building. I saw many workers of the Central Committee apparatus at their posts. I also remember that before the arrival of the Soviet paratroopers and the KGB, I kept looking at the telephones on my desk, as if expecting that someone could still call to say this was all just a big misunderstanding.

In the meantime, several hundred, maybe several thousand people gathered on the wide embankment above the river in front of the Central Committee building. Mostly young, they carried national flags, and I heard them calling my name and singing the national anthem, even the Internationale. What bitter irony!

At around 4:00 A.M., a black Volga limousine led a column of tanks and armored vehicles from the north across the Hlavka Bridge over the Vltava and toward the building. The crowd broke open before the vehicles moving on it, but not fast enough, and a clash occurred in which the Soviets fired machine guns. A young civilian was killed in front of our eyes. Smrkovsky, standing at my side, angrily grasped one of the telephones, dialed a number, and shouted at somebody on the other end of the line to stop the killing. I thought he was talking to Chervonenko, but then I realized that Smrkovsky was speaking in Czech, and Chervonenko didn't know any Czech.

Then we watched the paratroopers—or "air infantry" to use the Red Army term—jump down from their vehicles, automatic rifles in hand, and quickly surround the building. Soon all telephones, including the inter-office network, went dead.

Dawn was turning into full daylight when a detachment, almost a platoon it seemed to me, led by several officers rushed into the building. It was almost 9:00 A.M. when about eight Soviet paratroopers and one or two lower officers burst into my office and closed and blocked the windows and connecting doors. It was like an armed robbery. Without thinking I made a move toward a telephone on my desk, but one of the soldiers aimed his tommy gun at me, grasped the phone, and tore the cable out of the wall.

I can't remember exactly how many of us were still in my office, but I know that Smrkovsky, Kriegel, Spacek, Sadovsky, and Simon certainly were, and probably also Mlynar and Slavik. Then the main door flew open again and in walked some higher officers of the KGB, including a highly decorated, very short colonel and a Soviet interpreter I had met before somewhere; I think he had been in Prague a few weeks earlier with Marshal Yakubovsky. The little colonel quickly reeled off a list of all Czechoslovak Communist Party officials present and told us that he was taking us "under his protection." Indeed we were protected, sitting around that table—each of us had a tommy gun pointed at the back of his head.

A KGB officer then ordered me, Smrkovsky, Kriegel, and Spacek to follow him. While we walked out, I saw Sojak, my office manager, and told him in a low voice to secure my briefcase, which contained papers I did not want the Soviets to get hold of. I did not know then that Sojak was one of the conspirators. When I returned a week later, I found my briefcase all right, but the papers I had worried about had disappeared.

The KGB man led us across the corridor to the office of Cestmir Cisar, the reformist Central Committee secretary, who had already gone into hiding, as I later learned. There we were awaited by several Soviet officers, as well as some civilians who turned out to be our own State Security "volunteers" assigned to formally arrest us. One of them said in a mechanical voice, as if he were an amateur actor, "I am placing you in custody in the name of the Workers' and Peasants' Government led by Comrade Indra." After a short pause, he added that within two hours we would be brought before a "revolutionary tribunal," also chaired by Comrade Indra.

Smrkovsky, short-tempered as he was, immediately fired off a derisive question about the legitimacy of this so-called tribunal. I thought it made no sense to talk with these people at all under the circumstances, and I said, "Forget it, Josef!"

We were seated along a rectangular table, each of us facing his own guardian, a colonel or lieutenant colonel. Some two hours more passed, until another KGB officer came in and ordered me to follow him. With my colonel behind me, I was led down the stairs and along the corridor to a rear door to the courtyard of the building, where I saw tanks and other military vehicles lined up. They ordered me to climb up on an armored carrier, a large vehicle on eight wheels with a round manhole on top, through which they pushed me. After a short while, Kriegel was shoved in, too, and the vehicle started to move. From the turns, I tried to guess where they were taking us. After a while I deduced that it was most probably Ruzyne airport. It crossed my mind that our destination could as well be the prison of the same name in the same area, a dismal place built in the early 1950s and a monument to the repression of that time. Still, I was not entirely sure where we were, and I decided to try a trick to find out.

I pretended to have breathing difficulties and asked our guards to open the manhole to let some air in. I noticed that my request made them nervous; their orders obviously were to bring me somewhere alive, wherever that somewhere was. So they opened the hatch, and, as they did so, I stood up and put my head through it. We were on a street I recognized, with apartment houses on both sides and people looking out the windows. Now I knew that they were taking us to the airport. Of course they pulled me down fast, but I had seen enough.

It was shortly after noon when we arrived at the airport. Kriegel and I were taken to an office on the ground floor. In adjoining offices they held Smrkovsky, Simon, and Spacek, but I did not know that then. All five of us arrested in the Central Committee building were now at the airport, some nine miles from the Old Town of Prague, and later in the day we were joined by Cernik, whom they had captured in the prime minister's office.

After several more hours of waiting, I asked the officer assigned to me whether I could get some fresh air. He hesitated for a moment, but then he nodded and led me out on the side of the building. It was evening but not quite dark yet, and soon I noticed people watching me from behind the glass walls of the building. I took hope from the fact that I had been seen. When I came back inside, I noticed that Kriegel was no longer there. I was alone with my guards. Night was setting in.

It was about nine when they ordered me to walk across the tarmac to an airplane, put me inside, and let me sit there for quite a while. At that point, I became aware that something had probably gone wrong with their plans, because they seemed not to know what to do with me. That impression got stronger after another hour or so, when they walked me to another plane. This one was larger, a Tupolev. (I had been unable to recognize the first one; it was probably an Antonov.) Not too long after I got into the second plane, it took off.

I lost track of how long we were in the air, somewhere between one and two hours. Then we landed on an airstrip surrounded by large heaps of excavated earth—apparently an unfinished airfield. I was sure I was somewhere in southern Poland; later I learned it was Legnica. They led me to a wooden barracks, where I saw the little colonel who had handled our arrest in Prague and had been present when the Czech State Security man told us about the revolutionary tribunal. Again I realized that something had gone wrong with their coup—otherwise, why all the changes and delays?

After the first stop there was another, shorter journey, until we arrived at an airport in the Subcarpathian Ukraine, probably in Uzhgorod, which is just beyond the easternmost border of Slovakia. Cernik and Simon were there, too, but I did not see Kriegel, Smrkovsky, or Spacek.

At the Uzhgorod airport, we were greeted by a detachment of very tall, heavyset, athletic-looking KGB officers in civilian clothes, who led us to several field vehicles waiting on the runway. Cernik physically resisted being pushed into one of the automobiles, and I jumped up and started to shout in Russian very loudly, "What are you doing? Don't you know this man is the prime minister of a sovereign state?" The big men stiffened for an instant, startled. They took their hands off Cernik, and he climbed into the car himself.

We drove uphill for about an hour, until we reached a complex of mountain chalets, where they put each of us into a separate room. And another day passed, Thursday, August 22.

As usual I needed little sleep and spent most of the time rethinking the whole chain of events since my capture. I was sure I was right that the Soviets had had to change their original intentions. What was happening now was not the simple liquidation plan they had announced at the beginning; this looked more and more like an improvisation. I also noticed that, in the last several hours, my guardians' behavior had become more relaxed and even more polite. In complete isolation, without access to newspapers or radio, I had no idea what was happening in Czechoslovakia and in the world, and could not even guess what had made the Soviets change their plans.

My suspicions were confirmed the next day. Shortly before noon they brought me out of my room, put a pair of opaque dark glasses on me, and led me to a car. The engine started, and the car began to move, this time downhill, no doubt along the road we had climbed the day before.

After about an hour we stopped. They led me inside a building and into an elevator, and, after a short ride up, they pushed me into an office where they finally took the black glasses from my eyes. I looked around and did not need long to figure out that I was in the office of a high local Party or Soviet official. Why all the clowning with dark glasses I've never understood. Under the circumstances, it made no sense whatsoever.

I soon inferred from the man's direct link to the Kremlin that I was in the office of the regional Soviet Party committee. I was sure there was no other connection like that in Uzhgorod. Soon the telephone on the secretary's desk rang, and I was told to answer it. At the other end was Nikolai Podgorny.

At that time, Podgorny was a full member of the Soviet Politburo, chairman of the Supreme Soviet, and a member of the very top Soviet leadership. Why they chose him to talk with me I cannot tell. In any case, I was unimpressed. He was very polite, even soft-spoken and in his own way almost polished—I think he even inquired how I was. But that did not surprise me. It was the way they behaved.

Podgorny said, "We will have to talk."

I retorted, "About what, and where?"

He did not respond to the first part of my question but said that we should talk in Moscow.

To that, I responded, "How do you expect me to get there? As a prisoner? First I need to know where the people are who were captured with me. I'm not willing to consider your proposition until we're all together."

He said that this would be arranged and that he would see me soon in the Kremlin.

He kept none of his word. They brought me to Moscow against my free will, as a prisoner, and without uniting me with the other captured people. There was nothing normal, fair, or voluntary in the so-called negotiations that ensued. Still, three days after they had occupied my country and threatened a revolutionary tribunal and possibly a firing squad, they needed to talk with me. Now I wanted to know why.

22

IN THE KREMLIN

I WAS delivered to the Kremlin around 11:00 P.M. Moscow time, on Friday, August 23. My watch had stopped somewhere in the Subcarpathians, so I had only a vague idea of what time it was. Today, however, I can reconstruct a rather accurate chronology of those days based on documents and testimony.

In the Kremlin, they gave me no time to wash away the dust and dirt of the previous three days. They led me directly to "a meeting," as one of the KGB men called it. I remember a tall door, an antechamber behind it, another door, and then a large office with a rectangular table. There I saw the four men most responsible for the criminal invasion of my country: Brezhnev, Kosygin, Podgorny, and Voronov. A "gang of four," one might jokingly say today, but the term was not yet coined in 1968. That was another time and another country.

I wondered why Michail Suslov was not there, and why Voronov had taken his place. Not that Voronov was any better, but Suslov, I believed, was a much higher authority. Voronov was then prime minister of the Russian federation, and that may be why they pushed him forward to sit at Kosygin's side.

I think the fact that they did not let me wash up beforehand was deliberate. They wanted me to feel humiliated and defeated, but, somehow, I did not. I wasn't, after all, the one who should have been ashamed.

No one said anything for a while, as Podgorny gestured to a chair for me on the other side of the table. There were no formal greetings and no handshakes.

They seemed to me to be trying to put on their best faces, but I don't think they were really embarrassed anyway: their overall arrogance hardly allowed for such sensitivity. Only normal people feel shame after wrongdoing. But Brezhnev, I recall, looked sideways, as if avoiding looking me in the eye, and Kosygin's chin was hanging somewhat lower than usual. Only Podgorny appeared quite casual. Of Voronov I have hardly any recollection. But they were all good actors.

I wondered why they wanted to talk with me alone. Shouldn't the other kidnapped members of our Presidium, especially Cernik and Smrkovsky, also be present? Then it crossed my mind that Brezhnev and his buddies might just be curious to see whether their "therapy" would work on me. It wouldn't.

I did not know then that President Svoboda and other high-ranking Czechoslovak officials had arrived in Moscow in the early afternoon and were in the Kremlin. Nor did I know that the Soviets had already talked with them at length. In fact, Svoboda and his group had arrived voluntarily: to come to Moscow was Svoboda's idea. According to reliable witnesses, it had occurred to him a day after the invasion, when he was under severe pressure from Ambassador Chervonenko to legitimize the "Workers' and Peasants' Revolutionary Government."

Some historians and political analysts have viewed the president's decision as tactically wrong and damaging to the cause of national resistance, but I don't look at it that way. Seventy-three-year-old Svoboda was not a politician but an old soldier through and through. His main concern was to avoid bloodshed between an unarmed populace and the army of occupation. He felt that something had to be done fast. Whether he considered options besides going to Moscow I do not know. Later he told me that he had said to Chervonenko that he would rather shoot himself than legitimize the junta led by Alois Indra.

At any rate, he must have felt cornered and desperate, with principal responsibility suddenly on his shoulders. So he decided to go to the source of the catastrophe to try to avoid the carnage of which, he had no doubt, the Soviets were perfectly capable. I can understand his frame of mind.

In truth, Svoboda held his ground rather well under the pressure of the first twenty-four hours following the occupation. At the outset, he was undecided on how to respond to the Soviet demand to legalize a puppet government. Fortunately, Chervonenko and his native helpers were not the only people the president could consult. A strong influence on Svoboda's decision to refuse Chervonenko's demands came from Minister of Agriculture Josef Boruvka. Svoboda had great confidence in this man, and when Boruvka told him that Indra's "government" must by no means be sanctioned by the president's authority, Svoboda responded, "Well, if you say so."

I also think that initially the Soviets were not very happy about the president's proposal to go to Moscow. They were bent on immediate extraction of his blessing for the installation of a quisling regime. It was only when they realized that a smooth transition from Dubcek to Indra was a pipe dream that they had to change their minds. The whole political justification for the invasion had turned into an international scandal, and they were not quite as unconcerned about that as some observers thought, and so they apparently began to like the idea of cosmetic negotiations. For that, of course, they needed not only Svoboda but also me and the others they had originally come to "terminate."

Thus, Brezhnev and the rest of the top Soviet leaders had talked with Svoboda first, then talked separately with other members of his group for at least eight hours before I was delivered to the Kremlin. The Soviets preferred one-on-one interrogations: this was, of course, a way to find out who stood where, in order to divide us.

Svoboda chose to bring with him to Moscow the minister of defense, General Martin Dzur; Deputy Prime Minister Gustav Husak; and Minister of Justice Bohuslav Kucera. Kucera was chairman of the Socialist Party, and he presumably represented the non-Communist segment of the National Front. These three men represented the Czechoslovak government, whose officials had found refuge at the Castle after the kidnapping of Prime Minister Cernik and the seizure of state offices in Strakova Akademie, on the left bank of the Vltava River.

Svoboda also decided to bring with him three members of the remaining Party leadership, and he let them decide who they would be. There were not many to choose from: in addition to Piller, Bilak and Indra were anointed. Now Brezhnev and his companions could learn firsthand from the plotters why their scheme had gone awry. As I say, I knew absolutely nothing about these arrivals when I sat down across from Brezhnev and his three accomplices. I was in no mood to "negotiate." I was simply angry, but trying to compose myself.

Recently I acquired a partial Soviet stenographic record of this meeting and was able to use it to refresh my memory. The transcript contains some holes—results of either censorship or technical difficulties—and stops after fifty-two pages, without recording how the session ended, but otherwise it seems an accurate account of what was said.*

Brezhnev, for some reason, addressed me with the Russian *ty*, the familiar second-person usage found in most European languages. We had never

---

* "Stenograma Peregovorov" (Stenographic Record of Talks), August 23, 1968, Document No. 302.

been on a first-name basis before that, so I found it odd, if not phony. In my answers, I used the more formal *vy*. He began by inquiring after Cernik's health but soon went on to a tortuous justification for the invasion. At times he masked his condescension with a positively fatherly air.

BREZHNEV: How is Comrade Cernik feeling?*
DUBCEK: All in all, bad.
PODGORNY: Bad health or mood?
DUBCEK: Bitter.
BREZHNEV: Let's agree not to bury ourselves in the past, but to discuss calmly, proceeding from the situation that has developed, in order to find a solution that will work to the benefit of the Czechoslovak Communist Party so that it can act, normally and independently, along the lines laid down by the Bratislava Declaration. Let it be independent. We don't want and we're not thinking of further intervention. And let the leadership work according to the principles of the January and May plenary sessions of the Central Committee of the Czechoslovak Communist Party.** We have said this in our reports and we're prepared to affirm it again. Of course, we can't say that you're in a good mood. But your moods aren't the point. We must sensibly and soberly direct our talks toward the search for a solution. It can be stated flatly that the failure to carry out fixed obligations impelled five countries to extreme and inevitable measures. The sequence of events that has materialized confirms entirely that behind your back (by no means do we wish to say that you were at the head of it) right-wing powers (we will simply call them antisocialist) prepared both the congress and its actions. Underground stations and arms caches have now come to light. All of this has now come out. We don't want to raise claims against you personally, that you're guilty. You might not even have been aware of it; the right-wing powers are broad enough to have organized it all. We would like to find the most acceptable solutions that will serve to stabilize the country, normalizing a workers' party without links to the right and normalizing a workers' government free from those links.

We don't need to conceal from each other that if we find the best

* This is apparently a reference to Dubcek's encounter with Cernik in Uzhgorod on August 22.

** Brezhnev intentionally ignored the most important session, in April 1968. It was at this session that the Action Program was approved and the new Presidium elected.

solution we will still need time for normalization. No one should have the illusion that everything will all of a sudden become rosy. But if we do find the correct solution, then time will pass and every day will bring us successes, material talks and contacts will begin, the odor will dissipate, and propaganda and ideology will start to work normally. The working class will understand that, behind the backs of the Central Committee and the government leadership, right-wingers were preparing to transform Czechoslovakia from a socialist into a bourgeois republic. All that is clear now. Talks on economic and other matters will begin. The departure of troops, et cetera, will begin according to material principles. We have not occupied Czechoslovakia, we do not intend to keep it under "occupation," but we hope for her to be free and to undertake the socialist cooperation that was agreed upon in Bratislava. It is on that basis that we want to talk with you and find a workable solution. If need be, with Comrade Cernik as well. If we stay silent we will not improve the situation and will not spare the Czech, Slovak, and Russian peoples from tension. And with every passing day the right-wingers will fire up chauvinistic emotions against every socialist country, and first of all against the Soviet Union. Under such circumstances it would be impossible to pull out the troops; it's not to our advantage. It is on these grounds, on this basis, that we would like to conduct the talks, to see what you think, what's the best way to act. We're ready to listen. We have no *diktat*; let's look for another option together.

And we would be very grateful to you if you freely expressed different options, not just to be contrary, but to calmly find the proper option. We consider you an honorable communist and socialist. In Cierna you were unlucky, and there was a breakdown. Let's cast everything that happened aside. If we start asking which one of us was right, it will lead nowhere. But let's talk on the basis of what is, and under these conditions we must find a way out of the situation, what you're thinking and what we must do.

DUBCEK: That was quite an introductory speech. I, too, Comrade Brezhnev, would like to say a few words, although I'm very depressed. I haven't been home for three days. I would also like to say, however, that it's true that we need to look ahead. It's true that there exists a definite and real situation.

PODGORNY: It's precisely for that reason that we want to talk, to look ahead.

DUBCEK: A definite situation has now arisen. But even in Cierna*, Comrade Brezhnev, I already sensed that we needed to look ahead. After Bratislava the situation in Czechoslovakia and in the Communist Party was at first favorable in all respects. . . . Thus my comrades and I couldn't understand why . . . military measures were implemented on the part of five countries. . . . These measures—without the notification of me personally, the president, the chairman of the government, the chairman of the National Assembly—were undertaken through extreme steps, extreme measures that, it seems to me, raised—not just before your Party or ours, but before the international Communist movement—the most complex problem that has ever faced the movement.

It's hard for me, given the trip and my bitter mood, to explain immediately my opinion about why we must reach a solution about the real situation that has arisen. Comrades Brezhnev, Kosygin, Podgorny, and Voronov, I don't know what the situation is at home. In the first day of the Soviet Army's arrival, I and the other comrades were isolated and then found ourselves here, not knowing anything. . . . I can only conjecture what could have happened. In the first moments, the members of the Presidium who were with me at the Secretariat were taken to the Party Central Committee under the control of Soviet forces. Through the window I saw several hundred people gathered around the building, and you could hear what they were shouting: "We want to see Svoboda!" "We want to see the president!" "We want Dubcek!" I heard a number of slogans. After that there were shots. It was the last thing I saw. From that point on I know nothing, and can't imagine what's happening in the country and in the Party. . . .

As a Communist who bears a great responsibility for recent events, I am sure that—not only in Czechoslovakia but in Europe, in the whole Communist movement—this action will cause us the bitterest consequences in the breakdown of, and bitter dissension within, the ranks of Communist parties in foreign countries, in capitalist countries.

Thus the matters at hand and the situation are, it seems to me, very complex, although today was the first time I read the newspapers. I can only say, think of me what you will, I have worked for thirty years in the Party, and my whole family has devoted everything to the affairs of the Party, the affairs of socialism. Let whatever

* The stenographic record reads "Chop," not Cierna, but that must be a simple error.

is going to happen to me happen. I'm expecting the worst for myself and I'm resigned to it.

BREZHNEV: Why talk that way?

DUBCEK: . . . Perhaps this will sound bad coming from my lips, but our Presidium had such strong support inside the Party and from the people, who haven't had a party of their own, perhaps, since 1948. . . . We must all discuss this together. But I would be acting wrongly, comrades, if I didn't tell the truth, that I believe that bringing in troops was a terrible political mistake that will have tragic consequences. . . .

In the history of the Czechoslovak people over the last century, the time of Russophilia, the relations of our people toward Russia have always been good, without a negative side. Now, it seems to me, something else has happened. . . .

I can only suppose, since I have no contacts and don't know what's going on there, but nevertheless I know the people, I know the Party, so I don't just suppose but feel sure that my words are valid.

Why do I say this? I'm not saying it merely to express anything more or less unpleasant, but simply in order to look at the reality of the circumstances, because if the appraisal of the situation on your part is somehow unreal, then the methods and solutions to the problem will be incorrect and the results will not be those you believe you are achieving.

There followed a seemingly improvised attempt to bring me up to date by citing various papers that Brezhnev and company had in front of them, while secretaries bustled in and out with still more reports. Much of this was for show. More than once, they lifted things straight off their papers that I knew to be nonsense and that only confirmed how little they really understood about our situation.

PODGORNY: They were shooting out of windows in Prague.

BREZHNEV: They were shooting from attics and windows in Prague and Bratislava. The houses were surrounded, but no one came out. Prague was the most active.

You should know, we can't conceal it. A congress was held yesterday, for one day. How it was organized should be noted here. They met in a car factory. I don't know if that's true or not, but they're announcing it officially.

PODGORNY: In the electric works.

BREZHNEV: The congress was held in the factory club. They're mentioning various numbers of delegates—eight hundred, nine hundred, a thousand people. We know that there weren't any Slovaks there. There were only five: Kolder, Simon, Piller, Sadovsky, and . . .

This cynical appeal to my Slovak national pride was as transparent as any of their obfuscations. No matter what the true number of Slovaks at the congress, of the four (not five) rattled off from this report, only one, Sadovsky, was Slovak.

PODGORNY: Not one member of the Presidium was there.

BREZHNEV: They had elections, it is reported, by open vote. What kind of plenary they elected isn't known, but this is the Czechoslovak Communist Party Central Committee they elected. (*He reads.*) All of them, that is, absolutely right wing. Neither Indra nor Bilak was there. That's the kind of delegates they elected. That was the membership they elected and proclaimed. . . . Someone worked it out thoroughly. Everything was prepared. The Presidium was elected by open vote.

DUBCEK: If things were going normally, everything would be fine with the congress.

Kosygin claimed that a conference of 25,000 Sudeten Germans was taking place in Cheb, a western Bohemian town. From reports several weeks old in our free press, I knew enough to reply that this was happening not in Cheb but in West Germany.

KOSYGIN: In Cheb, under your tenure, a conference of Sudeten Germans is convening. What does that mean? That you allowed it.

DUBCEK: It couldn't be.

KOSYGIN: How could it not be? It was publicized. Twenty-five thousand people have gathered in Cheb and were to convene in three days' time.

DUBCEK: When?

KOSYGIN: In three days.

DUBCEK: In West Germany.

KOSYGIN: In Cheb.

DUBCEK: Did anything happen there?

Thrown into confusion, Kosygin offered, lamely, "In the meantime our troops went in and nothing happened. But it was publicized under you."

Systematically they confused Gustav Husak with Milan Klusak, who was President Svoboda's son-in-law and head of our diplomatic mission in New York. At another point, they told me that the Soviet Army had rescued Oldrich Svestka, allegedly detained by his own editors in the editorial building of *Rude Pravo*, the Party newspaper. In reality, as I later learned, they had found him dead drunk in his office and taken him to the Soviet Embassy, where he'd been told to sleep it off.

Most deceptive were their fabrications regarding Svoboda's trip to Moscow. They pretended that he was not already there but was about to arrive. Why they lied about it I still don't know.

BREZHNEV: Ludvik Ivanovich displayed initiative in coming to us. We were quick to tell him that we were delighted to meet such a great friend and on whatever terms he wanted—him alone or with other delegates. He announced that he would leave by plane at 9:30 A.M. Prague time. Right now he's on the plane. I don't have confirmation, but he said that before his flight he would make an announcement that he was flying to the Soviet Union on an official visit at his own request. . . .

I had a talk with our ambassador in the morning today, since yesterday at 11:30 P.M. Ludvik Ivanovich had sent for him and said that he wanted to fly to Moscow. . . . We don't know the details because our connection is breaking all the time. It's restored, then breaks again. The last we know for sure is that he's in the air. It just isn't known whether or not he made an announcement, what he said he'd say or not. It will probably be clear in a little while since he couldn't have flown out in complete silence.

PODGORNY: There's a lot of noise about him having been arrested.

BREZHNEV: Some underground radio station or other is broadcasting that he's been arrested. How is he flying? At first it was thought that he was flying straight here, and flying with a group: Bilak, Piller, Indra, Kucer [sic], Novak [sic]. But at the last moment we were informed that he's flying to Bratislava to pick up Klusak. He decided to bring him, and we don't object. I don't know Klusak. . . . That's the group the president decided to bring with him. We . . . haven't named a single candidate. There have been no personal ties between us and him. He passed everything on through the Soviet Embassy. We greeted him officially at the airport, as president. * We

* EDITOR'S NOTE: This sentence is in the past tense, which is entirely out of context with the rest of the record, as if it did not belong here.

haven't severed diplomatic relations and we never considered doing so. We will receive him with all customary honors. . . . We will house Comrade Svoboda in the Kremlin. Where to house the other comrades, we ask. Probably in the Kremlin too. . . . I don't know why Ludvik Ivanovich is bringing this delegation. When he comes we'll find out. . . . We've heard that the healthy forces are uniting, that there is life.

In spite of all their obfuscations, I did learn some significant facts. The Fourteenth Congress had assembled clandestinely in Prague, as Bohumil Simon and I had discussed shortly before my kidnapping. They had elected a new leadership, in which, of course, there was no place for traitors. From that I could also draw some wider conclusions: that the Soviets' plan to replace legal bodies of the state and Party had failed, and that there must be widespread passive resistance throughout the country. The initiators of the intervention were now looking with some desperation for a "solution."

> BREZHNEV: . . . we must find an acceptable solution. The more ener-getically we discuss, the more candidly and realistically we ap-proach all this, the sooner we'll find the correct solution. . . .
> PODGORNY: A way out must be found.

Implicitly they were offering me a prominent role in their solution when they talked about the "conspiracy" behind my back. At the same time, they did not hesitate to use veiled threats. Of the four Soviet leaders, the most ag-gressive and rude was Kosygin. He and the others made a number of clearly anti-Semitic innuendos and allusions, particularly to Frantisek Kriegel and Ota Sik. Simon is usually considered a Jewish name in Russia, so, although Bohumil Simon was not Jewish, he was also presumed to be so by my inter-locutors, with all the anti-Semitic overtones such presumption entailed.

> BREZHNEV: What we're saying is that we're not blaming you—a lot went on behind your back, and you couldn't have known it all.
> PODGORNY: Alexander Stepanovich . . . there was such an uproar around the meeting at Cierna. . . . The events that occurred around Cierna were organized by you-know-who, they collected signatures, namely Kriegel and others. No one informed the people that it needed to have been that way.
> BREZHNEV: Because after the meeting there was a conference of Si-mon, K———, which took place without you, where a question was raised about whether or not to allow the troops to enter. . . . We

have the time to show you how all of this was organized and which people were working on it.

DUBCEK: Is Cernik coming?*

BREZHNEV: Yes, soon.

DUBCEK: And Smrkovsky?

BREZHNEV: In a few hours. Everyone's alive, everyone's healthy, they're at a place of rest.

DUBCEK: I'm in such a state—soldiers, guns pointed at me all the time, I couldn't get out of the car for seven hours, men with machine guns on both sides, armored cars. You think it was easy?

BREZHNEV: It was a matter of your security.

KOSYGIN: . . . I came to Karlovy Vary, and you gave me five bodyguards. I wasn't worried. On the contrary, I was grateful.

DUBCEK: Comrade Kosygin, there's no comparison. You were being protected voluntarily, and here it's a question of force.

Brezhnev tried to cite the example of Hungary as a lesson from which we could learn:

BREZHNEV: Let's remember the Hungarian events. It was worse then. There was no one but Kadar. Over the years our friendship has grown stronger, and now, in these days of trouble, everything is normal in Hungary. I spoke with Kadar today. The people have grown, learned.

But the prospect of the "fraternal" troops of the Warsaw Pact giving my countrymen instructions in socialism brought to my mind other lessons of history:

DUBCEK: You realize that in Slovakia the Hungarian Army will teach the Slovaks . . . a Slovak soldier who lived through the war, fought as a partisan, and participated in the Slovak National Uprising must now surrender his arms to a Hungarian soldier.

BREZHNEV: All that must be overcome.

DUBCEK: . . . German forces come in and we give our men instructions to obey them—you must understand that psychological moment.

At great length they fretted and harangued about the surreptitiously convened Fourteenth Congress.

---

* EDITOR'S NOTE: This question proves that Dubcek could not have known at this time that Cernik was already in Moscow as well. It contradicts Cernik's assertion that the two had come to Moscow several hours earlier and had met there before Dubcek's interrogation.

BREZHNEV: Holding the congress is pointless now. How could the
     congress be held?
DUBCEK: Desire is one thing, reality another.
BREZHNEV: Then it's a fictitious congress.
DUBCEK: The majority of the delegates have a right to be there.
PODGORNY: Who convened the congress?
DUBCEK: Evidently they themselves. One has to know the situation in
     the country.
PODGORNY: Many of the Slovaks weren't at the congress, so who could
     have convened it? No one in the whole Presidium took part.
KOSYGIN: But they didn't do anything at the congress, they didn't hear
     any reports. They just had elections.
DUBCEK: . . . Because the Presidium was no longer in existence.
PODGORNY: It still isn't.
DUBCEK: At home.

Finally Cernik entered the room, and the whole scenario had to be
repeated for his benefit. Bewilderingly, they threw around accusations,
speculations, and conjecture about the political stance of this or that of our
leaders, all aimed at ferreting out reformers and identifying potential stooges.
Earlier in the meeting Brezhnev had singled out Zdenek Mlynar for praise:

BREZHNEV: When they invited him to the congress, Mlynar said that
     he wouldn't take part. . . . I don't know if it's true.

And they counted up those who had not yet let them down:

BREZHNEV: Dzur, Rusel, and Mukha have behaved well and
     calmly. . . . I don't know where Husak was.
DUBCEK: Evidently in Slovakia.

By the time the meeting started to wind down, they were again harping
on the Fourteenth Party Congress. Cernik had taken almost no part in the
exchanges. The stenographic record has him speaking only twice briefly,
and, when he agrees to the Soviet demand to cancel the Party congress in
Prague, he is not quoted directly but only, apparently, by Podgorny. I say
apparently because on this point the transcript is quite confusing.

DUBCEK: There was never a situation in which the congress could have
     convened prematurely. Events created that situation when your
     Party leadership decided to send in troops.

KOSYGIN: You can justify that congress?

PODGORNY: The question is whether it can be considered lawful or not.

Alexander Stepanovich believes that, in his words, it can't be helped—the congress took place.

Cernik believes that the congress should never be recognized as legal.*

KOSYGIN: Recognizing the congress as legal would mean that in a month, and perhaps sooner, Czechoslovakia would be bourgeois. Look at its makeup: Sik, Goldstuecker. It brought together a particular group of people with their eyes set on a Western regime and who are waging a struggle against the socialist camp and the Soviet Union. Do you really think that we can send in the army and afterwards come to terms with that crowd? . . . They were obviously preparing for it a long time, even when you were still there. The fact is that it was well planned, the forces were in place, the auditorium was ready. . . . They didn't ask for your opinion about whether to convene or not.

DUBCEK: They didn't know where I was.

KOSYGIN: They were preparing the congress when your telephone was still working. We have that information. They could have asked, you were at the Central Committee, you couldn't leave, did you give the go-ahead or not?

DUBCEK: The go-ahead was given to prepare for the congress of September 9. I think that it must have happened afterwards.

KOSYGIN: There wasn't time, in twelve hours, to assemble congress delegates from all over Czechoslovakia. . . . It was all prepared earlier. What's still unknown is whether they conducted the congress with or without your consent. . . . There were people there who behind your back were working against you and against everything progressive. . . . If the congress is declared lawful, they will overturn all your policies, the whole political structure of Czechoslovakia, and transform Czechoslovakia into a bourgeois republic. This will be done instantaneously. They have the support of Western governments, and thus the goal established a long time ago will be achieved: to separate Czechoslovakia from the socialist countries and create a bourgeois republic of the Masaryk type.

---

* In the transcript, this sentence can be interpreted as though spoken by Cernik himself. Given Podgorny's speech and textual evidence, however, it seems that the stenographer may have attributed it to Cernik by mistake.

In a last attempt to throw sand in our eyes, they raised the specter of an American plot:

> KOSYGIN: Reports came out from radio stations that you were no longer alive, that you had been killed. It was done by one agency, an agency that counted on the fact that if you weren't around a new leadership would be needed.
>
> PODGORNY: I'll bring you a report from an American agency. The American information agency broadcast a report saying that a ham radio operator in the USA had received a transmission from a ham radio operator in Czechoslovakia claiming that Dubcek was killed. As UPI declared, some ham radio operator in the state of ---- received a message from a ham radio operator in Czechoslovakia saying that Dubcek had been killed two hours before. A similar radiogram in Morse code was received by another radio service.
>
> KOSYGIN: We must now quickly find out how they organized all this, and we must act against them decisively, because there won't be another way out. If we don't take measures, the matter will lead to civil war in Czechoslovakia, and responsibility for the civil war will, of course, be borne by you. And it will break out because steps weren't taken. It's a very dangerous moment.
>
> Sik is in England.
>
> DUBCEK: In Yugoslavia.
>
> KOSYGIN: The minister for foreign affairs, who was in Yugoslavia, has now gone to America to make a protest. Your friend found himself some friends in America too.

The whole meeting had lasted more than two hours, and we now also have a record of what Brezhnev thought of it. Here I quote from a Polish record of a briefing he held in the Kremlin the following day, Saturday, August 24, for Ulbricht, Gomulka, and the rest of the Warsaw Five.*

"Dubcek assumed a worse attitude than Cernik," Brezhnev said to his accomplices. "If we do not manage to solve the situation with Dubcek, then let Indra be at the head of the Central Committee. . . . But it is important that Dubcek agree to declare the Congress invalid. If he agrees to that, let Indra become second secretary. Then it will be possible to replace Dubcek."

Gomulka subsequently remarked, "In Czechoslovakia, the [Commu-

---

* Protocol from a meeting of Party and government delegations of Bulgaria, GDR, Poland, Hungary, and the USSR in Moscow, August 24-26, 1968; Archives of New Sources, Warsaw, "Secret," no number.

nist] Party does not exist anymore. It turned itself into a group of Social Democrats and allied itself with the counterrevolution."

At the end of the meeting, with no conclusions reached, the four Soviets remained seated behind the table while I was led to another doorway, opposite the one I had entered. I can't recall if Cernik came with me. I found myself in a spacious antechamber and was surprised by all the familiar faces. Immediately, I spotted the white-haired head of President Svoboda and turned to him spontaneously. I was genuinely happy to see him there. I realized that I was no longer alone.

Svoboda and I had had a very cordial relationship for many years, and we had a great deal of respect for each other. We had agreed on practically all the aspects of Prague Spring; Svoboda was a sincere supporter of reforms. He had had his bitter experiences with the old regime, and he appeared to understand the importance of the changes for which I was striving. Therefore, I expected from him as much joy and relief on seeing me as I felt on seeing him, despite the deplorable circumstances.

But, as I looked in his eyes, I was shocked by his stiff and cool expression. Svoboda, to tell the truth, never seemed totally at ease; he always had the rigid bearing of a military man. But at that frozen moment he seemed to exude an almost hostile air, as if something had changed his deepest feelings. Later I nearly forgot the experience, and I regret that I never asked him about it.

This strange moment did not last more than a second or two, and I am not sure that anyone else took notice of it. Svoboda's countenance soon relaxed, and we started to talk, to exchange information about ourselves and the situation back home.

Here I learned, for the first time, about the Soviets' demand that we sign various documents constituting an agreement of sorts on how to solve the impasse, and a list of obligations, presumed mutual. What they really wanted from us, I easily guessed, was a *post factum* justification for their aggression. I said I absolutely refused to take part in such a charade. I pointed out, among other things, that we had no constitutional authority to make any deals with the Soviets behind the backs, and without the approval of, the government and parliament. Svoboda tried to change my mind, arguing that an extraordinary situation justified such extralegal steps.

I could not bring myself to accept what I viewed as a legally impermissible, humiliating, and entirely unfair process. I was filled with anger, and I told them that I would rather resign, which would take me out of the picture completely.

At this point Svoboda and the others, while considering compromise, were not yet ready to accept an act of capitulation dictated by the Soviets;

even Svoboda seemed to be quite firm in defending our position. It was somewhat later that he became more accommodating, as he tired and slipped into impatient resignation.

Cernik thought there was no way but to try to talk with the Soviets, and he hoped to achieve an honorable compromise. Smrkovsky, whom they brought to the Kremlin the next day, held a similar position. I was simply unable to overcome my feelings and stuck stubbornly to my refusal to participate in any negotiations with the Soviets.

During the conversation with Svoboda—it was already about 3:00 A.M.—I felt unwell, as the tensions and fatigue of the previous days started to overcome me. A member of Svoboda's party offered to let me rest in one of the rooms assigned to the president's group, but the Soviet officials there flatly refused it. "The Kremlin is not a hotel," one of them said. So they led me down to a car and took me to a guesthouse of sorts where I could sleep. I later learned that the other kidnap victims—Smrkovsky, Kriegel, Cernik, Simon, and Spacek—were also kept outside the Kremlin.

I slept most of the day Saturday, and was awakened in the late afternoon and instructed to get ready to go back to the Kremlin. I still did not feel well, and was even more tired than the day before. Somebody asked me later whether I had been treated by a Soviet physician in the guesthouse. If it happened, I must say I have no recollection of it.

Back in the Kremlin, I met the Czechoslovak group again, and I was urged, once more, to take part in "negotiations" with the Soviets. Again, I refused. But I also thought about ways of gaining time. The Soviets obviously needed a swift solution, and I calculated that delays might help us gain some concessions. Anyway, I proposed that the remaining members of our Party leadership be brought to the Kremlin. Otherwise, we could not act in an official capacity.

At that point I had to lie down, and I was taken to one of the rooms reserved for Svoboda's staffers. While I was resting there, the Soviets quickly accepted my demand and flew six other people to Moscow: Mlynar, Lenart, Barbirek, Jakes, Rigo, and Svestka. Mlynar came to see me and gave me a sketchy report on the situation back home—the passive resistance, the discussions at the Party congress, and so on. An informal meeting with the Russians took place after I left our group Saturday night, and Smrkovsky came to tell me about the proceedings. He also told me more news from home, where it was extremely tense. The Soviets were apparently unable to silence the radio, and dozens of free newspapers continued to be published and distributed under the noses of the occupation forces.

I also learned that the traitors were in complete political isolation. Practically all existing political and professional organizations stood firmly behind the reform policies of Prague Spring and had demanded the withdrawal of foreign troops and a safe return from Moscow of the whole leadership, especially those known to have been kidnapped.

We also enjoyed wide international support, I learned, including that of the majority of Western Communist parties. Soviet aggression against Czechoslovakia had been brought before the Security Council of the United Nations by the United States, and our foreign minister, Professor Jiri Hajek, had interrupted his vacation in Yugoslavia to appear there to protest the invasion.

All of this was heartening, of course, but it did not change the basic facts that our country was occupied by a huge military machine and that there was no force in the world that would chase it out. At the same time, the unanimous character of the resistance had already forced the collapse of the political framework for intervention. That left the Soviets facing the unwelcome necessity of a direct military government. This alternative, however, was unacceptable ideologically as well as politically, both at home and abroad; it would expose the whole operation for what it really was—the naked conquest of another country.

So they had to shift gears and try to impose on us these negotiations, which they now publicized in their usual deceptive way. When Svoboda had arrived in Moscow, for example—I learned this while still there—the Soviets had quickly prepared an "enthusiastic" welcome for him, with half of the Politburo, Brezhnev included, lined up at the airport. Then Brezhnev and Podgorny drove with him through Moscow in an open limousine among cheering crowds, who had been ordered to fill the sidewalks along the way. That drive was transmitted by Soviet television and radio for the whole world to see that all was just an act of "friendship." (A few hours afterwards, Brezhnev and Podgorny were conducting their charade for me about Svoboda being "in the air.")

Despite such publicity, the Soviets were ill prepared for a "negotiated" outcome. The negotiations themselves—as I learned from Smrkovsky and Cernik—were chaotic and lacked any clear purpose in their early stages. Until the last day, Sunday, August 25, there was no formal meeting of the two "delegations." The contents of the final document that concluded this second stage of the drama took shape slowly in separate conversations between individuals or among very small groups.

I took no direct part in these exchanges. At the beginning, it was Svoboda who talked with the Soviets. Later, when they changed their minds about what to do with me and the other five kidnapped Presidium members, it was mainly Cernik and Smrkovsky who conducted these talks. As for traitors like Bilak and Indra, even the Soviets did not seem to take them seriously anymore. My offer to step down as first secretary was rejected by most other members of our group, who insisted repeatedly that I remain in position and participate in the talks. Svoboda was particularly assertive, arguing with me forcefully several times about the necessity to reach a compromise. As time passed, I got the impression he was prepared to make almost any concession to diffuse the explosive situation.

Cernik was too optimistic. He thought our position was strong enough to force the Soviets to retreat on matters of substance. Smrkovsky, I think, was more realistic, and as always inclined to look at all sides of a question. He recognized how important it was for the Soviets to get me involved in the outcome of the talks, and he encouraged me to stay out of the process until a reasonably acceptable compromise was in sight.

With their failure to replace our legitimate leadership with an obedient Party-state hybrid on the 1956 Hungarian model, the Soviets' assertion that *we* had asked for the invasion lost all credibility. Now they strove to legitimize the aggression by having us concede officially that it was "necessary" and that there had been a "counterrevolution" in Czechoslovakia. This was a crucial ideological point, and one could see how important it must have been for them.

They also kept hectoring us to admit the validity of the admonitions in the Warsaw Letter and our error in refuting them. To us, these doctrinal refinements were maddening and capricious, but to the Soviets they were serious stuff. Ritual and ideology had become one and the same in the Stalinist system, and they could not swallow the fact that a "brotherly" Party could hold to its own opinion: it might encourage others to do the same.

The biggest bone in their craw was our policy of reform and its embodiment in the Action Program. This was an especially sticky problem for them, because they could not really attack the program directly and in specific terms. They had never published its text in their media, and their criticism had always been vague, wrapped in dogmatic and distorting references. In their own backyard they were still striving to reverse Khrushchev's reforms without appearing to do so, since that might jeopardize their simultaneous grasping after "respectability" on the international stage. Since our reforms were a logical extension of their own earlier de-Stalinization, they had to choose indirect ways to attack our Action Program and use the sort of double-talk at which they excelled. Muddy or not, they wanted their reservations included.

There were two further demands. First, they wanted us to declare void and invalid the Fourteenth Party Congress, which had started meeting secretly in Prague the second night after the invasion. The congress, as I have mentioned, had already elected a new Central Committee, without

Soviet stooges on it. Second, they demanded that we ask the U.N. Security Council to withdraw from its agenda the question of Warsaw Pact aggression against Czechoslovakia.

Since I did not directly participate in the talks, I can only give a secondhand account of them. But I should say that at no point in these exchanges was I really an outsider. Our people—Smrkovsky, Cernik, Spacek, Simon, and others—kept me informed. They asked my opinion on various issues, and I never refused to give it. So indirectly I was part of the dealings, but I could not bring myself to direct participation. I have always been a spontaneous creature, and my indignation at the Soviets' skulduggery was too deep.

Nevertheless, I was not blind to the fact that a way out of this situation had to be found. I shared, in general terms, President Svoboda's apprehension that the longer the uncertain conditions existed, the greater the danger of a bloody conflict at home. I did not, however, share his inclination to sacrifice so much—all our ideas and principles—just to end the impasse. That is why I stayed offstage, relying mainly on our principal negotiators, Cernik and Smrkovsky, to inject my suggestions.

The first stage of these preliminary contacts lasted about thirty hours— from the arrival of the president's party in Moscow to the night of Saturday, August 24. We felt we had obtained a realistic idea of what the Soviets really wanted, and now we could reflect on our own further steps. It took the next stage, however, for us to sort out the possible from the impossible.

23

THE MOSCOW DIKTAT

O N Saturday night, August 24, or Sunday morning, August 25, we agreed that the time had come for a counterproposal. Cernik led the way with Smrkovsky but followed that up in detailed ongoing discussions with me. We differed in our expectations of the likely outcome of this step, but we basically agreed on our position.

The contents and tone of our proposal were similar to those of our answer to the Warsaw Letter back in July, except more subdued, reflecting the reality of the occupation. Still, it repeated our refusal to recognize the existence of counterrevolution in Czechoslovakia, it firmly defended the Action Program, it characterized the invasion as a "tragic misunderstanding" or "tragic error"—I am not quite sure which—and it demanded a Soviet commitment to withdraw their troops. We felt that this was a dignified negotiating position. Whether it was also realistic under the circumstances is another matter.

During the day Sunday, Smrkovsky came to inform me that the Soviets had answered our proposal with arrogance and threats, flatly refusing practically all of our main points. They characterized Cernik's proposal as an "ultimatum," and Kosygin told Smrkovsky that we were in no position to make demands. Time was on their side, Kosygin maintained, and they could wait as long as it took for us to understand that.

Obviously, the Soviets were aware of the divisions emerging in our group and were trying to make use of them. Here I am referring not to the Bilak-Indra crowd, who were already out of the picture, with neither side paying them any attention, but rather to President Svoboda's overriding worry about finding a solution and his growing impatience with our resistance to the worst Soviet demands. And, most important, there was the gradual defection of Husak.

I learned from Smrkovsky and Cernik that Husak was almost certainly shifting to the Soviet side. It was his surprise support for the Soviet demand that the Fourteenth Party Congress be declared void that split our ranks and forced us to accept this Soviet claim. Not only did we lose that crucial point but our whole negotiating position was significantly weakened.

As a pretext for his shift, Husak claimed that there were not enough Slovak delegates at the congress. This was subterfuge; the fact was that the occupation had disrupted the country's transportation system to such an extent that it was physically impossible for many delegates to get to Prague. The fact is that the congress Husak was disowning, if fully attended, would have consisted of nearly 30 percent Slovak representatives. And, ironically, it elected Husak himself, for the first time since the early 1950s, a member of the Czechoslovak Party Central Committee.

As the meetings went on, Husak frequently assumed so-called objective and realistic positions, clearly signaling to the Soviets that, unlike most of us, he was cooperative and "reasonable." His rewards were to come later. Now, at any rate, I understood why Kosygin had tried to make such an issue out of "only five Slovaks" being elected to the congress.

Neither Svoboda nor Husak was a member of the Party Presidium at this time, so they had no real business participating in our discussions. But this was an extraordinary situation, and the Soviets themselves readily characterized the talks as a "Party-state" affair. This was both expedient—in that it allowed them to make use of any collection of people on our side willing to accept their conditions—and deliberate—since it seemed to justify their meddling in both Party and state affairs.

In this setting, Svoboda's presidential office gave him clout far beyond his customary role and actual constitutional powers. Husak was only a deputy prime minister, but with his long-standing reputation at home as a Slovak nationalist and his recently acquired one as a reformer, it was expected that he would soon be elected first secretary of the Slovak Party to replace the toadying Vasil Bilak. This prospect strengthened his hand significantly. After that he would be elected to full membership in the Czechoslovak Presidium. That he owed his rise in Slovak Party ranks to playing the reformist card until hours before the invasion added no little salt to the wounds he now inflicted.

A few hours after rejecting Cernik's draft of an agreement, the Soviets sent over their own document, later known as "the protocol." It was worse than anyone had expected, and much longer than the document signed later. This "proposal" restated the Soviet demand that we acknowledge the existence of counterrevolution in Czechoslovakia and the legitimacy of the invasion. It pointedly ignored any reference to the withdrawal of their army from Czechoslovakia. Further, they demanded we declare the Fourteenth Party Congress invalid, reinstitute censorship, and replace the current managers of radio and television. One section insisted we retain traitors like Indra and Bilak, and another listed people they wanted removed: among them Kriegel, Cisar, and at least three members of the government— Deputy Prime Minister Ota Sik, Foreign Minister Jiri Hajek, and Interior Minister Josef Pavel.

In this form, the protocol was unacceptable to us, and we told the Soviets so. At least they had finally come out into the open with their inventory of demands, and this changed the situation qualitatively. We could assume that this list represented the maximum of their demands: we took it as the baseline for a better deal. From this point on, we strove for corrections, changes, and deletions in the Soviet draft.

In the process of this paperwork, which took place the whole day of August 25 and into the twenty-sixth, a text emerged that still looked terrible but was a considerable improvement on the original. The Soviets agreed, for example, to drop their insistence that we recognize the legitimacy of the invasion and the existence of counterrevolution. But they would not allow any language committing them to withdraw their forces. Especially galling to us was the tone they insisted on using, which sought to give the impression that we were doing everything voluntarily, if not on our own initiative.

As with the Bratislava Declaration, we accepted some points because the vague and pretentious language at least afforded more than one interpreta-tion. One example was Point 5, in which the Soviets promised to withdraw their troops gradually "as soon as the threat to socialism passed." In our opinion, there had never been any such threat, and in its wording the point at least spelled out the temporary nature of the occupation. In the long run, of course, this double-talk brought us very little, but in the short run it looked less hopeless.

At a meeting in the Kremlin during the early morning hours of Monday, August 26—a meeting I still did not attend—a majority of our group was ready to sign. That majority included the Bilak-Indra group, joined by Lenart, Piller, and then Czechoslovak Ambassador to Moscow Vladimir Koucky, a longtime secretary of the Central Committee under Novotny, and, more significantly, President Svoboda, Husak, General Dzur, and Dr. Kucera, the non-Communist minister of justice. Thirteen out of twenty possible representatives were therefore ready to sign, and of the remaining seven at least one, Prime Minister Cernik, was strongly inclined to join them. The rest were Smrkovsky, Spacek, Simon, Mlynar, Kriegel, and myself.

Kriegel was a special case in that he too had not taken part in direct negotiations with the Soviets, but his immediate circumstances were somewhat different from mine. Until August 26, he had had no freedom of decision, for he had been kept in isolation somewhere outside the Kremlin, and we were not sure of his whereabouts. To the many questions that Smrkovsky, Cernik, Svoboda, and others asked concerning him, the Soviets always responded elusively, saying only that he was all right and safe.

Not until later did I realize that we should have pressed Svoboda to tell the Soviets that without Kriegel we would not talk about anything. But there was no formal meeting of both groups before the night of the twenty-fifth. All previous discussions had been conducted informally in countless individual conversations or small conferences. It wasn't until the morning of Monday, August 26, that the Soviets finally yielded to our demands and brought Kriegel to the Kremlin.

I was still in my room and only learned about Kriegel's arrival after he was gone. Smrkovsky briefed him on all the developments and let him read the draft of the protocol. Then Cernik and Svoboda talked to him. Kriegel resolutely refused either to participate in any negotiations or to sign the document and asked instead to be taken back to his quarters.

Of course, I fully understood Kriegel's stand. Had I been in his position, I would undoubtedly have done the same. The Soviets later suggested that Kriegel should attend the final meeting of both groups. I sensed immediately that their intention was to use his negative stand to lay open the disagreements within our group and thus weaken our efforts for further improvements in the draft document. I flatly refused this proposal; Kriegel's decision to stay out of the negotiations had to be respected.

Although we were as one in refusing to attend the meetings, Kriegel's and my situations were different. For many people at home—and abroad—my name had become the embodiment of the Prague Spring and of our struggle to defend it against Soviet pressure. Hence I had a clear and undeniable personal responsibility for the lives of thousands of people at home, who would almost certainly take my refusal to sign the "agreement" as encouragement to active resistance. I did not believe I had the right to allow that, for it would only lead to a bloodbath. Many years later I saw my conclusions confirmed: I learned from high Soviet representatives, especially General Yershov, a member of the Soviet High Command in 1968, that the Soviet Army was only waiting for a sign of active resistance in order to suppress it indiscriminately.

The real threat of suppression at the time shows how little our decisions could be considered "voluntary." What we had before us was a classic example of an uneven treaty, imposed by force and intimidation. For Czechs and Slovaks such a treaty had eerie qualities of déjà vu: it seemed almost a carbon copy of the Protectorate of Bohemia and Moravia imposed on the last prewar Czechoslovak president, Dr. Emil Hacha, by Hitler in Berlin on March 15, 1939.

In Moscow, all that we could responsibly do, I felt, was try to limit the damage and save as much space for further independent action as possible. I thought that by Monday there was little purpose in prolonging the tug-of-war about words and turns of phrase. I tried to assess the potential of the concessions the Soviets had made in comparison with their original demands and thought I saw a certain room to maneuver in the future. The last draft did not legitimize the invasion; it did not admit the existence of counterrevolution in Czechoslovakia; it did not restate the argumentation of the Warsaw Letter; and it did not refute our reform policies.

We even managed to make the Soviets implicitly confirm these reforms as the basis of our future course. This was the meaning of a reference to the decisions of the May 1968 Czechoslovak Communist Party Central Committee, which had confirmed about 98 percent of the Action Program. The Soviets agreed to define the May resolutions as the foundation of our subsequent policy.

These grudging concessions did not keep me from loathing everything that remained in the protocol. It was still a diktat through and through. One of the fifteen points even declared the protocol secret "in the interest of both communist parties" and their "friendship"—as if secrecy were going to be possible under the circumstances. The language was pretentious, and all references to "our intentions" or "our decisions" were false. In view of the hard-won loopholes, however, I am still convinced that without internal treason we would have been able to save a fair part of the reforms.

In the end I decided to attend the "plenary" meeting with the Soviet leadership scheduled for late afternoon Monday—it would be my first meeting with them since our encounter on Friday night—and to sign the protocol after some more changes in wording. Most important, I wanted to have language stating that the occupation was temporary and specifying the conditions of withdrawal of Soviet troops.

When we entered the conference room, the Soviet Politburo were already seated along a long rectangular table, and we occupied chairs facing them. I had Cernik on my left and Smrkovsky on my right. One would have expected a businesslike meeting, devoted strictly to a review of the draft document. Brezhnev, however, opened the session with a cliché-ridden speech. I tried to keep my eyes on the table, letting his words go in one ear and out the other. But when he described the sorrow with which his Politburo had decided to send in their tanks, I felt sick and angry. Nevertheless, I did my best to stay detached.

We had agreed to have Cernik make the opening remarks on our side. In a cool and matter-of-fact way, avoiding any polemics, he defended the reform policy and pointed out the negative effects of the invasion for the cause of socialism.

A member of the Soviet Politburo, I believe Pyotr Shelest, first secretary in the Ukraine, interrupted Cernik's presentation at one point with an offensive remark, and Brezhnev cut in as soon as Cernik finished, objecting to his negative characterization of the invasion. At that point, I felt impelled to take the floor.

I did not expect to change the minds of the men on the other side of the table, but I felt it was my obligation to restate our case openly, directly, and honestly. We were soon to sign an act of surrender packed with falsehood and pretense, and it was being imposed upon us by brute force and threats. For the record I felt obliged to give things their real names before that final humiliation.

I had no prepared notes; I was speaking from my heart. Unlike Cernik, I could speak in Russian, and I noticed that the somber looking Soviet Politburo listened attentively. At least none of them tried to interrupt.

I pointed out that our reforms had been long overdue and absolutely necessary. Socialism, and the Communist Party, had been seriously discredited by the previous policies, and we could not go on without significant changes in all spheres—political, economic, and cultural. The Action Program was the basis of these reforms, and it enjoyed the overwhelming support of the Party and the general public. Our reforms in no way threatened, but rather solidified, our commitment to socialism, which also meant our commitment to the Soviet alliance. From the beginning, I said, Soviet criticism of our reform policies had been rooted in ignorance of our internal situation; that was the reason we rejected it. The invasion was a tragedy, and its aftereffects might never be corrected in the minds and hearts of our people. The document before us, I concluded, gave this tragedy an even larger dimension. We might be forced to sign it, but let it be understood that it would not solve any problems. In the long run, it would make them even worse.

There was a brief silence after I finished; then Brezhnev spoke. This time he left all flowery references to comradely solidarity and eternal friendship aside and instead resorted to pure Realpolitik. Now he made it clear that ideas and ideals were quite secondary. He simply came at us with Mao Tsetung's proverbial "barrel of the gun." Here he revealed himself and his whole Politburo for what they were: a bunch of cynical, arrogant bureau-crats with a feudal outlook who had long since ceased to serve anything but themselves.

He said that since the end of the last war Czechoslovakia had been a part of the Soviet security zone, and that the Soviet Union had no intention of giving it up. What had worried the Soviet Politburo most about Prague Spring had been our tendency toward independence: that I did not send him my speeches in advance for review, that I did not ask his permission for personnel changes. They could not tolerate this, and, when we had not submitted to other forms of pressure, they had invaded the country. He looked very pleased with what he was saying. Brezhnev always seemed able to move himself—even to tears.

I realized that in this crazy-house setting nothing made any sense—not the ideals I cherished and I thought we shared, not the treaties we had concluded, not the international organizations we were both part of. I deeply disagreed with what he said and told him so, before even attempting to argue for my point of view. But Brezhnev suddenly stood up, his face turned red, his thick eyebrows beetled down, and he started to shout at me that all our negotiations were apparently good for nothing. Then he turned around and slowly walked out of the room, followed by his entire Politburo in almost military fashion.

While they marched out, I quickly rethought the whole situation and my place in it. Brezhnev's bottom line was that we were his country's colony, and it was his business, not ours, to decide how to run our affairs. Our understanding of our own situation did not matter. It was entirely irrelevant whether we did things right or wrong. What mattered was whether they approved or not. Did it make any sense, under these circumstances, to sign another worthless "agreement" with them?

As soon as the door closed behind the last Soviet Politburo member, I said, "I do not think that these negotiations make any sense. You heard what I heard. What confidence can we have in them?"

There was no answer, and I added, "It makes no difference whether we sign anything or not. They'll do whatever they want, anyway. I am not signing that protocol."

There was a commotion where we still sat; then everybody stood up and started talking. Svoboda came toward me to tell me that it was too late and that I had to sign. Cernik took up the practical side: if we did not sign now, they might force us to sign something much worse next time. Smrkovsky was not sure but said that, all things considered, we had no choice but to sign. After a short pause, he brought up the parallel to 1939, when Presi-dent Hacha returned from Berlin. "They managed to slow things down and to save a lot of people," he said. In a way, this looked like the end of Smrkovsky's lifelong belief in socialism, for he now saw little difference between the Nazis and the Soviets.

After much discussion and persuasion from almost everybody, I reluctantly came back around to where I'd been in the morning. In the meantime, it had become night, and a new meeting had to be arranged. We met in the same conference room and at the same table.

At this last meeting, there were no more speeches, probably to avoid another outburst of disagreement. We proceeded directly to the review of the document, paragraph after paragraph. The Soviets accepted several changes that we proposed. My sole concern, at that point, was the question of troop withdrawal. This was carried out by a reformulation of Point 5 of the protocol, albeit not as distinctly as I would have preferred.

Unfortunately, in order to get Soviet acceptance of an eventual, if unspecific, troop withdrawal, including a promised fast pullout from large cities, we had to make our own concessions: in personnel and in withdrawing the invasion question from the U.N. Security Council agenda. Brezhnev and the others had been insisting on both points in each of the multitude of encounters over the past days. For reasons of their own, the Soviets did not want the personnel changes they were demanding spelled out in the document. But orally Brezhnev was very explicit about who had to be dismissed and whom (of the traitors) he was forcing us to retain in their old positions. He also made it very clear that any Soviet concessions were contingent upon our compliance with these demands.

A few other issues outside the scope of the document were settled. Of these the most important, in my view, was the drafting of certain members of the Central Committee elected by the invalidated Fourteenth Party Congress into the old existing body. I told Brezhnev that declaring the congress void was not such a simple matter, because it had been attended by a large majority of delegates, and their will had to be respected in some way. One solution was to bring some of them into the existing Central Committee. Brezhnev did not reject this directly. In this way, we succeeded in defining a "gray zone" within and around the document where I could maneuver.

But I was unable to foresee the practical importance of the last changes we had achieved. I was sad, tired, and humiliated. These feelings were strongest when they brought the redrafted and retyped document for signature and let in a crowd of television cameramen and photographers. Brezhnev remembered public relations, but he obviously overlooked a sticky detail: here we were signing a document that was presumably secret!

It was shortly before midnight, and we were supposed to leave for a flight back home at 3:00 on Tuesday morning. As we were served some refreshments, I looked around to see whether Kriegel had already joined us. I did not see him and asked loudly where he was. Why wasn't he with us now?

It came up that the Soviets did not want him to return with us to Prague. Brezhnev argued that the presence of the only man who did not sign the protocol could cause political difficulties. I refused to leave Kriegel behind, and Svoboda supported me energetically, as did Smrkovsky, Simon, and others. Finally Brezhnev gave in. We were about to leave for the airport, and Brezhnev promised that Kriegel would be there too. When we arrived, we refused to board the plane until we ascertained that Kriegel was waiting for us in the aircraft. The new era was not opening with a great deal of trust.

As we took off, all our thoughts turned to home. It was clear to us that this was no glorious return. Very few would like the news we carried. We had lost a war, figuratively speaking, and six of us were returning from captivity, not from a junket. But the message we brought could hardly be unexpected.

Moreover, there were strict limits to what we were permitted to say publicly about the protocol. That, I thought, was the toughest part of what I saw immediately ahead of me as the airplane slowly descended: how not to tell the whole truth, yet avoid lying.

24

THE ONSET OF
"NORMALIZATION"

T HE period that began at the end of August gained historical notoriety as
the era of "normalization." Few of those who remember this time can think
of it without repugnance and bitter irony.

For the Czech and Slovak people, one of the most perplexing aspects of
those days must have been the abrupt change in public communication.
Words that had been used freely in their natural sense were suddenly turned
upside down to produce a perverted "newspeak" imposed on us by the
Soviets. It was a colossal masquerade, of course, and behind this facade the
struggle went on.

The term *normalization* first appeared in the Soviet draft of the Moscow
Protocol, but it did not arouse any particular reaction on our side. We were
focusing on the issues we believed could hurt us most, like the legitimacy of
the invasion and the absence of a statement defining the occupation as
temporary. Compared with these issues, the use of the term *normalization*
did not immediately imply anything sinister; it seemed to us that to bring
things back to normal after an invasion was a natural requirement. But the
Soviets had a different idea of what was normal.

Not only the protocol but the whole era was filled with ambiguities as we
tried to give the policies the Soviets were imposing upon us a different
direction. Several times they told us with arrogant self-assurance that time
was on their side—no matter what we did. I had no doubt that their
intention was to put the lid on completely as soon as conditions permitted.
We were determined to resist the encroachment as long as we could.

We were now at something of a standoff: on the one hand, our country
was at the gunpoint of a huge occupation army, and the protocol had been

imposed under threat of a bloodbath. On the other hand, they had signally failed to find an acceptable political solution that would sanction their aggression. As a way out of the stalemate, they had had to release us unharmed and even reinstall us in our positions. Here was the old truth of the limited value of bayonets: you can do many things with them, but you cannot sit on them.

We were, however, surely the weaker wrestler, although our situation was not entirely hopeless. There were a number of ways we could continue to resist, but everything depended upon unity within our ranks—at the top and between us and the Czech and Slovak peoples.

As for unity at the top, the situation was complicated by the traitors we were obliged to retain and the reformers we were being forced to replace. In the early normalization period, we had some freedom to choose replacements for those who were not acceptable to the Soviets, and the traitors in our ranks were at least well known, entirely isolated, and thus able to be effectively neutralized.

To preserve unity between ourselves and the people at large was a more serious challenge. Official information about what had happened in the Kremlin was presented in the form of a "bilateral" communiqué issued by the Soviets and stuffed with lies and nonsense. Our stay in Moscow was described as a "comradely visit," and the tug-of-war about the wording of the protocol was characterized as a "comradely discussion." Among our people, this created the impression that we had deserted the common cause of a humanized socialism and completely surrendered.

The onerous duty of explaining the new situation fell mainly upon my shoulders. We had agreed that the first to make a radio address would be President Svoboda. Cernik would inform the government, and Smrkovsky would inform the National Assembly. My task was to appear the day of our return, Tuesday, August 27, at 5:30 P.M., on radio and television to report to the general public. Public appearances for Cernik and Smrkovsky were scheduled for the following days.

By the time the draft of my speech was finished, I knew what President Svoboda had said. In contrast to his behavior in Moscow, Svoboda had struck an overly optimistic—almost defiant—note. He said that we would not retreat—not even "one step"—from our previous policies. He also asserted, inexplicably, that we had reached an agreement with the Soviets on a gradual and complete withdrawal of their troops, a misstatement bound to evoke unfulfillable expectations. Perhaps he was tired and had not taken the time to review what his speech writers had prepared for him.

I put everything else aside, changed the draft prepared for me substantially, and even made a few more revisions when reading the text on the air.

The pressure was enormous. Every television set and radio in the country was turned on. Even children listened. I was overwhelmed not only by the thought of the size of the audience but also because I understood what their state of mind had to be at that moment. I was severely restricted in what I could say, but one thing I decided not to do was stir up illusions. In language deliberately skewed by caution, I made four main points.

First, without provoking the Soviets, I tried to express my gratitude for the support from the people during our ordeal. Second, I made it clear that we had lost our freedom of action, stating that in the future our activities "would be conducted in a situation that would not depend upon our will alone." Third, I declared that a complete withdrawal of foreign troops as early as possible was the most important objective of all coming efforts. That, I thought, would put Svoboda's earlier statement into more realistic perspective, since we had no "pledge" in principle but only the characterization of the occupation as "temporary." Finally, I emphasized the need to stand together: "Only a unity of action can secure the success of our further policy." This was more than a statement, it was a plea.

I found it extremely difficult to control my emotions, especially when reading the parts of my speech in which I knew it would be apparent I was not telling the whole truth. Two or three times, I had to pause and fight back tears. I counted on the trust I had earned from my audience in the years before the invasion. I was sure they understood that even at this difficult moment I was not telling them lies but simply could not say more than I did.

On the whole, I believe I conveyed a realistic picture of where we were and what lay ahead. The borders were still open, and all those who feared the future were free to leave. I had no intention of initiating an exodus. It was the invasion alone and its consequences that were responsible for the flight of over 100,000 people in the next weeks.

Within a day or two of our return, I met with the Central Committee elected at the clandestine Fourteenth Congress, which had been in permanent session from August 22, the day after my abduction, until our return. The Congress had been meeting in a large factory building in Vysocany, an industrial district on the northern outskirts of the capital. The Soviets had either not located or dared not attack this first fully reformist body while we were negotiating in Moscow. The meeting place had been defended by segments of the Workers' Militia, itself largely an opponent of reforms.

The new Central Committee was led by Professor Venek Silhan, a distinguished Czech economist who had been entrusted by the congress to stand in for me as first secretary. I informed them of the obligations the Soviets had imposed on us, including the annulment of the results of the Congress. I explained my stand on that question and shared with them my ideas on how to get around this stricture. They professed their full understanding and promised their support.

Hostility toward the occupation forces was rising. The public knew the Soviets had failed to install a quisling government and had been internationally condemned for their aggression. The invaders had silenced television, but radio was on the air twenty-four hours a day, and newspapers, even weeklies, continued to publish freely even though their editorial premises had been seized. They simply went underground.

Apparently our position was being perceived by the public at large as much stronger than it actually was. After our return from Moscow, the National Assembly, the Czech National Council, the Central Committee of the National Front, and the Presidium of the Trade Union Council all adopted resolutions that put the departure of foreign troops at the head of their demands. Justified as they were, there was nothing to enforce these resolutions. The Soviets meanwhile started to set new conditions, even for leaving inhabited centers, the presumed first stage of their departure. In Prague, for example, they now insisted that all posters, notices, and graffiti be removed from public places before they would start to move out.

The population everywhere was showing its hostility toward the army of occupation in many ways. Towns, cities, and even villages were full of signs and slogans rejecting the occupation. Traffic signs throughout the country were removed or misplaced to confuse the Soviets. Verbal confrontations went on everywhere, and we knew that the Soviets had already killed and wounded dozens of unarmed citizens in both Slovakia and in the Czech lands. The situation was truly explosive. We had good reason to be afraid of bloodshed.

We decided to issue a rather urgent appeal asking for the public's understanding and cooperation in creating the conditions for Soviet withdrawal. The appeal was signed by the president, the chairman of the national assembly, the prime minister, and myself on behalf of the Central Committee. Simultaneously, we established a special committee, composed of representatives of all top government and Party bodies, to handle technical problems arising from the presence of the occupation forces. Part of this group was a military committee for liaison with Soviet headquarters: we badly needed a mechanism for handling specific local problems, some of which threatened to get out of control.

I was in constant consultation with Cernik, Smrkovsky and Svoboda. The full Presidium, including all secretaries (only Indra was missing, presumably sick in a Moscow hospital) met briefly on the night of our return, and again on Wednesday, August 28, still at the Castle. The Central Committee offices continued to be occupied by Soviet troops, as were many other buildings, including publishing houses, editorial offices, and even the Academy of Sciences.

One of the first steps we had to take was to instruct our Minister of foreign affairs, Professor Hajek, to ask for the withdrawal of the Czechoslovak issue from the agenda of the U.N. Security Council. If we did not meet this imperative, the Soviets would not even talk about removing any troops. Similarly, we had to cope with the Soviet demand for "control of the press and other mass communications." The Russian text of the protocol used the term *vladenie* for "control," and that could not be translated into Czech or Slovak as anything other than *ovladani* or *ovladanie*, which is in fact stronger even than the English *control*, more like *possession* or *domination*, which of course perfectly fit the Soviet concept of how to handle the media.

My reform colleagues and I could not accept this concept, at variance even with the Soviet constitution. Not only had freedom of the press been constitutionally guaranteed in Czechoslovakia since the previous spring but we had prohibited censorship. To regress in this area was now illegal in our statutory system, as we had pointed out in Moscow. Indeed, some historians believe that a primary purpose of the invasion was to crush our freedom of the press.

At any rate, we had to do something to show the Soviets we were taking steps in this direction while striving to remain faithful to our principles and abide by our laws. Ironically, the presence of foreign troops helped us in this balancing act. The clumsy formulation of Point 1 of the protocol, concerning the invaders' forces, allowed us to advance the concept of "temporary control of the press" as related to the "temporary occupation" of the country.

So the government established a temporary Office for Press and Information. An editor known for his sympathy to our reforms was asked to chair the institution, and he accepted. This office worked, at least at the beginning, on the basis of voluntary restraint. It was not an organ of prepublication censorship and was not intended to be.

Naturally, the Soviets did not think it was enough, and they constantly pressured me to impose not only a strict, Novotny-type censorship but also the complete control over the media employed during the Stalinist years. I never gave in on these points; the Soviets had to wait more than eight more months until my successor, Husak, did what they wanted.

As we returned from Moscow, an extraordinary two-day congress of the Slovak Communist Party took place in Bratislava. The congress, which ended Thursday, August 29, was imbued with the liberal spirit of the weeks before the invasion and was strengthened rather than daunted by the occupation. This congress voted a new Slovak leadership, totally excluding known traitors. The most striking result was the expulsion of Vasil Bilak from the post of Slovak first secretary, and the election of Gustav Husak in his place.

Husak had, of course, posed as a dedicated supporter of democratic reforms until the day before the invasion, and he was viewed by most delegates as the very opposite of Bilak. It is true that Bilak and Husak disliked each other. Bilak considered Husak a closet liberal to the end. For his part, Husak, who fashioned himself an intellectual, found it hard to conceal his disdain for the unimaginative Bilak.

In any event, the congress would have never elected Husak first secretary had he not repeatedly and emphatically declared his devotion to democracy and his personal loyalty to me, or had they known of his behavior in Moscow. He had returned directly from his equivocations there to address the congress as follows: "I am fully behind Dubcek's policies, I took part in their creation, I will support him completely. I will either stay with him or leave with him." The congress ended with unanimous approval of an open letter to me, which read,

> Dear Comrade Dubcek!
> We were with you during the difficult moments of your struggle against the regime of subjectivism of power, as well as during your struggle for the new and healthy [changes] after January [1968]. We were on your side during the arduous moments of the last days. We were with you in our thoughts and we will be with you in our deeds. We know that there are many tasks before you which will not be easy. We want to solve them with you, under your leadership.

Husak led the vote approving the letter.

Husak's reformist stand in spring and summer 1968 was taken to be a natural result of his bitter nine years in jail under the old regime. In his speech to the Slovak Party congress, Husak estimated that a Soviet withdrawal could come within "several months." Such optimism certainly sounded good, but it was absurd, and he knew it.

Party propaganda had boomeranged: the accusation against Husak of bourgeois nationalism had been transformed from a crime to an asset in the eyes of Slovaks. Husak was certainly aware of how unearned his new reputation was. In Moscow and immediately after, he started to play the national card strongly, knowing that the Soviets now approved. After August 1968, the Soviets saw Slovak autonomy, on which they had frowned in 1945, 1948 and even 1967, as a means of weakening, if not defeating, the reform movement in Czechoslovakia. Husak was to be their point man.

The Slovak Party congress also voted a resolution demanding the federalization of Czechoslovakia, as embodied in the Action Program. This was an old and justified demand that would now, unfortunately, be accomplished under deplorable circumstances and used to facilitate the defeat of reform policy.

Two days later, August 31, the Czechoslovak Party Central Committee met at Prague Castle. The one-day meeting had two main agenda items: first, to inform the committee about the "negotiations" in Moscow and obtain its approval of them and, second, to carry out personnel changes—both those demanded by the Soviets and those we had in the meantime proposed.

I made the chief report on the first point, giving much more detail than I could in my public broadcast. I made it entirely clear that there was nothing voluntary in our acceptance of the protocol, but I also explained why we thought that, even with the conditions in the diktat, we still had some chance to defend our reforms, though their pursuit would be much slower. Our priority remained complete withdrawal of occupation forces as soon as possible.

After a short statement by President Svoboda, Smrkovsky presented the contents of the protocol. A brief discussion followed, but the Central Committee now had a clear picture of the realities of both our talks in Moscow and the current climate of normalization. The meeting voted approval of the protocol, two of whose conditions most directly affected Party affairs: the invalidation of the recent Fourteenth Party Congress and the postponement of the next congress until after normalization.

The Central Committee also decided to create a commission to prepare a congress of Communists in the Czech lands. This was an important step in the direction of federalization and a more equitable political system in the country as a whole. There was no Czech Communist Party at that time, only a Communist Party of Czechoslovakia and a Communist Party of Slovakia; the latter was a collective member of the Czechoslovak Communist Party and in many ways subordinate to it. So the idea of founding a Czech Communist Party was welcome to both the Czechs and the Slovaks, because it would replace the old overcentralized system with two truly independent and equal parties free to create joint federal Party bodies as needed. There was nothing in the protocol to preclude such a step, but the Soviets would later not permit it.

A certain excitement was caused in the Central Committee by the demands of several antireform plotters—such as Bilak, Kolder, and Jakes—to make statements. Bilak and his accomplices avoided saying that they had not asked the Soviets to come and rescue their political sinecures. Instead, they "solemnly pledged on their honor" that they had never, not even in the last ten days, "done anything wrong." The audience was more amused than impressed. Bilak, in his memoirs written some fifteen years later, makes it clear that the whole troupe had been preparing a coup in collusion with the occupying forces, and that they continued to collaborate until the final act of treason in April 1969. So much for these people's "honor."

The personnel changes I proposed—Point 2 of the agenda—were of substantial importance if our reforms were to survive. As we had planned, several delegates from the clandestine Fourteenth Party Congress were present. Priority was given to those who had been elected to the Central Committee by the recent congress. I sought to incorporate eighty of them into the existing committee and to restructure the Presidium along similar lines. Both steps, I believed, would at least partially recognize the validity of the will of democratically elected delegates, solidify the positions of the reform forces in the Party leadership, and strengthen our hand in coming disputes with the Soviets about the interpretation of the protocol.

From the tactical point of view, it was important that the protocol did not explicitly prohibit this procedure; nor had it explicitly objected to the convening of the extraordinary Party congress or the election of the delegates. It only demanded the postponement of the congress until the situation in the country was "normalized." The delegates elected to the Fourteenth Congress had consequently not lost their mandates, and we were not obliged to hold new elections of delegates. Fortunately, the Central Committee approved both my proposals. I was also able to add to the Central Committee seven candidate members from the old Committee.

In its new composition, the Central Committee then reshaped the Presidium, dropping three of the Bilak-Indra team on whose retention the Soviets had not explicitly insisted—Kolder, Rigo, and Svestka—along with a fellow traveler of the group, Antonin Kapek. On the negative side, at Soviet insistence, Frantisek Kriegel had to leave the Presidium, and Cestmir Cisar the Secretariat. But the Central Committee added fifteen new members to its Presidium, including President Svoboda, who was elected an honorary member.

All new members had clearly professed, during the months of Prague Spring, their full support for our reforms. The new Presidium included Evzen Erban, a former Social Democrat who now assumed Kriegel's position as the chairman of the National Front. Husak also became a Presidium member as the new first secretary of the Slovak Party. On the whole, these measures amounted to a significant weakening of pro-Soviet forces in the top bodies of the Party. The Central Committee also fired conspirator Oldrich Svestka from his post as editor of the Party newspaper, *Rude Pravo*.

Just before the vote on the addition of the new members, I was summoned to the telephone by a call from Brezhnev. Somebody was obviously keeping him informed about the course of the meeting.

"What is going on there?" Brezhnev said in an impatient tone. "Whom are you trying to bring into the Central Committee?"

It would have been nice to tell him that it was none of his business, but our situation made me resist the temptation. Instead I stuck to my game plan. "We are going to expand the Central Committee by eighty-seven new members," I replied. "Seven of them are from the ranks of the old candidate members. The rest have been proposed by regional secretaries from among the delegates for the Party congress."

"It is not a democratic way to change the composition of the Central Committee," he retorted.

I liked *him* talking about democratic ways: his latest one had come in the shape of tanks rolling across the bridges in Prague!

"It is a necessary compromise," I said. "But I told you I would do that."

"You did not say there would be so many," Brezhnev shot back, raising his voice.

I said, "Nor did you say how many they should be. So I thought eighty-seven would be the right number."

I could visualize his rising eyebrows as he said: "They are too many, and I don't like it."

"It's too late to do anything about it now." I held my ground. "If I proposed a change at this moment, everybody would know you had ordered it. They know you called me."

Apparently he realized this, so he had to retreat.

Meeting the remaining Soviet demands for personnel changes was up to the government. They insisted on replacing the minister of the interior, Josef Pavel. His position was taken by the regional Party secretary in Pilsen, Jan Pelnar, a moderate and certainly not an opponent of reforms. The directors of radio and television, Zdenek Hejzlar and Jiri Pelikan, were also removed, but we did not permit their replacement by known traitors. As an actual bonus of the demanded changes, we were able to replace the heads of CSTK (the Czechoslovak News Agency) and the Ministry of Communication, who had exposed themselves as Soviet agents during the night of the invasion.

With the reorganization of the Central Committee, its Presidium, and the Secretariat, and with the personnel changes in the government and mass communications, the first spell of "normalization" came to its end. On balance, we were confirmed in our belief that not everything was entirely lost, and that by moderate and well-considered action we could hold some ground. Any tacit resistance was made possible by the unity still prevailing in our camp. I was keenly aware of the need to preserve that unity. But so was the enemy.

25

THE RETREAT

S OON after I came back from Moscow, Anna returned from the hospital, and we had a family reunion of quiet emotion. It had been a close call for me, hadn't it? My father called; he did not feel well, and what happened had shattered all he believed in. He died a year later.

Admittedly, I haven't said much about family affairs in these pages, but that should not be understood as a failure to enjoy and appreciate family life. After all, I have never had a private life other than with my family, and I strongly believe that private life is exactly what it is supposed to be; even a politician's right to privacy should be respected.

My sparse references to members of my family should not make the reader think I do not treasure and rely on their support. Above all, my wife was always there when I needed her, and so was my mother as long as she lived. When we all met at the end of August 1968, we knew we would be even more severely tested in the future than we had in the past.

After the invasion came a period of retreat. It could not have been otherwise. We were managing the affairs of an occupied country where the barrel of a Soviet gun was trained on our every move. But, as I have said, there were limits to the power of that gun.

Speaking of retreat, one thing may need to be made clear: at no point before April 1969 was this like Napoleon's disastrous retreat from Moscow. At least on the part of my allies and me, it was an organized retreat, in which no inch of territory was given up without calculated resistance. Until Husak was installed as Czechoslovak Party first secretary, there were no purges, no arrests, and no persecution. We even managed to continue rehabilitating the victims of earlier repressions. In spite of everything, the press was still relatively free, no journalist or scientist was washing windows to make a living, cultural life was picking up again and even foreign travel was virtually unrestricted. To maintain all this required political will and a determination to fend off the growing pressure to implement neo-Stalinist measures.

It was not a glorious time, to be sure. We could not continue expanding democratic ways; we could only defend what was left of previous achievements. Painful and humiliating concessions had to be made to prevent, or at least postpone, something much worse. I cannot say that I am proud of that time or that I remember it without bitterness, especially toward desertions in our ranks and the emergence of new traitors.

The reader will recall our four basic points of resistance at the Moscow meetings: no recognition of the legitimacy of the invasion and occupation, no admission of "counterrevolution," no acceptance of Warsaw Letter criticisms, and no abandonment of the Action Program. I felt I had to stand fast on all four points or resign. To give up on any one, I reasoned, would open the floodgate for repression. In my public statements, I referred, somewhat cryptically, to "immense consequences" should we give up on these principles. Unfortunately, I was right.

The loss of such loyal supporters of reform as Frantisek Kriegel, Josef Pavel, and Ota Sik brought special pain. We all understood the necessity of yielding to Russian pressure on this point. Cernik or I met with each departing colleague, and without exception they understood. We found decent jobs for all of them in the state administration. Quite a few others were sent abroad as diplomats: Jiri Pelikan, for example, was named a counselor at our embassy in Rome.

Kriegel had already decided to give up his membership in the Presidium and his position as chairman of the National Front. He remained a member of the Central Committee and a deputy of the National Assembly. I have to concede not only that Kriegel was—justifiably—skeptical about the prospects of a long resistance but also that he thought the whole policy of "organized retreat" made no sense. At the same time, he could offer no sensible alternative, and, from my pragmatic viewpoint, that was difficult to understand. So we disagreed, but stayed friends. I assured him that as long as I was first secretary I would never allow him to be persecuted, and I was able to keep that promise.

The question arose, of course, what to do next. While we managed to keep out of the Moscow Diktat the worst provisions, the protocol as a whole (with the occupation army to enforce it), made any positive policy very difficult. But we needed exactly that—a positive policy, something we could aim for, something to ward off a complete demoralization. It was also extremely important for the Czech and Slovak public. Soon after the Central Committee meeting at the end of August, I initiated an inventory of those points of the Action Program that could still be pursued. The occupation meant that ambitious moves to guarantee civil rights, such as freedom of association and official encouragement of new voluntary organizations, were out of the question. We could only maintain and defend what we already had. But I did see two areas in which I felt it was possible to advance the Action Program without risking an immediate clash with the Soviets: the plan to federalize the state and the reorganization of the economy.

Steps toward federalization were undertaken immediately. A delegation of the Czech National Council went to Bratislava for discussions as early as September; a draft of the relevant constitutional law was approved by the government at the beginning of October, and a few days later it was submitted to the National Assembly. The parliament approved the law on October 27. President Svoboda signed the document in a solemn ceremony at Bratislava Castle three days later.

The timing coincided with the fortieth anniversary of the creation of the Czechoslovak Republic in 1918. The Soviets grumbled but did not interfere. They had their ways of emptying the federal system of any meaning and would apply them once they had restored an obedient power center in Prague. But, for the time being, federalization was a great achievement for us. It helped keep the Action Program alive, and it responded to the historic aspirations of the Slovak nation. In the short run, it was to suffer deplorable setbacks, but it would survive the era of Brezhnev and Husak.

One political effect of federalization should have been the creation of a Czech Communist Party; this would have made the new political structure of Czechoslovakia more balanced. In the future, the Czechoslovak Party was supposed to act as an integrating and coordinating body but with no power to meddle in the internal affairs of either national Party. It is no wonder that we would soon run into direct Soviet opposition, which cast a shadow over preparations for the next Czechoslovak Central Committee session.

Naturally, the Soviets pushed ahead relentlessly toward complete encroachment. They interfered constantly at all levels, aggressively lobbying our ranks and "fishing for souls." We defended our cause with all the means we could. By the end of September, we had achieved a significant gain: Soviet Army units left the cities and larger towns, a move that somewhat limited their use of direct force. Brutal and clumsy intervention had not been unusual in the first weeks of the occupation. In Ostrava, for example, a detachment of the Soviet Army reoccupied the editorial offices of the regional Party newspaper, *Nova Svoboda*, in mid-September, abducted its editor, Ivan Kubicek, and threatened him with a firing squad if he did not give up his journalistic activities. We achieved his release only after energetic protests.

But even as the Soviets left urban areas, somewhat easing the pressures on our social and political structures, their techniques for paralyzing us from inside Party and government structures grew steadily stronger. For instance, they renewed efforts to impose on us a "treaty" legalizing the presence of their troops on our territory. Since their quisling agents had failed to do the job for them, they decided to push it through by direct intimidation.

At the beginning of October, they peremptorily summoned Cernik, Husak, and me to Moscow for "talks." They did not even give us the customary right to choose a delegation; they chose it themselves, ignoring Smrkovsky. It was the first time that I did not have this closest ally at my side when facing the Soviets.

We met on October 3. Much as before, Brezhnev, Kosygin and Podgorny pushed their view of normalization, showing no interest in my responses. I presented my point of view anyway. There was no discussion of a possible "treaty" regularizing the Soviet troop presence on our territory. On October 10, the Party Presidium deliberated on the results of our trip, and there was still no sign of what was to come.

Then, on October 14, Kosygin ordered Cernik to return to Moscow on very short notice. There they told him that a treaty on Soviet troops in Czechoslovakia had to be signed within two days. They made it a strictly government-to-government affair, ignoring me and the Party leadership completely. Cernik had barely returned when Kosygin landed in Prague with Marshal Grechko at his side and bluntly informed President Svoboda that the treaty had to be signed immediately. They made it clear that the alternative would be a reoccupation of Prague and other cities.

Svoboda put up no resistance. Desperately we tried to figure out how to reject the latest diktat, but Kosygin and Grechko permitted us no time to subject the treaty to the normal procedures of approval. It had to be signed on the spot, and in the same manner the National Assembly was forced to ratify it.

Under normal circumstances, three parliamentary committees would have carefully examined the text of the document separately. Under Kosygin's pressure, they were called to a joint meeting. Informed ahead of time of the draft's particulars by a deputy minister of foreign affairs, the three committees refused it.

Cernik and Smrkovsky were immediately threatened with all kinds of consequences if resistance continued. Grechko threatened to order his troops to reoccupy inhabited centers and to put their quislings directly in charge of the government, which would have meant widespread arrests, since nowhere at the local, district, or regional level were Soviet sympathizers in control anymore. All these threats were made verbally, and not recorded. We decided, hurriedly, that, provided the treaty clearly defined the occupation as temporary, it should be approved. In the light of international law regarding uneven treaties, it was illegal anyway.

On October 18, a depressed National Assembly, which had 306 deputies, reluctantly approved the treaty with four votes against and ten abstentions. Like most deputies, Smrkovsky and I voted yes for tactical reasons. I knew that many men and women of good faith felt betrayed by my vote, even if they understood the brutal blackmail that compelled it. Personally, I viewed voting yes as our best chance to avoid a reoccupation of our cities and the conflagration that would inevitably follow. And, since the treaty continued to call the occupation temporary and was arrived at under such patently extralegal means, I saw it as neither legitimizing the occupation nor inherently valid. But none of this is to say that it was not a very painful vote to make.

During October and the first half of November, I visited factories in the Czech lands and in Slovakia where I discreetly tried to explain our position and the conditions under which we were operating. I was distressed to see that many people, while still supporting us wholeheartedly, did not understand the complexity of the situation. Naturally they detested all concessions to the Soviets. But some people acted as if the country was not occupied, as if we were free to do what we wanted. There was a growing lack of natural, open communication.

At that same time, the Soviets launched a campaign directly accusing the reform forces in the Party of "criminal activity." First, they coined the term *healthy forces*, intended to encourage the traitors. Extremists started to organize themselves with Soviet support. Soon my allies and I found ourselves in a cross fire of enemies who knew exactly what they wanted, while we, deprived of the candid communication we had enjoyed in the recent past, were unable to find our way through the battlefield.

In this atmosphere, we attempted to prepare for the November session of the Czechoslovak Central Committee. As the only agency capable of directing further development, its decisions would be of crucial importance.

In the Presidium, there was still a sufficient majority supporting me in the pursuit of reformist preoccupation policy. We drew up a draft resolution incorporating the points I considered essential.

We flatly condemned the political practice of the old regime before January 1968, an important point considering the fact that the clear purpose of the invasion had been to restore that practice. We continued to emphasize economic reforms and spelled out our reasons for pursuing them. And the Action Program as a blueprint for future policy was reconfirmed.

We argued that we were doing nothing in violation of the Moscow Protocol, but there were inevitable setbacks. For one thing, we were forced to slow down the organizing of a national Czech Communist Party, which stayed at its initial preparatory stage. We did create an Office for the Administration of Party Affairs in the Czech Lands. Unhappily, Lubomir Strougal, a former reformer now revealed as a leading quisling, was elected to head this institution. I did not interfere because, as a Slovak, I did not wish to initiate the selection of officials for the embryonic separate Czech Party. Strougal's stature in the Party leadership was unfortunately increased. His further behavior can only be compared with that of Husak. Those two were the most responsible for breaking our defensive lines.

The outcome of the November Central Committee session cannot be characterized as altogether negative. We were still able—three months after the invasion—to defend the essence of Prague Spring, something not always appreciated in critical accounts of that meeting.

Simultaneous with this session in Prague was a Congress of the Polish Communist Party in Warsaw, which Brezhnev also attended. I conceived the idea of taking our draft resolution to Warsaw for Brezhnev's formal sanction. Under the circumstances, I saw nothing humiliating in this. I viewed it as a tactical move: Brezhnev's stamp of approval could slow down the rise of the ultraconservative wing in the Czechoslovak Communist Party. Indeed, I believed that Brezhnev, as I had learned to know him, would be flattered to see that we finally understood that we needed his consent and advice.

In that respect I was right. Brezhnev found nothing objectionable in the draft. However, I had made the mistake of taking Husak along in addition to Cernik. My rationale was that it would help if we were the same trio Brezhnev had chosen for our last visit to Moscow. I did not expect any trouble from Husak because he had been consulted several times as the resolution was being prepared, and he had expressed no reservations. In Warsaw, however, without telling me in advance, he said to Brezhnev that he thought the resolution should contain a condemnation of "rightist opportunism." Brezhnev, predictably, liked the idea very much and insisted on its inclusion in the document. After Cernik hesitantly conceded, I had no option but to go along.

Husak knew perfectly well what he was doing. He was positioning himself as a lackey of Brezhnev. It was not the first time or the last. "Rightist opportunism" was, of course, meant to single out those who were opposed to further concessions and who stood firmly behind our reform policy. I knew perfectly well that I was one such rightist opportunist, even if it had not yet been spelled out.

I had never liked the derogatory jargon employed by the Communist movement since Lenin's time. I regarded terms such as *revisionism* and *counterrevolution* as vague, questionable, and even dangerous as pretexts for repression. *Rightist opportunism* fell into the same category, of course. I worried that accepting such a formula might be a serious mistake, and I knew that my supporters would be disappointed, but in the end I thought that it was not an acceptance of the Soviet "counterrevolution" slogan and that it was worth Brezhnev's support for the resolution as a whole. Politics is seldom a simple business.

We returned from Warsaw early in the morning, and the resolution was soon passed by the Central Committee without significant opposition. Even the Stone Age warriors, after learning that Brezhnev had given his blessing, voted for it. In line with our determination to carry on with the Action Program, the document was optimistically titled "The Main Tasks of the Party in the Next Period."

To my dismay, the resolution evoked a strong wave of public disagreement, especially in the Czech lands. College students in Prague and in Brno went on a three-day strike, and several intellectual unions, focusing on the document's conciliatory aspects, criticized the November session of the Central Committee as a betrayal of Prague Spring. I was very saddened by all this, because I did not see things that way. Lines of communication and understanding between various components of the reform front were further weakened.

I should admit that I did not always see eye to eye with the Czech reformers. In many cases, I held a more sober position, and I believe I was more stable and reluctant to act impulsively. My inherent Slovak caution was at times incorrectly interpreted as hesitation.

At the end of 1968, public attitudes of Czechs and Slovaks were diverging. In August anger at the Soviet invasion was equally strong in both parts of the country. Now Czech attitudes were becoming increasingly radical, tending to disregard the rational limits to our resistance. In Slovakia, the situation was much more stable. I do not think such relative calm represented either accommodation or resignation, or was a response to Husak's maneuvers. It stemmed rather from different priorities and, eventually, from a greater appreciation of our real circumstances, which does not make it one with Husak's cynical "realism." Also, except for Husak and Bilak, malice did not mark the relationships among opposing Slovak politicians the way it so often did among their opposite numbers. There were, in effect, two different political cultures. After April 1969, resignation spread much faster in the Czech lands than in Slovakia, acquiring a kind of nihilism.

Three weeks after the November plenum, we were summoned to the Soviet Union again, this time to Kiev. Yet again Brezhnev wanted "to discuss our situation." As before, the Soviets "suggested" the composition of our delegation: Svoboda, Cernik, Husak, Strougal, and myself. I was slowly being "contained" by the accommodationists.

Before we left, there was no disagreement in the Presidium on how to present our case. When the meeting started, I made a report about our domestic situation in line with the resolution Brezhnev had so recently approved. Discussion proceeded calmly, and it looked as if there would be no unpleasant surprises. Then, suddenly, Strougal said, "We should put our personnel problems in order, especially at the district level."

He had given me no warning of his intention to make this dangerous proposal. Its sum and substance was clearly that we should force out of office thousands of local officials elected during Prague Spring. In other words, we should launch a purge at the local and district levels, which would inevitably continue upward.

For me, this was entirely unacceptable, but Brezhnev, of course, was enthusiastic. He said, clapping his palm on the table, "Vot eto pravilno shto tovarish Strougal rekomenduyet! (Well, what Comrade Strougal is recommending is right!)" Husak hurriedly expressed support for Strougal's proposal. We were clearly split. Svoboda did not say anything, as if he were absent. Cernik was also completely passive. I alone opposed the idea, arguing along legal norms and Party rules. I felt sick.

After this disastrous trip, I started again to think seriously about resigning as first secretary. Support for our reform policies was eroding. New traitors like Husak and Strougal, calling themselves realists, were closing ranks with the old traitors of August. The people, especially in the Czech lands, were increasingly confused about whom and what to support. The retreat that had started as an organized and coordinated policy was in danger of turning into a rout.

I shared my thoughts with my closest associates and allies, including Smrkovsky. The question was what would happen if I stepped down now? Such a move would undoubtedly strengthen the ultraconservatives and accelerate a retreat from reform. Smrkovsky argued that my resignation would soon be followed by the purges already demanded by Strougal and Husak, with more persecution to come. Smrkovsky and the others felt that the longer we held on, the better those threatened by the coming coup could prepare themselves.

I listened and pondered. As I saw it, there were two kinds of defeat. It was one thing to be crushed by the Soviets and quite another to be sold out by self-interested traitors. So I decided not to give up yet. I am still not quite sure where and when I should have quit. After all, my decision to remain bought only another five months before the gangsters took over.

Christmas 1968 was a troubled one.

26

A HARVEST OF TREASON

O N Christmas Day, Husak appeared on television to demand that the next chairman of the parliament be "a representative of the Slovak nation."

His move was timed to coincide with the coming into effect of the new federal framework. The National Assembly was to become the Federal Assembly on January 1, 1969. The new body was to be divided into two chambers: a Chamber of People and a Chamber of Nations. There was also a provision to preclude parliamentary domination of the Slovaks by the more numerous Czechs: any bill would have to have a majority not only in the Chamber of People but also in both sections of the Chamber of Nations to become law.

Husak used the transition to federalization as justification for demanding that the four top political positions in the country be equally divided between the Slovaks and the Czechs. The offices of president, prime minister, and chairman of the parliament were then held by Czechs: Svoboda, Cernik, and Smrkovsky. Only the position of Czechoslovak first secretary was held by a Slovak—myself.

Husak had not discussed his "initiative" with me; he made his demand suddenly—a gambit sure to enhance his position in Soviet eyes. I suspected that he had advised the Soviets in advance. They must have been delighted.

One would have expected Husak to set his sights on the office of prime minister rather than chairman of the parliament. However, he was not really striving to establish a principle of equal distribution of top offices, as was proved later. To ask for a Slovak to replace Prime Minister Cernik would have gained Husak little. Cernik was then already vacillating, and

Husak did not view him as an obstacle to his further plans. No, his move was aimed at my chief ally, Smrkovsky. The Soviets also disliked Smrkovsky, and he was frequently attacked in the Soviet press. Indeed, a subversive pamphlet, no doubt inspired by the Soviets, had just appeared all over Czechoslovakia attacking Smrkovsky as "a Politician with Two Faces." Now the Russians would have their way.

Husak's skulduggery was exemplary. However hollow his nationalism, on the surface his demand was justified. It put me in a particularly difficult position: it was politically impossible for me to refute his argument without losing my base of support in Slovakia, although not refuting it would cost me dearly among the Czechs. I could foresee the sad and inevitable consequence. After losing his position as chairman of the Federal Assembly, Smrkovsky would also lose his seat in the Party Presidium. Long-standing practice had tied the positions together. Husak's stab in the back was the worst of all the betrayals between August 1968 and April 1969.

Smrkovsky was in no doubt about Husak's intent and immediately volunteered to step down to spare me difficulties. Peter Colotka, a Slovak who had just been nominated deputy prime minister in the first federal government, was named to replace him. Smrkovsky was then elected first deputy chairman of the Federal Assembly and chairman of the new Chamber of People.

Colotka, a new man in the top leadership, was a lawyer in his mid-forties. Since 1966 he had been a member of the Central Committee of the Communist Party of Slovakia, and since 1962 he had held the post of commissioner for justice of the Slovak National Council. He was also the Czechoslovak representative on the International Court of Justice in The Hague. His rise in 1969 was mainly a result of his support of Husak. It certainly paid off: in April 1969 Colotka replaced Smrkovsky in the Czechoslovak Presidium, and then he held top jobs in the regime of occupation until its demise in 1989.

The maneuver to remove Smrkovsky was greeted with nationwide dismay. Protests were strongest in the Czech lands, where he was a national hero. He bravely went on television, asking the public to understand the situation, to accept his replacement as chairman of the parliament, and to avoid protest strikes and demonstrations.

His fall evoked a deep bitterness and disappointment in many honest supporters of Prague Spring, who felt humiliated and betrayed. In this agitated atmosphere, a young philosophy student at Charles University, Jan Palach, immolated himself in the center of Prague on January 16, 1969, and, taken to the hospital, lay dying for two days.

Palach's sacrifice shocked the whole country. Never before had such a one-man auto-da-fé occurred in Czechoslovakia, or I believe, anywhere in Europe. It testified to the terrifying desperation of the people, especially the very young, in the face of an overwhelming foreign force that was imposing its degenerate ways on their country. A young man in Pilsen followed Palach's example in a few days; then two more fiery suicides occurred, in Brno and again in Prague. These later cases were less known because the government tried to suppress the news to avoid more public turmoil.

I was appalled by these deaths. The day of Palach's fateful gesture, I was chairing a Central Committee meeting during which one member, Vladimir Koucky, proposed annulling the August 21 declaration condemning the Soviet invasion. Fortunately, his proposal was rejected, but his daring to raise the question was a clear sign of what was coming.

I was exhausted. I doubted the wisdom of my December decision to stay on, and I caught a paralyzing flu with a high fever. The day after the Central Committee meeting, January 18, I went to Bratislava, and after a day or two at home I had to enter the hospital. I was there when Jan Palach died. I was unable to attend any official functions until February 4 and for another two weeks struggled with the effects of the virus.

In the meantime, Palach's funeral turned into a mass demonstration in defense of our reform policy and in protest against the Soviet occupation, showing once again the depth of popular support for Prague Spring. Briefly, our domestic enemies slowed their onslaught; their public isolation was still too obvious. In spite of their creeping penetration into the highest positions in the country, they did not have either the strength or the daring to deliver the final blow to Prague Spring. For that they still needed "brotherly assistance" from the Soviets.

In March came the annual world ice hockey championship, which took place in Stockholm that year. On March 21, the whole country watched as Czechoslovakia played the Soviets: it was much more than ice hockey, of course. It was a replay of a lost war, and I was ecstatic when we defeated the Soviets 2–0. It was like a national holiday, and thousands of people took to the streets to celebrate. The anti-Soviet overtones could not be missed by anyone. But that was nothing compared with the second victory of our team over the Russians a week later. This time we won 4–3 and took over the world title from the Soviets. Many more people went out to celebrate this second victory; in Prague alone, an estimated 150,000 gathered. It turned out that the Soviets and their agents in our secret police were prepared to take advantage of just such an eventuality.

In Wenceslas Square, the main artery of downtown Prague, a team of police agents under cover as city workers had unloaded a heap of paving stones in front of the offices of Aeroflot, the Soviet airline. The whole action, we now know from police documents, was supervised directly by the Czech minister of the interior, Josef Groesser, a Soviet agent. What they then needed, of course, was a victory by our team, and a safely predictable celebration in the square.

It would take an improbable stretch of the imagination to presume that the Soviet team had actually been "advised" to lose the game, but the fact is that in doing so they performed an important service for Soviet foreign policy. As the television broadcast of the game ended, the streets quickly filled with people, and Wenceslas Square was packed. We now know that State Security agents who were mingling with the crowd began to throw the conveniently placed stones at the Aeroflot office. Few Czechs followed their lead. Glass was broken, but otherwise nothing happened. Still, this was the first act in a chain of events that led to decisive moves against us, moves that had all been well prepared and coordinated.

By 11:00 P.M., the Soviets were asking the Czechoslovak military to intervene in the streets. Before midnight, General Dzur, minister of defense, called and asked my permission to use the army against the demonstrators. I told him that as long as I was in office I would never agree to the use of armed forces against our own people. In the end, regular police handled the situation without much difficulty.

But the Soviets and their lackeys sensed the opportunity and decided to strike. On March 31, without informing our authorities, Marshal Grechko landed in Milovice, the military airfield some 25 miles northeast of Prague that the Soviets had held since the invasion. He brought with him V. S. Semyonov, Soviet deputy foreign minister in charge of military affairs. The next day Grechko and Semyonov set to work. Grechko went before the Defense Ministry's Military Council to make arrogant demands of a strictly political nature: first, we were to institute censorship; second, we were to employ our own armed forces to suppress the "counterrevolution." He also said that, in case of further demonstrations, Soviet troops would use their weapons in a perimeter around their garrisons.

Dzur informed me about these new demands shortly before I was to meet both Grechko and Semyonov at the Castle. Semyonov handed me the Soviet shopping list, and he was, I must say, even more arrogant than Grechko. I told them that the Czechoslovak people had the right to express publicly their joy or grief. We were already using sufficient, if moderate, means to maintain public order. We were determined not to use violence and had the situation safely under control.

There was no reaction. Semyonov repeated his demands mechanically, as if I had said nothing, and he made several very negative comments about "the political leadership." With that I knew that they had decided to impose the personnel changes they needed to break our resistance.

I thought about his remarks for a few moments, then asked him whether he would elaborate. His reply, in its entirety: "*Kontrarevolusii nuzhno snyat golovu* (The counterrevolution must be beheaded)." Now that was crystal clear. The reformers, above all I myself, were their target. I did not see how, largely isolated, I could further withstand their pressure.

Among our senior leaders, the situation had deteriorated significantly since November. Smrkovsky's departure was imminent. He was still a member of the Presidium, but his reduced status and the continuing Soviet attacks on him had diminished his role. He was immensely popular, but that did not count for much against those "riding the Soviet tank." As for Svoboda, he was increasingly subdued, passive, even detached. Cernik, dismayed by it all, had become increasingly accommodating. I knew I could not expect to fight the good fight anymore.

The pro-reform group in the Presidium was gradually disintegrating, and my own support had eroded to the point that it hinged on one or two votes. I knew that I would have to give up, after all. But I still desperately tried to think of ways to fend off repressions.

In that mood, I proposed that Semyonov visit me once more in my office for a talk before he left. He accepted, and we met on April 11. The day before, to increase the heat on me, Marshal Grechko had informed our chief of staff, General Rusov, that 8,000 more Soviet troops were being brought into Czechoslovakia.

Semyonov started with new demands, of which the most outrageous was that we punish Academician Josef Macek, a historian and editor of a recently released collection of documents on the Soviet invasion known as *The Black Book*. Publication of Macek's work was a vivid symbol of the extent of the freedom of the press we still had over seven months after the invasion.

Instead of reacting to Semyonov's words, I did what he had done to me at our earlier meeting and ignored them. I had the impression he still expected me to cave in and meekly carry out their bid to restore the police state of yore. They obviously thought I was the best choice: that way our reforms would be destroyed by the person with whose name they were most commonly associated.

That, of course, I would never do, and I think that by then it should have been sufficiently clear to them that I was not their man. So I paused for a moment, then told him that I needed to reflect on how to proceed so that the Soviets would be satisfied and I would remain true to my own principles. I was no more specific than that, and he did not ask me to be. I only noticed that his expression changed somewhat as I talked, and he looked as if he were searching me.

Soon after Semyonov left, I called in my two longtime secretaries, Jozef Gadjos and Oldrich Jaros, close associates who had worked with me years before I came to Prague. I told them that I had arrived at the conclusion that I had to resign. Otherwise the Soviets would set up another provocation that could lead to further public turmoil and even a bloodbath. I said that I would tie my departure to certain conditions in an attempt to secure for at least a little longer the course of passive resistance laid down by the Central Committee in November. That would prevent the wide-scale repression that I most feared.

Both my associates agreed that the Soviets would try dirty tricks to bring me to my knees and that a voluntary departure, if well prepared, was one way to avoid that. How long repression could be delayed once I stepped down was a question none of us could answer.

That day I went to inform Cernik, Svoboda, and Smrkovsky. Cernik, to my surprise, not only showed no emotion but seemed downright eager to affirm my decision. He had also given no thought to the situation after my resignation. I was disappointed, but he had been with me from the beginning and was closely connected with the reforms. And under the circumstances there was no other leader I could still realistically propose as my successor.

Svoboda took longer than Cernik to respond, and it was clear to me that it was not easy for him to react one way or the other. But after a while he joined his hands on the table, looked me in the eye, and said, "I can see your point. There is probably no other way."

Finally, it was Smrkovsky's turn. He, I must say, never lost his fighting spirit, but at that time he too thought that we had held our positions honorably and long enough. "Let us see what we can still do after your resignation. They haven't yet got our skins, have they?" he asked.

The day I was preparing for my departure, Husak made a speech in Nitra in which he finally launched a direct attack on me, announcing that the time had come to put the Republic in order and criticizing my "weakness" in refusing to do so. His act was well synchronized with his masters. As I later learned, he had recently had a secret meeting with Brezhnev in Uzhgorod, where he had apparently been encouraged to grab the office of Czechoslovak Communist Party first secretary.

On April 12 I formally informed the Presidium about my decision to step down. I made the announcement a part of my report on the preparations of the next session of the Central Committee, scheduled for April

17. The brief discussion that followed focused on the problem of succession.

There was already a large group of Husak supporters within the Central Committee. They included not only the well-known opponents of any reform but, surprisingly, a number of members I had brought in last August from the "illegal" Fourteenth Party Congress. This group was headed by Milan Huebl, a historian and personal friend of Husak who, for reasons of his own, believed that Husak would defend our reform policy even more effectively than I had. Three years later Huebl found himself in jail, where his friend Husak kept him for six years.

I was, of course, upset by the idea that Husak might step into my shoes. I tried to block his election as far as I could and, during the Presidium meeting on April 12, proposed Cernik as my successor.

Cernik, however, refused even to be considered for the job, and that left Husak as the only candidate. At that point I decided to state openly, in Husak's presence, why I was opposed to his succession. Longer than most, I said, I had perceived his serious character flaws and unscrupulous ways. They had been on full display in the immediate postwar years. Recent weeks had shown, I said, that he had not changed much, in spite of his bitter experience with the Stalinist regime. I was afraid that he would lightly abandon everything we had managed to defend in Moscow in August, and even the limited reforms we were still defending.

The Presidium took no final decision at this meeting. But support for Husak's candidacy was strong, even though I knew that even some of those who leaned toward him shared my misgivings.

Before the next Presidium meeting, I went to the Castle once more to talk to Svoboda. I was not optimistic, but I thought that he, with his unquestionable authority, might still somehow change the balance in the Presidium.

I told him again why I was so afraid of Husak. I said that he was capable of anything, that he would betray all our principles, serve the Russians without restraint, and not refrain from a policy of repression.

Svoboda listened, but he seemed somehow not disposed to talk about Husak, as if he had some difficulty concentrating. Instead, I saw him suddenly slip down the sofa on which he was sitting, very low, as if he wanted to kneel before me. In this unusual position he inclined his face to me and said, "For God's sake, Sasha, forgive me, but I must tell you this. I have already promised Grechko that you would soon resign."

He was unable to talk about anything else. I felt sorry for the old man. He was clearly too tired to do what I had hoped for. For different reasons, we were both somewhat embarrassed as I left.

At the next Presidium meeting, April 17, I was cornered. I had no option other than to accept Husak as my successor. Out of nineteen votes, there was one abstention besides mine.

My last move before the vote was an attempt to renew our pledge not to abandon the four basic principles of our post-invasion policy. Continued adherence to these principles would be the only possible safeguard against repression. I said that this was my condition for consent to Husak's election.

One after another, all present expressed their agreement.

Further possible roles for me were also discussed, and I was urged to stay on as a member of the Presidium. Husak proposed that I assume the chairmanship of the Federal Assembly. I hesitated before accepting the offer. I really had only one motive in agreeing: by staying on, I hoped, I might be able to restrain the policies Husak undoubtedly had up his sleeve.

On the same day the plenary session of the Central Committee formalized these changes. My resignation was accepted, and Husak was elected first secretary by a sufficient majority. A new Presidium was also elected; in it reformers were, for the first time since April 1968, in a clear minority.

27

THE DEATH OF
PRAGUE SPRING

M Y worst fears were realized soon after Husak took office. Many editors were quickly dismissed and replaced by obedient people, and publications that could not be otherwise brought under control—*Listy*, the writers' weekly; *Reporter*, the journalists' weekly; and *Studentske Listy*, a weekly published by the Union of University Students—were terminated. The first arrests came, especially in the Czech lands. Regional Party secretaries known for their support of reforms were removed, most significantly in Prague and Brno. Newly appointed regional secretaries started to remove reformist officials at the district level. News of the suppression of various organizations was published almost every day.

In those weeks, Husak operated mainly through the Czechoslovak Party Secretariat, which he hurried to "reorganize" according to his needs. During the rare Presidium meetings I still attended, I disagreed with almost everything on the agenda. But I was a lonely voice there, and I was gradually withdrawing from all Party activities. At the May session of the Czechoslovak Central Committee, I opposed the expulsion of those who stood in Husak's immediate way—Kriegel, Slavik, Sik, Vodslon, and others.

The next day my father died, and I left immediately to make arrangements for his funeral. He was buried in the cemetery in Uhrovec, his and my birthplace. Hundreds of people attended the funeral, but it was a quiet, sad ceremony. I couldn't help feeling that everything my father had believed in had died with him.

The Party publications, especially *Rude Pravo* under a new, extremist chief editor, and *Tribuna*, edited by a vengeful Oldrich Svestka, now

(Left): Well-wishers greet Dubcek as he arrives at Bratislava Station for the August 3, 1968 conference that will be seen as a setback for the Soviets. *Archive Photos (Below):* Brezhnev's arrival at the Bratislava conference. For Dubcek the bouquet was more than ceremonial. *CTK Uncredited photos are from the author's collection.*

(Above): A reaffirmation of friendship? Warsaw Pact leaders at the Soviet war memorial in Bratislava after talks, August 5, 1968. *Miroslav Vojtek, Narodna Obroda*
(Left and below): On the eve of the invasion, symbolic support from the unaligned: Dubcek and Svoboda with Tito and Ceaucescu. *CTK (both)*
(Opposite): The "friends" invade: August 21, 1968. *Miroslav Tuleja, Narodna Obroda*

(*Above and left*): August 21, 1968: Prague. *Miroslav Tuleja, Narodna Obroda* (*both*)
(*Below*): August 21, 1968, Bratislava: Lone man against tank. *Ladislav Bielik*, Narodna Obroda

(Above): Soviets guard the Central Committee building, where Dubcek and colleagues were held prisoner, while hard-liners Indra (left) and Bilak (right) front for the invaders. *CTK (all)*

(*Above:*) Clandestine Fourteenth Party Congress, held in a factory building in the Vysocany district of Prague two days after the invasion. *CTK*

(*Left*): August 26, 1968: Postinvasion meeting in the Kremlin between Soviets and Czechoslovaks. No Czechoslovak photographers or journalists were allowed. *CTK*

(Top): Dubcek during his emotional August 27 television address to the Czechoslovak people about the "negotiations" in Moscow. *CTK*
(Bottom): Loyalty in defeat: Dubcek being embraced by a Moravian steelworker, September 1968. *CTK*

(Left): October 1968: Signing the "agreement" on the temporary stay of Warsaw Pact troops. As Kosygin and Cernik sign, Svoboda, Smrkovsky, Husak, and Dubcek look on. *CTK*

(Below): Jan Palach's funeral, February 1969. *Miroslav Tuleja, Narodna Obroda*

Dubcek with his
opportunistic
successor, Gustav
Husak.
(Below): Husak
being applauded
two years later by
Czech hard-liner
Strougal. Svoboda
is in the middle.
CTK

(*Above*): Dubcek and a friend at Senec Lake building a vacation cottage, 1971. *Oldrich Jaros*
(*Left*): Dubcek in a moment of relaxation.

(Top): Dubcek's house in the hilly Slavin district of Bratislava. *Vlado Krajci*
(Bottom): Dubcek working for the Slovak Forestry Administration.

(Right): November 26, 1989: Dubcek responds to cheers in Wenceslas Square after twenty years of political exile. *CTK*
(Below): Dubcek with Pope John Paul II, in Rome.
(Opposite page, below left): Dubcek being embraced by Vaclav Havel. *Mike Abrahams/Network*
(Opposite page, below right): A far more pleasant trip to Moscow: Dubcek meets Gorbachev, May 1990. *CTK*

(Top): Anna. *Pavel Breier*
(Center): Dubcek at his wife's grave. *Vladimir Benko*
(Right): Dubcek with Havel in August 1991, as Czechs and Slovaks threaten to go their own ways. *Jana Kosnarova*, Narodna Obroda

(Above): Dubcek's mangled BMW
after the September 1, 1992, accident.
CTK
(Right): Dubcek's funeral. *Miroslav*
Vojtek, Narodna Obroda

When will they leave? Dubcek outlasts the state watchdogs. *Pavel Breier*

launched a campaign against me. I was accused of all kinds of crimes, errors, and failures, in the denunciatory style of the early 1950s. Repeatedly I demanded the right to answer them, but, as I had expected, they ignored me completely.

In the Federal Assembly, where I was elected chairman toward the end of April, there was a depressed and resigned mood. Of the agenda I hardly remember more than the state budget for 1969, delayed because of the events of the previous year. Everybody there seemed to understand that, contrary to the intentions of the Action Program, the role of the parliament would not grow but revert to its earlier feeble stature.

In the assembly, I was at least close to Smrkovsky again. He was still hanging on as deputy chairman and as chairman of the Chamber of People. We talked about the inevitable moment when we both would have to leave altogether. Smrkovsky thought that there was no need to make it easier for Husak. Let's wait for the last fight, he said. Frankly, I wasn't so sanguine, but fatalistically I stayed on.

I attended very few public functions at the time. I spoke before a commemorative gathering in Terezin in northern Bohemia, site of the Nazi concentration camp known as Theresienstadt. I had to have a formal audience for Soviet Ambassador Chervonenko in my office in the assembly, a most annoying obligation. Twice more I saw President Svoboda: once when he received me after my election to my new office and once in Bratislava, at the celebration of the fiftieth anniversary of Comenius University. Svoboda seemed melancholic and withdrawn, like someone only mechanically fulfilling his duties.

On July 24, I attended my last Presidium meeting, during which Husak worried about the need to maintain public order on the first anniversary of the Soviet invasion. No specifics were discussed. Soon after this meeting, Smrkovsky and I each received instructions from Husak to stay out of Prague until further notice.

Smrkovsky went somewhere in the Low Tatras in Slovakia for a rest. I returned to Bratislava, where my family had moved in April. Of course, the Federal Assembly was not in session and not scheduled to meet until September, so neither Smrkovsky nor I had any official justification for being in Prague. Nor had we been planning to be there, despite Husak's paranoia.

As we know today, Husak's regime had for weeks been preparing to suppress any public demonstration during the August anniversary. I had received no information about it, since it was a secret operation handled by the Party Secretariat and the Ministry of the Interior.

Husak's hectic preparations were elaborate. The army was assigned to detach and train special units for street control. Special police forces were formed for the same purpose. From the arsenal of Gomulka's ZOMO, the special Polish antiriot police, came tear gas, plastic shields, and oversized truncheons. Husak was obviously anxious to show Brezhnev how tough he was.

In July I was interviewed by a correspondent from the French daily *Le Monde* who asked whether my opinions had changed from the previous year. No, I told him, I still adhered to the ideas of Prague Spring. The story apparently displeased Husak, and, about a week before the anniversary, I received from him a demand that I send to the Secretariat a written "correction" of my opinions. I decided to ignore the demand.

I spent most of August at the lake in Senec, a recreational area about an hour's drive east of Bratislava where I was building a family cottage with my sons and some friends. My only public appearance at the time—and my last before the anniversary day—was in my electoral district of Senica nad Myjavou, in the White Carpathians, where I had been invited long before. I was very cordially received by the local populace and officials, but I was saddened to observe how depressed they were over the shattering of the previous year's hopes.

Then came the anniversary. There were public protests in over thirty cities, the largest taking place in Prague, Brno, Bratislava, and Kosice. Husak's regime marshaled more than 35,000 soldiers, policemen, and militiamen to attack the unarmed demonstrators, and at least five (and more likely ten times that number) were eventually killed. Three of the victims, including a fifteen-year-old boy, were under twenty years of age.

The radio carried only sketchy reports, but as the death toll started to rise, Husak sought to have martial law declared by the executive body of the Federal Assembly, its Presidium (not to be confused with the Party Presidium). By thus justifying the terror, he sought to wash his hands of the blood he had already spilled.

Legally, however, there was no one in Prague authorized to convene the Assembly Presidium. That was the prerogative of either the chairman of the assembly—me—or one of the two deputy chairmen, Smrkovsky or Dalibor Hanes. Hanes was out of the country, and Smrkovsky and I had been ordered to stay out of Prague.

Husak, of course, cared little about legal "formalities." He found a willing servant in Jozef Gabriska, a deputy in the Chamber of People who took over this administrative arm of the Federal Assembly. Illegally, Gabriska convened the Assembly Presidium on the morning of August 21, a Thursday. However, because of the recess, there was no quorum that day or the next, when they were still two votes short.

A deputy minister of the interior, Jan Majer, a colonel in the State Security, arrived to brief the Assembly Presidium about the situation and extracted from it an illegal approval of the government's actions. But this was not enough for Husak. He needed more.

On Friday, August 22, he convened that other, more powerful Presidium, of the Czechoslovak Communist Party. There a draft of the proposed martial law was discussed and approved. It was presented by Cernik, who by now was doing all he could to please Husak and save his skin. (Alas, not for long.) The norm approved by the Czechoslovak Communist Party Presidium, Law 99, sanctioned the suppression of opposition under martial law and became known as the truncheon law.

I was not present at this meeting, nor was I invited to it. Husak was well aware that I would have resolutely opposed his measure, and I believe that he didn't even want to listen to my objections. At that stage, of course, the proposal would have been easily approved whether I was there or not.

This meeting occurred shortly after noon, as I can reconstruct from documents now available. Husak immediately sent the draft to Gabriska in the Federal Assembly, but apparently with the instructions not to act on it right away. At this point Husak decided that I should be there to make everything look more legitimate.

I was still in Senec that day, where they caught up with me and demanded that I immediately report to Prague in my capacity as chairman of the Federal Assembly. I left hurriedly and arrived in Prague, by air, at about 4:00 P.M.

When I entered my office, Gabriska was waiting for me with an urgent order from Husak to have the draft law passed by the Presidium at once. I wasn't as impressed as they thought I would be, and I took some time to study the text of the proposed law. I did not like it at all.

The law itself, however, was only one aspect of the matter. I found out that before my arrival the rules of parliamentary procedure had been completely ignored, and I now insisted they be observed. I demanded that the draft first be reviewed by legislative experts of the assembly. We had to know if it was in agreement with the constitution and other laws. Only after we had such a legislative finding, I said, could the Assembly Presidium and I responsibly consider the document.

I raised these objections before the other members of the Assembly Presidium, who had by now ordered themselves into a "permanent session." I also raised my political reservations: was such a draconian law needed at all? Didn't we have enough appropriate laws already?

My views met with practically no support from the members of the Presidium who were there. Only Cestmir Cisar expressed any doubts about legality of the draft law, but only in terms of the rights of the universities, which itself was a very limited part of the issue. No one else raised objections to the draft. On the contrary, they seemed eager to approve it without any respect for regular procedures, and some started attacking me quite rudely.

Nevertheless, I continued to use my prerogatives to call a break so that the legal experts could examine the proposal. I could do nothing more at that moment, saving the question of an insufficient quorum for later.

Shortly afterwards, Husak arrived and forced his way into the meeting. He was not a deputy of the assembly and had no reason to be there. I would never have behaved like that when I was first secretary—and I was an elected member of the Chamber of People. But in Husak's eyes, the parliament was a rubber stamp, no more than a "transmission handle" of the Party, as Lenin had taught. And he was furious that I was trying again to throw doubt on this long-established Communist practice.

He had hardly taken a seat when he started to shout at me that I would be responsible for the further loss of lives if the draft law was not quickly approved and publicized. Large crowds in the streets of Brno, he said, were on their way from a bicycle race to a soccer match and threatened to explode unpredictably. The law, he said, was needed immediately to make it possible to cancel the soccer game and turn people away from the stadium.

Husak pointed a finger at me and repeated that I would be personally responsible for further casualties if I continued to delay approval of the law. Other Assembly Presidium members hurried in with their loud support. It was at this point that I gave in, tired and resigned. But I did not vote for the law. I simply presided over its approval. The fact that, in procedural terms, it was all entirely illegal added to the pain.

My great error was that I signed the law at all. Signing laws, I must say, was the chairman's routine task, whether they approved of the laws or not. But this was not a routine situation, and I should have refused to sign it. But it was a hectic, nervous moment; I was completely isolated there, and at the time I did not think through the consequences. I'll never stop regretting it. I am not trying to excuse myself; I can only explain the situation.

Husak left immediately, wearing a cool, sarcastic expression He had, as he saw it, achieved a great victory: Law 99 was promulgated the next day in all the media, signed by Svoboda, Cernik, and myself. The funeral announcement of Prague Spring was published with the signatures of the three people whose names were most closely associated with it. For millions of people, it was depressing news, and some even refused to believe it.

It took little time for my regrets to set in. I read the law again and again. In a letter sent September 8, I urged Cernik to issue, as soon as possible, procedural regulations that would prevent any abuse of the general definition of "antisocial activity" in paragraph 4 of Law 99. I never received an answer.

Two weeks later, in my absence, the Czechoslovak Communist Party Presidium decided to remove me from the office of chairman of the Federal Assembly and expel me from the Party Presidium. The decision was formalized at a Central Committee meeting on September 25 and 26. There Cernik made a humiliating recantation of his support for Prague Spring, for which he was rewarded by a few more months as prime minister. After that period of grace, he was fired and replaced by Lubomir Strougal, who formed a "triumvirate" with Husak and Bilak for most of the ensuing years.

At that meeting, I was given the same opportunity as Cernik—to recant, to humiliate myself, and to quench what for most of our people had been a beacon of hope. For that, as I later learned, they were ready to reward me with some small sinecure, perhaps the mayoralty of Bratislava.

I refused and instead used this last opportunity to speak before that body to restate firmly my views. I defended all my actions from October 1967, particularly my policies during Prague Spring. I offered them no regrets and no self-criticism but held my ground to the last. I walked out before the end of the session and a week later sent them a letter of resignation from membership in the Czechoslovak and Slovak Party central committees.

The September plenary session of the Czechoslovak Central Committee also completed the process of normalization. It was the culmination of the drama of the last twenty months: Husak now overtly removed two of the four fundamentals on which our resistance had stood and, in fact, repudiated all four: the invasion was reclassified as an act of "international assistance" that had prevented the success of a "counterrevolution." The Czechoslovak Presidium declaration of August 21, 1968, was decreed void. And, finally, the convening of the Fourteenth Party Congress right after the invasion was declared an illegal, "anti-Party" act. These were the very moves I had feared most. The floodgate of purges and mass persecution had opened.

A number of members of the Central Committee, including Smrkovsky, were immediately expelled. At the same time, they apparently decided not to repress me completely. Husak, it seems, did not yet feel confident enough. As it turned out, he needed another eight months.

28

"EXILE" IN TURKEY

B EFORE the Central Committee session ended, I returned to my house in the hilly Bratislava neighborhood of Slavin. The whole family had moved there for good in April. So we were back in our old home on Misikova Street, and I was glad that I finally had time to start putting everything in order there. I had been used to doing my own odd jobs and home repair, but since autumn 1967 I had had no time for such things.

It was clear to me that I would have to be looking for a job. I was just forty-nine years old and the retirement age in Czechoslovakia was sixty. I was in no hurry, though, and needed to rest a few weeks and pull myself together. I could also expect that "they" would not permit me to take a job of my choice. Things were moving back to the practices of Novotny's times, and Husak would certainly be inclined to decide everything—including my future employment and wage—himself.

It was as I expected: in mid-October I was summoned to Vasil Bilak's office in Prague. In my time he had lost his position as Slovak Party first secretary, but after the invasion the Soviets had compelled us to keep him in the Czechoslovak Party Presidium. Now he also was the secretary of the Central Committee in charge of foreign relations.

Bilak treated me with a tinge of superiority, sitting behind a large desk and coming directly to the point. He informed me that the Presidium had decided to dispatch me, as ambassador, to Ghana.

I would have been much less surprised if they had decided to put me in charge of a chicken farm. I wondered why they had chosen Ghana. The "sympathetic" regime of President Nkrumah had been overthrown three years before, and some military men unfriendly to the Soviet Union were in control. That would hardly make it easier for them to keep an eye on me. On second thought, I could see that it really didn't matter where they sent me—as long as it was somewhere far away.

I told Bilak flatly that I was not interested in his offer, that I had no intention of going to Africa or anywhere else. With that, the conversation was over, and I returned home.

There all was not well. Anna had become something of a nervous wreck, increasingly sensitive to what was happening around us. She took the mounting public attacks against me very badly. And the situation aggravated her chronic gallbladder problems. I was extremely distressed to see her like that.

It was a depressing time, to be sure. The political underworld, led by traitors from the time of the Soviet invasion, popped up on all sides as normalization proceeded. Prague Spring was now condemned as "non-Marxist." All decisions defending our independence and opposing the Soviet intervention were declared void by the Party, the government, the parliament, and a dozen large public organizations.

Very few of my previous supporters were willing to stay in their positions at the price of renunciation of all their previous principles. Oldrich Cernik in the government and Cestmir Cisar at the head of the Czech National Council worked for the new masters. They were held in general contempt and were soon thrown out anyway.

Shortly after I refused Bilak's proposal to go to Ghana, I sent a letter to the Czechoslovak Party Presidium, a sharp rejoinder to the attacks on me in the media. I demanded that the letter be shared with all members of the Central Committee.

Two weeks later I received an answer from Husak refusing my demand. Instead he ordered me, in a menacing way, to inform the Presidium within fourteen days whether I was in agreement with the Party's current political course. It was obvious that he was getting ready for his next move against me, expulsion from the Czechoslovak Communist Party. But for some reason he still hesitated, possibly worrying that there might be unexpected political complications.

Every night during those weeks I had long discussions with Anna about our situation. When I told her that Bilak had offered me a diplomatic position abroad, she seized on the idea as a way of escaping our situation, at least for some time. She was simply desperate. I tried to explain to her that it was probably a trap. They would let me leave, then would not permit me to return. While I respected everybody's right to leave the country, I could not imagine how I could live in exile. Anna remained unpersuaded, however, and I had very bad feelings about this argument.

I suspect that our house was bugged, and that the leadership was informed of our disagreement. Very soon I was called to Prague again and offered another diplomatic post—this time in Ankara. When I told Anna about it, we had another long discussion. She argued with great persistence that I should accept the offer and soft-pedaled the idea of a trap. Very reluctantly, I agreed. Anna was the sole reason I made the decision.

For a few weeks I reported to the Ministry of Foreign Affairs in Prague to receive basic instruction on diplomacy and information on Turkey. On December 15, it was publicly announced that I had been appointed ambassador to the Turkish Republic. I thought ironically about another politician exiled to Turkey: Trotsky, in 1929. But at least I would never wind up in Mexico, or have to fear an ice pick.

Our departure was scheduled for January 16, 1970. Before we left, I answered Husak's letter in which he had demanded that I express my agreement with his policy. I rejected his implicit threats and again protested the slanderous media campaign against me.

President Svoboda invited me to a private dinner shortly before my departure. He went out of his way to show me his friendship, but I could not avoid the feeling that the occasion was mostly for his own reassurance.

It was customary that departing new ambassadors be received by the Czechoslovak Party first secretary. Husak, however, showed no interest in seeing me. Had he been capable of normal emotions, I would have said that he wanted to spare himself embarrassment.

On January 16, Anna and I traveled straight to Ankara on Czechoslovak Airlines. The airplane was half empty, and I suspected that many of the other travelers were State Security officers. There were two flight attendants, both young Czech girls, and they could not hold back their tears when they saw me and my wife boarding the plane. Throughout the flight they were very attentive and friendly, and we were deeply touched by that. The authorities, duly informed, thought differently. As I later learned, both girls were suspended immediately after their return, then fired.

Our arrival at the Ankara airport was unforgettable. Friday is a Moslem holiday, and huge crowds of friendly people came to welcome me. There were also dozens of journalists and photographers. The Turkish police had to call for reinforcements to keep the situation under control, and they had us wait in a reception room until a passage from the airport to the city could be cleared. A photographer broke a window in the room to take our pictures, cutting his hand. The representative of the Turkish government did not get to me at all, only the Czechoslovak chargé d'affaires, Knapp, somehow managed to get through the crowd.

It was over an hour before we could leave. I was quite astonished by what

I saw—all these friendly strangers who came on their own to show me their sympathy for my country and my cause.

The ambassador's residence in the Ankara embassy was comfortable, but even after several months we had the feeling that we were staying in a hotel—it was not really a home. The embassy was small, with only five or six on the diplomatic staff and a few other employees such as drivers and technicians. I had personally known only one of the embassy staff, a driver who happened to have worked at the regional national committee in Banska Bystrica in the early 1960s.

I didn't worry too much about who stood where in the embassy. I just assumed that they all worked for the Ministry of the Interior back home. They all treated me politely, with the exception of an overly obvious gumshoe who arrived shortly after I did. His only task seemed to be to watch my every move.

When I presented my accreditation at the Turkish Ministry of Foreign Affairs, I was received by officials at the highest levels, including President Cevdet Sunay. The Turkish officials made every effort to demonstrate their sympathy. I have never forgotten their friendliness and understanding. I met with similar sympathy everywhere I traveled outside Ankara. In Istanbul, that remarkable city, former capital of the Byzantine Empire, news of my presence spread quickly. Wherever Anna and I stopped—even for a quick meal—a crowd of friendly people gathered, anxious to greet me and assure me of their sympathy.

More than twenty years later, when I was once again the chairman of the Czechoslovak parliament, I visited Turkey at the government's kind invitation. Before going I recalled that, at the time of my abrupt departure in June 1970, I had not returned my diplomatic pass to the Turkish foreign office. So I took it with me and gave it to the Turkish officials with my apology. The next day they brought it back and asked me to keep it as a souvenir.

Husak tried in many ways to make my stay in Ankara unpleasant. I could hardly read this as other than a clumsy attempt to force me to ask for political asylum. They even sent a special commission, allegedly to investigate the situation in the embassy. I succeeded in ignoring this pressure to defect. I was determined to endure.

A number of Western governments offered me their hospitality in case I decided not to return to Czechoslovakia. I shall not forget the generosity of the United States, Canada, England, France, Australia, Sweden, and others. I explained to the diplomatic representatives of these countries that I had to return home. I felt obligated to remain on board no matter what. My place was with the people of my country.

However, getting back home proved easier said than done. In April and May, I learned enough from various sources to deduce that Husak and his accomplices intended to prevent my return. Quickly, I made efforts to secure a ticket to Prague on Czechoslovak Airlines. When they told me for the third time that there was no space available—on a flight that was rarely fully booked—I saw my worst expectations confirmed. I had to find another way, and I had to be devious. I kept up the pretense that I was still waiting for a place on a Czechoslovak Airlines flight. Then I confided in Anna and prepared her to stay behind for a while, so that it would appear that I was still there, too.

I was lucky to get help from several Czechoslovak technicians, who were installing export machinery in Turkish industrial plants. One man, a Skoda Works engineer with whom I had worked in Dubnica during World War II, was particularly helpful. With the assistance of these good people, I bought a ticket for a flight on Hungarian Airlines from Istanbul to Budapest. From there, I knew, it would be easy to get across the border to Bratislava.

One night I crept secretly out of the embassy, took a cab to the railroad station, bought a ticket to Istanbul, and got there in time to catch the Hungarian plane. In fact, I encountered few difficulties on this clandestine trip. I sighed with relief when we were in the air.

It was the beginning of June when I landed in Budapest. The Hungarians, however, proved to be friendly only to a certain point. I have never had any doubt that it was Kadar himself who had to determine what to do with me as soon as he learned that I was on my way to Budapest. And it was certainly he who decided to inform the Czechoslovak authorities.

That explains why I was awaited at the airport in Budapest by Frantisek Dvorsky, a former regional secretary of the Slovak Communist Party in western Slovakia. He had come with an official limousine, and he would take me not home to Bratislava but directly to Prague and an appearance before the Czechoslovak Communist Party Central Auditing Commission. Centralized power had been quickly reestablished under Husak; his practices demonstrated how much he really cared about Slovak autonomy.

I do not recall what Dvorsky's official position was at that time, but he belonged among Husak's new allies. We did not talk much during the ride to Prague—if it was for any reason other than the presence of the driver, I cannot tell.

In Prague I was informed that I had been expelled from the Party. To drive me there for that purpose alone was, I think, a bit of overkill. At the time they usually just published news of an expulsion in the newspapers. But at least I could now return to Bratislava, to my home. Their plan to force me into exile had failed.

About two weeks later, the Czechoslovak Central Committee publicly formalized my expulsion, but that worried me far less than the fact that Anna was still in Ankara and encountering great difficulty in her attempt to get back. As she later told me, she had to endure a whole month of torment from embassy officials, who were infuriated that I had escaped them. Fortunately, she had closely befriended a Turkish housekeeper, and I'm sure this lady was the source of information about my wife's predicament that soon appeared in the Turkish and foreign press. The international publicity forced Husak to give up any idea of holding Anna hostage.

I asked the Ministry of Foreign Affairs in Prague to permit one of our sons to go to Ankara to help his mother pack up and move, but they did not bother to answer. When Anna returned, she was exhausted, but the humiliation she had had to endure evoked a new defiance in her.

It made for a touching bit of consolation that a friendly Turkish crowd had gathered at the embassy gate the day she was taken to the airport and poured water on the automobile's wheels, a traditional gesture of goodwill in Turkey. For years to come, we needed all the luck and good wishes we could get.

29

LIFE UNDER RESURRECTED BIG BROTHER

S OON after I came back from Turkey, I started to look for a job. I sought something as a manual laborer because I knew I could not expect to be cleared for anything else. At least I have always been good with my hands and had not forgotten the craft I learned in my young years. I had modest demands, mostly for a workplace reasonably near my home.

I looked through classified ads, and I made a list of some twenty factories and workshops looking for locksmiths, welders, and lathe workers. Because of the relative overemployment, there was a general shortage of laborers, and I anticipated little trouble.

I should have known better. It did not take long to find out that "they" had built an invisible wall around me. For me, there was no job anywhere. It was not up to me to decide how I would make a living. Much later I learned that the new Party leadership had made me a priority; they deliberated over my fate several times in those weeks. Of course, they wanted to get me as far away from public attention as possible.

At the time there was a whole army of people like me who had been professionally displaced and were moving into new and less desirable jobs. During the 1969-70 purges, almost half a million members of the Communist Party were expelled or suspended and forced to leave their previous employment. The same fate met many non-Party people who had shown sympathy for the reforms. The purge was particularly vicious in the Czech lands, but that is not to say that Slovak "normalizers" showed less zeal: in Slovakia the situation was different, and the normalizers used more subtle means of coercion.

The most affected professions were those of journalists and historians, but no trade was really spared. Even many army officers were expelled from the armed forces. Many writers were silenced, and many academics were forced out of their faculties. There was hardly any field in which the best and most honest people were not dismissed or blacklisted. I was therefore in good company, one of hundreds of thousands who refused to humiliate themselves, to deny their hearts and recant their beliefs. I, of course, got special attention, because in the eyes of the new rulers I was an especially dangerous "counterrevolutionary."

At home we calculated how long we would be able to survive if I didn't work at all. We had only meager savings— 75,000 crowns, to be accurate, equal to about $3,000 on the black market. We had a year-old Simca car, and we had also put some savings into the cottage at Senec. Our financial reserves were very limited for a family of five. Pavol, our eldest, was twenty-one, a student in the medical school of Comenius University. Both younger boys were in high school. Eventually they would be allowed to finish their studies, but they then had no freedom to choose employment, and they could not travel abroad. My mother was still with us, and she helped us with her modest old-age pension. Anna was not feeling well and was not fit to take a full-time job. They would have made it difficult for her even if she had tried. It was up to me to provide for the family.

My mother died a year later at the age of seventy-four. She was a lifelong Party member, and when the purges were launched she knew they would soon call to ask her whether she agreed with the occupation. Only an affirmative answer qualified for further membership. She did not wait for that call but returned her Party card with a long, touching, handwritten letter in which she explained, in plain but eloquent language, why she could not continue to be a Party member under Soviet occupation. I might add that of the several thousand pre-World War II Communists who were still living in 1969 or 1970, a large number acted in a similar way.

Sometime toward the end of October 1970, I was summoned to the Central Committee of the Slovak Communist Party in Bratislava and brought before Jozef Lenart, the new Slovak Party first secretary. He had finally been rewarded for his treason by return to high office in both Prague and Bratislava. It would have been more appropriate for me to be interviewed by someone of much lower rank than Lenart, but obviously he couldn't pass up the pleasure of seeing me down and out.

Lenart informed me that I had been expelled from the Party—a rather superfluous piece of news considering that I had been present for my expulsion. Then he said that they were choosing a job for me and that I should wait until I was notified.

I could do nothing but submit myself to their verdict. At least I still had the freedom to refuse employment I found distasteful.

In the next few weeks they offered me at least three jobs that I refused, mainly because the workplaces were too far from the city and I would have to spend, in one case, three hours commuting to work. In the end they offered me a position as a mechanic in the local Forest Administration in Krasnany, just outside the city limits of Bratislava. This offer I accepted, and I started to work there in December 1970.

I was generally responsible for the maintenance and operation of machinery of various kinds, from bulldozers and scraper loaders to chain saws. After some months I was assigned to the workshop, where I was mainly occupied fixing chain saws of Western manufacture, such as Stihl or Husqvarna, and welding broken equipment.

My starting salary was 2,200 crowns per month ($74 at the black market rate), which was average pay in industry at that time. Like the rest of the employees, I got a small end-of-the-year pay raise most years, so that I made about 3,000 crowns when I retired in 1981.

When I began work, I was well received by both management and my fellow laborers. The director of the Forest Administration named Miroslav Hanak whom I had known from the past. During 1971, however, I came under increasing persecution. I was constantly under secret police surveillance which had to affect my relationship with my co-workers. The authorities took even further steps to turn me into a nonperson: I was gradually expelled from all the organizations of which I had been a member, including the Hunters' Association, the trade unions, and even the Union of Anti-Fascist Fighters, an association of participants in the World War II resistance. I wrote formal protests against these actions but never received any answers.

The friendly Mr. Hanak was soon replaced by a rude and hostile person named Duris—undoubtedly put there largely to keep an eye on me. Once he summoned me to his office, where I saw a mailman standing in the corner. Duris had a bunch of foreign letters for me, all registered, on his desk, and he told me that I had to sign the receipts. I knew that all mail addressed to me or my family, especially foreign mail, was subject to police control. In fact, for many years I was not permitted to receive any mail from abroad. Here the catch was that these were registered letters, and a foreign sender was entitled to compensation, in hard currency, by the Czechoslovak postal administration for "lost" letters. That was why, I think, they wanted to compel me to sign the receipts—with no intention of letting me have the letters.

I took the pencil and wrote the date first, watching Duris closely. He thought that I had already signed and quickly raked the letters into his drawer. I looked at him with amusement, dropped the pencil, and left the room. I did not get the letters, but he did not get my signature either.

Soon I learned that these letters were from France and Italy, from organizations expressing solidarity with the victims of repression in Czechoslovakia. They sent me repeated invitations to visit.

From the fall of 1970 until 1989, I was constantly under police surveillance, and so was my wife. I assumed that they were also keeping an eye on my mother and my sons. For over three years, an unmarked State Security car was parked directly in front of my house. Later they parked about a hundred feet up the street. Quite frequently one or two plainclothes officers or a uniformed policeman stood in front of our entrance gate. At times they prevented any person outside my family from coming to visit us; at other times they simply demanded to see the visitors' identification cards. By the second half of the 1980s, the surveillance was becoming less obtrusive, but it continued one way or another, until November 1989, when their regime collapsed like a house of cards.

Every day on the streetcar to and from work, there were at least three plainclothes officers following me. Two of them virtually boarded with me, each standing at a different exit and keeping me in sight all the time. The third officer drove behind the streetcar, and sometimes he had another man with him. It was quite an operation.

After a few weeks, I remembered the faces of most of these men, who made little effort to hide their identity. Naturally, many people recognized me and greeted me. Often strangers came up to me, inquired after my well-being, and tried to express their sympathy. Soon I noticed that anyone who had greeted me was followed by one of the agents as soon as he or she stepped off the car. Then I learned from some of those who had received this attention that they were stopped, had to show their ID's, and a few days later were called for interrogation. Some were threatened with the loss of their jobs if they talked to me again. This practice depressed me, and I decided to avoid further contacts, because I did not want to see anyone hurt just for a simple expression of sympathy. So in a way they achieved what they wanted—to isolate me from other people.

Once I approached one of the agents I had seen many times on my tail. I said, "With the two of you always following me and the others in an automobile, wouldn't it be more economical if you simply drove me to work?" He looked at me, thought a while, and replied, "That would be against regulations." They were everywhere with me—even in the hospital when my daughters-in-law delivered my grandchildren, and later when I took my grandchildren for walks. This happened a lot, because in due time

I had three granddaughters and a grandson, and they frequently stayed with us.

My wife was never alone either, any time she left the house. Once she was returning from grocery shopping, carrying heavy bags, when she saw two young, healthy agents shadowing her. She could not overcome her anger and waited around a corner until one got close. She snapped at him, "At least you should help an old woman with her bags." But he pretended not to know what she was talking about.

They also kept an eye on us at our summer cottage in Senec, where it was easy to spot their observation posts. There I was occasionally visited by dissident friends, some of whom came from Prague. My loyal supporter Vaclav Slavik and I met there several times—usually treading water in the middle of the lake. Zdenek Mlynar also came to see me in Senec once or twice before he left for Austria in 1977, and we, too, used the lake for a private conversation. this made the police uneasy, and they had to resort to a rowboat. Once a policeman, tired of rowing around us, shouted at me, "How long are you going to stay there?" I shouted back, "Certainly longer than you will!"

At the Forest Administration, I encountered one particularly ironic situation. There was a constant problem with spare parts for our technical equipment, especially chain saws. To get hold of these was sometimes almost impossible, and the official whose responsibility it was to supply us with spare parts was occasionally quite desperate.

Finally he turned to me for help: I told him I would try, and I did. With the permission of our unhappy director, Duris, they provided me with a car and a driver, and I made shopping trips to various hardware stores outside Bratislava, mostly in western Slovakia. As it happened, I always brought back what was needed. There were good people everywhere, and they gladly reached under the counter when they saw me. Another time, we needed a high-pressure boiler for heating the workshops. Again, I was dispatched to find one, and I did—in Zilina. I doubt that Husak or Bilak would have had such good luck as I.

Once—just once—I had to go as far as Bohemia, where, not far from Prague, the central reserve stock of spare parts for Husqvarna and Stihl chain saws was located. It was beyond the radius allowed for Forest Administration cars and I had to go there by train.

Discreetly, using the workshop telephone instead of my home phone, I had contacted my former assistant Dr. Jaros, who lived in Prague and was working as a bricklayer. His wife, Vera, also a historian, was working as a driver for another enterprise. She was waiting for me when I arrived in Prague, and she took me to that warehouse. I got what I was looking for, and she delivered me back to the railroad station. My movements, however, had been monitored by the StB, and the following week Vera lost her job as a driver and was assigned to the storeroom. It was after this trip that the authorities finally ordered Duris to stop sending me out on acquisition junkets. No more travel for Dubcek. So from then on I stuck to my job in the workshop.

Throughout the period of normalization (later they called it consolidation), my family was the target of eavesdropping as well as surveillance. Quite a few purged people had lost their telephone licenses under various pretexts, but I was spared. Not only did they let me keep my home telephone but I received a new instrument, much nicer than my old one, allegedly a gift from an old friend for my fifty-first birthday in 1972. Initially I did not suspect foul play. In fact, I discovered the special properties of this equipment only by deduction. Shortly after I had the new telephone set connected, I noticed that the police car that used to park in front of the house had moved farther away. Nevertheless, as soon as somebody rang the doorbell, the police were immediately there. Before long I started to suspect a connection between my fancy new telephone and the new behavior of my guardians.

My technical know-how was not sufficient to understand the electrical subtleties involved, so I discreetly asked a friendly expert to examine the phenomenon. It was quite simple: my telephone was connected with the doorbell. As soon as the doorbell sounded, the bug in the telephone picked it up and alerted the surveillance team.

So we quietly disconnected the new set and reconnected the old one. While doing so, I complained loudly on the phone that my telephone was malfunctioning again—nothing unusual in the outdated Czechoslovak telephone system. After we replaced the set, it was dead for a few seconds, but then its tone started up. And soon the police car was back in front of the house.

Some time later an acquaintance of mine, a forester, offered to give me a new television set from the Orava television factory. It was not uncommon for a new model to be put in several dozen households for test use, on the condition that the person using the set would regularly report on its performance.

But I was increasingly suspicious at that time, and after a few weeks I disconnected the set and started using my old one. Very quickly the forester called and asked me whether I liked the new set, whether it was working well, and whether I was recording its performance. At first I told him that everything was all right and that I was making notes of my viewing. But a few days later he called again and asked me the same stupid questions, so I told him that the set had suddenly gone dead and that I had had to put my old one back into service. Then he asked me at least to return the cabinet. Highly amused, I told him that I had already given it away to a radio amateur. I was not surprised when my radio friend found an eavesdropping device inside the set.

From then on, I was particularly cautious, especially after we found a bug in a small butane lighter. I told my wife not to accept any new appliances. One day, however, the oven stopped working, and Anna, without telling me, called a repairman to fix it. The problem was a broken thermostat. On his way to get a new thermostat, the repairman was picked up by the StB and taken to their regional administration, where they installed a bug in the thermostat. They then ordered him, under various threats, to go back to our house and mount the "new" part in our stove.

When Anna finally told me about it a few days later, I knew immediately what kind of thermostat we had. As soon as I could, I bought a regular thermostat and brought it home. Then, with music playing to keep my wardens happy, I disconnected the equipment supplied by the StB and put the normal thermostat in its place. I saved every bug that we found in the house during those years as souvenirs, but I do not think we found them all. A few might still be there, rusting in the walls.

While I tried to stay above all these chicaneries, I could not remain calm as easily when my wife was a victim of mistreatment. Still unemployed, Anna was busy taking care of the house and of our little "farm" behind it. We kept chickens and rabbits, and this, with the vegetable garden, was Anna's domain. It all helped us to make ends meet. In addition, I built a small vineyard, which yielded around twenty gallons of good wine each year.

Anna continued to have painful problems with her gallbladder. In the past it had always helped her to take a cure in a health resort that specialized in those diseases. The best one was Karlovy Vary, in western Bohemia, but for us it was all but impossible to get a permit for treatment there, since permits were issued only by the trade unions, from which I had been expelled.

According to law, all people had the right to a course of treatment at the health resorts, but in reality the regime controlled effectively who could and who could not use that right. So I had virtually no recourse. However, in 1976 a friendly woman who worked in the trade union office in Krasnany and whom I had told about Anna's health problems gave us a permit for a cure in Karlovy Vary. I was very happy, and in a few weeks I took Anna to the railroad station and put her on a train to Bohemia.

Her trip, of course, did not escape the attention of the police. Anna had company all way to Karlovy Vary, and after she got there she was separated from the other patients and put in a very small, poorly furnished room under the roof. Anywhere she went, StB agents were behind her. She went through the treatment, but the stressful conditions made real healing virtually impossible. The trade union employee who gave me the permit was fired within a week.

Years later—during the mid-1980s—Anna again badly needed treatment, but I was unable to get it for her, no matter how I tried. Then the possibility of a solution arose. There is a smaller health resort in Dudince, in southern Slovakia, which was recommended for gallbladder diseases. We could not get a permit for treatment there, but the Forestry Administration had a gamekeeper's lodge nearby where our employees could occasionally stay and rest for a limited time. A lady who worked with me in Krasnany acquired a permit to stay there for herself and another woman, and they offered to take Anna with them. While there, Anna could take the baths at the spa without staying in the health facility. All she needed was her physician's report and recommendation.

But those procedures applied only to "normal" people, not to my wife. In a flood of tears, she returned from Dudince the same day she left. What happened? I asked her. Sobbing, she told me that when she went to the main facility to have her treatment scheduled, she was informed that it was out of the question because Mrs. Lenart, the wife of the Slovak Party first secretary, was there. That this circumstance excluded only Anna was confirmed by the fact that the two women with whom she went to Dudince had no problems taking their baths. Health care was apparently a political category for us at the time.

This era was called *Realsozialismus*, "real socialism," to distinguish it from the dreamworld of the old thinkers and us reformers. The term, I think, originated in Ulbricht's East Germany, which is why it sounded a little like *Endlösung*, "final solution." *Realsozialismus*: in Czechoslovakia, chief propagandists of the regime of occupation, like Bilak or Jan Fojtik, frequently used the term. They succeeded in one respect. Any notion of a socialism different from their perverted system disappeared from the minds of millions.

Realsozialismus was the ultimate stage of the Soviet system, which was slowly dying before our eyes although we were not yet aware of it. I had not for many years believed that that system could drag on for long without deep, substantial changes. When my friends and I were forcibly prevented from carrying out such changes, I knew that the crisis of the system had only deepened and, paradoxically, its end accelerated. When a glimpse of light finally appeared at the end of the tunnel, I was pleased, of course, but not surprised.

30

THE PATHS OF HISTORY

By now, I had for many years believed that the kind of social order practiced in the Soviet Union and in Eastern Europe was a dead-end enterprise. Socialism, or any other modern social system, could not exist without democracy. That was the essential course correction that I was trying to carry out in 1968. But since we were brutally prevented from realizing our plans, I knew that the agony of the Soviet system would only further deepen and accelerate.

Nevertheless, our dictatorship was still powerful in the early 1970s, with a thorough web of control mechanisms constantly perfected to check its decay. So it would have been rash to expect that some miracle would soon give us another opportunity to free ourselves.

Previous experience had also shown that future changes would almost entirely depend on developments in the Soviet Union itself. I therefore became more intensely interested in Soviet internal affairs than ever before.

Since my return from Turkey in mid-1970, I had had very little time to follow developments even at home, much less in the Soviet Union. I was working full-time, and I was frequently dog tired when I came home in the evening. In my free time, I had to work around the house and take care of my family. In truth, I had adjusted to these new conditions with little difficulty, and I did not feel any misgivings. There were rewarding sides to this routine, such as the additional time I could spend with my family and my hobbies—gardening and odd jobs around the house.

To follow developments, both domestic and external, was not easy. I read the local press and listened to local radio and television news, but it was mostly propaganda, largely devoid of information. There were some alternatives, to be sure. Occasionally we tuned in to Vienna for television news because Austrian television came through loud and clear to southern Slovakia. That, of course, was refreshing. I knew people who viewed nothing else. However, tuning in Western radio stations was almost impossible, as jamming became more and more effective. I can remember just a very few times that I managed to listen to Radio Free Europe, for example. Under the circumstances, I had only limited and irregular access to objective information. Mostly I had to rely on experience and instincts.

The early 1970s were truly depressing. The group of traitors whom the Soviets put in power in Prague were consolidating their positions, and the central theme of their deafening propaganda was that they would be there forever. That was the very essence of *Realsozialismus*: that and only that was real, nothing else existed.

The first event to disrupt the rulers' fantasy of eternity was the conference on security and cooperation in Europe in Helsinki in 1975. For us, the most important aspect of the documents adopted there was the Soviet concession on human and civil rights. What the Soviets, and the sour-faced representatives of our regime, signed there was in complete contradiction of their ongoing policies. Even if the Soviets had no serious intention of applying the accords in their own backyard, we understood that the obligations they had formally undertaken were important. The treaty brought about a qualitative change in the whole situation. After Helsinki, what the Soviets and their lackeys in Eastern Europe continued to do was illegal under international law.

A year before the Helsinki conference, I had sent long personal statements to the Federal Assembly, the Slovak National Council, and the Czechoslovak Communist Party leadership in which I condemned the systematic suppression of basic civil rights in Czechoslovakia. I said that I viewed as most detrimental the fact that people had again been deprived of their right to speak out freely and without fear about public affairs. I emphasized the deadly consequences of the crisis into which our society had been thrown.

It is important to point out that the Czech and Slovak societies did not react to normalization in precisely the same way. To be sure, general attitudes were the same—quiet rejection of the occupation and contempt for the rulers installed by a foreign power. But in the specifics there were significant differences.

In Slovakia, my own case was an exceptional extreme. On the whole, fewer people were directly affected by the purges in Slovakia than in Bohemia; punishment was rather rare, and the sentences were not as long. It was easier in Slovakia for the victims of the purges to find some acceptable alternative existence. Quite a few Czechs who were crushed at home found it easier to exist in Slovakia in those years. Consequently, resistance in Slovakia was less radical and less desperate than in the Czech lands. In Slovakia, there was nothing comparable to Charter '77, the civil rights movement that openly challenged Husak's regime. Out of some 2,000 signatories of the charter, there were only three Slovaks, two of whom lived in Prague.

The charter was, of course, a courageous initiative in the tradition of Czech political and cultural defiance going back to Austria-Hungary. In Slovakia, we viewed it with great sympathy. Many of my personal friends in Bohemia and Moravia signed the charter—most of its signatories, after all, were former Czech reform Communists.

I am occasionally asked why I did not sign the charter myself. The question results mainly from a lack of understanding of the difference between Czech and Slovak realities. The charter was a Czech response to the situation. In Slovakia, we agreed with virtually every idea in it, but we had our own ways to support these ideals.

I continued to send personal statements to political organs in Prague through the years of the Soviet occupation, repeatedly protesting the imprisonment and other forms of persecution of dissidents. I denounced the mistreatment of Vaclav Havel and other leading Charterists: Rudolf Battek, Petr Uhl, Ladislav Lis, Jiri Dienstbier, Vaclav Benda, and others. I never changed my views, never recanted, and never stopped restating my rejection of the policies of normalization. I did not have to rush to declare myself a dissident by means other than those that I had decided to use. The Slovak response to the changing external situation was different from that in the Czech lands. Instead of a public action such as the charter, there formed, gradually and quietly, an underground opposition composed mainly of Catholic activists and former reformers who had left the Communist Party during the purges. These groups were mutually supportive. I took part in their activities, and my friends always found ways of informing me about significant developments.

Around 1980 I started to sense the first winds of change in the Soviet Union. Of course, I had taken note of the gradual breakup of Brezhnev's Politburo, especially the departure of people responsible for the invasion of Czechoslovakia in 1968, such as Podgorny, Kirilenko, and Kiril Mazurov. I also noticed the rise of some new men, steady in the case of Andropov, uncertain in those of Tikhonov, Romanov, or Chernenko. It was a changing landscape, but I was still skeptical about the ability and will of any of these new Soviet leaders to part with Stalinist ways—for a long time, I must say, I was equally skeptical about Gorbachev.

The end of the Brezhnev era was foreshadowed by events in Poland and the invasion of Afghanistan. The rise of Solidarity in Poland cannot be overstated as a factor underlying the general crisis of the Soviet system. Even the installment of Jaruzelski's military dictatorship in Poland in December 1981 I saw as a defeat and not a victory for the Soviets. With bitter irony, I remembered Gomulka and his role in the destruction of Prague Spring. How could he, with all his life experience, have been so blind to the situation in his own country?

In January 1982, Suslov died, which I considered a very important event. He was the last direct living link to Stalin in the Politburo, and I had always believed that he was the most powerful man there. Immediately after Suslov's funeral, as I later learned, Andropov launched an attack on Brezhnev. In recent months I had watched Brezhnev in occasional television shots, visibly fading. Now the KGB had moved to undermine his authority even before he died, by involving his daughter in a corruption scheme. When Brezhnev died in November 1982, Andropov—not Brezhnev's designated heir, Chernenko—assumed the office of general secretary.

I watched Brezhnev's funeral on television. I had retired the year before and had more time to read and think. I watched the live transmission with astonishment as it became obvious that the grave they had dug was too short for Brezhnev's coffin, so that they had to slip it in by lifting one end and lowering the other. Suddenly, the coffin slipped too far and too fast, hitting the side and the bottom of the grave with a hollow sound. My God, I told my wife, they do not even know anymore how to bury their head of state!

I read with close attention Andropov's first public speeches and began to realize that something more was happening than a regular changing of the guard. Conditions for another attempt at reforming the Soviet system had apparently emerged. How far this process would go was, of course, impossible to guess. At least I could see that very powerful segments of the Soviet bureaucracy were being forced to acknowledge the need for change. Obviously, the system was not working, and there must have been a significant decline in the overall performance of the Soviet economy and other signs of crisis. Only such serious signals could have moved these forces to recognize the necessity for changes.

I also watched Andropov's unexpected illness and death, the subsequent misery of the brief Chernenko regime, the rise of Gorbachev, and finally his takeover in February 1985. Soon I noticed a direct line connecting Gorbachev's course to that of Andropov. I am convinced that had Andropov enjoyed vigorous health, he would have done the same things Gorbachev did, at least in Gorbachev's early years as general secretary.

As glasnost and perestroika started to evolve inside the Soviet Union in 1986 and 1987, their fallout quickly reached Czechoslovakia. Here we had a fossilized variant of the system Gorbachev was trying to reform. Since 1969 Husak's policies had all been based on a rigid rejection of reform. The very notion of reform had been made synonymous with counterrevolution. Gorbachev's policies inevitably and swiftly undermined the whole rationale of the Husak-Strougal regime.

Perestroika was diluted tea compared with our Action Program of 1968, and glasnost could not compare with the freedom of the press we had instituted at the same time. However, important similarities were obvious to everybody. I savored a joke then making the rounds: "What's the difference between Gorbachev and Dubcek? Twenty years!"

The Prague regime reacted with embarrassment. They did not dare, certainly not until early 1989, say anything openly critical of perestroika; after all, they depended entirely upon continued Soviet support. They chose instead to offer reserved and selective approval. At one point they started to refer to "different conditions" between the two countries, a notion forbidden since 1969. They felt betrayed and cornered.

This last stage of the Husak regime was also marked by the failures of its domestic policies becoming increasingly obvious. In 1969 all efforts to deal with the accumulated problems of the society and the economy ceased. The worst of the old practices were revived with catastrophic consequences. By the mid-1980s, everything in Czechoslovakia was deteriorating, most notably environmental conditions and public health. The regime, which had never enjoyed any respect, was also quickly losing its authority.

Gorbachev visited Czechoslovakia in the spring of 1987. Many people hoped that he could somehow lift the mantle of oppression laid down by his predecessors, but his visit resulted in general disappointment. He did nothing that could be interpreted positively. Outwardly, at least, he evinced full support for Brezhnev's orphans ruling in Prague. By then, however, nothing could slow down the demise of the regime. In December 1987, the Czechoslovak Party leadership desperately decided to carry out a cosmetic change. Husak was recalled as Party first secretary, while holding on as president of the Republic. His Party office was taken over by Milos Jakes, a traitor of 1968 vintage.

This shuffle made the situation even worse. It revealed one basic fact: that the purges of 1969 through 1970 had successfully eliminated all reform-minded forces in the Czechoslovak Communist Party. Nobody was left to press for a new course. In 1987 the Communist Party could neither change nor put on a better face. Jakes was a pitiful figure, good only to feed the grapevine of endless jokes. The stage was set for the end of normalization.

My personal situation, by contrast, was changing only slowly. I was still under strict police surveillance, frequently shadowed by five different unmarked police cars, each with two agents. People who talked with me continued to be detained for identification.

I never stopped protesting this harassment; I sent twenty such protests to the office of the general prosecutor between 1971 and 1989. I described each case in detail, not forgetting to supply license plate numbers. After a long delay, I always received the same answer: "No reason has been found to start any action on the basis of your complaint dated . . ."

I continued to be the defenseless prey of rude attacks and slander in the media as the regime's propagandists increased the shrillness of their condemnations of Prague Spring. In 1985 Vasil Bilak attempted to carry this practice abroad, attacking me in an interview for the German weekly *Der Spiegel*. At that point I decided to fight back, and, with the help of an Italian journalist, Luciano Antonetti, I sent my rejoinder to *Unita*, the daily newspaper of the Italian Communist Party. It was immediately published, and *Der Spiegel* took pains to reprint my answer in full.

In spite of the continuing surveillance and attacks on me in the domestic press, I could observe certain small changes. The people I met in public places were much less frightened than before. The wind had started to blow from a different direction.

At the time of Husak's replacement by Jakes, I decided to test the situation and made two or three trips to Prague. I stayed with friends who were signatories of Charter '77, such as Oldrich and Vera Jaros or Vaclav and Vera Slavik. I went for a walk in downtown Prague, and my friends took me to the theater during these visits. I was followed by StB agents at every step, but that was all they did. Hundreds of unknown people came up to me in public places, greeted me, and shook my hand. At the theater, people applauded when they recognized me, and some actors even came to greet me.

In May 1988, I received a letter from the University of Bologna informing me that they had awarded me an honorary doctorate. I was invited to Italy to accept it. The fact that I had received the letter at all was a small miracle, but it was characteristic of the changing situation. I applied for a passport and an exit visa, and shortly I received them. It was by now August. I went to Prague to apply for the Italian entry visa, which I received immediately. Vaclav Slavik accompanied me to the Italian embassy, with a whole convoy of police cars and StB officers behind us.

I was supposed to go to Italy in November, but before I left I sought assurance that I would be permitted to return. I sent a query to the minister of the interior, a man by the name of Vajnar. I had decided not to go to

Bologna without such an official assurance. To my pleased surprise, I received it in October. It was then arranged that University of Bologna would send a car to Bratislava for me. Luciano Antonetti volunteered to come, but they did not let him across the Czechoslovak border, so he waited for me in Austria.

To describe my reception in Bologna—and everywhere else in Italy—is almost impossible. Everywhere I went I was surrounded by friendly crowds. To receive so much public respect and sympathy after so many years of hostile oblivion was overwhelming. The courtesies from strangers were especially touching. As I waited in front of a bookstore for the official car to pick me up, a man recognized me and absolutely insisted on driving me back to the university. There was no way to refuse.

In my speech during the ceremony at the university—the oldest university in the world—I firmly defended the reform policies of Prague Spring and was able to express in public my solidarity with those hundreds of thousands people in Czechoslovakia still suffering from repression. I added that I fully understood those of our citizens who had chosen exile over humiliation at home.

During my two-week stay in Italy, I was received by the chairwoman of the Italian parliament, Nilde Iotti, by the leaders of the Communist and Socialist parties, Achille Occhetto and Bettino Craxi, and finally, in the Vatican, by Pope John Paul II.

I was returned to Bratislava by car on a gloomy day toward the end of November. The situation at home was very tense because of growing police mobilization. Shortly after I returned, I received several more invitations to visit institutions in Western Europe. I decided to apply for permission to go to Madrid for a lecture and to France to attend the celebration of the 200th anniversary of the French Revolution in July 1989. Both applications were briskly rejected. They did not want me to go abroad anymore.

Their time was running out, no matter what they did. In Prague the actions of Charter '77 grew bolder, and in Bratislava the opposition demonstrated against continuing breaches of freedom of religion. Vaclav Havel was arrested again on January 16, 1989, when he attempted to put flowers on the place where Jan Palach had suffered twenty years before. I immediately sent strong protests to both Jakes and Husak. I wrote, "If you still want to do something, I would advise you to start doing it by releasing Havel."

In April 1989, the Jakes regime decided to retreat before a wave of protests from abroad as well as at home. They let Havel go home, and I went to Prague to visit him. With the help of my contacts among the Czech Charterists, it was not difficult to arrange the visit. When Vaclav Slavik took me to Havel's apartment building, on the banks of the Vltava slightly south of the National Theatre, a police team shadowed me, and there was another police team "protecting" Havel's house, but they did not prevent me from going in.

Havel was greatly pleased to see me. Our meeting was extraordinarily friendly, reflecting our mutual respect. We discussed the situation for a while, and we were both optimistic. Havel proposed that we call the poet and playwright Pavel Kohout in Vienna, a mutual friend who had been forced to leave the country almost ten years before. In 1967 Kohout was one of the Czech writers Novotny had expelled from the Party. During Prague Spring, his Party membership was renewed, but then, like me, he was expelled again by Husak. Now he was on the line, and Havel and I both talked with him. I like to remember that evening.

The drama leading to the collapse of all the Soviet-modeled regimes in Eastern Europe in the fall of 1989 started with the attempt of masses of East Germans to escape via Czechoslovakia and Hungary to West Germany. The scenes in and around the compound of the West German Embassy in Prague must still be vividly remembered worldwide.

The German exodus had phenomenal impact in Czechoslovakia. Here the fiction of *Realsozialismus* was definitely and finally destroyed. By the end of September, Prague was filled with thousands of abandoned East German automobiles, gladly left behind as soon as trains started taking their owners to the West—with the humiliated consent of the Honecker regime.

The Soviets did not seem to care anymore about their Eastern European possessions. Poland was all but lost already, and in Hungary reform had grown rapidly into revolution. Soviet leaders were much more concerned with maintaining control at home. The East German regime crumbled in October. It did not require clairvoyance to know that the regime in Czechoslovakia would soon follow. On the surface, the situation still looked quiet. There were no strikes or other signs of mass protest. Police mobilization reached its peak, and it looked as if the Jakeses were prepared to have a bloodbath to save their skin.

Then all was suddenly otherwise.

On November 17, the fiftieth anniversary of the Nazi assault on Czech universities during the German occupation, the authorities permitted a commemorative student manifestation. A march was planned in an area outside the center of Prague. But then the marchers changed direction and moved toward the city center. How it happened is still not quite clear.

By coincidence, I was in Prague that day. I was supposed to meet a deputy of the European parliament. The Slaviks were taking me to Dr. Jaros's apartment, where the meeting was supposed to take place. On the way there we were surrounded by the police and taken to a police station. There we were held until the late evening hours.

In the meantime, the riot police attacked the students, who were marching toward Wenceslas Square, and several students were brutally beaten. This launched a chain of events that led to the collapse of the old regime within two weeks.

I returned to Bratislava the next day and took part in that city's first protest demonstrations in response to the events in Prague. The numbers of people joining these demonstrations grew from day to day in cities and towns throughout the country, and in Prague the crowds soon reached almost a million. Prague, of course, had to play the leading role. It was the capital of the Republic and the seat of all the main government offices; the outcome of the conflict could not be decided elsewhere.

During these revolutionary days, two new movements emerged as representatives of the opposition: Civic Forum in Prague and Public Against Violence in Bratislava. Both were loose alliances of opposition forces from dissident Communists to Catholic activists. Direct contacts between these groups were quickly established, and their further actions were closely coordinated. The opposition presented three crucial demands: to revise the valid constitution by removing the clause postulating "the leading role" of the Communist Party; to abolish the National Front as an obstacle to free formations of political parties and movements; and to terminate Marxism-Leninism as the only permissible state ideology.

Under growing pressure from the public, and clearly deserted by the Soviets, the Jakes leadership decided to retreat. Within a few days the government—still the old one—presented the relevant proposal to the parliament—also still the old one—and it was approved on November 29. This day, I believe, marked the death of the old regime.

Further developments took the form of negotiations between representatives of Civic Forum and the government. Here the specific forms of nonviolent transfer of power were agreed upon. The term "Velvet Revolution" was derived from the nonviolent nature of this process.

It was on November 26, 1989, that Vaclav Havel and I appeared, side by side, on the famous balcony of the Melantrich publishing house on Wenceslas Square. We symbolized the alliance of Czech and Slovak opposition forces in their struggle against the remnants of the Stalinist system.

I treasure that moment in fond memory. I recall that there was some argument in the room leading to the balcony about who would introduce us. It was a silly idea in itself, but the building was the property of the

Czechoslovak National Socialist Party, and its leader wanted to get some credit. Then somebody energetically pushed both Havel and me onto the balcony. It was Stanislav Milota, a well-known cinematographer cameraman who was then the chief coordinator of Civic Forum.

The powerful roar of the crowd as we appeared still echoes in my ears. Several hundred thousand people stood there cheering. My thoughts ran back twenty-one years to that May Day parade of 1968: I could compare this moment with nothing else.

And that, for me at least, closed the circle of historic events that had started in October 1967, when I launched the revolt against Novotny. So many things had happened—times of hope, times of defeat, times of patient resistance. Now I was standing on this balcony, at the side of a Czech dissident almost a generation younger than I, and we both knew that the crowd down there was giving us the power to bring the cause of freedom to its final victory in our country.

EDITOR'S AFTERWORD

T HIS afterword is written under circumstances drastically different than expected. Mr. Dubcek wished to conclude his memoirs with an epilogue reflecting on the period after November 1989, which in a sense was the capstone of his political life. We discussed the contents after the June 1992 elections in Czechoslovakia, and again in mid-August. It was left until close to the final deadline to write this last word. In the meantime, the fatal car accident occurred, on September 1, 1992. Alexander Dubcek never recovered from his injuries; he died nine weeks later.

For that epilogue, he projected no detailed recapitulation of either the events of the last three years or his personal history in that time. He simply wanted to offer his own summary of these events. While I shall respect the author's intentions as much as I can, his passing necessitates certain added commentary from me.

From December 1989 until June 1992, Alexander Dubcek was chairman of the Federal Assembly. With the presidency and the post of prime minister, this was one of the three key offices in Czechoslovakia under its constitutional system. It was in the Federal Assembly that the revolutionary changes of 1989 were ratified in legal and constitutional from. There, Dubcek devoted all his energies to helping build the foundations of a democratic state. In particular he directed the reconstruction of the assembly from a rubber stamp parliament to an active, independent legislature. That was no easy undertaking, especially in the interregnum between December 1989 and June 1990, when the first democratic elections in Czechoslovakia since 1946 were held.

Dubcek was an important part of the coalition of democratic forces that gradually forced the Communists, in December 1989, to surrender all the key offices in the country, a movement that culminated in the reluctant resignation of Gustav Husak and the election of Vaclav Havel to the Czechoslovak presidency on December 29, 1989. Dubcek, who had been elected chairman of the legislature only the day before, presided over this act, as he did when Havel was reelected on July 5, 1990.

Under Dubcek's chairmanship, the parliament reestablished multiparty democracy; reenacted full religious freedom, freedom of the press, and freedom of enterprise; and abrogated the "treaty" that had formally legalized Soviet occupation—to name only its most important acts.

With no delay, Dubcek also initiated actions to bring Czechoslovakia back into Europe. One of his first official trips abroad was to Strasbourg, the seat of the European parliament. In Prague, he received dozens of foreign statesmen, among them George Bush, François Mitterrand, Margaret Thatcher, Boris Yeltsin, Lech Walesa, and Turkish President Turgut Ozal. Dubcek himself traveled to many countries, including Japan and the United States, to establish better, stable relations and to facilitate a widening cooperation.

In the June 1990 elections, Civic Forum and Public Against Violence, the Czech reform movement and its Slovak equivalent, won decisive victories in their respective lands. Soon after that, a gradual political differentiation among members of both movements led to their breakup, while the political mainstreams in the two republics moved in different directions.

In Slovakia, the main current stayed left of center, as before the elections. Caution about introduction of a market economy and concerns about the future of the welfare state played important roles. One must remember that contemporary Slovak political culture grows out of the nation's historic experience, which is of long-lasting, widespread poverty and unemployment. Macaulay thought that historical memory, if bad enough, could live through five generations.

In contrast, the political mood in the Czech Republic moved to the Right after June 1990. This showy display of rightist attitudes was unprecedented in this historically liberal land. It can only be compared with the early post-Munich period, when such a manifestation was a helpless reaction to the betrayal of the Western allies. The reemergence of this disposition in 1990 was probably a belated reaction to twenty years of Soviet occupation, a time of humiliating self-accommodation.

As the sometimes self-proclaimed political Right became a significant attraction in the Czech Republic, former dissidents, mostly left-of-center liberals who assumed leading political positions in the early postrevolutionary period, gradually lost support. New leaders emerged, unbranded with a dissident past, which had for years been viewed by most as bizarre anyway. The result: shock treatment for the economy, enhanced by a strongly consumerist public philosophy and a hard line toward Slovak demands. The fact is no one presented any more sensible option, and the plan has a much better chance to work in the Czech Republic than in Slovakia. At any rate, a distinctly Czech national agenda was set.

These opposing tendencies in the two parts of Czechoslovakia took shape at a time of renewed Slovak efforts to assert equality and to increase the Slovak share in the federal power structure. Czech politicians and public, always burdened with the memory of Munich and Slovak separation in March 1939, reacted with irritation. The trends collided, creating a complex situation, aggravated by poor mutual understanding.

These problems became the most sensitive internal political issue during 1991 and the electoral campaign in the spring of 1992. Dubcek devoted unlimited time and energy to finding a reasonable solution. In endless meetings, he strove to achieve agreement on crucial problems of the constitutional setup of the state and the division of powers between the federation and the national governments. He was a realist and a very practical politician. He disliked noisy gestures and pointless polemics. He worked quietly but tirelessly for a basic consensus at the federal level, seeing that the negotiations between the national governments and assemblies were failing. While it proved impossible for the two sides to agree on a new constitution, he tried at least to amend the basic articles of the old to strengthen and preserve the federation.

Dubcek always weighed his steps on the merit of their acceptability in the legislature. At the same time, he tried to discourage others, including President Havel, from making proposals he knew were "unpassable." The defeat of such proposals would make the situation still worse, he believed. In the end, his own proposals had a better chance of success than any others. The failure of his efforts should not be seen as the measure of their worth.

It deserves note that even in the June 1992 elections, Dubcek was still running for, and elected to the *federal* parliament. That in itself was a political gesture.

I first met Alexander Dubcek in April 1964, when Ahmed Ben Bella, the Algerian president, visited Czechoslovakia. As a reporter, I had covered the Algerian war and had met Bella before, so I was assigned to cover his visit.

After a two-day stay in Prague, Bella went on to Bratislava. The contrast was remarkable. The state functions I had attended in Prague had been ritualized and stiff. Bratislava seemed another world. Dubcek was youthful, relaxed, and natural. Formalities were kept to a minimum. Discussions lacked any doctrinal undertones. Even the weather cooperated; it was a beautiful, warm spring day, and Dubcek took his guest for a stroll along the Danube.

I was anxious to talk with Dubcek alone, since I was curious about this man who did not fit at all the widespread image of a Communist Party official. But time was pressing, and the few minutes I passed with Dubcek were devoted exclusively to his questions about Algeria.

The next few times I met Dubcek were in April and May 1968, during Prague Spring, and then briefly two or three times between August 1968 and April 1969. Soon after that he was named ambassador to Turkey and I found myself welding garage doors in northern Bohemia. In the summer of 1974, I was forced to leave Czechoslovakia. Dubcek, back from Turkey and reduced to the status of a nonperson, stayed behind, in seclusion in Bratislava.

When we met again sixteen years later, he was the new chairman of the Czechoslovak Federal Assembly. The prospect of our collaborating on his memoirs came up, and we agreed on how to proceed.

Then I traveled to Prague several times, including a stay of almost six months, and interviewed Dubcek extensively. We covered not only his life but those of his parents and the many events of the last seventy years. I confess that, like many Czechs, I was fairly ignorant about Slovakia when I started to work with Dubcek on his memoirs, and I had to read extensively to prepare for the job.

There were times in the writing of this book when my interpretation of events differed from Dubcek's, especially in the period following the Soviet invasion in August 1968, but I believe I have recorded his views faithfully. For the most part, I found it easy and natural to follow his narrative, his arguments, and explanations. I never saw him hesitate with an answer or digress. Each time he made a point, I saw that he was doing so honestly and sincerely. Even when I did not agree with a view, he at least made me understand and respect it.

While others had surely known Dubcek longer and better, I realized quickly that he was an extraordinary man, certainly for a politician, which he was in every inch. Some of his essential traits made my task much easier.

For one thing, Dubcek was completely without cynicism. He tried to see the good side of everything. He sincerely believed in the good, and he always assumed that everyone had good intentions. He was often let down, but that never changed his basic nature. In time he became more cautious in his political behavior, but he remained, for better or worse, a trusting person.

Dubcek was a moral man, with the deeply ingrained Lutheran traditions and family rules of his ancestors. He loved one woman all his life and was a kind, patient, and gentle husband and father. The devious morals of Leninist "dialectics" never seems to have affected his honesty, personal attitudes or behavior. Even in his many encounters with dangerous and powerful opponents, he remained quite sincere, albeit cautious and restrained.

He was invariably truthful. I meticulously checked his facts, and not once did I find any substantive discrepancy between his account and the documentary record. He didn't always remember the exact date and hour of an event, but he was true in describing its substance.

The question must arise as to how Dubcek could have become a high Communist official with these characteristics, but that can only be answered in terms of his whole extraordinary life. Like most Slovak and Czech Communists during wartime and the early postwar era, he was no Bolshevik. He was a socialist, whose beliefs were easily compatible with his Lutheran family principles. Simply put, he believed in social equality and justice. He had no academic, philosophical, or legal training before the 1950s. The Party he joined did not advertise that it was a criminal organization. The goals it claimed to strive for made him like his parents before him believe that he was becoming part of a movement to realize the centuries-old dream of a fair deal for all. One must also remember that the illegal political party he joined was hunted by the police of the Tiso regime. In due time he found out that the train he was on was moving in the wrong direction, and he worked for years, with sagacity and courage, to change its direction. His efforts failed only because what he found there was a single, one-way track.

As a politician, Dubcek was a consistent Fabian: he almost invariably avoided direct conflicts, tirelessly looking for consensus. This trait, unique among high Communist officials, was in fact an early indication of the political direction in which he was moving.

Dubcek's understanding of freedom underwent a labored development. Initially he perceived freedom in very practical terms: freedom from fascism; freedom from poverty and unemployment; the right to work, health care, and social security; the right to a decent living. But in time he learned to see the importance of democracy in modern society, the importance of cultural freedoms and freedom of the press. From the moment he came to power, he worked consistently to achieve these goals.

The main reason the Soviets decided to invade Czechoslovakia in August 1968 was the Action Program initiated by Dubcek in October 1967. The program has often been criticized as limited in scope. But Dubcek once told me, "I was not so naive as not to see that it would only take time before the changes we made yielded to a full multiparty democracy. I knew that, and Brezhnev knew that, of course. So why won't the critics see it?"

In his last years, Dubcek identified entirely with the ideas of European Social Democracy. He met with Willy Brandt, whom he greatly admired, and in early 1992 he assumed the leadership of the Social Democratic Party in Slovakia. By then he believed that the whole Leninist and Soviet phenomenon was a tragic miscarriage of history. He viewed with satisfaction the transformation of the Slovak Communist Party into a moderate party of the Left, but he was angry that the Czech Communist Party showed no signs of similar intentions. In his characteristic way, he observed: "They should have the decency to dissolve themselves. They have nothing to do here anymore."

While he arrived at an understanding of democracy and the electoral process, Dubcek never changed his basic belief in justice-social justice-for all. He saw clearly that there was no substitute for a market economy, but he believed that public, municipal, and cooperative ownership should play a significant role within that economy. He repeatedly emphasized that the market cannot, by itself, solve most human and social problems. When a part of the Czech public seemed to become obsessed with Thatcherism in the first months after 1989, he worried that the lessons of the past might be forgotten. He believed that a market economy must be wisely regulated by an enlightened government and an effective legal system with solid guarantees for all citizens.

During the two and a half years of his tenure as chairman of the Czechoslovak Federal Assembly, he worked longer hours than anyone around him, often sleeping only two or three hours a night. Several times he returned from his office to his temporary home in Prague, a government villa, and fell asleep with his clothes on. He once did so, in late fall 1991, under a wide open window on a freezing night and caught a terrible cold, from which he never fully recovered. He had little time to eat and did so very irregularly. Several times I saw him biting on the same piece of fried carp wrapped in aluminum that he kept in his refrigerator for weeks.

The stress became especially acute after Dubcek's wife died in September 1991. He was never quite the same without her. When she was dying, he spent hours sitting silent and motionless by her side in the hospital. Anna's death was an unhealed wound for him.

In the weeks after his accident, physicians discovered that Dubcek had not only a broken spine but also pneumonia, stomach ulcers, and an inflamed pancreas. In November 1989 he was a very healthy man for his age, as close friends remember. It was the hectic time following the revolution and his complete disregard for himself that undermined his health, even before his tragic and untimely fatal car accident.

*　　*　　*

After many months of collaboration with Alexander Dubcek, I do not think it presumptuous to imagine certain thoughts he would have wanted to express in this epilogue. He would, in the first place, have reiterated his deep satisfaction at having lived long enough to witness the end of the Soviet occupation of his country and the realization of his longtime hopes for Czechoslovakia—so brutally interrupted in August 1968. He would have expressed his belief that democracy was firmly established in both Slovakia and the Czech lands no matter what economic and social policies were to follow.

Dubcek would also have stated his disappointment and sorrow at that unexpected and unwanted outcome of the Velvet Revolution, the breakup of Czechoslovakia. But other things saddened him, too. He deplored the disrespect of a large part of society, especially in the Czech lands, for those who had for many years openly opposed the old regime while the majority passively collaborated. He believed that the veterans of Prague Spring and the signatories of Charter '77 deserved much more respect and gratitude.

Dubcek also lamented the behavior of some people with whom he interacted during the last three years of his life. But he was a very considerate man, a man of delicacy, and he would surely have avoided publicly criticizing even those who in these years disappointed, deceived, or hurt him. I am certain that all he would have wished to say about such behavior would have been low-key and simple. He would have liked to call for more decency and tolerance in public life and, above all, for more mutual understanding between Czechs and Slovaks.

The lack of this understanding was most painful for him, because he was both a Slovak and a Czecho-Slovak patriot. He believed that a union of Slovaks and Czechs should be preserved as the best guarantee of the national interests of both; he never forgot the potential external dangers that separation might render more actual. Commenting once on the political leaders conducting the negotiations leading to the breakup of the state, he said, "Obviously they did not learn geography."

Until his last active days, Dubcek never ceased striving to preserve a federation of Czechs and Slovaks. He was deeply saddened to witness the union fall victim to uncontrollable currents on both sides. But still he didn't lose hope. That, as he often said, dies last.

JIRI HOCHMAN
Columbus, Ohio,
November 1992

PRINCIPAL FIGURES

Bacilek, Karol—First secretary of the Slovak Communist Party, 1954–1963; Czechoslovak minister of national security, 1952–1954.

Benes, Edvard—Czechoslovak president, 1935–1948 (in exile in London, 1939–1945).

Bilak, Vasil—Pro-Soviet member of the Czechoslovak Communist Party Presidium in 1968–1970.

Cernik, Oldrich—Member of the Czechoslovak Party Presidium in 1968; prime minister, 1968–1970.

Cisar, Cestmir—Secretary of the Czechoslovak Communist Party Central Committee in 1968.

Clementis, Vladimir—Czechoslovak minister of foreign affairs; executed with Rudolph Slansky in 1952.

Gottwald, Klement—Leader of the Czechoslovak Communist Party, 1928–1953; Czechoslovak president, 1948–1952.

Hendrych, Jiri—Deputy to Antonin Novotny in the 1960s; secretary of the Czechoslovak Communist Party Central Committee.

Husak, Gustav—Purged in the early 1950s; deputy prime minister and Soviet collaborator in 1968; Czechoslovak president, 1973–1989.

Indra, Alois—Secretary of the Czechoslovak Communist Party Central Committee in 1968; Soviet collaborator.

Jakes, Milos—Pro-Soviet chairman of the Czechoslovak Party's Central Auditing Commission; the last first secretary of the Party, 1988–1989.

Kolder, Drahomir—Head of the commission (1962–1963) to rehabilitate victims of the 1950s purges; member of the Czechoslovak Communist Party leadership in the 1960s; pro-Soviet in 1968.

Kriegel, Dr. Frantisek—Member of the Presidium in the Dubcek government; alone in refusing to sign the Moscow Protocol.

Lenart, Jozef—Czechoslovak prime minister in the 1960s; ally of Antonin Novotny; Soviet collaborator in 1968.

Masaryk, Tomas—First president of Czechoslovakia, 1918–1935.

Mlynar, Zdenek—Secretary of the Czechoslovak Communist Party Central Committee in 1968.

Novomesky, Ladislav—Slovak poet and Slovak Communist Party leader; jailed on false charges in the 1950s.

Novotny, Antonin—Hard-line Czechoslovak party leader, 1953–1968, and president of Czechoslovakia, 1957-1968. Ousted by Dubcek et al. in the thaw preceding Prague Spring.

Pelikan, Jiri—Director general of Czechoslovak television in 1968.

Piller, Jan—Member of the Czechoslovak Communist Party leadership in 1968.

Sik, Ota—Spearhead of Czechoslovak economic reform in the 1960s; deputy prime minister during Prague Spring.

Simon, Bohumil—First Secretary of the Prague city committee of the Communist Party; kidnapped to Moscow with Dubcek.

Siroky, Viliam—Czechoslovak prime minister, 1953–1963.

Smidke, Karol—Slovak Party leader, purged in 1951.

Smrkovsky, Josef—Chairman of the National Assembly, 1968–1969; member of Dubcek's leadership.

Spacek, Josef—Regional Party secretary in Brno, Moravia; member of Dubcek's leadership, and kidnapped with him to Moscow.

Strougal, Lubomir—Deputy prime minister in 1968; turned pro-Soviet after the invasion.

Svestka, Oldrich—Novotny disciple; chief editor of the Party newspaper, *Rude Pravo*; Soviet collaborator in 1968.

Svoboda, General Ludvik—Czechoslovak president, 1968–1973. Took part in negotiations in Moscow.

Tiso, Father Josef—Nazi puppet president of the Slovak State from 1939 to 1945; executed 1947.

The Soviets and Their Allies

Brezhnev, Leonid—General secretary of the Communist Party of the Soviet Union, 1964–1982.

Chervonenko, Stepan—Soviet ambassador to Prague in 1968.

Gomulka, Wladislaw—General secretary of the Polish Communist Party in 1968.

Kadar, Janos—General secretary of the Hungarian Communist Party in 1968.

Khrushchev, Nikita—General secretary of the Communist Party of the Soviet Union, 1953–1964.

Kosygin, Alexei—Soviet prime minister and member of Brezhnev's Politburo in 1968.

Podgorny, Nikolai—Chairman of the Presidium of the Supreme Soviet and member of Brezhnev's Politburo in 1968.

Suslov, Michail—Member of Brezhnev's Politburo in 1968.

Ulbricht, Walter—General secretary of the East German Communist Party in 1968.

Voronov, Gennadii—Prime minister of the Russian Federation and member of Brezhnev's Politburo in 1968.

Zhivkov, Todor—General secretary of the Bulgarian Communist Party in 1968.

Others

Ceausescu, Nicolae—General secretary of the Romanian Communist Party in 1968.

Tito, Josip Broz—General secretary of the League of Communists of Yugoslavia and president of Yugoslavia in 1968.

EDITOR'S NOTE ON
DOCUMENTATION

T HIS work is based on Alexander Dubcek's narration, which I recorded, translated into English, and edited. We proceeded chronologically, from the story of his parents through his growing up in the Soviet Union to the twenty years following the suppression of Prague Spring.

Occasionally, the author was not quite sure about dates, names, or other details, and he asked me to find those facts and fill in the gaps in his narration. All hard facts, however, were verified to assure maximum accuracy. Where verification was not possible, Mr. Dubcek decided either to leave the fact out or to make it clear that his point was rather in the range of probability. Such cases were very few.

In one case only, unfortunately after the author became disabled, did I run across a serious discrepancy between available archival sources and his narration. This concerned the sequence of events on August 23, 1968, when Mr. Dubcek was transported from captivity in Ruthenia to Moscow. Specifically, his memory of arriving in Moscow differed from the testimony given by former Czechoslovak Prime Minister Oldrich Cernik by about ten hours. Since Mr. Dubcek died shortly after my discovery of this discrepancy, I could not question him directly. After a careful study of the case, which included an examination of the Soviet stenographic record of Mr. Dubcek's interrogation in the Kremlin, I decided in agreement with the author's estate and the publishers to accept Mr. Dubcek's version as more probable. The discrepancy is of no substantial importance in the context of the whole book.

Mr. Dubcek finished reading the working translations of the first twenty chapters of the manuscript and made occasional written corrections in the text as well as comments and complementary notes on the margins or at the end. On the whole, corrections were rare, and each was incorporated in the English text.

The manuscript was also reviewed by Dr. Oldrich Jaros, the head of the office of the chairman of the Czechoslovak Federal Assembly between December 1989 and June 1992. Dr. Jaros had worked closely with Alexander Dubcek since the early 1960s, especially in 1968–69. Selected parts of the work were also read by Dr. Vera Jarosova, but her prolonged illness prevented her from reviewing the entire manuscript.

In the final stages, the work was reviewed as well by Dr. Jan Uher, a Slovak political scientist in Bratislava, who paid special attention to the last ten chapters, which Mr. Dubcek, because of the accident, was unable to read himself. Dr. Uher's corrections have been incorporated.

A variety of sources was used to verify details missing in the narration, most notably the rich documentation gathered by Dr. Vera Jarosova in Prague and the archives of the Czechoslovak Government Commission for the Investigation of the Events of 1967–1970.

THE ACTION PROGRAM OF THE COMMUNIST PARTY OF CZECHOSLOVAKIA

Adopted at the Plenary Session of the Central Committee of the Communist
Party of Czechoslovakia, April 5, 1968
Complete Text
[*Rudē Prāvo*, April 10, 1968; translation revised from ČTK, Prague,
April 1968]

The Czechoslovak Road to Socialism

The social movement in the Czech lands and Slovakia during the 20th century has
been carried along by two great currents—the national liberation movement and
socialism.

The national liberation struggle of both nations culminated in the emergence of
an independent state in which for the first time in history Czechs and Slovaks were
united in a single state. The founding of the Czechoslovak Republic marked an
important step forward in the national and social development of both nations. The
democratic order eliminated old monarchist remnants and created favorable conditions for fast progress in all spheres of national life.

The pre-war bourgeois order, however, did not settle the onerous class antagonisms and was not able to lay reliable foundations for the lasting prosperity of the
new economic entity or guarantee workers and employees full employment and a
secure existence. Its nationalist regime, though liberal toward the minorities,
ignored the individuality of the Slovak nation and did not succeed in eliminating
the influence of extreme nationalism and in introducing harmony among all
nationalities of the Republic. Under the conditions prevailing at that time in
capitalist Europe, not even the independence of the Czechoslovak Republic could
be permanently safeguarded.

The progressive forces tried to respond to these shortcomings. Their most
energetic component was the Communist Party of Czechoslovakia which was
striving for a socialist conception of Czechoslovak society.

As a consequence of the anti-Fascist movement—which originated in connection with the breakup of pre-war Czechoslovakia—and even more of the national
liberation struggle, the integration of socialism with the national and democratic
movement began to take shape.

During the national and democratic revoluton of 1944–45 the national and
democratic values of socialism were united for the first time. The democratic and
national movement began to be socialized and socialism became truly national and
democratic. Czechoslovakia's road to socialism, which began with the Slovak
National Uprising and the Prague Uprising in 1944–45, is the source of the most
progressive traditions of modern Czech and Slovak history.

The Republic, whose liberation was the result of the heroic fighting of the Soviet
Army and the national liberation struggle of the Czechoslovak people, was restored

on new foundations which facilitated the solving of the most acute national problems: The existence of the Republic as a state was ensured by close alliance with the Soviet Union. By nationalization the Republic gained an economic system providing conditions for rapid restoration and for the further development of the economy toward socialism. The considerable expansion of informal political freedoms was the true culmination of the whole democratic tradition of Czechoslovakia's development. Socialism became the embodiment of the modern national program of the Czechs and Slovaks.

Czechoslovakia was the first industrial country to put socialist reconstruction into practice. The policy of Czechoslovakia's road to socialism from 1945 to 1948 was an expression of the attempt to respect the complexity of the specific internal and international conditions of Czechoslovakia. It contained many elements which can contribute toward achieving our present aim of democratizing the socialist order.

We identify ourselves with traditions of the liberation struggle in which patriots participated at home and in various parts of Europe and the world. 375,000 men and women gave their lives for these ideals. We will support a scientific examination of the history of both nations, the conclusions of which cannot be decreed by anyone, but can only be the result of the study of history itself. The February victory of the working people was an important milestone in the socialist development of post-war Czechoslovakia; it created the conditions necessary for accelerating the advance to socialism. After February 1948 the Party took a new road of socialist construction backed by confidence and support of the broadest strata of the population.

It was a difficult road. In a divided world in the grips of the cold war, our nations had to increase their efforts to safeguard their hard-won national existence and therefore concentrate on reinforcing their own defense system and that of all the other socialist states. Building the new Republic, which lacked many of the internal resources essential for developing the economy, was closely connected with the progress and problems of the whole socialist camp. The inclusion of the Republic in the system of socialist states brought substantial changes in the direction of development of the national economy and also in its internal structure, in the character of the state and the social order. We therefore respected the common tasks of those countries in which combating problems of economic and cultural retardation and creating new forms of ownership played a leading role.

All this influenced the speed, form, and content of the profound economic, social, and political reconstruction which the Republic experienced during the building of socialism. They called for an exceptional exertion of energy from the working class and the whole people, great sacrifices from Communists, and the dedicated work of tens of thousands of functionarires.

The unusual size, quality, and challenge of the changes, however, gave rise to the contradictions, grave shortcomings, unsolved problems, and deformations of socialist principles which are known as the personality cult.

The construction of the new social system was marked by insufficient experience, lack of knowledge, by dogmatism and subjectivism. Many signs of the times, conditioned by heightened international tension and the compulsory acceleration in building industry, were understood as the generally valid forms of life and development in a socialist society. The stage of development of the socialist states at the beginning of the fifties and the arrest of the creative development of knowledge concomitant with the personality cult, conditioned a mechanical acceptance and spreading of ideas, customs, and political conceptions which were at variance with Czechoslovak conditions and traditions. The leading bodies and institutes of the Party and the state of that time are fully responsible. The centralist and directive-administrative methods used during the fight against the remnants of the bourgeoisie and during the consolidation of power under conditions of heightening international tension after February 1948 were, in this situation, unjustifiably carried over into the next stage of development and gradually grew into a bureaucratic system. Sectarianism, suppression of the democratic rights and freedoms of the people, violation of the laws, signs of licentiousness, and misuse of power became apparent in the internal life of the Republic, undermined the initiative of the people, and, what is more, gravely and unjustly afflicted many citizens—Communists and non-Communists alike. The irreparable losses suffered by our movement at that time will forever remain a warning against similar methods.

The extraordinary strength of our people led to great historic successes. Basic socialist social changes have been accomplished and the socialist order has sunk its roots deeply and firmly into our land. Our society, in which the means of production are mainly in the hands of the socialist state or of workers' cooperatives, has got rid of capitalist exploitation and the social wrongs connected with it. Every citizen of the Czechoslovak Socialist Republic has the right to work and enjoys basic social security. Our society has emerged from a period of industrialization with an extensive industrial base. We have acheived noteworthy successes in the advancement of science and culture. The broadest strata of the people have unprecedented opportunities for gaining a suitable education. The international status of the Republic among the socialist countries is firmly secured.

At the end of the fifties our society entered another stage of development. The political line which we wish to apply and develop began to take shape at that time. The following features are characteristic of the present stage:

• antagonistic classes no longer exist and the main feature of internal development has become the process of bringing all social groups closer together;

• methods of direction and organization hitherto used in the economy are outdated and demand urgent changes, i.e., an economic system of management able to enforce a turn toward intensive growth;

• the country must be made ready to join the world scientific-technical revolution. This calls for especially intensive cooperation of workers and agricultural workers with the technical and specialized intelligentsia and will place high demands upon knowledge and qualifications and the application of science;

• a broad scope for social initiative, a frank exchange of views, and the democratization of the whole social and political system have literally become a necessity if socialist society is to remain dynamic. They are also a condition for being able to hold our own in world competition and fulfill our obligations toward the international workers' movement honorably.

Surmounting the Causes of Profound Social Crisis

Even when this Party line was in the formation stage and just starting to be applied, it ran up against a lack of understanding for the new tasks, a relapse into methods of work from the time of sharp class struggle, and the opposition of those who in one way or another found the deformations of socialist reality convenient.

We need a frank statement of what these mistakes and deformations were and what caused them so as to remedy them as soon as possible and concentrate all forces *on the fundamental structural change in our lives* which we are facing at the present time.

After the 20th Congress of the Communist Party of the USSR, which was an impulse for revival of the development of socialist democracy, the Party adopted several measures which were intended to overcome bureaucratic-centralist sectarian methods of management or its remnants, to prevent the instruments of the class struggle from being used against the working people. Many Communists and whole working collectives tried to open the way for a progressive development of the economy, the standard of living, science and culture. The clearer it was that class antagonism had been overcome and foundations for socialism laid, the greater was the stress placed upon promoting cooperation among all working people, social strata, groups, and nationalities in Czechoslovakia and on making fundamental changes in methods employed during the time of acute class struggle. They rightly judged the development of socialist democracy to be the main social condition for realizing the humanistic aims characteristic of socialism. However, they met with a lack of understanding, various obstacles and, in some cases, even direct suppression. The survival of methods from the time of the class struggle caused artifical tension among groups, nations, and nationalities, different generations, Communists and nonparty people. Dogmatic approaches impeded a full and timely re-evaluation of the character of socialist construction.

The measures adopted did not therefore bring the anticipated results. On the contrary, over the years, difficulties piled up until they closed in a vicious circle. Subjective conceptions which held that construction of the new society was dependent only upon an accelerated and extensive development of production were not overridden in time. This led to a precipitate expansion of heavy industry, to a disproportionate demand on labor power and raw materials, and to costly investments. Such an economic policy, enforced through directive administrative methods, no longer corresponded to the economic requirements and possibilities of the country and led to exhaustion of its material and human resources. Unrealistic tasks were allotted to the economy, illusory promises were made to the workers. All these factors intensified the unfavorable structure of production, which fell out of step with national conditions: skilled labor could not be put to sufficient advantage, production suffered considerable technical retardation, the development of public services was slowed down, the equilibrium of the market upset, the international status of the economy worsened (especially in foreign trade). The result was stagnation and, in certain cases, a reduction in the living standard of the people.

These shortcomings were directly caused by the maintenance and constant restoration of the old directive system of management. Economic tools of supply and demand, and marketing ties were replaced by directives from the center. Socialist enterprise did not expand. In economic life, independence, diligence, expertise, and initative were not appreciated, whereas subservience, obedience, and even kowtowing to higher ups were.

A more profound reason for keeping the outlived methods of economic management was deformations in the political system. Socialist democracy was not spread in time. Methods of revolutionary dictatorship deteriorated into bureaucracy and became an impediment to progress in all spheres of life. Political mistakes were added to economic difficulties and a mechanism created which resulted in helplessness, conflict between theory and practice. Many of the efforts, activities, and much of the energy of workers of the Party, the state, the economy, science, and culture were squandered. The adverse external circumstances of the early sixties brought things to a head, and a serious economic crisis followed. This period saw the start of the difficulties with which the workers are still confronted daily: the slow increase in wages after many years, stagnation of the living standard, and especially the constantly increasing retardation of the infrastructure in comparison with advanced industrial countries, the catastrophic state of housing and insufficient construction of houses and apartments, the precarious state of the transportation system, poor quality goods and public services, a low quality living environment, and, in general, conditions which tangibly affect the human factor, opportunities for developing human energy and activities, which are decisive for a socialist society. The people grew bitter. They began to feel that despite all the successes which had been achieved and all the efforts exerted, socialist society was making headway with great difficulty, with fateful delay, and with moral and political defects in human relations. Quite naturally, apprehensions arose about socialism, about its human mission, about its human features. Some people became demoralized, others lost perspective.

The main link in this circle was that of remnants or revivers of the bureaucratic, sectarian approach in the Party itself. The insufficient development of socialist democracy within the Party, an unfavorable atmosphere for the promotion of activity, the silencing or even suppression of criticism—all of this thwarted a fast, timely, and thorough rectification. Party bodies took over tasks of state and economic bodies and social organizations. This led to an incorrect merging of the Party and state management, the monopolized power-position of some sections, unqualified interference, the undermining of initiative at all levels, indifference, a cult of mediocrity, and unhealthy anonymity. Irresponsibility and lack of discipline consequently gained ground. Many correct resolutions were never fulfilled. This adversely affected theoretical thinking, making it impossible to recognize in time the shortcomings and danger connected with the outdated system of management. Reform in the economy and politics was held up.

All of these questions became a focus for clashes between forces insisting upon fundamental changes and the bearers of the old conception. The situation was clarified, and essential social progress pushed ahead. At the December and January sessions of the Central Committee, thorough, concrete criticism was made of the main causes of the aforementioned shortcomings and their backers, and corrective measures were instigated in the leading bodies of the Party themselves. One of the immediate causes was said to be that inside the Party there was too great a concentration of decision-making power, that certain individuals, and above all A. Novotny held exceptional positions. This criticism allowed the whole Party and society to start overcoming old approaches and sectarian bureaucratic practices on the basis of self-critical evaluation of the work to date, from top to bottom, so as to create real unity of Czechoslovak society on the basis of social democratism, to implement thoroughly the principles of the new system of economic management, to modernize and rationalize life in Czechoslovakia, to open up long-term perspectives of gradually including Czechoslovakia in the scientific-technological revolution—so that in all spheres of society the strength of socialism might be revived and start out along a new road of socialist development.

A Policy of Unity and Confidence

Decisive for the socialist development of this country was the creation of a broad alliance of progressive forces of the town and country headed by the working class and the combined Czech and Slovak nations.

The resolution of the 13th Congress of the Communist Party of Czechoslovakia set the task of "continuing to strengthen the unity of the working class, which is the leading force in the society, with agricultural cooperative workers and the socialist intelligentsia as the political base of the state, helping the mutual rapprochement of classes and strata of the nations and nationalities in Czechoslovakia, and consolidating their unity." The sense of the present policy is to provide continuous stimulation for democratic relations of cooperation and confidence among the various social groups without differentiation, to harmonize their efforts, to unite their forces on the basis of the development of the whole society.

All social classes, strata, groups, both peoples and all nationalities of the society agree with the fundamental interests and aims of socialism. One of the great advantages of socialist development to date is that a decisive factor in assessing the standing and activity of the people in this society is what they accomplish at work and their progressive social activity, not their membership in this class or that stratum. The Party resolutely condemns attempts to oppose the various classes, strata, and groups of the socialist society to each other and will eliminate everything that creates tension among them.

On behalf of unity and the interests of the whole society, there can be no overlooking the various needs and interests of individual people and social groups according to their work, qualification, age, sex, nationality, and so on. In the past we have often made such mistakes.

Socialism can flourish only if enough scope is given to the various interests of the people. It is on this basis that the unity of all workers will be brought about democratically. This is the main source of free social activity and development of the socialist system.

The Party is backed, and will continue to be backed, by the *working class*, which has shown that it is able to carry the main weight of socialist endeavor. Under prevailing conditions, we rely especially upon those, who, with their awareness, i.e., profound understanding of the real interests and tasks of the working class in the revolutionary reconstruction of the whole society, with their qualifications, and their cohesion with modern technology, with the high effectiveness of their work and their social activity, contribute markedly to the further progress of Czechoslovak production and to the society as a whole. The working class began the revolutionary struggle so as to abolish every sort of exploitation, erase all class barriers, facilitate the liberation of all people, and transform the conditions of human life and the character of human labor, make way for the full self-realization of man, and by all this to change even itself. These long-term interests of the working class have not yet been fully realized. The workers, however, now have in their hands new technical, social, and cultural means which allow them to continue changing their working and living conditions and developing elements of purposeful creative endeavor in their work. We are determined to develop all the creative and by far not fully utilized energy which the working class possesses for these tasks.

In the past, workers did not always have an opportunity to develop their own interests. Therefore the Party will strive to activize the social life of the workers, to provide scope for profiting from all their political and social rights through political organizations and trade unions, and to strengthen the democratic influence of collective teams of workers in the management of production. It will strive for the alleviation of extremely tiring jobs, the humanization of work, and the improvement of working conditions.

One of the most significant results of the transformation of the social structure was the creation of social groups which organically coalesce with the workers—*agricultural cooperative workers*. This fact must be appreciated politically. The Party will strive for the absolute economic equalization of agriculture with industry and appreciation for the social importance of agricultural work. In accordance with the conclusions of the 7th Congress of Agricultural Cooperatives we shall support the setting up of all-state agricultural cooperative organizations and increase their political authority; we want to abolish all administrative, bureaucratic obstructions which impede the independent initiative of agricultureal enterprises, everything that endangers the security of cooperative enterprise and results from a lack of confidence in the ability of agricultural cooperative workers to act independently and in a socialist way.

Likewise it will be necessary to understand that the character of our *intelligentsia* has gradually changed; it has become an intelligentsia of the people, a socialist intelligentsia. It represents a force which takes a creative part in the development of society and makes the wealth of science and culture available to all people. Today, workers will find in the intelligentsia an integral part of their own inner strength. The constantly closer collaboration of the technical intelligentsia with workers in productive collectives is further proof of how we have been surmounting former class barriers. The Party will support the growing unity between the intelligentsia and the rest of the working people. It will combat the recent under-estimation of the role of the intelligentsia in our society. It will combat everything that upsets relations between the intelligentsia and the workers. It will strive for just remuneration of complex and creative mental labor.

Just as with the working class, so with the agricultural workers and the intelligentsia, the Party will rely mainly upon those who best understand and most activly further social interests and who, by effective work, most markedly contribute to social progress. Cooperation among all groups of socialist society will be effective and possible only when everyone has become aware of his responsibility to everyone else and does not give preference to narrow professional interests.

Czechoslovak statehood is founded on the voluntary and equal co-existence of *Czechs and Slovaks*. The establishment of socialist relations will provide for the strengthening of the fraternal co-existence of our nations. Our Republic can be strong only if there are no sparks of tension or signs of nervousness and suspicion in relations between the Czech and Slovak nations and among all our nationalities. We must therefore resolutely condemn everything which has occurred in the past which might undermine the principles of the equality and sovereignty of both socialist nations. The unity of the Czechs and Slovaks can be strengthened only on the basis of an unhampered development of their national individuality in harmony with economic progress and objective changes in the social structure of both nations, and on the basis of absolute equality and voluntariness. The more developed the two nations, and the greater use made of the enormous economic and cultural resources in Slovakia, the stronger our Republic will be. Indifference to national intersts or even endeavors to suppress them is considered by the Party to be a gross distortion of its program and political course. The Party will consistently defend the Leninist principle that overlooking the interests of a smaller nation by a larger is incompatible with socialist relations between nations. It will oppose any kind of endeavor to denigrate the continuous search for the best methods of developing the consitutional relations between our nations on the basis of equal rights and voluntariness. Communists of both nations and all nationalities in this country defend the principles of internationalism; the Communists of each nation and nationality are themselves surmounting nationalistic relics in their own surroundings.

Under socialist conditions, each of the national minorities—Hungarian, Polish, Ukrainian, German, etc.—has a right to its own national life and a thorough realization of all other constitutional rights.

The Party stresses it will oppose all expressions of anti-Semitism, racism, and any antihumanistic ideology, tending to set people against one another.

Various *generations* of our society have grown up under different conditions and naturally vary in their outlook on many questions pertaining to our life. The Party strongly renounces endeavors to play off the interests of these generations against one another and will devote special care to harmonizing and satisfying the needs of the different age groups.

It is true that thanks to the dedicated work of the older generation, our system has provided better conditions for the young people than the pre-Munich Republic. Nevertheless, we still owe much to our youth. Shortcomings and mistakes in political, economic, and cultural life, just as in human relations, make an especially strong impression on the young. Contradictions between words and deeds, a lack of frankness, a phrase-mongering bureaucracy, attempts to settle everything from a position of power—these deformations of socialist life must painfully affect students, young workers, and agricultural workers and give them the feeling that it is not they, their work, their efforts which are decisive for their own future life. Restoring contact with young people everywhere and making them responsible (socialism gives them this responsibility) for their independent work is an urgent task.

This especially applies to improving working conditions and opportunities for young people to be active in social and cultural life and thoroughly erasing everything that evokes a lack of confidence in socialism among young people. We are all glad about youths' enthusiasm and their positive and critical initiative, necessary conditions if they are to see their cause and future in socialism and communism.

Neither should we overlook the material conditions and social esteem, which give the older generation a dignified and well-merited retirement. This society should pay great attention to ensuring adquate security for the active members of the resistance movement, to whom everyone owes respect.

To deformations of Party and state policy belongs blame for the fact that in the past the problem of women, especially those in employment, was not considered a serious political matter. In state, economic, and cultural policy, women should have access to positions which comply with principles of socialist democracy and the significant role taken by women in creating material and spiritual values of the society.

In the further development of our society we must count on the activity of all strata of the population in public life and constructive endeavor. We can say quite openly that we are also reckoning with believers, who, on the basis of their faith, wish, as equals, as builders of a socialist society, to take their part in helping to fulfill all our exacting tasks.

Developing Democracy and Eliminating Equalitarianism

Using and unifying the manifold interests of social groups and individuals calls for the elaboration and implementation of a new political system in our lives, a new model of *socialist democracy*. The Party will strive to develop a state and social order that corresponds to the actual interests of the various strata and groups of this society and gives them a chance to express their interest in their organizations and voice their views in public life. We expect that in an atmosphere of mutual confidence between people and their institutions civic responsibility will grow and the norms of human relations will be respected.

Meanwhile, the Party will strive to link the democratic principles of the social system with expert and scientific management and decision-making. In order to be able to judge responsibly what is in the interest of the whole society, we must always have before us several alternatives for appraisal and expertly drawn-up proposals for solving all disputable matters, and we must ensure that the people get a greater amount of candid information.

Today, when class differences are being erased, the main criterion for evaluating the status of people in society is how the individual contributes toward social progress. The Party has often criticized equalitarian views, but in practice leveling has spread to an unheard of extent and become one of the impediments to an intensive development of the economy and raising the living standard. The harmfulness of equalitarianism lies in the fact that it gives careless, idle, and irresponsible people an advantage over dedicated and diligent workers, the unqualified over the qualified, the technically backward over the talented and initiative-oriented.

Though attempting to replace equalitarianism with the principle of appraising actual achievements, we have no intention of forming a new privileged stratum. We want the remuneration of people in all spheres of social life to depend upon the social importance and effectiveness of their work, upon the development of initiative, and upon the degree of responsibility and risk. This is in the interest of the development of the whole society. The principle of appraising actual achievements raises the technical standard, profitability, and productivity of labor and the respect and authority of the managers responsible. It stresses the principle of material incentive and the growing importance of high qualifications for all workers.

One of the key conditions of the present and future scientific, technical, and social development is to bring about a substantial increase in the qualifications of managers and experts at all levels of economic and social life. If the leading posts are not filled by capable, educated socialist cadre experts, socialism will be unable to hold its own in competition with capitalism.

This fact will call for a basic change in the existing cadre policy, in which education, qualifications, and ability have been under-rated for years.

To apply the principle of remuneration according to the quantity, quality, and social usefulness of work we must put an end to income leveling. This is not to be understood as an excuse to neglect the interests of citizens in the lowest income group, the interests of families with many children, citizens with reduced working ability, pensioners, and certain categories of women and youth. On the contrary, a thorough application of the principle of differentiated remuneration according to actual work achievement is the only effective means for developing resources which enable the standard of living to rise and, according to the spirit of socialist humanism, determine and ensure good living conditions for all strata of the society. We want to make it quite clear that honest work for the society and efforts to improve qualifications are not only duly remunerated but must also enjoy due respect. A socialist society respects those who achieve exceptional results, who are active and show initiative in advancing production, technical, cultural, and social progress; it respects talented people and creates favorable conditions for them to make themselves felt.

The Leading Role of the Party—A Guarantee of Socialist Progress

At present it is most important that the Party practice a policy fully justifying its leading role in society. We believe that this is a condition for the socialist development of the country.

The Communist Party, as a party of the working class, won the struggle with capitalism and the struggle to carry out revolutionary class changes. With the victory of socialism it became the vanguard of the entire socialist society. During the present development the Party has proven its ability to lead this society; from its own initiative it launched the process of democratization and ensured its socialist character. In its political activity the Party intends to depend particularly on those who have an understanding of the requirements of the society as a whole, who do not see their own personal and group interests as opposed to those of socialism, who use and improve their abilities for the benefit of all, who have a sense for everything new and progressive and are willing to help advance it.

The Communist Party enjoys the voluntary support of the people. It does not practice its leading role by ruling society but by most devotedly serving its free, progressive socialist development. The Party cannot enforce its authority. Authority must be won again and again by Party activity. It cannot force its line through directives. It must depend on the work of its members, on the veracity of its ideals.

In the past, the leading role of the Party was often conceived as a monopolistic concentration of power in the hands of Party bodies. This concept corresponded to the false thesis that the Party is the instrument of the dictatorship of the proletariat. This harmful conception weakened the initiative and responsbility of state, economic, and social institutions, damaged the Party's authority, and prevented it from carrying out its real functions. The Party's goal is not to become a universal "caretaker" of the society, to bind all organizations and every step taken in life by its directives. Its mission lies primarily in arousing socialist initiative, showing the ways and real possibilities of Communist perspectives, and in winning over all workers to them through systematic persuasion and the personal examples of Communists. This determines the conceptional character of Party activity. Party bodies do not deal with all problems; they should encourage activity and suggest solutions to the most important ones. At the same time the Party cannot turn into an organization which influences society only by its ideas and program. Through its members and bodies it must develop the practical organizational methods of a political force in society. Political and organizational Party activity coordinates the practical efforts of the people to turn the Party line and program into reality in the social, economic, and cultural life of the society.

As a representative of the interests of the most progressive part of all strata—and thus the representative of the prospective aims of the society—the Party cannot represent the entire scale of social interests. The political expression of the many-sided interests of the society is the National Front, which expresses the unity of the social strata, interest groups, and of the nations and nationalities of this society. The Party does not want to and will not take the place of social organizations; on the contrary, it must take care that their initiative and political responsibility for the unity of society is revived and flourishes. The role of the Party is to seek a way of satisfying the various interests which does not jeopardize the interests of the society as a whole, but promotes them and creates new progressive ones. The Party policy must not lead non-Communists to feel that their rights and freedom are limited by the role of the Party. On the contrary, they must interpret the activity of the Party as a guarantee of their rights, freedom, and interests. We want to, we must achieve a state of affairs where the Party at the basic organizational level will have informal, natural authority based upon its ability to manage and the moral qualities of Communist functionaries.

Within the framework of democratic rules of a socialist state, Communists must continually strive for the voluntary support of the majority of the people for the Party line. Party resolutions and directives must be modified if they fail to express the needs and possibilities of the whole society. The Party must try to ensure for its members—the most active workers in their spheres of work—suitable weight and influence in the whole society and posts in state, economic, and social bodies. This, however, must not lead to the practice of appointing Party members to posts, without regard to the principle that leading representatives of institutions of the whole society are chosen by the society itself and by its individual components and that functionaries of these components are responsible to all citizens or to all members of social organizations. We must abolish discrimination and "cadre ceilings" for non-Party members.

The basis for the Party's ability to act is its ideological and organizational unity based upon broad inner-Party democracy. The most effective weapon against methods of bureaucratic centralism in the Party is the consolidation of the influence of Party members in forming the political line and the reinforcement of the role of really democratically elected bodies. Elected bodies of the Party must first of all guarantee all rights of its members, collective decision-making, and ensure that all power will not be concentrated in a single pair of hands.

Only down-to-earth discussion and an exchange of views can lead to responsible decision-making by collective bodies. The confrontation of views is an essential manifestation of a responsible multilateral attempt to find the best solution, to advance the new against the obsolete. Each member of the Party and Party bodies has not only the right, but the duty to act according to his conscience, with initiative, criticism, and different views on the matter in question, to oppose any functionary. This practice must become deeply rooted if the Party is to avoid subjectivism in its activity. It is impermissible to restrict Communists in these rights, to create an atmosphere of distrust and suspicion of those who voice different opinions, to persecute the minority under any pretext—as has happened in the past. The Party, however, cannot abandon the principle of requiring that resolutions be put into practice once they are approved. Within the Party, all its members are equal regardless of whether they hold any post in Party bodies or in the bodies of state and economic organizations. Nevertheless, anyone who occupies a higher position also carries greater responsibility. The Party realizes that a deeper democracy will not take hold in this society if democratic principles are not consistently applied in the internal life and work of the Party and among Communists. Decisions on all important questions and on filling cadre posts must be backed by democratic rules and secret ballot. The democratization of Party life also means the strengthening of work contacts between the Party and science. In this line we shall make use of consultations and exchanges of opposing and contrary views, since the role of science does not end with the preparation of analyses and documents. It should continue on Party grounds by observing the innovations produced by various resolutions and by contributing to their materialization and control in practice.

The Central Committee of the Communist Party of Czechoslovakia set out on this road at its December and January sessions and will make sure that in the months to come questions of the content and democratic methods of Party life and relations between elected bodies and the Party apparatus are clarified throughout the Party and that rules will be elaborated to define the authority and responsibilities of the individual bodies and links of the Party mechanism, as well as the principles of the Party's cadre policy, which will ensure an effective, regular change of leading officials, guarantee to keep its members well informed, and regulate relations between Party bodies and Party members in general. In preparing the 14th Party Congress the Party will ensure that Party statutes correspond to the present state of its development.

For the Development of Socialist Democracy and a New System of the Political Management of Society

In the past decade, the Party has often put forward the demand for the development of socialist democracy. Measures taken by the Party were aimed at enhancing the role of elected representative bodies in the state. They emphasized the importance of voluntary social organizations and of all forms of popular activities. Party policy initiated a number of laws which increased the protection of rights of every citizen. It was clearly stated in the theses of the Central Committee of the Communist Party of Czechoslovakia prepared for the 13th Party Congress that "the dictatorship of the working class has fulfilled its main historical mission in our country" and guidelines for further development of our democracy were given no less clearly–"the system of socialist democracy—the state, social organizations, and the Party as the leading force—endeavors to bring out the different interests and attitudes of working people to social problems in a democratic way and to settle them within social organizations with regard to nationwide needs and goals. The development of democracy must proceed hand in hand with strengthening the scientific and professional approach to social management."

Nevertheless, *the harmful characteristics of centralized directive decision-making and management have survived into the present.* In relations among the Party, the state, and social organizations, in internal relations and methods among these components, in the relations of state and other institutions to individuals, in the interpretation of the importance of public opinion and of keeping the people informed, in the practice of cadre policy—in all these fields there are too many elements embittering the life of the people, obstructing professionally competent and scientific decision-making, and encouraging highhandedness. The reason may be sought, first and foremost, in the fact that the relations among these bodies in our political system have been built up for years to serve as the instrument for carrying out the orders of the center, and hardly ever made it at all possible for the decision itself to be the outcome of a democratic procedure.

The different interests and needs of people not foreseen by the system of directive decision-making were taken as an undesirable obstacle and not as new needs to be respected by politics. The often well-meant words of "an increase in the people's participation in management" were of no avail, because in time "participation of the people" came to mean chiefly help in carrying out orders, not in making the decisions. Thus it was possible that views, measures, and interventions were enforced even though they were arbitrary and did not comply either with scientific knowledge or with the interests of the various strata of the people and individual citizens. Centralized decision-making put into effect this way could not be effective. It led to a number of resolutions not being fulfilled and a weakening of goal-oriented management of social development. This, in turn, has in many cases kept positions occupied by people who were incapable of any other type of "management," who consistently revive old methods and habits and surround themselves with people who humor them and not with people whose capacities and character would guarantee the successful filling of their posts. Although we consistently condemn the "personality cult," we are still unable to eradicate certain characteristics of our society which were typical of that period. This undermines the people's confidence in whether the Party can change the situation, and old tensions and political nervous strain are revived.

The Central Committee is firmly determined to overcome this state of affairs. As noted above, for the 14th Congress we must cast the fundamental issues of the development of the political system into a concept meeting the demands of life, just as we have established the fundamental concept of the new economic system.

We must reform the whole political system so that it will permit the dynamic development of socialist social relations, combine broad democracy with scientific, highly qualified management, strengthen the social order, stabilize socialist relations, and maintain social discipline. The basic structure of the political system must, at the same time, *provide firm guarantees against a return to the old methods of subjectivism and highhandedness from a position of power.* Party activity has not been directed systematically to that end, and in fact, obstacles have frequently been put in the way of such efforts. All these changes necessarily call for the *commencement of work on a new Czechoslovak Constitution* so that a draft may be thoroughly discussed among professionals and in public and submitted to the National Assembly shortly after the Party Congress.

But we consider it indispensable to change the present state of things immediately, even before the 14th Congress, so that the development of socialism and its inner dynamics will not be hampered by outdated factors in the political system. Our democracy must provide more leeway for the activity of every individual, every collective, every link in management, at lower and higher levels and in the center too. People must have more opportunity to think for themselves and express their opinions. We must radically change the practices that allow the people's initiative and critical comments and suggestion from below to meet with the proverbial deaf ear. We must see to it that the incompetent but readily adaptable people are replaced by those who strive for socialism, who are concerned with its fate and progress and the interests and needs of others, not with their own power or privilege. This holds for people both "above" and "below." It is going to be a complicated process, and it will take some time. At all levels of management, in the Party, in state and economic bodies, and in social organizations, we must ascertain which body, which official, or which worker is really responsible, where to look for guarantees of improvement, where to change institutions, where to introduce new working methods, and where to replace individuals. The attitude of individual Party officials to new tasks and methods, their capability of carrying the new policy into practice, must be the basic political criterion.

No Responsibility Without Rights

Which body and which official are responsible for what, and the rights and duties involved, must be perfectly clear in our system of management in the future. It is the basic prerequisite for proper development. To this end, each component part should have its own independent position. Substitution and interchanging of state bodies and agencies of economic and social organization by Party bodies must be stopped. Party resolutions are binding for the Communists working in these bodies, but the policy, managerial activities, and responsibility of the state, economic, and social organizations are independent. The Communists active in these bodies and organizations must take the initiative to see to it that the state and economic bodies as well as social organizations (notably the Trade Unions, the Czechoslovak Union of Youth, etc.) take the problem of their activities and responsibilities into their own hands.

The whole *National Front,* the political parties which form it, and the social organizations will take part in the creation of state policy. *The political parties* of the National Front are partners whose political work is based on the joint political program of the National Front and is naturally bound by the Constitution of the Czechoslovak Socialist Republic. It stems from the socialist character of social relations in our country. The Communist Party of Czechoslovakia considers the National Front to be a political platform which does not separate political parties into government and opposition factions. It does not create opposition to state policy—the policy of the whole National Front—or lead struggles for political power. Possible differences in the viewpoints of individual component parts of the National Front or divergency of views as to a state policy is to be settled on the basis of the common socialist conception of National Front policy by way of political agreement and unification of all component parts of the National Front. The organization of political forces to negate this concept of the National Front, to remove the National Front as a whole from political power, was ruled out as long ago as 1945 after the tragic experience of both our nations with the pre-war political development of the Czechoslovak government; it is naturally unacceptable for our present republic.

The Communist Party of Czechoslovakia considers the *political leadership* of the Marxist-Leninist concept of the development of socialism as a precondition for the proper development of our socialist society. It will assert the Marxist-Leninist concept as the leading political principle in the National Front and in all our political system by seeking, through the means of political work, such support in all the component parts of our system and *directly among the masses of workers and all working people* that will ensure its leading role in a democratic way.

Voluntary social organizations of the working people cannot replace political parties, *but the contrary is also true. Political parties in our country cannot exclude common-interest organizations of workers and other working people from directly influencing state policy,* its creation and application. Socialist state power cannot be monopolized either by a single party, or by a coalition of parties. It must be open to all political organizations of the people. *The Communist Party of Czechoslovakia will use every means at its disposal to develop such forms of political life that will ensure the expression of the direct voice and will of the working class and all working people in political decision-making in our country.*

The whole existing organization, its activities, and incorporation of various organizations into the National Front must be revised and restructured under the new conditions and built up so that the National Front may carry out its qualitatively new tasks. *The National Front as a whole and all its component parts must be granted independent rights and its own responsibility for the management of our country and society.*

Voluntary social organizations must be based on truly voluntary membership and activity. People join these organizations hoping they will express their interests, and they therefore have the right to choose their own officials and representatives, who must not be appointed from outside. These principles should form the foundation of our unified mass organizations. Although their activities are still indispensable, their structure, their working methods, and ties with their members must respect the new social conditions.

The implementation of the *constitutional freedoms of assembly and association* must be ensured this years so that the possibility of setting up voluntary organizations, special-interest associations, societies, etc., is guaranteed by law and the present interests and needs of various strata and categories of our citizens are tended to without bureaucratic interference and without a monopoly by any individual organization. Any restrictions in this respect can be imposed only by law and only the law can stipulate what is antisocial, forbidden, or punishable. Freedoms guaranteed by law and in compliance with the constitution also apply fully to citizens of various creeds and religious denominations.

The effective influence of views and opinions of the working people on the policies and a firm opposition to all tendencies to suppress the criticism and initiative of the people cannot be guaranteed if we do not ensure constitution-based freedom of speech and political and personal rights to all citizens, systematically and consistently, by all legal means available. *Socialism cannot mean only liberation of the working people from the domination of exploiting class relations, but must provide for a greater degree of self-fulfillment than any bourgeois democracy.* The working people, who are no longer ordered about by a class of exploiters, can no longer be dictated to by any arbitrary interpretation from a position of power as to what information they may or may not be given, which of their opinions can or cannot be expressed publicly, where public opinion may play a role and where it may not. Public opinion polls must be systematically used in preparing important decisions and the main results of such research published. Any restriction may be imposed only on the basis of a law stipulating what is antisocial—which in our country is mainly determined by the criminal code. The Central Committee of the Communist Party of Czechoslovakia considers it urgently necessary to define in a press law and more exactly than hitherto in the shortest possible time when a state body can forbid the propagation of certain information (in the press, radio, television, etc.) and exclude the possibility of preliminary factual censorship. It is necessary to overcome the holding up, distortion, and incompleteness of information, to remove any unwarranted secrecy of political and economic facts, to publish the annual balance sheets of enterprises, to publish even alternatives to various suggestions and measures, and to increase the import and sale of foreign newspapers and periodicals. Leading representatives of state, social, and cultural organizations are obliged to organize regular press conferences and give their views on topical issues on television, radio, and in the press. In the press, it is necessary to make a distinction between official standpoints of the state, Party organs, and journalists. The Party press especially must express the Party's life and development along with criticisms of various opinions among the Communists, etc., and cannot be made to coincide fully with the official viewpoints of the state.

The Party realizes that ideological antagonists of socialism may try to abuse the process of democratization. At the present stage of development and under the conditions of our country, we insist on the principle that bourgeois ideology can be challenged only in open ideological struggle before all of the people. We can win people over to the ideas and policy of the Party only by a struggle based on the practical activities of Communists for the benefit of the people, on truthful and complete information, and on scientific analysis. We trust that in such a struggle, all sections of our society will contribute actively towards the victory of truth, which is on the side of socialism.

At present the activity and responsibility of publishing houses and editors-in-chief, of all Party members and progressive staff members of the mass communication media, must be to push through socialist ideals and implement the policy of the party, of the National Front, and of the state.

Legal norms must provide a more precise guarantee *of the freedom of speech for minority interests and opinions* also (again within the framework of socialist laws and in harmony with the principle that decisions are taken in accordance with the will of the majority). The *constitutional freedom of movement*, particularly that of travel abroad for our citizens, *must be precisely guaranteed by law.* In particular, this means that a citizen should have the legal right to long-term or permanent sojourn abroad and that people should not be groundlessly placed in the position of emigrants; at the same time it is necessary to protect by law the interests of the state, for example, as regards the drain of some categories of specialists, etc.

Our entire legal code must gradually solve the problem of how *to protect in a better and more consistent way the personal rights and property of citizens,* and we must especially remove those stipulations that virtually put individual citizens at a disadvantage against the state and other institutions. We must in the future prevent various institutions from disregarding personal rights and the interests of individual citizens as far as personal ownership of family houses, gardens, etc. is concerned. It will be necessary to adopt, in the shortest possible time, the long-prepared law on compensation for any damage caused to any individual or to an organization by an unlawful decision of a state organ.

It is a serious fact *that hitherto the rehabilitation of people*—both Communists and non-Communists—who were the victims of legal violations in the past years, *has not been always carried out in all its political and civic consequences.* On the initiative of the Communist Party Central Committee bodies, an investigation is under way as to why the respective Party resolutions have not been fully carried out, and measures are being taken to ensure that the wrongs of the past are made good wherever it has not been done yet. No one having the slightest personal reason from his own past activity for slowing down the rectification process may serve in the political bodies or prosecutor's and court offices that are to rectify unlawful deeds of the past.

The Party realizes that people unlawfully condemned and persecuted cannot regain the lost years of their life. It will, however, do its best to remove any shadow of the mistrust and humiliation to which the families and relatives of those affected were often subjected, and will resolutely ensure that such persecuted people have every opportunity of showing their worth in work, in public life, and in political activities. It goes without saying that even in carrying out full rehabilitation of people, we cannot change the consequences of revolutionary measures made in the past years in accordance with the spirit of class law aimed against the bourgeoisie, its property, economic, and social supports. The whole problem of the rectification of past repressions must be approached with the full responsibility of the state bodies concerned and based on legal regulations. The Central Committee of the Communist Party of Czechoslovakia supports the proposal that the procedure in these questions and the problems of legal consequences be incorporated in a *special law*.

A broad democratic concept of the *political and personal rights of citizens*, their legal and political safeguards, is considered by the Party to be a prerequisite for the necessary strengthening of social discipline and order, for a stabilization of social relations. A selfish understanding of civil rights, an "I'm all right, Jack" attitude toward social property, the policy of placing one's particular interests over those of the whole society—all these are features which Communists will oppose with all their might.

The real purpose of democratization must be the achievement of better results in day to day work due to wider possibilities of purposeful activity and a concern for the interests and needs of the people. Democracy cannot be identified with empty speechmaking. It cannot stand in opposition to discipline, professionalism, and effectiveness of management. But arbitrariness and an obscure definition of rights and duties make such a development impossible. They lead to irresponsibility, to a feeling of uncertainty, and hence also to indifference towards public interests and needs. A more profound democracy and greater measure of civic freedoms will help socialism prove its superiority over limited bourgeois democracy and make it an attractive example for progressive movements even in industrially advanced countries with democratic traditions.

The Equality of Czechs and Slovaks Is the Basis for the Strength of the Republic

Our republic, as a joint state of two equal nations—Czechs and Slovaks—must continually check to be sure that the constitutional arrangement of relations between our fraternal nations and the status of all other nationalities of Czechoslovakia develop as required to strengthen the unity of the state, foster the development of the nations and nationalities themselves, and correspond to the needs of socialism. It cannot be denied that even in socialist Czechoslovakia, in spite of outstanding progress in solving the problem of nationalities, *there are serious faults and fundamental deformations* in the constitutional arrangement of relations between the Czechs and Slovaks.

Let it be stressed that the very asymmetrical arrangement was unsuited by its very character to express the relations between two independent nations, because it expressed the standings of the two nations differently. The difference was mainly in the fact that the Czech national bodies were identical with the central ones which, having jurisdiction over all the state, were superior to the Slovak national bodies. This prevented the Slovak nation, to all intents and purposes, from taking an equal share in the creation and realization of a country-wide policy. The objective shortcomings of such a solution were underlined by the existing political atmosphere and practice, which adversely affected the standing and activity of Slovak national bodies. Under such conditions, the activities of Slovak national bodies were weakened, both in the fifties and in the fundamental conception of the 1960 Constitution of the Czechoslovak Socialist Republic. Thus the Slovak national bodies found themselves in a position from which their influence on the state machinery could be only of peripheral importance. These shortcomings, especially in view of the unsound elements of the political atmosphere of the recent past could not be overcome even by the 1964 joint document of the Central Committee of the Communist Party of Czechoslovakia and the Central Committee of the Communist Party of Slovakia on a strengthening of the role of the Slovak National Council.

This development necessarily caused misunderstandings to arise between our two nations. In the Czech lands lack of national bodies made the Slovak national bodies seem superfluous. In Slovakia the people were convinced that it was not the Slovaks who governed their own house but that everything was decided in Prague.

In the interest of the development of our socialist society it is therefore absolutely necessary to strengthen the unity of the Czechoslovak people and their confidence in the policy of the Communist Party of Czechoslovakia, *to effect a crucial change in the constitutional arrangement of the relations between Czechs and Slovaks* and to carry out the necessary constitutional changes. It is essential to respect the advantage of a *socialist federal arrangement* as a recognized and well-tested legal state form of the coexistence of two equal nations in a common socialist state.

For reasons of organization, the final federative arrangement must be preceded, as an integral part and its developmental stage, by *the removal of the most flagrant shortcomings in the present unsatisfactory state of things* in the legal relations between the Czech and Slovak nations. It is therefore necessary *to draw up and pass a constitutional law* to embody the principle of a symmetrical arrangement as the goal to work toward after the 14th Congress. On the basis of full equality, this law will settle the status of Slovak national bodies in our constitutional system in the nearest future—before the elections to the National Assembly and the Slovak National Council. It will have to

• constitute *the Slovak National Council as a legislative body, the Slovak Council of Ministers as a collective executive body,* and ministries as individual executive organs of the Slovak National Council, widening the real powers of all these organs so that the division of legislative and executive powers between statewide and the Slovak bodies may essentially comply with the principles of the Kosice government program;

• *entrust the management of national committees in Slovakia to Slovak national bodies* and, in connection with an efficient arrangement between the state center and the Slovak national bodies, set up a full-scale Slovak ministerial office for internal affairs and public security;

• *adjust the competence of Slovak national bodies so that they may draw up and approve an economic plan and budget for Slovakia* in all its items including the relevant economic tools. Set up a suitable structure of ministerial economic executive bodies in the Slovak National Council and modify the organizational pattern of the material and manufacturing base in Slovakia accordingly;

• *renew the institution of state secretaries* in central departments, especially in the ministries of foreign affairs, foreign trade, and national defense, and make the secretaries members of the government;

• *exclude, politically and constitutionally, the possibility of outvoting the Slovak nation* in legal issues concerning relations between the Czechs and Slovaks and the constitutional status of Slovakia;

• in addition, outside the scope of the constitutional law, *effect in terms of concrete political practice the principle of equal rights of both nations in appointments to central bodies, diplomatic service, etc.*

In preparing the 14th Congress of the Party and the new constitution, it is necessary to submit a professionally and politically backed proposal for a constitutional arrangement of relations between our two nations that will fully express and guarantee their equality and right of self-determination. The same principles shall be applied to the pattern of the Party and social organizations.

In the interests of strengthening the unity, coherence, and *national individuality of all nationalities in Czechoslovakia—of Hungarians, Poles, Ukrainians, and Germans*—it is indispensable to work out a statute stipulating the status and rights of the various nationalities, guaranteeing the future of their national life and the development of their national individuality. The Central Committee of the Communist Party of Czechoslovakia realizes that, in spite of indisputable achievements in solving the problems of nationalities, serious shortcomings exist. We deem it necessary to stress that the principles of our program with respect to our two nations extend also to other nationalities. To that end, it is necessary to stipulate constitutional and legal guarantees of a complete and real political, economic, and cultural equality. The interests of nationalities will also have to be safeguarded from the point of view of the pattern of state, regional, district, municipal, and local organs of state power and administration. It is necessary to see that the nationalities are represented, in proportion to their numbers, in our political, economic, cultural, and public life, in elected and executive bodies. Active participation of the nationalities in public life must be ensured in the spirit of equality of rights and according to the principle that the nationalities have the right to independence and self-administration in provinces that concern them.

The Power of Elected Bodies Emanates from the Will of the Voters

With the coming *elections* begins the onset of implementation of the principles of this Action Program in the work of the elected bodies of the state.

Although efforts were made in the past few months to improve the preparation for elections, it proved to be impossible to have the elections organized by the originally proposed deadline if we wished to meet the requirements of the principles of an advanced socialist democracy. It is therefore necessary to work out an electoral system that will take the changes in our political life into account. An electoral law must lay down exactly and clearly democratic principles for the preparation of the elections, the proposal of candidates, and the method of their election. The changes in the electoral system must be based, in particular, on the new political status of the National Front and the elected bodies themselves.

The *national committees* make up the backbone of the whole network of representative bodies in our country, the democratic organs of state power. It must be in the national committees that state policy is formed, especially in districts and regions. In their work the principle of socialist democracy is to be fully applied. The various interests and requirements of the people must be expressed and united in the general, public interest of communities, townships, districts, and regions.

The Party regards the national committees as bodies that have to carry on *the progressive traditions of local government and people's self-administration.* They must not be taken for local bureaucratic offices supervising local enterprises. The essential political mission of national committees is to protect the rights and needs of the people, to simplify the process of settling all matters with which the people turn to the national committee, to pursue public interest and oppose efforts of some institutions to dupe the people and ignore their requirements.

The Party regards the National Assembly as a socialist parliament with all the scope for activities the parliament of a democratic republic must have. The Communist deputies must see to it that the National Assembly draws up a number of concrete measures before the new electoral period, measures that will put into actual practice the constitutional status of the National Assembly as the supreme organ of state power in the Czechoslovak Socialist Republic. It is necessary to overcome formalism in negotiations and the unconvincing unanimity concealing factual differences in opinions and attitudes of the deputies. From this point of view it is necessary to settle, as soon as possible, the relations between the National Assembly and Party bodies and a number of problems regarding internal activities of the National Assembly, particularly those of organization and competence. The result must be a National Assembly which actually decides on laws and important political issues, and not only approves proposals submitted. The Party supports a strengthening of the controlling function of the National Assembly in our entire public life and, more concretely, with respect to the government. The controlling machinery must be in the hands of the National Assembly, which will establish it as its own body. Together with closer bonds between the National Assembly and our public opinion, all of this may, in a short time, increase the role and the prestige of the National Assembly in our society.

Separation and Control of Power: Guarantee Against Highhandedness

The Communists in the government, too, must ensure as soon as possible that the principle of responsibility of the government towards the National Assembly covering all its activities is worked out in detail. Even under the existing practice of political management, the opportunity afforded for independent activity of the government and of individual ministers was not sufficiently made use of; there was a tendency to shift responsibility on to the Party bodies and to evade independence in decision-making. The government is not only an organ of economic policy. As the supreme executive organ of the state it must, as a whole, deal systematically with the whole scope of political and administrative problems of the state. It is also up to the government to take care of the rational development of the whole state machinery. The state administration machinery was often underrated in the past. This machinery must consist of highly qualified people, professionally competent and rationally organized; it must be subject to systematic, democratic supervision; and it must be effective. The oversimplified idea that these could be attained by underrating and decrying the administrative machinery in general has done more harm than good.

Within the whole state and political system, it is necessary for us to create such relations and rules that would, on the one hand, provide *the necessary safeguards to professional officials* in their functions and, on the other hand, enable *the necessary replacement of officials* who can no longer cope with their work by professionally and politically more competent people. This means establishing legal conditions for the recall of responsible officials and providing legal guarantees of decent conditions for those who are leaving their posts through the normal way of replacement, so that their departure does not amount to a "drop" in their material and moral-political standing.

The Party is based on the principle that no undue concentration of power must occur, throughout the state machinery, in one sector, one body, or in a single individual. It is necessary to provide for such a division of power and a system of mutual supervision that can rectify the faults or encroachments of any of its links with the activities of another link. This principle must be applied not only to relations between the elected and executive bodies, but also to the inner relations of the state administration machinery and to the standing and activities of courts of law.

These principles have been infringed mainly by undue concentration of duties in the existing ministry of the interior. The Party thinks it necessary to turn it into a department for internal state administration, to which the administration of public security also belongs. All those areas in our state which were traditionally within the jurisdiction of other bodies and with the passage of time have been incorporated into the ministry of the interior must be withdrawn from it. It is necessary to elaborate proposals as soon as possible to transfer the main responsibility for investigation to the courts of law, separating prison administration from the security force, and hand over the administration of press law, archives, etc., to other state bodies.

The Party considers the problem of a correct incorporation of the security force in the state as politically very important. The security of our lives will only benefit, if everything is eliminated that helps to maintain a public view of the security force marred in the past period by violations of law and by the privileged position of the security force in the political system. That past period impaired the progressive traditions of our security force as a force advancing side by side with our people.

These traditions must be renewed. The Central Committee of the Communist Party of Czechoslovakia deems it necessary *to change the organization of the security force* and to split the joint organization into two mutually independent parts—State Security and Public Security. *The State Security service* must have the status, organizational structure, men, equipment, methods, and qualifications which are in keeping with its work of defending the state from the activities of enemy centers abroad. Every citizen who has not been culpable in this respect must know with certainty that his political convictions and opinions, his personal beliefs and activities, cannot be the object of attention of the bodies of the State Security service. The Party declares clearly that this apparatus *should not be directed toward or used to solve internal political questions* and controversies in socialist society.

The Public Security service will combat crime and keep public order. It is to this end its organization, men, and methods must be adapted. The Public Security force must be better equipped and strengthened; its precise functions in the defense of public order must be laid down by law and will be directed by the national committees. Legal norms must create clearer relations of control over the security force by the government as a whole and by the National Assembly.

It is necessary to devote the appropriate care to carrying out *the defense policy in our state.* In this connection it is necessary to work for our active share in the conception of the military doctrine of the Warsaw Treaty countries, strengthening the defense potential of our country in harmony with its needs and possibilities, a uniform complex understanding of the problems of defense and all problems of the building of socialism in all our policy, including defense training.

The legal policy of the Party is based on the principle that in a dispute over rights (including administrative decisions of state bodies) the basic guarantee of legality is proceedings in court which are independent of political factors and are bound only by law. The application of this principle requires a strengthening of the whole social and political role and importance of courts of law in our society. The Central Committee of the Communist Party of Czechoslovakia will see to it that work on the complex of the required proposals and measures proceeds so as to find the answer to all the necessary problems before the next election of judges. In harmony with and parallel to that, it is also necessary to settle the status and duties of the public prosecutor's office so that it may not be put above the courts of law, and to guarantee full independance of lawyers from state bodies.

Youth and Its Organization

We regard young people as those who are to continue the socialist transformation of society. Present political activity and the part young people are taking in the revival process prove that the reproaches often leveled against them are without any foundation. A decisive part of the working and student youth is, thanks to its energy, critical approach, matter-of-factness, and initiation, a natural ally and important factor in the creation and implementation of the program aims of the

Party. For this reason, it is indispensable *to open wide and confidently the doors of our Party to young people.*

At the same time it is necessary to give young people of all social categories, according to their age and abilities, the opportunity to have a voice in all their own and public matters in elected bodies; their organization should be recognized as partners of Party and social organizations, economic bodies, national committees, and administration of schools in solving social, working, study, and other urgent problems of youth and children. Young people must be given an opportunity to apply their knowledge, qualifications, and talents in appropriate places—including leading positions. Cultural, sporting, and recreation facilities must be built with their cooperation so that they may spend their leisure time in a healthy and effective way. The work of voluntary and professional trainers, coaches, instructors, and other workers who sacrifice their time and devote their abilities to children and youth must be regarded as socially highly beneficial and praiseworthy.

In this connection, let us say *a few words of self-criticism on the relations of the party and the Czechoslovak Union of Youth.* Until recently, we expected the latter or its representatives to pass on to the young people more or less ready-made instructions, often the result of subjective opinions, which tactlessly interfered with the internal affairs of the youth organization. We did not sufficiently encourage young Communists to take part in the creation of Party policies by making them consistently defend, develop, and express the interests, needs, requirements, and viewpoints of the youth as a whole and of its individual categories. Thus the initiative of the youth and the role of its organization were impaired in public and political life. This tendency was exacerbated by the incorrect principle of direct Party control of the Czechoslovak Union of Youth.

However, the independence of the youth and children's movement does not eliminate, but in fact presupposes ideological guiding, a systematic interest of the whole Party in the problems of youth and of children's education, the practical assistance of Communists in children's and young people's collectives, and tactful attention to young people in everyday life.

The multiformity of needs, interests, and frequently changing inclinations of young people, increased many times over by variations in age, social strata, qualifications, etc., require *a diversified and well-differentiated organization of children and young people.* Apart from partial interests and inclinations of the moment among various categories of young people, there are pressing immediate and prospective needs and interests affecting the whole younger generation, which can be expressed and pushed through only by *joint action of all the important youth categories; this calls for a suitable form of organization and social representation of young people.* We are of the opinion, without, of course, wanting to prescribe any pattern of youth organization, that a form of federation would be most fitting for the present needs and situation of youth and children's movements.

To a great extent it is up to the present officials of the Czechoslovak Union of

Youth and of other social organizations to assist in this process, to prevent both
the suppression and unnecessary diversification of the sound initiative of young
people, to make good use of all their experience and all possible opportunities in
the search for the optimum development of our socialist youth and children's
movement.

The National Economy and the Standard of Living

The 13th Congress approved conclusions stating that the improvement of our
economy and the transition to intensive economic development cannot be
achieved by traditional approaches or partial improvements of the directive system
of management and planning, that a basic change of the machinery of socialist
economy would be necessary. The idea which prevailed was the idea of an
economic reform based on a new economic system, the revival of the positive
functions of the socialist market, necessary structural changes of the economy, and
a profound change in the role of the economic plan would cease to be an
instrument for issuing orders and would become an instrument enabling society to
find the most suitable long-range trends of its development by scientific methods; a
change from an instrument designed to enforce subjectively determined material
proportions to a program of economic policy, ensuring an effective development of
the economy and the growth of the standard of living. The implementation of the
first important steps of the economic reform has met with the active support of the
working people, experts, and the broad public.

Certain features of the economic development over the past two years, better
utilization of production factors, a drop in the share of material costs in the social
product, the growing demands placed by consumers on the technical level and the
quality of products, etc., fully confirm the validity of the conclusions adopted by
the 13th Congress. These positive features of economic development have not yet
begun to better satisfy the needs of society or reduce the tension in the internal
market because former tendencies are still strongly apparent, the old structure of
production and foreign trade still survives, and adaptation of production to the
changes and growing demands of the market is moving forward very slowly. This is
connected with many inconsistencies and gaps in implementing the program of
economic reform.

Instead of a consistent effort to establish more objective market criteria which
would expose the economic backwardness and old deformations of the economic
structure and gradually eliminate their existence, there are still considerable efforts
to deform these criteria, to adapt them to the given conditions and thus create a
situation in which the backwardness and the deformations would remain con-
cealed, could survive and thrive at the expense of us all.

The system of protectionism—furthering economic backwardness, and maintained by our policy of prices, subsidies, and grants and by the system of surcharges
in foreign trade—continues to prevail in our economic policy. This confused system
of protectionism creates conditions under which ineffective, poorly managed, back-

ward enterprises may not only exist but are often given preferences. *It is not possible to blunt the economic policy forever by taking from those who work well and giving to those who work badly.* It is therefore necessary to be objective about value relations. Differences in income between enterprises should reflect actual differences in the level of their economic activities. *Nor is it politically correct for the consumer to pay indefinitely for inefficiency either directly in high prices and taxes or indirectly by different forms of siphoning off material from efficient enterprises.*

Enterprises facing a demanding market must be given a free hand in making decisions on all questions directly concerning the management of the enterprise and its economy and must be allowed to react in a creative way to the needs of the market. A demanding market, together with sound economic policy, will thus put pressure on production to become more effective and to introduce healthy structural changes. Economic competition, especially with advanced foreign firms, must be the basic stimulus for improving production and reducing costs. This competition cannot be replaced by subjective adjustments of economic conditions and by directive orders of superior bodies.

Socialism Cannot Do Without Enterprising

The democratization program in economy links economic reform more closely with the process facing us in the sphere of politics and the general management of society, and stimulates the determination and application of new elements to develop the economic reform even further. *The democratization program of the economy places special emphasis on ensuring the independence of enterprises and enterprise groupings and their relative independence from state bodies, the full implementation of the right of the consumer to determine his consumption and his style of life, the right of a free choice of working activity, the right and real possibility of various groups of the working people and different social groups to formulate and defend their economic interests in shaping the economic policy.*

In developing democratic relations in the economy we at present consider as the most important task the final formulation of the economic position of enterprises, their authority and responsibility.

The economic reform will increasingly push whole working teams of socialist enterprises into positions in which they will directly feel the consequences of both good and bad management. The Party therefore deems it necessary that the whole working team which bears the consequences should be allowed to influence the management of the enterprise. We must set up democratic bodies in enterprises and vest them with limited rights with respect to the management of the enterprise. Managers and head executives of the enterprises, which would also appoint them to their functions, would be accountable to them for the overall results of their work. These bodies must become a direct part of the managing mechanism of enterprises, and not a social organization (they cannot therefore be identified with trade unions). They would be made up of elected representatives of the working team and representatives of certain components outside the enterprise, thereby ensuring the influence of the interests of the entire society and an expert and qualified level of decision-making; the representation of these components must be subordinated to democratic forms of control. It is likewise necessary for us to define the degree of responsibility of these bodies for the results of the management of socialist property. These principles raise many concrete questions; at the same time it will be necessary to propose a set of by-laws to cover them, using certain traditions of our factory councils from the years 1945–48 and experiences in modern enterprising.

This naturally in no way reduces the indivisible authority and responsibility of the leading executives in managing the enterprise which, together with their qualifications and managing abilities, is the basic precondition of successful enterprising.

In this connection it is also necessary to reassess the present role of trade unions. In the centralized system, their function of supporting directive management coincided with defending the interests of the working people. Moreover, they also performed certain state functions (e.g., labor legislation). The resulting situation was that on the one hand they took inadequate care of the interests of the working people and on the other they were accused of "protectionism." Even a socialist economy places working people in a position in which it is necessary to defend human, social, and other interests in an organized way. The central function of trade unions should be to defend the professional interests of the workers and the working people, and act as an important partner in solving all questions of economic management; on this platform, the trade unions would be more effective in developing their function of organizing workers and employees for a positive solution of the problems of socialist construction and their educational function connected therewith. Communists in trade unions will take these principles into account and take the initiative to ensure that the trade unions themselves analyze their position and the functions and activities of the central and union bodies on the basis of the whole Action Program of the Party, that they evaluate the internal life of trade unions as an independent democratic organization and work out their own political line in solving these questions.

The enterprise must have the right to choose its organizational pattern. Supra-enterprise bodies (like the present general and branch managements) cannot be imbued with state administrative power. The individual branches, with due regard to their conditions, must be transformed into voluntary associations, on the basis of the economic interest and enterprise requirements. Enterprises must have the right to decide the activities of these associations, the right to leave them and become independent and to join associations which will better ensure the functions resulting from the concentration and specialization of production and integration processes.

The withdrawal of enterprises from the existing supra-enterprise agglomerations and their free association cannot begin before the rules for this process are outlined by the government. During the transition period it will be necessary to ensure that even after becoming independent the enterprises will fulfill precisely predetermined financial and cooperation obligations which result from their previous membership in the supra-enterprise body.

It is necessary to put an end to the previous simplified, schematic approach to formulating the organizational structure of production and trade. The structure of enterprises must be varied, just as are the demands of our market. It is therefore necessary to take into account the development of small and medium-sized social-ist enterprises, whose importance lies first and foremost in competitive production, a fast supply of new items to the market, and in a flexible reaction to different customer demands. In the development of the organizational structure of produc-tion and trade it is necessary to open up scope for economic competition among enterprises of all sorts and forms of enterprising, above all in the production and supply of consumer goods and foodstuffs.

Agricultural production contributes to a great extent to the consolidation of our national economy. The latest period and particularly the future needs of the economy clearly emphasize this positive role of agriculture. Agriculture should develop in such a way as to gradually ensure a rational structure of nutrition to the population. This is why the Party considers it necessary to raise and concentrate the aid of the state and of all branches, especially the chemical and engineering industry, in ensuring the growth of crop and animal production. This is and continues to be the foremost task of our economic policy.

Cooperative enterprises in agricultural production are of exceptional importance for the development of our economy. The Party supports the conclusion of the Seventh Congress of Unified Agricultural Cooperatives, particularly the creation of a national organization of cooperative farmers, the right of unified agricultural cooperatives to do business also in other branches, and the possibility of selling part of farm products directly to the population and to retailers. The state bodies will help to ensure all-year employment for the farming population.

The Party considers the development of agricultural production in cooperatives and in state farms to be the decisive line of large-scale production in agriculture. It would be expedient for Communists to prepare proposals which will develop new forms of closer contact between agricultural producers and supply and sales organi-zations of agricultural products so that these new forms may ensure direct contact of agricultural production with suppliers and the market and would be to a certain extent similar to the former farm cooperatives.

We shall support the development of different forms of credit for farming and recommend that the whole credit system in the agricultural economy be re-examined. At the same time, the Central Committee recommends that agri-cultural and other state managing bodies seek and support other forms of enterprise in utilizing land in mountainous, hilly, and border regions. In the border regions it is necessary to strive for the creation of further suitable conditions designed to intensify economic activities, i.e., to make better use of existing small workshops, to extend recreation possibilities, and engage in further capital construction. This should help stabilize the settlement of the border regions and normalize their life. Even though the production of individual farmers constitutes a relatively small part of overall production, it is important to facilitate their work, improve their economic conditions, and aid their cooperation with cooperative and state enterprises.

In keeping with the proposals made at the 13th Congress of the Communist Party of Czechoslovakia, it is also necessary to create possibilities for cooperative enterprising wherever cooperatives earn the money for their activity. It will be expedient to make individual cooperatives independent economic and social organizations with full rights, abolish the impractical administrative centralization of cooperatives, and create only such bodies over cooperative enterprises whose economic activity is advantageous for them. In connection with the development of cooperative enterprises, it appears to be expedient to elaborate more thoroughly the co-ownership relations between cooperative farmers and cooperative property.

A serious shortcoming in our economic life has long been the low standard and shortage of services of all sorts which reduces the standard of living and arouses justified discontent among the population. The improvement of communal services (water, gas, sewerage, municipal transportation, road cleaning, etc.) will require considerable investments and can be achieved only gradually if their profitability is to be ensured. The unsatisfactory state existing in other services is caused by the way they are organized and administered, by low interest of the workers in their economic result, by the fact that certain services are unprofitable, by bad supplies of material, and low and poor investments.

Neither the standard of productive forces, nor the character of work in services, repairs, and artisan production warrants the present high degree of centralization in their management and organization which involves quite unnecessary administration and burdens the services with inexpedient costs. This is why it is necessary to take immediate measures for improving and extending all existing forms of services (cooperative, communal enterprises) and simplify their management and organization in the spirit of the principles of the new system. In the sphere of services it is particularly justified to make individual shops independent and to remove unnecessary administrative links of management. Small-scale individual enterprising is also justified in the sphere of service. In this respect it is necessary to work out legal provisions concerning small-scale enterprises, which would help fill the existing gap in our market.

The Role of the State in Economy

Spreading social wealth is the concern of our entire society. The actual tasks and responsibility fall both on enterprises and on managing bodies, particularly on the government. It is therefore in their common interest to make use of the growing political activity of the working people, which has been taking place since the December and January plenums of the Central Committee, and to win them over to the path leading toward the consolidation of the national economy.

To achieve this it is necessary to recast the entire organism which implements the economic policy of the state. The appropriate organizational questions must be solved by state and economic bodies. The party considers it desirable that the final setup should correspond to the following principles:

Decision-making about the plan and the economic policy of the state must be both a process of mutual confrontation and harmonization of different interests— i.e., the interests of enterprises, consumers, employees, different social groups of the population, nations, etc.—and a process of a suitable combination of the long-term development of the economy and its immediate prosperity. Effective measures protecting the consumer against the abuse of the monopoly position and economic power of production and trading enterprises must be considered as a necessary part of the economic activity of the state.

The drafting of the national economic plan and the national economic policy must be subject to democratic control of the National Assembly and specialized control of scientific institutions. The supreme body implementing the economic policy of the state is the government. This presupposes an institutional setup of central management which enables the decision-making process to express and unify special interests and views and to harmonize the operation of individual economic instruments and measures of the state in the implementation of the economic policy. At the same time, the institutional setup of the bodies of economic management must not allow opportunities for the assertion of departmental and monopoly interests and must ensure a marked superiority to the interests of citizens as consumers and sovereign bearers of the economic movement. In all central economic bodies it is indispensable to ensure a high level of specialization, rationalization, and modernization of managerial work, even if changes in cadres are required to do so. All this must be the concern of the government bodies which analyze the national economy, work on alternative solutions of its development and that of the national economic plan, compare planned development with actual market development, and proceeding from these findings, take effective economic measures etc., and thus consistently and purposefully influence the real course of economic development (i.e., the activity of enterprises and their associations) in the direction outlined by the economic policy of the state. State bodies approach enterprises and their associations and integrated groups in the same way as they approach other independent legal subjects. The means at the disposal of the state are the result of the work of all the people and must be used for satisfying the needs of the entire society in a way which society recognizes to be reasonable and useful.

An important part of economic management must be a well-conceived technical policy based on an analysis of world-wide technical progress and its own conceptions of economic development. The purpose of this policy will be to regulate the technical level of the production base and to create economic conditions which would arouse strong interest in seeking out and using the most up-to-date technology.

In this connection it would be useful for the state bodies concerned to examine all kinds of public expenditures and for the government to work out a program of state and public measures designed to reduce them. The state budget must become an instrument for restoring the equilibrium and not for its weakening. The Central

Committee considers it necessary and possible to reveal and reasonably utilize extraordinary internal and external resources for achieving a speedy restoration of the economic equilibrium.

At the same time, the Central Committee appeals to all enterprises, their associations, plants, and workshops to work out and implement, using their enhanced economic authority, a program for rationalizing all managing, production, and business activity, in order to ensure their smooth running and reduce production costs. Such a program is the precondition for an economic evaluation of existing capacities and for technical modernization of production.

We are putting great hope into reviving the positive functions of the market as a necessary mechanism of the functioning of socialist economy and for checking whether the work in enterprises has been expended in a socially useful way. However, we have in mind not the capitalist, but the socialist market, and not its uncontrolled but its regulated utilization. The plan and the national economic policy must appear as a positive force contributing to the normalization of the market and directed against tendencies of economic imbalance and against monopolistic control of the market. Society must plan with due insight and perspective, it must use science to work out the possibilities of its future development and choose its most reasonable orientation. This, however, cannot be achieved by suppressing the independence of other subjects of the market (enterprises and the population), since this would on the one hand undermine the interest ensuring economic rationality and on the other deform information and decision-making processes which are indispensably necessary for the functioning of the economy.

The economic structure of Czechoslovakia, its technical standard, concentration, and specialization must be developed in a way enabling it to react quickly to economic changes at home and in the world.

The level of the adaptability and flexibility of the national economy is also the result of the skill and the technical and cultural standard of the working people, their ability to adapt themselves quickly to the changing technical and economic conditions of production. From the point of view of the resources for economic growth in Czechoslovakia, manpower, its abilities and quality, technical and cultural standard as well as its adaptability and mobility, are of quite exceptional importance. Even from the point of view of future economic growth, the Czechoslovak economy does not possess more promising resources than its great human resources. Czech and Slovak workers and farmers have always been known for their know-how, their skill and creative approach to work. As a result of the directive method of management, the new generation has only partly taken over these qualities from the older generation. Instead of a feeling of satisfaction from well done work, this directive system encouraged indifference, mechanical fulfillment of tasks, and resignation to situations caused by management incompetent and without initiative. The Party believes that the prime condition for eliminating these losses is to give leading positions to people who are really capable and who are able to secure natural authority in working teams by their professional and human level.

More Effective Participation in International Division of Labor

Experience resulting from our economic units' many years of isolation from the competitive pressure of the world market has clearly shown that such isolation creates exceptional conditions for the activity of economic units, conditions causing a relative lagging behind in rate of technical progress and in structural economic changes that this progress creates, a loss in competitiveness of our products on the world market and undue tension in external trade and payment relations. The limited raw material base of our economy and the limited size of the home market make it impossible to implement the changes in the material base of production brought about by the scientific and technical revolution without widely integrating our economy into the developing international division of labor.

The development of international economic relations will continue to be based on economic cooperation with the Soviet Union and the other socialist countries, particularly those aligned in the Council of Mutual Economic Assistance. It should be understood, however, that the success of this cooperation will increasingly depend on the competitiveness of our products. The position of our country in the development of the international division of labor will strengthen with the more general convertibility of our products. In our relations with the CMEA countries we shall strive for the fuller application of criteria of economic calculations and mutual advantage of exchange.

We shall also actively support the development of economic relations with all other countries in the world which show interest in such relations on the basis of equality, mutual advantages, and without discrimination. We support the development of progressive forms of international collaboration, especially cooperation in production and in the pre-production stage, the exchange of scientific and technical know-how, business in licenses, and suitable forms of credit and capital cooperation with interested countries.

Opening our economy to the pressure of the world market makes it continually necessary to rid the foreign trade monopoly of administrative conceptions and methods and to eliminate directive management in foreign trade transactions. In this sphere, the Central Committee considers it necessary to carry on an effective state commercial and currency policy, based on economic rules and instruments of indirect management.

The Central Committee considers it indispensable to raise the authority and responsibility of enterprises in the concrete implementation of international economic relations. Production and trading enterprises must have the right to choose their export and import organizations. At the same time it is necessary to formulate conditions which would entitle enterprises to act independently on foreign markets.

Our economy's many years of isolation from world markets has divorced home trade price relations from price relations in the world market. Because of this situation, we consider it necessary to enforce a policy of bringing the home and world market prices gradually closer together. In practice this means a more energetic policy of removing various surcharges and subsidies from prices of the foreign market. Enterprises must be aware that it is only temporary protection they are receiving from the state and that they cannot count on it indefinitely. They must therefore work out a program of changes in production which will enable them in the next few years to do without subsidies and surcharges. Another side of this policy of eliminating price surcharges and subsidies must be a more broad-minded approach to those branches and enterprises in the national economy which from the point of view of the national economy are capable of selling their products effectively in foreign markets. The Party considers it expedient to speed up the necessary changes in the present system of price relations and put them gradually in order both by the pressure of the market forces and by creating a proper rational price system based on a well-conceived state economic policy. This policy must be accompanied by energetic measures designed to ensure the internal stability of the currency. This presupposes the production of effective and good-quality stocks of products marketable in foreign markets, achievement of equilibrium in the internal market of commodities, money, and labor, an effective restrictive investment policy, achievement of equilibrium in our balance of payments, and creation of necessary currency reserves.

The phased opening of our economy to the world market, the final aim of which is to create conditions for the convertibility of our currency, must be carried out to an extent that would not cause too many social problems nor endanger the growth of the standard of living. However, it must be realized that we are living in conditions of sharp competition and that every concession today will worsen the prerequisites of effective economic development and of the growth of the standard of living in the future.

Problems of the Standard of Living—An Urgent Task of the Economic Policy

The basic aim of the Party in developing the economic policy is the steady growth of the standard of living. However, the development of the economy in the past has been one-sidedly focused on the growth of heavy industry with long-term return-ability of investments. This was done to a considerable extent at the expense of the development of agriculture and consumer goods industries, the development of the production of building materials, trade, services, and non-productive basic assets, particularly in housing construction. This one-sided character of our economic development cannot be changed overnight. If, however, we take advantage of the great reserve existing in the organization of production and work, as well as in the technical and economic standard of production and products, if we consider the possibilities offered by a skillful utilization of the new system of management, we can substantially speed up the creation of resources and on this basis raise the growth of nominal wages and the general standard of living.

As far as the growth of the standard of living, special emphasis must be placed on the growth of wages and salaries. However, the growth of average wages and salaries cannot be speeded up in such a way that enterprises will raise wages regardless of the real economic results. It will be continually necessary to apply the principle that the development of wages depends on finished products which have proven their social value. The methods of influencing the development of wages will have to take this into account. In keeping with the growth of wages in production, it is at the same time necessary to ensure the growth of wages in education, health services, and other non-productive branches.

The present system of retail prices is markedly divorced from the costs of production, gives an incorrect orientation to the structure of personal consumption of the population—including the consumption of food—and reduces the possible degree of satisfying their requirements. Under these conditions, we must do much more to remove existing disproportions in prices so as to create prerequisites for a faster growth of the standard of living. The solution of these questions will require shifts in prices of individual products and their groups—the prices of some articles will have to be raised; the prices of others will have to be reduced. Rational price relations cannot be fixed and proclaimed by a state authority; it is necessary to enable market forces to influence their creation. This naturally involves a certain risk that changes in price relations will occur with a certain growth in the level of prices, because in the situation we have taken over from the directive system of management overall demand is greater than supply. While opening up the required scope to internal price shifts, the central bodies must therefore regulate general economic relations so as to ensure an excessive growth of the price level and prevent the growth of real wages by at least 2.5–3 per cent per year.

It is impossible in the near future to effect a substantial raise in claims for appropriations from social funds, since this could not be done without substantially weakening remunerations for work. However, in the spirit of the resolution adopted by the plenary meeting of the Central Committee of the Communist Party of Czechoslovakia in December 1967, it is possible to solve the most urgent problems of social policy, such as the raising of low pensions, the extension of paid maternity leave, and aid to families with children. It is also possible to outline the principle that social pensions will grow in keeping with the growth of the cost of living. The Central Committee demands that state bodies ensure the removal of obstacles which weaken the interest of citizens in permanently continuing active work after qualifying for old age pensions. We also want to examine the justification of certain measures carried out in connection with the reorganization of the social security system in 1964 (e.g., taxation of pensions and the possibility of its gradual removal, introduction of a higher base for granting scholarships, etc.). We consider it necessary to raise the social security allowances of those who participated in the national struggle for liberation. We shall also elaborate the conception and the further course of improving the wage tax system so that after 1970 we can make fairer decisions concerning the taxation of women, mothers, and persons who have brought up children and further strengthen measures promoting a more favorable population development.

An important factor in determining standard of living and style of life is health care. In our society, we have introduced a number of measures in health care which capitalism was unable to develop. However, there are still many untapped possibilities, both in the organization of health care and of spa services as well as in the working conditions of doctors and health personnel. The Central Committee appeals to Communists in the health services and to other health workers to take the initiative and submit proposals designed to solve the problems which unnecessarily embitter citizens and health workers and which are the result of bureaucratic methods in medical care.

From the point of view of preventive care designed to strengthen the health of the people—particularly children and youth—and the effective use of spare time, we consider it indispensable to duly appreciate the social importance of all forms of physical and military training and recreation. We are in this respect expecting a principled stand from the government and the educational administration as well as initiative from social organizations.

An important qualitative aspect of the standard of living will be the general introduction of a five-day working week, for which it is necessary to create technological, organizational, economic, and political conditions in order to enable its operation by the end of 1968.

It is a serious shortcoming that the housing construction program was not carried out in past years. At present we regard the solution of housing construction problems as essential for the standard of living. We consider it necessary to concentrate forces in this sphere and secure the necessary support of the government and of state bodies for substantially raising the annual number of flats built by building organizations and for utilizing the initiative of the population in building family houses. At the same time, we must work out a long-term housing policy to correspond to changing social conditions, which will gain the confidence and support of the population, promote the interest of citizens in building and modernizing flats, and influence the development of the material basis and capacity of the building industry. For a transitional period it also will be expedient to endeavor to employ building organizations and manpower of other countries and concentrate construction in places where the need is most urgent.

It is characteristic of the bureaucratic and centralist tendencies applied over and over again in our life in the past that one of the places most affected by insensibility toward people is the center of our Republic—Prague. The capital city, with its experienced and highly qualified cadres of workers, technicians, scientists, artists, organizers of socialist construction and which boasts an immense wealth of monuments and cultural values, has paid dearly for sectarianism in economy and politics, for the low standard of responsible officials. Its facilities and amenities are not in keeping with its social functions, growing tourism, and the requirements of the life of its inhabitants. It is indisputably necessary to speed up housing construction in the capital and, in addition, to concentrate efforts on at least some of the other problems which annoy the people in Prague most: municipal and suburban transportation facilities and keeping the city clean. We must also solve the problems of the capital city of Slovakia—Bratislava. We must see to it that as many children as possible from these cities spend their holidays outside the capital in view of the present lack of adequate recreation facilities in Prague.

The Central Committee is of the opinion that despite the faster growth of the standard of living, neither present results nor even these measures meet existing needs. Nor do they correspond to our real economic possibilities; however, the low effectiveness of our economy is creating barriers which in the process of the further satisfaction of personal and social needs can be overcome only by efforts to mobilize the reserves and to develop resources in production. The elimination of the shortcomings in economy will require time. But we are convinced that consistent implementation of the economic reform and activation of all Communists and nonparty members will enable our country to embark upon the road of a fast, modern development of the economy.

Rational Utilization of Resources in Slovakia Will Lead to the Prosperity of the Republic

The economy of the Czechoslovak Socialist Republic is the integration of two national economies which makes it possible to multiply the economic potential of our entire society. This is contingent on a rational utilization of the resources and growth of the reserves of both our national political regions in the interest of an effective development of the Czechoslovak national economy as well as on the creation of a social and economic balance between the various regions. The new constitutional setup must firmly rely on the integration base and further integration tendencies in the economy of the entire state.

The past development of Slovakia within the unified Czechoslovak economy was marked by major changes in the economic and living standard. Slovakia has become an industrially advanced, agriculturally developed part of the Republic. For further development of an integrated Czechoslovak economy it is not important to make partial adjustments. We must work out the rational integration of the national political regions into the economic complex of the entire state.

However, the undeniable achievements were accompanied by the emergence of serious problems. Although Slovakia's share in the creation of the national income increased from 14.2 per cent in 1948 to 24.4 per cent in 1965, it is not adequate when compared with the possibilities of growth which exist in Slovakia: favorable geographic position, qualitative changes in the fund of manpower, possibilities of space concentration, new basis of chemistry, metallurgy, fuels and power, agriculture, natural resources.

The process of creating a balanced social and economic level between Slovakia and Czech lands is characterized by internal contradictions. An undeniable success of Party policy has been elimination of social and economic backwardness and a decrease of relative per capita differences. However, the faster rate of growth has not been sufficient to reduce absolute differences. The process of creating a balanced level was not based on the conception of the economic effectiveness of the development of the Czechoslovak economy.

The existing problems are caused mainly by the fact that the extensive economic growth of the Czechoslovak Socialist Republic was also enforced in the economic development of Slovakia. A potential source of growth was not used rationally, either in industry or in agriculture. The tertiary sphere, particularly the build-up of scientific research and development bases, has lagged greatly behind. Slovakia's development was not sufficiently coordinated; it proceeded along departmental lines, without the internal integration relations of modern entities.

The intensive development of Slovakia's economy is contingent on a complex of measures connected with the solution of short-term factual problems, the clarification of conceptual questions of long-term development, the effective operation of the new system of management, and the definition of the competence and authority of the Slovak national bodies.

The measures designed to speed up Slovakia's economic development by 1970 constitute the starting point for a fundamental change in Slovakia's integration into the process of transition of the Czechoslovak economy to the road of intensive growth. At the same time it is necessary to seek possibilities of solving acute problems: employment, the lagging behind of micro-regions with special regard to those which are inhabited by Hungarian and Ukrainian fellow-citizens, specific problems of the standard of living, particularly the housing problem, etc.

It is of decisive importance for Slovakia's long-term economic development to raise substantially Slovakia's participation in the creation and the utilization of the national income and to solve the task of creating a balanced economic level by 1980.

This necessitates faster economic development in Slovakia than the national average, and we must therefore give strong support to progressive structural changes, intensify agricultural production and the interconnected processing industry, develop the tertiary sector in all spheres, purposefully concentrate production and the infra-structure.

The development of Slovakia is taking place within the new system of management. However, this system in its present form has not created scope for the development policy of national political regions. Past adjustments of the plan and of economic instruments are not sufficient. It is therefore necessary to elaborate the system of management in such a way as to ensure that territorial and national aspects of development also become equal organic components of the system of management of the entire economy.

The Development of Science, Education, and Culture

At the present stage we must base the development of our society to a much greater extent on the progress and application of science, education, and culture. Their wealth must be used fully and completely to the benefit of socialism, and our people should understand the complicated claims connected with creative work in these spheres.

The Importance of Science in Our Society Is Growing

Socialism originates, holds out, and wins by combining the working movement with science. There is no relationship of subordination and compromise between these forces. The more resolute and impartial the advancement of science, the more it is in harmony with the interests of socialism; the greater the achievements of the working people, the bigger is the scope opened to science. The development and application of science to the life of socialist society shows how much the working people are aware of their historical tasks, to which extent they really enforce them. Socialism stands and falls with science, just as it stands and falls with the power of the working people.

Just now, at the beginning of the scientific-technological revolution in the world, the social position of science is changing considerably. Its application to the entire life of society is becoming the basic condition for the intensive development of the economy, care for man and his living environment, culture of the society and growth of the personality, modern methods of management and administration, the development of relations between people, and the solving of various problems raised by the current period. It is in the field of science and technology where the victory of socialism over capitalism is decided in long-term perspective.

Therefore the Party regards it as one of its primary tasks to provide an ever greater scope for the promotion of creative scientific work and for a timely and more efficient application of its results in social practice.

Relatively complete foundations of basic, applied research and development unprecedented in extent and importance have been built up in this country together with the construction of socialism. A number of qualified scientific workers who are respected throughout the world have made important contributions to building up this country. In spite of this, the opportunities offered by socialism for development of science and especially for application of its results to the benefit of society are, for the time being, far from being fully used, partly because of the still existing branch barriers between science, technological development, and production. The inflexibility of the system of management by directives, connected with the low-level qualifications of managing personnel is one reason for this. In the sphere of research the reasons are mainly differences in the levels of applied research institutes due to a lack of scientifically trained staff.

To improve existing conditions we shall continue making substantial improvements particularly in the *material conditions of our basic research* so that in the decisive branches it can permanently remain at a world level. The development of science must take into consideration the real possibilities of Czechoslovakia as a middle-size country, which can ensure top-level scientific research only by efficient specialization and concentration of energy plus extensive international cooperation and exploitation of the results of world science. Therefore it is also necessary to develop a system of evaluating scientific workers in such a way that selected progressive, scientific, and socially important directions of research can be supported more fully by a system of moral and material incentives.

If the social sciences are really to become an official instrument of scientific self-knowledge in socialist society, we must respect their internal life and ensure them a position and conditions that will enable them to achieve a high scientific level. Party organs will take the initiative in encouraging the development of social sciences and contributing to their orientation toward important social problems; but they will not interfere with the process of creative scientific work and in this respect will rely on the initiative and social responsibility of scientists themselves.

In addition to creating favorable conditions for the development of science *we must strive to surmount all obstacles between science on the one hand and social practice on the other*. Even though the full and consistent application of the new system of management is expected to bring the fundamental solution, we shall help further this process with new measures at the level of central management. The Party will especially support the development of feasible stimuli for applying the results of science in production and other social practices and for a rapid improvement of the qualifications of slowly developing applied research institutes. At the same time we shall also support a more profound examination of the social function of science, especially the problem of its effectiveness and the relationship between science and economy in Czechoslovak conditions.

The development of socialist society is at the same time a process of constant increase of the social involvement and responsibility of science and its application in managing and shaping the entire society. We shall strive on a broader scale than hitherto for the participation of scientists in the work of representative bodies and in the activities of other bodies of social management. We shall intensify the active participation of scientific institutions and scientific workers in drawing up proposals for political and economic measures. We shall encourage the broadest possible placement of scientific workers in social management and the educational system and create favorable social and economic conditions for their activity in these fields. We shall prepare without delay to introduce a binding system of scientific expertise and opposition on important proposals. This will contribute to qualified decisions at all levels of management.

Quality of Education—The Aim of Our Educational System

The progress of socialist society is contingent upon the growth in education of the people. This is a precondition for solving initial tasks of the scientific-technological revolution, promoting the relations and institutions of socialist democracy, and further asserting the cultural and humanistic character of socialism and the development and employment of every man in it.

Therefore we regard further progress in education as a primary task. In this respect we proceed from the traditions of the education of our nations and from the good results by which the socialist stage of development has improved our school system, especially by its broad democratization and the introduction of coeducation. It is still necessary to surmount the consequences of past shortcomings, when the quantitative development of education was frequently achieved at the expense of the quality of teaching. Nor was sufficient care given to the qualitative training of teachers. The frequent reorganization in the past did not contribute to the desirable improvement of the standard of education. On the contrary, this was the reason why, in many respects, it was lagging behind the existing needs and future demands. Therefore it is a foremost task today to concentrate the main attention and strength on a purposeful improvement of the standard, demands, and value of education and especially on improving and raising the standard of general education, expanding the base for more efficient ways of finding and training special talents, and modernizing the content, forms, and means of education.

The dynamic development of our economy and of the whole society requires an end to the underevaluation of education and of the needs of schools and teachers; it requires that a much bigger proportion be set aside from social resources for the development of education. We shall ensure that educational bodies in cooperation with the broad masses devote much thought to developing projects which will enable our economy to keep pace with the dynamics of the development of science and technology and with the needs of the time. We consider the following tasks as the most urgent ones:

a) To draw up a draft hypothesis on the long-term development of the educational system which will make it possible to stabilize the development of the educational system at all levels, and design its personnel and material base in advance so as to gradually eliminate the uneven development of education in individual regions of the country.

To prepare a new concept in harmony with the long-term project of basic polytechnic education, which would be based on a logical grasping of the subject, take advantage of the independence and initiative of students, and make it possible to fully apply the principle of differentiation according to interests and talents, solve the urgent problems of secondary general education schools by extending the base and time of secondary general education, and thereby improve preparations for later university studies while preparing those secondary school students who will not study at universities to take practical jobs.

To form and gradually introduce a system of additional education for young people who start working at 15 years, to increase the thoroughness of the preparation of young skilled workers in harmony with the technological and structural changes in our economy by improving the theoretical, specialized, and general education of young apprentices, to take advantage to a greater extent of the resources of plants and enterprises for the construction and equipment of apprentice centers of the new system of management of the national economy and in justified cases also to grant state subsidies, and not to allow a further decrease of material investments in these establishments. The same criteria should also be applied by National Committees in the construction and equipment of apprentice schools.

b) To create material and personnel conditions at secondary schools and universities for all young people who fulfill the necessary requirements and have proven themselves in the course of their earlier education eligible to be enrolled for studies. Therefore the system of enrollment at secondary schools and universities should be made more flexible. Administrative methods should be replaced by economic and moral stimuli, a sufficient amount of information, and improved educational advice, which will help regulate sensitively the influx of students to particular branches and bring closer together the abilities and interests of individuals and the needs of society. Meanwhile secondary and university education should not be understood only as training for a certain profession, but as a means of improving the extent of education, the cultural level of man, and his ability to solve new situations in the production process as well as in the economic, social, and qualification structure of society. This requires simultaneously an increase in the social responsibility of economic, cultural, and political institutions and of every individual for the application of education in practice.

c) In the management of universities, democratic principles and methods should be consistently applied. The prerequisites of scientific work, unity of teaching and research, should be continually strengthened; the authority and autonomy of university scientific councils should be increased. Universities should be given preference regarding modern equipment, the possibilities of scientific work should be improved, all-round cooperation between research, universities, and secondary schools should be intensified, expensive equipment should be taken advantage of jointly by research institutes and universities. Universities should be given broader access to foreign literature and more opportunities for study and training visits abroad in view of their pedagogical and scientific work, while understanding correctly the importance of acquiring knowledge for the development of science and flexibly applying the principles of profitability of foreign currency resources.

d) The structural changes in the national economy will also require retraining and complementing of the general or specialized education of adults. Therefore it will be necessary for schools, enterprises, social organizations, and mass information media (press, radio, television) to cooperate in order to improve and intensify the system of education for adults.

e) The complexity of education management should be safeguarded by legal arrangements so as to raise the role of school administration. In this connection it will be desirable to ascertain the effectiveness of university law so as to strengthen the democratic relations in the internal and external management and the social position of universities. The authority of Slovak National Council bodies in education in Slovakia should be applied fully in view of the importance of education as a basic element of national culture.

f) Equal study and development conditions should be consistently ensured for young people of all nationalities. An end should be put to the belittling approach towards solving problems of nationality education, and legal and institutional preconditions should be created to allow the nationalities to have something to say on the specific issues of nationality education.

The Party appreciates the work of our teachers in educating the young generation. Teachers belong above all to the school and young people, and their work must not be disturbed. Educational work is of nation-wide and society-wide importance. Therefore the social position of teachers must be safeguarded in the first place by the respective state bodies and National Committees. Efforts to provide conditions essential for their work must also follow this pattern. This means ensuring a high standard of training of teachers, developing wage relations of teachers and other school staff in harmony with the growth of real wages of workers in other branches, and also solving other urgent material needs of teachers so that they can perform their responsible profession with full concentration. In projects and the materialization of school capital construction, it is essential to ensure its complex character, including flats for teachers. The Party regards this as part of its policy to increase the prestige, authority, and social importance of the educators of the young generation.

The Humanistic Mission of Culture

The development of culture in the broadest sense is one of the basic conditions for the dynamic and harmonious development of socialist society. The culture of socialist Czechoslovakia consists of independent and equal Czech and Slovak cultures, together with the cultures of the other nationalities. The arts and culture are not a mere decoration of economic and political life; they are vital for the socialist system. If culture lags behind, it retards the progress of policy and economy, democracy and freedom, development of man and human relations. *Care for culture, material and spiritual, is not only the concern of the cultural front; it must become an affair of the entire society.*

It was an important tradition of the Communist Party from the start that it was able to unite the best men of culture and art around itself. This is proved not only by the socialist orientation of our pre-war artistic vanguard, but also by the fact that most of the cultural intelligensia sided with the left or were in the ranks of the Party after the liberation in 1945. Later, especially in the early fifties, certain representatives of culture were discriminated against, some were subjected to unjustified political repression, and the cultural policy of the Party was deformed.

The documents of the 13th Congress should have been a starting point of a new cultural policy, which would proceed from the best traditions of the past and from much positive experience acquired after 1956 and after the 12th Congress of the Communist Party of Czechoslovakia. However, the surviving bureaucratic attitudes and old methods of management prevented the impetus of the Congress from developing. The contradictions between proclaimed and practiced policies created tension and restricted the involvement and development of socialist culture. The Central Committee will investigate all the reasons for these conflicts and will create favorable conditions to normalize the situation.

We reject administrative and bureaucratic methods of implementing cultural policy, we dissociate ourselves from them, and we shall oppose them. Artistic work must not be subjected to censorship. We have full confidence in men of culture and we expect their responsibility, understanding, and support. We appreciate the way in which cultural workers helped instate and create the humanistic and democratic character of socialism and how actively they participated in eliminating the retarding factors of its development.

It is necessary to overcome a narrow understanding of the social and human function of culture and art, overestimation of their ideological and political role, and underestimation of their basic general cultural and aesthetic tasks in the transformation of man and his world.

The Party will guard and safeguard both the freedom of artistic work and the right to make works of art accessible.

To administer culture socially means, first of all, to create favorable conditions for its development. Disputes, which will naturally arise, will be solved by discussion and democratic decisions. *Independent decisions* of cultural workers in the spheres of their activity must also be an expression of the necessary autonomy of culture and art. They must be indispensable partners for state bodies. We are convinced that Communist intellectuals and all other leading workers in the sphere of culture and art are capable of cooperating in the formation and responsible, independent implementation of the policy of the Party in state, social, cultural, and interest group institutions, that they are a guarantee of the socialist, humanistic orientation of our culture.

Of course, the social effect of culture does not occur outside the political context. We shall ensure that the freedom of different views, guaranteed by the Constitution, is fully respected. However, the Communist Party cannot give up its inspiring role, its efforts to make art, too, efficiently help form socialist man in the struggle for the transformation of the world. The Party will apply consistently its political program; it will stimulate the development of Marxist thinking.

Socialist culture is one of the primary agents of the penetration of socialist and humanistic ideas in the world. *It helps unite the humanistic streams of world culture. It has the capacity of bringing closer the socialist nations and of strengthening the cooperating and fraternal relations of nations and nationalities.* Culture is a traditionally important value for our nations; it has always been of service to us in proving our vitality and individuality to the world. But the interpretation of the national traditions of the culture of the Czechs and Slovaks was one-sided in many respects, and whole important periods were artificially omitted from it. We give our full backing to the humanistic traditions of national cultures, and we shall support all efforts to endorse this heritage in the present psychology of Czechs and Slovaks.

We are supporters of both internationalism and national uniqueness of culture. We think it inevitable to take efficient measures without delay so that culture in Slovakia has the same conditions and possibilities as those in Bohemia, so that disproportions do not grow, but disappear. *The equal position of national cultures* also requires an equal position of national institutions. The competence of national bodies in Slovakia includes the management of the decisive instruments of national culture, such as radio, television, film, scientific institutes, artists' unions, book publishing, care for historical monuments, etc. It is necessary to secure the representation of Slovak national culture abroad; to increase the exchange of information and cultural values between the Czech and Slovak nations; to ensure the cultural life of the Slovaks in the Czech lands and of the Czechs in Slovakia in their native tongue.

Similar principles must be applied also towards the cultures of all the nationalities in Czechoslovakia, while realizing that they are specific cultures and not Czech and Slovak culture translated into another language. *The culture of nationalities* is an organic part of Czechoslovak socialist culture, but it is also in context with the general culture of its own nation, with which it is inseparably linked. Material conditions and personnel problems of the further development of national cultures must be guaranteed institutionally; scientific and cultural institutions and offices must be established with a view to nationality needs. The decisive role and care for the material base of national cultures pertains to state bodies, National Committees, together with the cultural unions of the various nationalities.

We shall take care not only of cultural work, but also of the system of *communication of cultural values*. We shall strive for the active participation of citizens in the development of socialist culture and in their *cultural education*, in the closest possible cooperation and complex influence of mass and local culture. We consider it urgent to examine the reasons for the catastrophic shortcomings of cultural and aesthetic education and to take measures to rectify them;—to create sufficient material, organizations, and other conditions of cultural activity, *to permit more flexibility in organizational forms;*—to allow the establishment of various cultural and hobby groups as well as their regional and national associations;—to complete an efficient network of cultural establishments with an active participation of National Committees, enterprises, social and group-interest organizations;—to purposefully build up new important *regional cultural centers* outside the capitals.

The entire sphere of culture must be responsibly safeguarded economically, in view of its importance, and protected from the uncontrolled nature of the market and from commercialism. We shall recommend, in the spirit of the 13th Congress resolution, that the government complete without delay the projected *revamping of the economics of culture*. Planned expenditures on culture must be stabilized and must increase progressively in harmony with the trend of national income. We shall also support voluntary combination of the means of industrial and agricultural enterprises, National Committees, and social organizations for culture. The means invested in culture can become an important instrument of its development if whoever makes use of them becomes a modern socialist customer.

Because they are dependent upon new distribution of the means for culture on a national scale the *following problems are most urgent*: to guarantee material care for the creators of important cultural values;—to eliminate discrepancies in the royalties, wages, incomes, and tax system in culture;—to cover the whole territory of the Republic with a good quality radio and television signal as soon as possible, to introduce a second television channel in 1970;—to overcome without delay the disastrous state of the printing industry;—to secure more paper in desirable assortments for the press and publishing houses;—to improve care of historical objects of art and save handicraft among other things by making way for cooperative or private enterprise in this sphere.

The planned expenditure on culture must *be concentrated in culture directing bodies* which must distribute it to cultural institutions. To increase the economic independence and responsibility of cultural establishments, enterprises, and groups is a prerequisite of the functioning economy of culture. Independent control will lead to a more rational exploitation of means and possibilities, to increasing the spirit of enterprise.

The International Status and Foreign Policy of the Czechoslovak Socialist Republic

We shall be putting the Action Program into practice during a complicated international situation, and its further development will influence the realization of certain important principles of the program. On the other hand, the process of the revival of socialism in Czechoslovakia will make it possible for our Republic to influence this international development more actively. *We stand resolutely on the side of progress, democracy, and socialism in the struggle of the socialist and democratic forces against the aggressive attempts of world imperialism. It is from this point of view that we determine our attitude toward the most acute international problems of the present and our share in the world-wide struggle against the forces of imperialist reaction.*

Proceeding from the real relationship of international forces and from the awareness that Czechoslovakia is an active component of the revolutionary process in the world, the Czechoslovak people will formulate its own attitude towards the fundamental problems of world policy.

The basic orientation of Czechoslovakia foreign policy was born and verified at the time of the struggle for national liberation and in the process of the socialist reconstruction of the country. *It is alliance and cooperation with the Soviet Union and the other socialist states. We shall strive for friendly relations with our allies— the countries of the world socialist community—to continue, on the basis of mutual respect, to intensify sovereignty and equality, and international solidarity.* In this sense we shall contribute more actively and with a more elaborated concept to the joint activities of the Council of Mutual Economic Aid and the Warsaw Treaty.

In the relationship to the developing countries, socialist Czechoslovakia will be contributing to the strengthening of the anti-imperialist front and supporting within its power and possibilities all the nations opposing imperialism, colonialism, and neocolonialism and striving for the strengthening of their sovereignty and national independence and for economic development. Therefore we shall continue supporting the courageous struggle of the Vietnamese people against American aggression. We shall also be in favor of enforcing a political settlement of the Middle East crisis.

We shall actively pursue the policy of peaceful co-existence towards advanced capitalist countries. Our geographical position, as well as the needs and capacities of an industrial country, require us to carry out a more active European policy aimed at the promotion of mutually advantageous relations with all states and international organizations and at safeguarding collective security of the European continent. *We shall consistently proceed from the existence of two German states, from the fact that the German Democratic Republic, as the first socialist state on German territory, is an important peace element in Europe, from the necessity of giving support to the realistic forces in the German Federal Republic, while resisting neo-nazi and revanchist tendencies in that country. The Czechoslovak people want to live in peace with all nations.* They want to develop good relations and cooperate with all states in the interests of strengthening international peace and security as well as mutual confidence in the economic, cultural, scientific, and technological fields. We shall also take more active advantage than we have done so far of our Republic's membership in international organizations, especially in the United Nations and its agencies.

Our science, culture, and art can do much more to strengthen and increase the international authority of socialist Czechoslovakia in the world. Czechoslovak foreign policy must provide conditions and extend the scope for the international application of our culture abroad. A broad application of our science and art abroad helps to prove efficiently the advantages of socialism and the possibilities of an active policy of peaceful co-existence.

Our foreign policy has not taken advantage of all opportunities for active work; it did not take the initiative in advancing its own views on many important international problems. The Central Committee of the Communist Party of Czechoslovakia, the National Assembly, the government, and the respective ministry must overcome these shortcomings without delay and consistently ensure that our foreign policy should express fully both the national and international interests of socialist Czechoslovakia.

A full development of the international role of socialist Czechoslovakia is inseparable from the education of citizens in the spirit of internationalism, which comprises both the grasping of common interests and aims of the world progressive forces and understanding of specific national needs. This is linked with the necessity of making prompt and detailed information on international problems and the course of our foreign policy available to the public and thus creating conditions for an active participation of Czechoslovak citizens in the shaping of foreign political attitudes.

The Communist Party of Czechoslovakia will be more active in the sphere of the international Communist and workers' movement. *We shall put special emphasis on friendly ties, mutual consultations, and exchange of experiences with the Communist Party of the Soviet Union, with the Communist and workers' parties of the socialist community, with all the other fraternal Communist parties.*

The Communist Party of Czechoslovakia will continue taking an active part in the struggle for the unity of the international Communist movement, for strengthening the active cooperation of Communist parties with all the progressive forces while regarding a resolute struggle against the aggressive policy of American imperialism as the most important task. The Communist Party of Czechoslovakia will take full advantage of its specific possibilities of establishing contacts with the socialist, peaceful, and democratic forces in the capitalist and developing countries. It will contribute to expanding the forms of cooperation and coordinating the work of Communist parties, while attaching great importance to international party consultative meetings. From this point of view it welcomes and supports the outcomes of the Consultative Meeting of Communist and Workers' Parties in Budapest. With dozens of fraternal parties the Communist Party of Czechoslovakia supports the proposal for convening an international Communist consultative meeting in Moscow late in 1968.

Comrades,

We are submitting to you quite openly all the main ideas which have guided us and which we want to adhere to at the present time. Everyone will understand that the proposals comprised in this Action Program are far-reaching and their realization will profoundly influence the life of this country. We are not changing our fundamental orientation. In the spirit of our traditions and former decisions we want to develop to the utmost in this country an advanced socialist society, rid of class antagonisms, economically, technologically, and culturally highly advanced, socially and nationally just, democratically organized, with a qualified management, by the wealth of its resources giving the possibility of dignified human life, characterized by comradely relations of mutual cooperation among people and free scope for the development of the human personality. We want to start building up a new intensely democratic model of a socialist society which will fully correspond to Czechoslovak conditions. But our own experiences and Marxist scientific knowledge lead us jointly to the conclusion that these aims cannot be achieved along the old paths or by using means which have long been obsolete and harsh methods which are always dragging us back. We declare with full responsibility that our society has entered a difficult period when we can no longer rely on traditional schemes. We cannot squeeze life into patterns, no matter how well-intended. It is up to us to make our way through unknown conditions, to experiment, to give the socialist development a new look, while leaning upon creative Marxist thinking and the experiences of the international workers' movement, relying on a true understanding of the conditions of the socialist development of Czechoslovakia as a country which assumes responsibility to the international Communist movement for improving and taking advantage of the relatively advanced material base, unusually high standards of education and culture of the people, and undeniable democratic traditions to the benefit of socialism and communism. No one could forgive us were we to waste this chance, were we to give up our opportunities.

We are not taking the outlined measures to make any concessions to our ideals—let alone to our opponents. On the contrary. We are convinced that they will help us to get rid of the burden which for years provided many advantages for the opponent by restricting, reducing, and paralyzing the efficiency of the socialist idea, the attractiveness of the socialist example. We want to set new penetrating forces of socialist life in motion in this country to give them the possibility of a much more efficient confrontation of social systems and world outlooks and allowing a fuller application of the advantages of socialism.

Our Action Program comprises tasks, intentions, and aims for the immediate future, up to the 14th Party Congress. We are aware that many of the shortcomings and difficulties which have accumulated over recent years cannot be fully overcome in a short time. *However, the fulfillment of this program can open up the way to solving other, more complicated and important problems of the organization and dynamic development of our socialist society in directions which could be only indicated until now; in the coming years, we want to start working out a long-term program, which will give form to and elaborate in detail the concept of the overall development of our socialist society in the stage we are entering, make clear the conditions and open up prospects of its Communist future.* After everything we have lived through over the past years we are obliged to give a reply to all our workers and ourselves as to how the Party imagines its aims can be achieved, how it wants to materialize the expectations and desires which are being invested by workers in their lives and in their participation in the Communist movement. We believe that our Marxist science has gathered and will gather now and in the future more than enough strength to enable it to prepare responsibly scientific preconditions for such a program.

We are not concealing the fact that difficult moments and extraordinarily exacting and responsible work face us in the coming months and years. For the fulfillment of the forthcoming progressive tasks it will be necessary to unite as many citizens of our Republic as possible, all who are concerned with the welfare of this country, with its peace efforts, with a flourishing socialism. The confidence, mutual understanding, and harmonious work of all who really want to devote their energy to this great human experiment will be needed. But the work and initiative of every Communist, every worker will be needed above all. We want to responsibly, consistently, and without reservations make room for this, remove all the barriers which stand in its way, set the creative capacities of our citizens, all the physical and moral capacities of society in motion. We want to create conditions so that every honest citizen who concerns himself with the cause of socialism, the cause of our nations, should feel that he is the very designer of the fate of this country, his homeland, that he is needed, that he is reckoned with. Therefore let the Action Program become a program of the revival of socialist efforts in this country. There is no force which can resist people who know what they want and how to pursue their aim.

The Central Committee of the
Communist Party of Czechoslovakia

THE MOSCOW PROTOCOL

[Svedectvi, vol. 9, nos. 34, 35, 36 (Winter 1969), pp. 228–231]

1. During the course of the talks problems were discussed concerning the defense of socialist achievements in the situation which has arisen in Czechoslovakia as well as the most essential measures dictated by the situation and by the stationing of allied troops in the CSSR. Both sides acted according to all the generally acknowledged norms for relations among fraternal parties and countries and according to the principles affirmed in the documents of the Cierna-nad-Tisou and Bratislava conferences. There was an affirmation of allegiance to the compacts of the socialist countries for the support, consolidation, and defense of socialism and the implacable struggle with counterrevolutionary forces, which is a common international obligation of all socialist countries. Both sides likewise affirmed the strong conviction that in the present situation the most important task is to put into practice the principles and tasks of the conference in Bratislava, from the agreement at the negotiations in Cierna-nad-Tisou and their concrete realization.

2. The Presidium of the CC CPCz announced that the so-called 14th Congress of the CPCz, opened August 22, 1968, without the agreement of the CC, violated party statutes. Without the participation of the members of the Presidium, secretaries, secretaries of the CC KSS, most of the delegates from the army and many other organizations, it is invalid. All measures pertinent to this problem will be taken by the Presidium of the CC CPCz upon its return to the CSSR. The delegation announced that a special 14th Congress of the CPCz will be convened after the situation has been normalized within the party and the country.

3. The KSC delegation reported that a plenum of the CC CPCz would be held within the next six to ten days with the participation of the party's control and revision commission. It will review problems of the normalization of the situation within the country, measures for improving the work of party and state organs, economic problems and problems of living standard, measures for consolidating all links of party and state rule, and it will discharge from their posts those individuals whose further activities would not conform to the needs of consolidating the leading role of the working class and the Communist party. It will carry out the resolution of the 1968 January and May plenums of the CC CPCz concerning consolidation of the positions of socialism within the country and further development of relations between the CSSR and fraternal countries of the socialist community.

4. The CPCz representatives declared the necessity for the speedy implementation of a number of measures fostering the consolidation of socialism and a workers' government with top priority to measures for controlling the communications media so that they will serve the cause of socialism fully by preventing antisocialist statements on radio and television, putting an end to the activities of various organizations with antisocialist positions, and banning the activities of the anti-Marxist social democratic party. Suitable and effective measures will be taken in the interest of accomplishing these tasks. The party and state organs will remedy

the situation in the press, radio, and television by means of new laws and measures. In this unusual situation it will be essential, if these tasks are to be accomplished, to take several temporary measures so that the government can have firm control over the ways and means of opposing antisocialist individuals or collectives. Essential personnel changes will be carried out in the leadership of the press and radio and television stations. Here, as at the meeting in Cierna-nad-Tisou, the representatives of the CPSU expressed full solidarity with these measures, which also conform to the basic interests of the socialist community, its security and unity.

5. Both delegations discussed problems connected with the presence of troops of the five socialist countries and agreed that the troops will not interfere with the internal affairs of the CSSR. As soon as the threat to socialism in the CSSR and to the security of the countries in the socialist community has passed, allied troops will be removed from the territory of the CSSR in stages. The command of the allied troops and the command of the Czechoslovak Army will immediately begin discussions concerning the removal and change in position of military units from cities and villages where local organs are able to establish order. Repositioning of the troops is to be effected in barracks, exercise grounds, and other military areas. The problem of the security of the Czechoslovak border with the German Federal Republic will be reviewed. The number of troops, their organization and repositioning will be effected in cooperation with representatives of the Czechoslovak Army. Material, technical, medical, and other provisions for the troops temporarily stationed in the CSSR will be determined by special agreement at the level of the Ministry of National Defense and the Ministry of Foreign Affairs. Problems involving matters of principle will be dealt with by the governments of both countries. A treaty concerning the conditions of the stay and complete removal of allied troops will be concluded between the government of the CSSR and the governments whose troops are on the territory of the CSSR.

6. Representatives of Czechoslovakia reported that the Czechoslovak armed forces were ordered to avoid incidents and conflicts with troops of the allied countries in the interest of peace and order. The Presidium of the CC CPCz and the government will adopt measures in the press, radio, and television to exclude the possibility of conflicts between the troops and citizens on CSSR territory.

7. The CPCz representatives announced that they would not tolerate that party workers and officials who struggled for the consolidation of socialist positions against antisocialist forces and for friendly relations with the USSR be dismissed from their posts or suffer reprisals.

8. An agreement was reached regarding the establishment in the near future of negotiations on a number of economic problems with an eye to expanding and intensifying economic and technical cooperation between the USSR and the CSSR, especially as concerns the needs for further development of the economy of the CSSR in the interest of fulfilling the plan for the development of the national economy with respect to the CC CPCz resolution.

9. There is full agreement that the development of the international situation

and the treacherous activities of imperialism, working against peace, the security of nations, and socialism, necessitate the further consolidation and increase in effectiveness of the defense system of the Warsaw Pact as well as of other existing organs and forms of cooperation among socialist countries.

10. The leading representatives of the CPSU and CPCz affirmed their resolve to scrupulously maintain the principle of coordinated action in international relations fostering the consolidation of unity in the socialist community and of peace and international security. Concerning European problems the USSR and the CSSR will follow as before a scrupulous policy in conformity with the interests of European security and offer strong resistance to militaristic, anti-Soviet, and neonationalistic forces, which follow a policy of revising the results of the Second World War in Europe and existing European borders. Both sides announced that they will scrupulously fulfill all the obligations resulting from the multilateral and bilateral treaties among socialist countries. In close cooperation with the rest of the countries in the socialist community they will continue in the future to struggle against imperialism's treacherous activities, support the national liberation movement, and work toward the easing of international tension.

11. In connection with the discussion of the so-called CSSR problem in the United Nations Security Council, the leading CPCz and government representatives announced that the CSSR did not request the Security Council to discuss this matter. The CPCz representatives reported that the Czechoslovak representative in New York had been instructed by the government of the Republic to lodge a categorical protest against the discussion of the CSSR problem in the Security Council or in any other United Nations organ and make a categorical request for the deletion of this issue from the proceedings.

12. The CC CPCz Presidium and the government announced that it would review the activities of those members of the government who were outside the country and made statements in the name of the government of the CSSR concerning internal and foreign policy, especially with regard to the maintenance of the policy of the CPCz and the government of the Republic. Suitable conclusions will be drawn from this review. In this connection the representatives of the CC CPCz consider it necessary to carry out several further personnel changes in party and state organs and organizations in the interest of ensuring complete consolidation within the party and the country. These problems will be considered from all points of view upon the representatives' return to their country. The activities of the Ministry of the Interior will also be examined, and measures will be taken to consolidate its leadership on the basis of the results.

13. An agreement was reached to set up an exchange of party and state delegations within a short period of time to further deepen attempts at reviewing and resolving the problems which arise in relations with one another and discussions of contemporary international problems.

14. The delegations agreed in the interest of both communist parties and friendship between the CSSR and the USSR to regard the contacts between the representatives of the CPCz and the representatives of the CPSU as strictly confi-

dential in the period following 20 August 1968, which therefore holds for talks just concluded.

15. Both sides pledged in the name of their parties and governments to promote all efforts of the CPSU and CPCz and the governments of these countries to intensify the traditional friendship between the peoples of both countries and their fraternal friendship for time everlasting.

INDEX

In this index, AD will be used for Alexander Dubcek.